'Lord, with whom Eros the Subduer
and the dark-eyed Nymphs
and radiant Aphrodite play,
as you roam across the high peaks of the mountains,
I beg you, come to me in kindness:
hear and accept my prayer.'

From an invocation to Dionysos by the poet Anakreon (6th century BC)

The Complete World of
Greek Mythology

Richard Buxton

with 330 illustrations, 139 in color

Thames & Hudson

Contents

Half-title: *Cameo, Hellenistic period.*

Title-page: *(left) The marble Tholos at Delphi, early 4th century BC, masterpiece of Theodoros of Phokaia.*
(right) Bronze statuette of Poseidon, 2nd–1st century BC; partially restored, including the trident.

This page: *One of the Moirai (Fates) strikes down her part-serpentine adversary. From the Battle of the Gods and Giants, north frieze, Great Altar of Zeus from Pergamon (c. 190–150 BC).*

© 2004 Thames & Hudson Ltd, London

First published in hardcover in the United States of America in 2004 by Thames & Hudson Inc., 500 Fifth Avenue, New York, New York 10110

thamesandhudsonusa.com

Library of Congress Catalog Card Number 2003110206

ISBN 0-500-25121-5

Printed and bound in Slovenia by Mladinska Knjiga

Introduction:
Myths in Context

Few monsters overcome by Herakles are more horrifying than Kerberos, the hound of the Underworld. The serpents growing from the beast's heads and paws intensify the terror. In this vase-painting (6th century BC) Eurystheus, who had commanded Herakles to perform his Labours, is nervously hiding in a big jar.

No group of stories exhibits greater richness and depth, and certainly none has been more influential, than the set of tales which we know as 'the Greek myths'. Narrative texts and visual images recording the exploits of the Greek gods and goddesses, and of the heroines and heroes, are already found early in the 1st millennium BC, and they have continued to be produced, in an apparently inexhaustible series of variations and reinterpretations, until the present day. The meanings which people have read into these stories have varied enormously over time, according to the contrasting perspectives from which different cultures have viewed the legacy of ancient Greece; indeed this chameleon-like capacity for adaptation has been a decisive factor in the myths' survival. Nor does the impact of the Greek myths show any sign of diminishing: the tireless efforts of Herakles to rid the world of monsters, as depicted on countless thousands of ancient vase-paintings, still find their echo in the latest films and software for interactive computer games.

The final chapter of this book explores some of the ways in which the Greek myths have been retold since antiquity. But before that the main focus will be on providing a detailed account of the myths as they were narrated within the contexts of ancient Greek culture. Quotations from Greek literary texts and reproductions of Greek artistic images therefore play a major part in the analysis. So also do illustrations of the Greek landscape, which was another crucial aspect of the world of Greek mythology. Many of the locations within which mythological episodes were said to have taken place – Mycenae, Delphi, Tiryns, Ithaca, the Athenian Acropolis – may still be visited today. Moreover, several types of landscape – mountain, river, cave, sea – played their own part in shaping the myths. In presenting the world of Greek mythology to the reader we shall frequently evoke the topographical contexts within which that mythology developed.

It is important to stress this objective of setting out the Greek myths in their Greek contexts. There is no shortage of dictionaries and handbooks of 'Classical mythology' – by which is meant the

Modern reworkings of the Greek myths introduce new and sometimes surprising variations on old themes. In a still from the Disney film Hercules *(1997), the great hero is seen riding on Pegasos, the winged steed which, according to ancient tradition, was the mount of Bellerophon.*

myths of Greece *and Rome*. It is true that there were significant continuities between the stories told in these two ancient cultures, but there were also major differences. Roman myth-telling is a fascinating topic in its own right, but it is not the main topic which will be addressed in the present volume (though see pp. 216–24, 'How Rome re-imagined Greece'): it is myth-telling by Greeks, and predominantly in the Greek language, which will be our central concern.

This Hellenic emphasis has relevance also for the form in which the names of mythological characters and places appear in this book. Until quite recently, scholars followed the convention of automatically Latinizing mythological names, even when everything about the context was Greek: not

Delphi: the location of
Apollo's oracle, which plays a
role in many Greek myths.

The following dating conventions are widely observed:

The Archaic period: 700–500 BC

The Classical period: 500–323 BC

The Hellenistic period: 323–31 BC

date	author/artist	key moments in verbal and artistic myth-telling
900–700 BC		'Geometric' pottery
?8/7th cent.	Homer	many epic poems were ascribed to him, incl. the *Iliad* and *Odyssey*; also *Homeric Hymns*
?8/7th cent.	Hesiod	poems incl. *Theogony* and *Works and Days*
625–475		Athenian black-figure vase-painting
c. 570		'François Vase' (see p. 25)
c. 555–c. 465	Simonides	lyric poems
530–300		Athenian red-figure vase-painting
c. 518–after 446	Pindar	lyric poems, esp. choral odes celebrating athletic victories
c. 525–c. 456	Aischylos	tragedies, incl. *Oresteia* trilogy
490s–c. 406	Sophokles	tragedies, incl. *Oedipus Tyrannos*, *Antigone* and *Elektra*
480s–406	Euripides	tragedies, incl. *Bacchae* and *Medea*
c. 450–380s	Aristophanes	comedies, incl. some involving mythological themes
c. 470		Temple of Zeus at Olympia
450		beginnings of S. Italian red-figure vase-painting
mid-5th cent.		white-ground vases known as *lekythoi*
c. 447–c. 430		building of Parthenon at Athens
c. 428–c. 348	Plato	philosophical works, incl. *Phaedo* and *Republic*
380		Temple of Asklepios at Epidauros
?late 4th cent.	Palaiphatos	rationalizing mythography
active 260	Apollonios of Rhodes	*Argonautica* (epic poem)
active 260	Kallimachos	many types of poetry, incl. *Hymns*
early 3rd cent.	Theokritos	pastoral poetry
active 300	Euhemeros	utopian 'novel' about how the gods had once been benevolent mortals
?c. 190		'Winged Victory of Samothrace' (sculpture)
?early 2nd cent.	Lykophron	*Alexandra*, recondite poem consisting of prophecies by Cassandra
c. 190–150		Great Altar of Zeus, Pergamon
active 150	Moschos	poems, incl. *Europa*
1st cent. BC	Diodoros of Sicily	'universal history' from mythological times
2nd cent. AD	Lucian	comic-ironical stories and dialogues, some with mythological content
?2nd cent.	Apollodoros	*Library of Mythology*
late 2nd cent.	Antoninus Liberalis	collection of metamorphosis tales
late 2nd cent.	Pausanias	*Description of Greece*
?3rd cent.	Quintus of Smyrna	epic poem filling the 'gap' between *Iliad* and *Odyssey*
?2nd/3rd cent.	Dictys Cretensis	account of Trojan War by an alleged Cretan eye-witness
5th cent.	Nonnos	48-book epic about Dionysos
?5th cent.	Dares Phrygius	account of Trojan War by an alleged Trojan eye-witness

Mycenae was said to have been the home of Agamemnon, conqueror of Troy. The city walls give an idea of the military and political might exerted by this ancient centre of power.

only would Kadmos (which is a literal transliteration from the Greek) appear as Cadmus, and Daidalos as Daedalus, but Zeus might even be referred to under the guise of his (partial) Roman 'equivalent' Jupiter, and Athene as Minerva. Unfortunately, there is no right answer to the problem of transliteration. It would seem over-fussy to call Athens by its ancient Greek name of 'Athenai', or Mycenae 'Mukenai'; so, where a commonly understood version of a place or a character is involved, that is the form which is adopted (thus the Latin form 'Oedipus' is preferred to the more puristically correct Greek form 'Oidipous'). In the case of relatively less well-known names, however, a more

'Hellenic' form is preferred (so 'Kreon', not 'Creon').

The plan of the book is straightforward. The first chapter, after posing the initial question of 'What is a myth?', investigates the general characteristics of Greek mythology, looking in particular at the kind of evidence we can draw on and – in keeping with one of our main emphases – the contexts within which Greeks told each other myths. The second chapter describes one particular category of tale: 'How things began'. The discussion deals with myths about the beginning of the universe, about the birth of the gods, and about the origins of humanity and its various communities. Chapter III analyses accounts of the powers and attributes of the Olympian gods. Chapter IV is devoted to some of the best-known tales of Greek heroism, including the legendary expeditions of the Greeks to Troy and of the Argonauts to capture the Golden Fleece. Chapter V once more concentrates on hero(in)es, exploring the strange and often terrifying events which befall these characters in their family relationships. Chapter VI examines a topic which will have been implicit throughout: the landscape within which Greek mythical narratives were imagined as having occurred. Finally, Chapter VII considers the fascination which Greek myths have exercised since antiquity, for, amongst others, artists, musicians, poets and scholars, not forgetting the impact of Greek mythology on other cultural media such as film and television. This fascination is as intense as it has ever been.

A final word may be added about the scope and

The Athenian Acropolis is dominated today, as it was in antiquity, by Athene's great temple, the Parthenon.

title of the book. One of the themes upon which we shall insist is the diversity of Greek myths. There are innumerable variations: between authors, between genres, between historical periods, between localities. Does this mean that the notion of 'completeness', which the title implies is the book's aspiration, must remain an unattainable ideal? If to be 'complete' means to chronicle every single variant of every single myth, then the answer has to be 'yes' – though this may be no great loss, since such an enterprise, if carried out to the letter, would drown the reader in a flood of detail. But what we can do is to offer a comprehensive picture of the *world* of Greek mythology – the imaginative contours and horizons, the motifs and recurrent concerns, which lent meaning to the stories. That attainable and worthwhile objective will be the goal of the pages which follow.

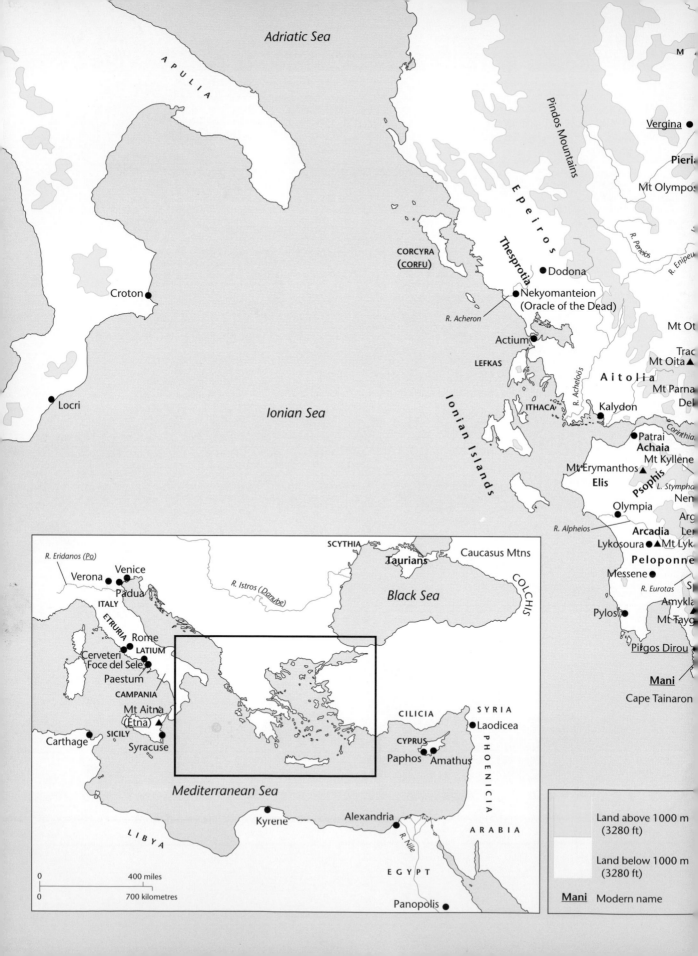

Adriatic Sea

A P U L I A

Pindos Mountains

Vergina ●

Pieria

Mt Olympos

E p e i r o s

R. Peneiós

R. Enipeu

CORCYRA
(CORFU)

Thesprotia

● Dodona

Croton ●

● Nekyomanteion
(Oracle of the Dead)

R. Acheron

Actium

LEFKAS

Mt Ot

Trac
Mt Oita ▲

Locri ●

Ionian Sea

R. Acheloös

A i t o l i a

Mt Parna
Del

ITHACA

● Kalydon

Corinthia

Ionian Islands

● Patrai
Achaia

Mt Kyllene

Mt Erymanthos ▲
Elis   Psophis   L. Stympha   Nen

● Olympia   Arg

R. Alpheios   Arcadia   Le

Lykosoura ● ▲ Mt Lyk

Peloponne

Messene ●

R. Eurotas   S

Amykla

Pylos ●   Mt Tayg

Pirgos Dirou

Mani

Cape Tainaron

R. Eridanos (Po)

SCYTHIA

Caucasus Mtns

Verona ●   ● Venice

R. Istros (Danube)

COLCHIS

Padua ●

ITALY

Taurians

Black Sea

ETRURIA

Rome ●

Cerveteri ●
Foce del Sele ●
LATIUM

Paestum ●

CAMPANIA

Mt Aitna
(Etna) ▲

SICILY

Carthage ●

Syracuse ●

CILICIA

SYRIA

● Laodicea

CYPRUS

Paphos ●   ● Amathus

P H O E N I C I A

Mediterranean Sea

A R A B I A

Kyrene ●

LIBYA

Alexandria ●

R. Nile

E G Y P T

Panopolis ●

0   400 miles
0   700 kilometres

Land above 1000 m
(3280 ft)

Land below 1000 m
(3280 ft)

Mani   Modern name

Rhodope Mountains

Black Sea

THRACE

ONIA

Mt Pangaion ▲

Kikonians

R. Hebros

Byzantium ●

Propontis

lla

Thessaloniki ●

Chalkidike

Olynthos ●

SAMOTHRACE

Hellespont

Troy/Ilion ●

Mysia

Phrygia

Mende ●

Pallene

Mt Ossa

LEMNOS

TENEDOS

Mt Ida ▲

Pelion ●

Iolkos ●

ai ●

asai ●

Magnesia

Aegean Sea

Antissa ●

Pergamon ●

hia

LESBOS

SKYROS

kis

rchomenos ●

Thebes ●

EUBOIA (EVIA)

Lydia

Boiotia

Chalkis ●

Smyrna ●

espiae ●

Mt Helikon ▲

Aulis ●

Mt Sipylos ▲

Kithairon ▲

Plataea ▲

chora ●

Attica

Marathon ●

Megara ●

Eleusis ●

Megarid

Athens ●

Brauron ●

Ephesos ●

lid

Isthmia ●

Mt Hymettos ▲

Corinth ●

Mycenae ●

SALAMIS

Epidauros ●

AIGINA

Miletos ●

Mt Latmos ▲

Troizen ●

LEROS

Caria

Tiryns ●

DELOS

Halikarnassos ●

SERIPHOS

NAXOS

PAROS

Cyclades

KOS

Cape Maleia

SYME

Lyci

THERA

(SANTORINI)

RHODES

KYTHERA

Lindos ●

N

CRETE

Knossos ●

Mt Ida ▲

Lyktos ●

Mt Dikte ▲

0   100 miles

0   150 kilometres

The Remaking of Tradition

We often speak, by a kind of shorthand, of 'the myth of…' – 'the myth of Oedipus', for example, or 'the myth of the Trojan War'. But in fact one of the central characteristics of the stories told by the Greeks was plurality. There was no single, canonical, orthodox version of a given tale which all its tellers had to repeat. Rather, each teller remade tradition according to the requirements of the particular social and artistic context. Of course there were overlaps between stories: many of the extant versions of, say, the story of Jason and the Golden Fleece have much in common with each other. But there was always the possibility for invention and – within the intangible limits of tradition – originality.

In this first chapter we shall describe some of the features of this narrative plurality. We shall set out the various and extremely diverse sources which have preserved the Greek myths, and we shall examine the different contexts, both domestic and public, in which myths were retold, whether orally, or in writing, or in visual representation.

Priam comes to Achilles' tent to ransom the body of his son Hektor, whom Achilles has slain in revenge for the death of his friend Patroklos. Achilles is eating a meal, with a knife in one hand and a piece of meat in the other; he has not yet noticed Priam. The focal point of the scene – Hektor's corpse – lies disregarded beneath the couch. Attic cup, c. 490 BC.

General Characteristics of Greek Myths

(Opposite) The Mycenaean citadel at Tiryns, in the Argive plain, is surrounded by massive defensive walls, whose 'Cyclopean' masonry is named for the one-eyed giants who were said to have carried out the building work. It was from the top of these mighty walls that Herakles allegedly hurled Eurytos' son Iphitos, when he slew him in a fit of fury.

The ruins of Mycenae in the northeastern Peloponnese are an inspiring reminder of the power and influence the great city once wielded. Mycenae features prominently in Greek myths: traditionally, it was the home of Agamemnon, conqueror of Troy.

Origins

No civilization has generated a richer or more abundant crop of myths than that of ancient Greece. The first myths for which we have direct evidence are found in texts of the poets Homer and Hesiod, usually dated to the 8th/7th centuries BC. However, traditions of myth-telling in Greece undoubtedly go back far beyond that date. Many aspects of the style of Homeric and Hesiodic poetry, especially the use of repeated 'formulaic' phrases (e.g. 'the wine-dark sea', 'Zeus the gatherer of clouds'), suggest that a long tradition of orally composed verse lies behind the poetry which we actually possess; moreover, the poems often allude briefly to mythical episodes with which the audience was evidently assumed to be already familiar. How far back we should push 'the origins' of Greek mythology is a question which is unanswerable in practice and, anyway, fatally flawed in principle – it is quite uncertain what such an alleged 'origin' is supposed to look like, and how we should know if we had found it. What we can assert with confidence, though, is that the myths which have survived from later Greece will have been shaped in a variety of earlier cultural contexts.

One such context is the late 2nd millennium BC civilization which modern archaeologists have labelled 'Mycenaean', adopting the name of one of that civilization's most remarkable sites. Many Mycenaean population-centres whose political importance subsequently declined – Orchomenos in Boiotia, and Tiryns and Mycenae itself in the Argolid – figure prominently in Greek myths; this strongly suggests a formative period of Mycenaean influence on the stories, even if – because of the absence of relevant written Mycenaean evidence – we cannot demonstrate the point conclusively. Another formative influence on the development of Greek myths may have been another 2nd millennium culture, the so-called 'Minoan' civilization of Crete (the name 'Minoan', now automatically applied by modern archaeologists, has its sole basis in mythology: Minos was a mythical king of Crete). Once more, lack of direct evidence prevents us from reaching definite conclusions about the possible role played by Minoan Crete in the development of Greek myths, but we cannot fail to register the

island's prominence in a number of mythological episodes: the Minotaur in the labyrinth (p. 128), the tale of Daidalos and Ikaros (pp. 92–93), the almost invulnerable bronze giant Talos (pp. 112–13), and many others.

Locations in which scholars have sought to find the well-springs of Greek mythology are by no means confined to what we regard today as 'Greece'. When, in the late 18th century, the British colonial presence in India resulted in the dissemination of knowledge of the Sanskrit language to Western linguists, comparisons between Greek, Latin and Sanskrit led to the hypothesis of an original Indo-European language. Moreover a common language might, it was felt, point to shared features of social life also. So it was that, when Friedrich Max Müller (1823–1900), a prodigiously learned German philologist, was appointed to a Chair in Oxford, he developed an approach which related the mythology of Greece to its assumed Indo-European origins; indeed, Müller argued that some myths which seemed to him not to make sense in their Greek form became lucidity itself when 'translated' back into Indo-European. The fact that so many of these translations involved reducing the rich complexity of Greek myths to rather banal allegorical utterances about elementary natural phenomena meant that Müller's comparativist theory failed to win lasting assent – although even at the beginning of the 21st century a few scholars continue to approach Greek mythology from an explicitly Indo-European perspective.

More broadly accepted than the Indo-European angle of approach is that which locates Greek myths against a background of Near Eastern – or, shifting the viewpoint, West Asiatic – civilizations, such as those of Assyria, Babylonia, the Hittites, ancient Israel, and so on. The two most influential contemporary voices which have articulated this case are those of the German scholar Walter Burkert and the British scholar Martin West. Their work and that of others has persuasively demonstrated major continuities between Greek storytelling and that of its eastern precursors, especially during the late Bronze Age (14th/13th centuries BC) and the so-called 'orientalizing period' (8th/7th centuries BC). Amongst the numerous significant parallels found are those involving cosmological accounts of the overthrow, by castration, of one supreme god by another (there are close similarities here between Hittite and Greek stories), and the monster-slaying exploits of the Greek hero Herakles (similar Mesopotamian myths exist). In some quarters, particularly in Greece itself, there has been opposition to this stress on West Asiatic parallels, on the grounds that such an emphasis might be felt to dilute the 'Hellenic' quality of Greek myths. As often, it is a question of striking a judicious balance: there should be room both for noting Near Eastern parallels and for asserting the

What is a Myth?

One widespread usage of the word 'myth' is exemplified by a sentence such as this: 'It's a myth that all English people drink tea at four o'clock in the afternoon.' A myth, on this definition, is just 'a widely held misconception'. However, such a simplistic definition, which defines a myth in terms of its falsity, does nothing to alert us to the imaginative richness and social significance of stories and story-telling. A different and more useful kind of definition – the kind with which we shall be operating here – goes like this: 'A myth is a socially powerful traditional story.'

(Above right) Frankenstein's monster contemplates his features in a pool: an engraving by Lynd Ward, from a 1934 edition of Mary Shelley's tale of terror, Frankenstein, or The Modern Prometheus, *1818. Thanks to its exploration of such themes as the creation of life and the dangers of excessive human ingenuity, this story has earned the right to be called a 'modern myth'.*

(Right) The legend of the ancient Celtic warrior Cuchulain is evoked in Oliver Sheppard's statue of the dying hero, located in Dublin at the site of the 1916 Easter Rising. Cuchulain's superhuman exploits, culminating in his early death, have been likened to those of Achilles.

There are three elements in this definition. The least problematic is the notion of *story*: a 'myth' is a narrative, a set of events structured into a sequence. The second element is *tradition*: the stories we shall be concentrating on were transmitted from teller to teller, and often from generation to generation; indeed, one way of characterizing a myth might be that it is a story whose origin has been forgotten. Thirdly, there is *social power*: our focus will be on narratives which occupy a highly significant position within the societies that retell them, in that they embody and explore the values, not just of individuals, but of social groups, and even whole communities.

In the light of this definition, we can see that myths – socially powerful traditional stories – have played and continue to play a focal part in the imaginative lives of very many societies. In modern Ireland, the legendary hero Cuchulain has been appropriated as an exemplar by adherents of both of the main, opposed, religious traditions, Catholic and Protestant. In the Balkans, the Battle of Kosovo – at which, in 1389, a Serbian force was said to have suffered a catastrophic defeat at the hands of an army of Ottoman Turks –has achieved mythical status for those who long to rediscover a Serbian nationhood. In a quite different register, but still exercising its own fascination, is the tale of Frankenstein's monster: thanks especially to diverse re-inventions in the cinema, this story-turned-myth explores one of the central anxieties of modern consciousness: how to deal with the capacity of technology to redefine life itself. The story of Frankenstein invites its readers or viewers to ask: what would the implications be if we could really create human life? Such a story is no longer just a story. Having become 'traditional', it belongs alongside such older tales as those of Robin Hood (what would it be like if the social order were inverted?) or, differently again, alongside the latest but already 'traditional' narratives about Superman. Myths are alive and well.

undeniable and distinctive contribution made by Greeks themselves.

The controversy about West Asiatic issues pales into insignificance beside another contemporary debate about Greek culture, including its mythology. Martin Bernal, a British scholar now teaching in the United States, has maintained that the key to understanding ancient Greece lies not in West Asia but in Africa, and specifically in Egypt, whose civilization, in his view, enormously influenced that of Greece in ways which only the racially motivated misapprehensions of generations of Western academics have masked. Many scholars would agree that Egypt's role as an 'origin' for aspects of Greek culture has been, for whatever reason, downplayed; nevertheless, the pan-Egyptian explanation advocated by Bernal has found complete favour only with the ideologically committed. Whatever the final verdict on Bernal's thesis, this controversy illustrates that Greek mythology is far from being a matter of merely 'academic' interest. As we noted in relation to contemporary Ireland and Serbia, myths may constitute some of the most dynamic and 'charged' aspects of any society. Correspondingly, those who interpret myths, whether ancient or modern, may expose raw nerves, and thus provoke hostility or even fury.

Where was Greece?

The word 'Greece' derives from the Latin 'Graecia'. It is probable that this name was first used of the Graikoi, a people living in Epeiros (in the northwest of present-day Greece), and that it was then taken over by the Italic peoples of the opposite, Adriatic coast, and used to refer, initially, to the Graikoi themselves, and later to a wider group of culturally and linguistically related peoples. Members of this wider group called themselves 'Hellenes', and called the territory in which they dwelt 'Hellas'. Accordingly, some modern scholars have adopted the terms 'Hellene/Hellas' in preference to 'Greek/Greece'. In the present book we shall retain 'Greece', while using 'Hellenic' and 'Greek' interchangeably. The word 'Hellenic' must, incidentally, be distinguished from 'Hellenistic', a term used conventionally (and in this book too) to designate the period from the death of Alexander the Great (323 BC) to the Battle of Actium (31 BC).

The stories that we know as 'Greek myths' were told over a wide and historically fluctuating area, by no means coincident with the territory labelled 'Greece' on modern maps. Already by the Archaic period (conventionally 700–500 BC), in addition to occupying the mainland north as far as Macedonia and east through Thrace to the Hellespont, Greek speakers had settled the Aegean islands and the western seaboard of Asia Minor (in present-day Turkey). In addition, the founding of overseas settlements further afield expanded the reach of all aspects of Hellenic culture, including its stories.

During the Archaic and Classical periods (the Classical period is conventionally dated 500–323 BC), the most significant destination for this type of expansion was 'Magna Graecia', a Latin term designating the parts of southern Italy and Sicily which came under Greek influence. From Apulia (mod. Puglia) and Campania as far north as Etruria (mod. Tuscany), we find ample evidence of the presence of Greek stories, not least thanks to the enormous quantities of painted pottery which have survived in south and central Italian tombs.

The export of Hellenic culture, myths included, extended further still. As early as the Archaic period, the north African coastal settlement of Kyrene (mod. Shahat) was a Greek foundation whose links with the homeland were expressed through mythology. As the poet Pindar (5th century BC) would put it later, celebrating the victory of the king of Kyrene in a chariot race in the Pythian Games at Delphi: 'Today, Muse, you must stand by a dear man, the king of Kyrene, city of fine horses – city of chariots on the silver-shining breast of the earth' (see also pp. 35–36).

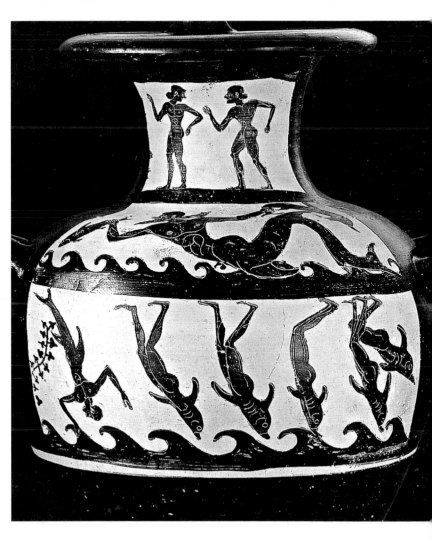

This Etruscan vase (late 6th century BC) illustrates a myth in which Dionysos turns a group of pirates into dolphins (see p. 82). The power of the god – discreetly evoked by the presence of vine-leaves at the far left – effects a miraculous transformation, depicted in the sequence of images in the lower section of the vase.

(Opposite) Part of the frieze of the Great Altar of Zeus from Pergamon portrays the victory of the Olympian gods over their monstrous adversaries, the Giants.

(Below) In this limestone relief (1st century BC) from Commagene in southeastern Turkey, King Antiochos I of Commagene clasps the hand of Herakles, who wields his trademark club.

The invasion of Greece by Persian forces in the early 5th century BC was the single most decisive factor in generating a sense of Hellenic identity. With the Persians repulsed, Greeks turned in upon themselves, tearing themselves apart in the protracted Athens–Sparta conflict ('the Peloponnesian War') in the last third of the 5th century. Then, in the 4th century, into the power-vacuum left by the weakened city-states of the southern mainland, there stepped a new and powerful force based in the northern Greek region of Macedonia. Hellenic expansion was to receive a totally unparalleled impetus thanks to the astonishing, albeit murderous energies of Alexander the Great, whose armies carried Greek culture as far as Egypt and Libya in the south and Afghanistan in the east. In the wake of military victory there followed civic consolidation, embodied in the buildings, customs and institutions which constituted the fabric of civic life: gymnasia, theatres, a common Greek language (the *koine*, 'common', 'shared'), as well as the stories which that language enabled to be retold. In the post-Alexander world of the Hellenistic kingdoms – ruled by dynasties founded by Alexander's generals, and handed on to their successors – many Greeks found themselves living at a greater distance than ever before from their ancestral hearth. In such a world, myths provided a vital means of retaining contact with cultural roots, while at the same time exploring new situations through a medium whose traditionality had always been open to constant adaptation, yet which was well on the way to becoming nostalgically regarded as 'classical'.

Region by region, the various parts of what had been Alexander's empire fell under the sway of Roman military and administrative power. The result was not the effacing of Greek myth-telling; on the contrary, Roman domination provided a framework for the survival of the Greeks' cultural heritage, including their mythology. One way in which this happened was that the Romans paid the Greeks the ultimate compliment of taking their literary and artistic works as models; the myths imperceptibly became not so much Greek as Greco-Roman.

What of the Greeks themselves under Roman power? Even when their cities had long since ceased to enjoy political independence, myth-tellers continued to narrate the ancient stories. Such harking back was not simply a product of inertia: it could make a strong ideological point. For example, the 2nd century AD Greek writer Pausanias incorporated into his description of a tour of Greece's ancient monuments countless references to the myths and rituals which he had come across, yet he virtually ignored the external political domination by Rome which provided the ever-present context for the life of this society. Pausanias came from Asia Minor – that is, from within the geographical area associated with 'Classical Greece'. But the world was now a bigger place. The satirist Lucian (2nd century AD), who exploited the old mythological themes with glee and panache, hailed from Samosata (mod. Samsât) on the Euphrates. As for Nonnos (5th century AD), author of a monumental 48-book epic (*Dionysiaca*) about the multifarious exploits of the god Dionysos, his homeland was Panopolis in Egypt. The geographical reach of the Greek myths was becoming ever more extensive. When the Romans' domination eventually ebbed away, the myths which they had inherited from the Greeks outlasted that domination, taking on ever newer guises, with an undiminished capacity for adaptation.

Sources of Evidence

Material Culture

Why have Greek myths continued to grip the imagination of later centuries? Part of the explanation lies in the richness and power of the visual images through which ancient artists depicted the stories. These images, which constitute one of our two principal sources of information for Greek mythology, may be divided into several main types: sculptures, wall-paintings, mosaics, vase-paintings and coins, not forgetting the evidence of such media as engraved gemstones and decorated mirrors.

Of these types it is sculpture, in both its free-standing and its architectural forms, which enjoys the highest status today. Most of what has survived is in marble; with a few spectacular exceptions – notably the 'Riace bronzes' recovered from the bottom of the sea off Calabria – works in bronze, or in even more precious metals, tended to be only too vulnerable to melting-down and re-use. Relatively few examples of ancient Greek sculpture remain *in situ*; most are now conserved and admired in

(Left) The Winged Victory of Samothrace (perhaps c. 190 BC, though many scholars date it earlier). The figure of Nike ('Victory') is shown alighting on the prow of a ship; in its original location in the sanctuary of the Great Gods on the island of Samothrace, the prow was set in the basin of a fountain. The statue, now in the Louvre, may commemorate a naval victory by the Hellenistic ruler who commissioned the work. Thanks to the sculptor's genius, Nike's posture and drapery express a miraculous sense of dynamism and grace.

(Right) The abduction of Persephone by Hades, depicted in a wall-painting from the 'Tomb of Persephone', a royal Macedonian tomb at Vergina, west of Thessaloniki (mid-4th century BC). Persephone struggles in vain when Hades seizes her for his bride and rides away with her in his chariot to the Underworld.

museums: the magnificent Parthenon (or 'Elgin') Marbles in the British Museum, London, for instance, or the statue of the Winged Victory of Samothrace, in the Louvre, Paris. In antiquity, too, sculptures representing the divinities, heroes and heroines of mythology were often regarded with awe by contemporaries. A classic case was Pheidias' legendary statue of Zeus at Olympia, now lost, but re-animated in lovingly detailed description by the ancient traveller Pausanias. 'When the statue was completed,' he observes, 'Pheidias prayed to the god to make a sign if the work was to his liking, and immediately a flash of lightning struck the pavement in the place where a bronze urn was still standing in my day.'

In contrast to sculpture, Greek wall-painting on mythological themes is represented by pitifully few extant examples. We know that many major works in this medium once existed: the invaluable Pausanias records a lengthy description of what must have been particularly sumptuous compositions, namely murals by the artist Polygnotos in the *lesche* ('conversation house'; see p. 28) of the Knidians at Delphi, depicting the Fall of Troy, and Odysseus in the Underworld. However, by comparison with what has perished – and indeed by comparison with the remains of the wonderful frescoes of Minoan Crete and the splendid wall-paintings preserved from the Roman period – Classical Greece has left us relatively little. But the few exceptions are the more to be cherished, as with the sensational portrayal of Hades' abduction of Persephone, on the walls of a Macedonian royal tomb near Vergina.

Decorated mosaic flooring is another medium for which Roman civilization offers us far more surviving material than does Greek. But from the end of the 5th century BC onwards, and increasingly in the Hellenistic period, the use of this means of decorating aristocratic or royal dwellings became more widespread; and some notable examples can still be appreciated. One of the main centres of Macedonian culture, the city of Pella, is a case in point; particularly fine is the image of the god Dionysos seated on a panther. To get a sense of what a Greek mosaic floor might have looked like in its ancient

Dionysos riding on the back of a panther-like creature: mosaic floor, Pella, late 4th century BC. Dionysos is often associated with 'exotic' wild beasts such as this one, signifying the god's ferocity and danger as well as his physical grace and beauty.

Bellerophon, riding on his winged steed Pegasos, vanquishes the fearsome fire-breathing monster, Chimaira. Centrepiece of mosaic floor from Olynthos in the Chalkidike peninsula, 4th century BC.

setting, a good place to go is the site of Olynthos, just north of the three-pronged peninsula of northern Greece known as Chalkidike. There, open to the elements in its original location, is a floor-mosaic of Bellerophon, mounted on the winged horse Pegasos and ready to slay the monstrous Chimaira.

Myth in vase-painting

With vase-paintings, our evidence increases a thousandfold. The term 'vase' is conventionally used by archaeologists to denote a wide range of ceramic containers, from oil flasks to perfume boxes, water jars and mixing bowls. Such containers figured in a variety of social contexts, including funerals, weddings, drinking parties (*symposia*) and sacrificial rituals, as well as all the humdrum needs of domestic life, such as storage and cooking. Most containers were undecorated, but many displayed painted embellishment, which was fired along with the clay and hence acquired amazing resilience. Sometimes a scene represented on a pot can be securely identified as mythological; sometimes it may be drawn from 'real life'; sometimes it is impossible to say whether life is being represented like

myth, or myth like life – a fact which in itself illustrates the central role which Greek mythological narratives played in the imaginative lives of those who told them. At all events, the evidence of painted pottery provides us with a rich harvest of mythological narrative. It would, indeed, have been possible to find a vase-painting to illustrate most of the Greek myths discussed in this book.

Coins, gems and mirrors

Whereas vases often depict a scene that is, in effect, the synchronic distillation of several episodes of a mythical narrative, an ancient Greek coin typically portrays a politico-religious image which in some way encapsulates the identity of the community who struck the coin. Often the image will evoke the community's foundation myth, or a god or goddess particularly associated with the community. The best-known examples are probably the 'owls of Athene', the birds which symbolize the identity of the patron goddess of Athens. But throughout the Greek world we find comparable examples. For instance, the city of Mende (in the Chalkidike peninsula) celebrated the

One of the most famous Greek artefacts depicting mythological themes, the 'François Vase' (c. 570 BC; named after its discoverer) was found in an Etruscan tomb near Chiusi in 1844. Among the numerous episodes which it represents are the slaying of the Kalydonian boar, the funeral games of Patroklos, and the wedding of Peleus and Thetis.

(Below left) Athenian coin, 5th century BC, showing Athene's owl. The bird symbolized the protection exercised by the goddess over the people of Athens. The owl also kept a watchful eye on Athenian trade and commerce from its vantage point on the reverse side of coins, which bore Athene's own image on the obverse.

(Below right) Dionysos perched on a donkey, coin from the city of Mende in Chalkidike (late 5th century BC). In artistic representations Dionysos is often associated with the donkey. Here the god's demeanour is particularly relaxed: the wine vessel in his hand alludes to the liquid which ideally suits him to be the emblem of a city famous for its wine.

fame of its local wine by issuing a type of coinage representing the god Dionysos seated on the back of a donkey.

Rarer than coins, but no less instructive in terms of their bearing of mythological images, are engraved gems and finger rings; some wonderful examples of this form of micro-artistry have survived. Another of the smaller-scale arts of antiquity was concerned with the engraving of the lids or covers of mirrors (typically made of copper alloy). Often the imagery borne by these fine objects had a mythological flavour, perhaps designed to

conjure up an ideal or heroized world to complement the role of the mirror in the beautifying of an individual. Especially intricate examples were made by the Etruscans, whose representations of mythology frequently have the added interest of filtering Greek stories through their own, distinctive imaginative structures.

Texts

Images can tell us a great deal. But they are often silent at the very moments where we most want them to speak. One has only to consider the countless, frustrating ambiguities generated by attempts to interpret the religious symbolism of Minoan and Mycenaean images without the aid of accompanying texts. From the Archaic period of Greek civilization onwards, by contrast, we do have texts, in marvellous abundance. These texts provide the second of our two main sources of evidence for Greek myths.

Sometimes we are lucky enough to have direct access to texts written in antiquity. In such cases, the place where the texts were deposited has been the decisive factor in their preservation, since only in very special circumstances have perishable materials been able to survive the ravages of the two millennia and more which separate us from the ancient Greeks. The prime example of such circumstances is provided by papyri, i.e. sheets made from

(Above) A decorated Etruscan mirror, late 4th century BC, depicting the Judgment of Paris. Turan (the Etruscan Aphrodite) is seated; facing her are Uni (Hera; cf. the Roman Juno) and Menrva (Athene; cf. the Roman Minerva). At the far right is Elcsntre (Alexandros, an alternative name for Paris); at the far left is Althaia.

(Right) Gold ring from a chamber tomb at Mycenae. This might represent a cult of the death-and-rebirth of vegetation. The central figure may be a divinity or a priestess; the figure on the right appears to be in mourning; the one on the left holds a tree ecstatically.

(Opposite above) Extract from Book 2 of Homer's Iliad, *from the 2nd–3rd century AD 'Hawara Papyrus', discovered in Egypt.*

(Opposite below) 10th-century AD codex of Book 3 of Homer's Iliad *in the library of San Marco, Venice.*

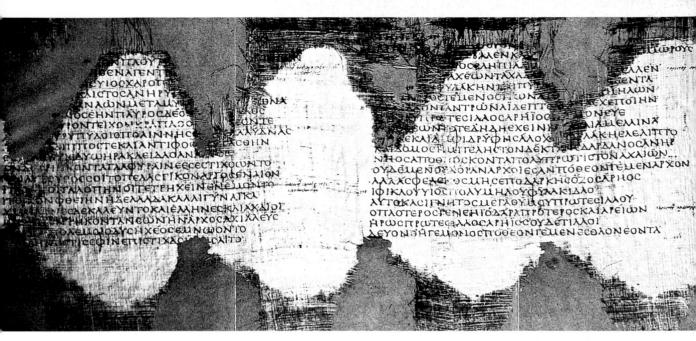

strips of the papyrus plant superimposed on one another to make a durable writing material. Although very occasionally papyri have been preserved in Greece, the bulk of them owe their survival to the bone-dry Egyptian sands: we have numerous, although often fragmentary, Greek writings from the Hellenistic period, when Greek civilization had expanded to include Egypt within its ambit. Given the importance of myths in Greek culture, it is no surprise to find that many papyrus texts relate or refer to mythological narratives. New finds of papyrus are still being made, and by no means all the papyri in the basements of our museums have been edited. The corpus of Greek mythology is not 'closed'.

Important though texts on papyrus are, they do not compare in quantity with a less direct source: the manuscripts that have survived complete, mainly from much later times. The advent and growing influence of Christianity within the Roman Empire meant that preservation of the great classics of the pagan world could by no means be guaranteed. That any writing at all has survived from Greek antiquity is due in large part to the civilization of Byzantium, where texts continued to be copied and recopied, enabling study of selected works from the great Hellenic past to form part of the Byzantine educational programme. When Byzantium at last fell to the Turks in 1453, many of these texts were brought westwards, to attain at last a less fragile existence thanks to printing. This complex process of transmission, which depended on a mixture of diligent commitment and pure chance, has resulted in the present availability of excellent and relatively intact texts of incomparable mythological documents.

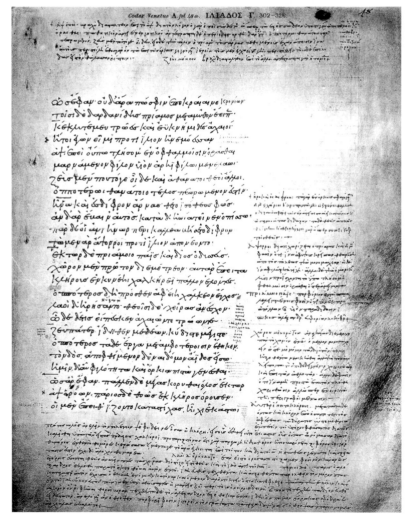

Contexts for Myth-telling

Myth-telling in everyday life

Greeks first experienced mythology as children, through the stories told to them by their elders; mostly our sources identify the tellers as the children's nurses, mothers or grandmothers. The point of some of these tales clearly lay in social control: threatening bogey-figures such as Lamia and Gorgo were invoked in the hope of getting the recalcitrant toddler to toe the line. But the exploits of the heroes and the Olympian deities figured also – indeed, Plato strenuously objected to the (as he saw it) anti-social results of letting children hear about violent dissension between Gods and Giants, and about bitter disputes among the Olympians themselves. Outside the home, once schools became a normal feature of Greek life (at least for boys), children's familiarity with the world of mythology was reinforced and extended in this context also: memorizing and reciting poetry formed a central part of the curriculum.

In later life, several different social and topographical contexts provided a framework for myth-narration. At the *symposion* – a kind of formalized drinking party for (principally) aristocratic, adult males – the participants sometimes exchanged songs and stories with a mythological slant, just as the vessels used by the drinkers often bore imagery with mythological resonance. Other typical contexts for story-telling were the cobbler's, the barber's, and the *lesche* (plural *leschai*), a communal gathering-place in which groups of (usually old) men would meet informally to talk and gossip; an anecdotal life of the poet Homer relates that he sang

(Left) The Gorgons were winged, female figures whose nightmarish expression provoked terror. One of the Gorgons was Medusa, mother of the winged horse Pegasos. In this terracotta relief (late 7th century BC) – perhaps part of an altar at Syracuse – Pegasos can be seen under the arm of his grotesque parent.

(Right) By defeating the rebellious Giants, the Olympians decisively consolidated their own power. On this Attic vase (mid-5th century BC) three Olympians take vigorous action: Zeus with his thunderbolt; at his side, Hera with her spear; finally Athene, protected by her awesome 'aegis', a snake-fringed cape bearing a Gorgon emblem.

(Above) Eleusis was one of the holiest places in Greece: it was the site of the 'Mysteries' in honour of Demeter and Persephone. These sacred rites drew participants from all over the Greek world. What the modern visitor sees here is the remains of the Roman rebuilding of the Telesterion ('Hall of Initiation').

(Left) Worship at Eleusis was mainly devoted to 'The Two Goddesses', Demeter and her daughter Persephone. On this relief (mid-5th century BC) Demeter is seated and holds three ears of corn. Standing before her is a younger figure, probably Persephone, holding torches. The contrast between darkness and illumination formed an important part of the initiatory experience at the Mysteries.

in, among other venues, a cobbler's shop and the 'leschai of the old men'.

Temples and other sites of ritual observance also provided contexts in which myths were narrated. In the case of many rituals, we can point to myths which in some sense 'went with' the action dramatized in the ceremony. For instance, the ritual complex known as the 'Eleusinian Mysteries' (Eleusis is west of Athens, in the direction of the Corinthian Gulf) finds its counterpart in the myth of the abduction of the goddess Persephone, best known to us from the version narrated in the *Homeric Hymn to Demeter*. As the myth related the seizing of Persephone by the god Hades and her eventual, albeit non-permanent, restoration to her mother Demeter, so the ritual at Eleusis, performed in honour of the 'two goddesses', i.e. Demeter and Persephone, enacted the contrast between the anxious gloom of the initiand and the joyful revelation experienced by the initiate. Unfortunately, in this case as in many comparable ones, it is not possible to say with certainty how or indeed whether the

(Below) Charon, ferryman of the Underworld, poles his boat towards a funeral stele (on the other side of the vase) beyond which is the figure of a woman; he will be offering her a passage to Hades. Charon's grim expression perfectly matches his occupation. The vase (5th century BC) is known as a lekythos, a type which often depicts Charon.

narration of the myth actually formed part of the rite. That said, analysis of myth-and-ritual complexes has been a productive growth area in the recent study of Greek myths. To take just one example, the Dutch scholar H. S. Versnel has thrown new light on the myth of Kronos – Zeus' primordial predecessor as ruler of the cosmos – by relating it to the Kronia festival, an in-between time of licence and topsy-turvy role-reversal during which slaves were waited on by their masters. As long as the festival lasted, 'old times' returned, with merry-making combined with chaos – a combination of positive and negative qualities which corresponded to a similar ambiguity in the character of Kronos himself. After the festival, the established order was reinstated, just as according to the myth Zeus had taken the place of Kronos. (On the myth of Kronos, see pp. 46–48.)

Narration of myths may be visual as well as verbal, and we can point to countless instances where the fixed imagery of temples, and the mobile imagery of cult vessels, evoked for the worshipper stories from the mythical past. So far as temple imagery is concerned, we need look no further than the marble metopes from the Athenian Parthenon: through their combination of dynamic energy and effortless permanence, these supreme sculptures illustrate the opposition between chaos and order, by juxtaposing the subversive aggression of the monstrous Centaurs with the controlled force of their heroic adversaries, the young Lapith men. As for the more mobile (but still amazingly durable) ceramic vessels used in various ceremonies, a typical example is offered by the small oil containing jars known as *lekythoi*, whose role in funerary ritual is complemented by the imagery which they commonly bear, imagery which, as often as not, evokes some aspect of death, for instance through the portrayal of the infernal ferryman Charon, or Hermes the Conveyor of Souls.

Myths in performance: Epic

If there is one thing which demonstrates conclusively that myths could be experienced as actively present in the lives of Greeks, it is the regularity with which mythical narratives were performed. Foremost among the mythological texts which survive from antiquity are the two towering epics ascribed to Homer: the *Iliad* and the *Odyssey*. The *Iliad* narrates a particular episode from near the end of the Trojan War when Achilles withdraws from battle, furious – the first word of the epic is *menin*, 'wrath' – because the Greek commander

An idealized marble bust of Homer – the poet. What relationship this sculpture (probably harking back to a Hellenistic original) bears to any real blind bard who ever sang in pre-Archaic Greece, it is impossible to say. But the quiet authority of this face suits the tremendous power of Homeric poetry.

Agamemnon has deprived him of his prize, the slave-concubine Briseis; only when his dear companion Patroklos has been killed by the Trojans does Achilles return to the fray. At last Achilles' anger abates – not completely, but just enough to allow him to restore the corpse of Hektor (Patroklos' slayer, slain in his turn by Achilles) to his inconsolable father Priam. Even such a brief summary indicates that the *Iliad* is about far more than one small episode in a war: it is a story of the precarious balance between pity and rage, and between heroism and all-consuming violence. And all this is played out under the eyes of the gods; although capable of feeling passionate involvement

Homer's supremacy amongst poets is expressed in a remarkable sculptured relief (2nd century BC) known as 'The Apotheosis of Homer'. Below a mountain-top dominated by Zeus, the Muses and Apollo, Homer himself is majestically seated on a throne (bottom left). Personified figures surround him, including Oikoumene ('The Inhabited World'), who places a wreath on his head; Mythos ('Myth'), the boy immediately in front of him; and Historia ('History'), to the right of Mythos, on the other side of a sacrificial altar.

(Left) Thanks to the authority conveyed by their staff and by their own eloquence, performers known as 'rhapsodes' held their audiences with recitations of epic verse. The painter of this vase (c. 480 BC) has included an inscription spelling out what the reciter's words were: 'So once in Tiryns...', part of a hexameter line from a mythological narrative as yet unknown to us.

Greek epic verse (for example its use of repeated 'formulae'), together with comparative evidence from modern societies where epic poetry is a living medium, have led scholars to conclude that the poems were, in all probability, originally composed orally. The Homeric poems themselves mention bards who sang heroic songs, to lyre accompaniment, at banquets in the residences of aristocrats and kings; it is by no means implausible that such contexts might have provided the setting for real-life performances of epic too. Performances at religious festivals are another likely context. In addition, we know that the Classical period saw professional reciters or 'rhapsodes' who performed excerpts from Homer in public competition. But smaller-scale settings also witnessed the performance of epic: Homer was said to have sung in a cobbler's shop and in the *lesche*. Add to all this the fact that ancient Greek schools placed considerable emphasis on pupils' learning to recite Homer aloud, and we can begin to get a picture of just how pervasive within society was the influence of these works of the poetic imagination.

Controversy continues about numerous aspects of Homeric poetry, not least whether the *Iliad* and the *Odyssey* were composed by one and the same poet, two poets, or many. But for the Greeks there was only one Homer – indeed he was referred to simply as 'the poet'. However, Homer was not the only great figure among the Archaic composers of epic verse (in the six-beat metre known as 'hexameter'). Regularly coupled with him was Hesiod, whose importance for the student of Greek mythology rivals that of Homer himself. Hesiod was said to have lived in the small village of Askra, near Mount Helikon in Boiotia. The two principal works

One of the contexts in which knowledge of the poetic mythological tradition was reinforced was the school. Here (Attic cup, c. 490 BC) a young man recites in front of his teacher, who follows the text on a papyrus roll.

with the fates of mortals, they are nevertheless ultimately remote, operating on a scale of time and power beyond human comprehension.

No less profound in its resonance is the other great Homeric epic, the *Odyssey*. Once more there is a strong and quite specific narrative core, namely the events surrounding the return home to Ithaca, after the Greeks' victory at Troy, of the endlessly resourceful hero Odysseus. But this is not just a tale of monsters vanquished and foes at home – that is, the suitors of his wife Penelope – duly despatched. It is also an exploration of what it means to be civilized, as expressed in the treatment of beggars, suppliants and strangers; and it probes emotions which are anything but straightforward, especially the ambivalence of Odysseus, drawn towards many different women yet simultaneously to one only. If the *Iliad* gives us only occasional glimpses of the peace that forms the framework for war, the *Odyssey* evokes a firmer sense of that world of solid and enduring normality – embedded above all in the practices of agriculture and in relationships within the family – with which even the greatest hero must come to terms.

How do we envisage these poems within their contexts? They were, of course, at some stage written down, when the need to preserve such acknowledged 'classics' was felt to be pressing. But epic poetry had a variety of performative contexts too; indeed, as we noted earlier, many features of

of his to survive are the *Theogony* and the *Works and Days*; usually dated to the 8th/7th centuries BC, these compositions are regarded by some scholars as even earlier than the epics of Homer.

As its name implies, the *Theogony* narrates the birth of the gods, tracing their origins back to the very beginnings of the universe; eventually, after a sequence of vicious struggles for succession, the Olympian divinities establish their power, under the at last unchallenged dispensation of Zeus. The *Works and Days* is a more varied and, if anything, an even more fascinating composition. The 'Works' referred to in the title are the labours which the peasant farmer must undertake if his crops are to survive and prosper; the 'Days' constitute a kind of informal calendar of the times within the year and the month when various practices – from ploughing to cutting one's nails – ought to be carried out. Weaving in and out of these themes is a recurring series of references to the sacred, including mythology. It is in the *Works and Days* that two enormously influential myths receive their earliest and most authoritative narration: the Five Races of Mankind (Gold, Silver, Bronze, Heroes, Iron), and the tale of Pandora, the gods' lovely but baneful gift to humanity.

(Above) The interior of an Attic cup (c. 460 BC) depicting a ritual celebration, with music, dancing and a burnt sacrifice. Poetry was often performed by a group of singers, who used mythology as a backdrop against which to explore personal experience.

Delphi: the ancient stadium, rebuilt in the 2nd century AD, is set high on the hillside. Victors in the 'Pythian' Games, held in honour of Apollo, were praised in choral song; mythology provided poets with a repertoire of themes for such celebrations.

Was Hesiod's poetry, like that ascribed to Homer, designed for 'performance'? It seems virtually certain that it was. There will surely have been opportunities to sing in local contexts such as the *lesche*; but real fame could only come from performance to a larger audience. According to one unverifiable but plausible tradition, Hesiod won a prize for one of his sung compositions at a contest in Chalkis in the isle of Euboia (mod. Evia), just over the water from his Boiotian homeland. The contest took place at the funeral of a local nobleman, the type of occasion at which a community could celebrate and explore its relationship with the past, thanks to the privileged voice of poetry.

Choral song

Homeric and Hesiodic poetry was performed by individuals. But another distinctive form of ancient Greek poetry was sung and danced by choirs. Such choral performances, to the accompaniment of the lyre, often had a competitive edge: we have particularly good evidence for competitions between choirs of young girls or young men. What differentiated this poetry from epic was the way in which, in contrast to the apparently more 'objective' voice of the epic narrator, the composer of choral lyric used mythology as a rich and resonant backdrop against which to explore personal experiences.

The context for such performances had a sacred aspect to it. We see this most clearly if we look at the type of choral lyric about which we know most, namely praise-poetry in honour of victors in the four great Games: at Nemea (northeastern Peloponnese), Isthmia (near Corinth), Delphi and Olympia. Each of these Games fell under the patronage of one of the gods: Poseidon at Isthmia, Apollo at Delphi, and Zeus at both Nemea and Olympia. Victorious competitors had their exploits celebrated in songs performed by a choir, whether at the site of the victory itself or in the victor's home community on his return.

Some of Greece's most illustrious poets were commissioned to immortalize such victories. The most famous of all was Pindar, who came from a village near Thebes in Boiotia. Pindar's rich and elaborate language bathed the physical prowess of contemporary athletes in the glow of their mythical antecedents. A typical example can

Olympia, home of the great Games in honour of Zeus; illustrated is the temple of Hera, the consort of Zeus. Athletes competed at the Games under the eyes of the gods. The achievements of the victors were immortalized in choral 'praise poetry'.

be found at the beginning of his ode (*Pythian* 9) praising a victory in the race-in-armour at Delphi. The victor, whose name was Telesikrates, came from the north African city of Kyrene (see p. 19), founded by colonists from the island of Thera (mod. Santorini), *c*. 630 BC:

I wish, with the aid of the deep-girdled Graces,
    to proclaim
the bronze-shielded Pythian victor: Telesikrates,
a fortunate man and a garland upon Kyrene, mistress
    of horses:
Kyrene whom once, from the windswept folds of Pelion,
    Leto's son Apollo, god of the flowing hair,
seized and carried away, a wild maiden, in his golden
    chariot.
He made her dwell as queen in a country rich in flocks,
    and all fruits,
blossoming and lovely, third root of the boundless earth.

Kyrene is at one and the same time a city and the homonym of a nymph loved by Apollo; the poet can thus borrow from the world of mythology images of beauty, wealth and fertility in order to enhance, by implication, the standing of the ordinary mortal Telesikrates.

Drama

Of all the Greek media for the performative narration of myths, none was more distinctive or influential than drama, an art-form which has bequeathed to us some of ancient Greece's most magnificent architectural constructions. Although the origins of Greek dramatic representation are obscure, what is not in doubt is that it was towards the end of the 6th century BC, in the city of Athens, that the theatre developed its characteristic features. Thespis, the dramatist who was linked with

this formative era, is hardly more than a name to us (though he has given us the word 'thespian'), but his successors Aischylos, Sophokles and Euripides (in tragedy) and Aristophanes (in comedy) span the next hundred years like mighty colossi of the imagination.

Their plays were put on in the Theatre of Dionysos, on the south slope of the Athenian Acropolis. Each year, in spring, around 15,000 people assembled for several days at the City Dionysia, a festival in honour of the god Dionysos. Three tragedians each put on a tetralogy of plays, consisting of three tragedies followed by a 'satyr play'. In a separate event, five comic dramatists each put on a single work. A jury of citizens, chosen by lot, voted to determine the winner in each competition. The context was both religious and civic: in the centre of the front row of the audience sat the priest of Dionysos, presiding over these astonishing examples of communal self-exploration by the citizen group.

Tragedy, satyr play and comedy shared at one level a common set of conventions: a few masked actors took the principal individual roles, while a chorus, also masked, provided continuity, commentary, and a more 'collective' perspective on the action. Other aspects of form were common to the three genres: dance and song, to the accompaniment of the *aulos* (double pipe), were crucial to the effect and the meaning. But the generic differences were as great as the similarities.

Tragedy: Tragedies dramatized events from the mythical past. Tales of the Trojan War and its aftermath figured large, as in Aischylos' *Oresteia* trilogy; *Philoktetes, Aias* and *Elektra* by Sophokles; and the *Trojan Women, Hekabe* and *Iphigeneia at Aulis*

The Theatre of Dionysos, below the Athenian Acropolis. It was here that the great tragedies and comedies were staged, in competitions witnessed by an audience of many thousands. In the centre of the front row sat the priest of Dionysos, embodying the god's keen interest in the dramatic events being represented.

of Euripides. But the exploits of other mythical heroes and heroines were replayed with equal power, notably the events surrounding Herakles (Sophokles' *Women of Trachis*; Euripides' *The Madness of Herakles*) and the family of Oedipus (as in the two *Oedipus* plays by Sophokles, and the same playwright's *Antigone*). More rarely, but with no less dramatic effect, episodes illustrating the relationships between the gods sprang into theatrical life before the eyes of the Athenian populace: the *Prometheus Bound* ascribed to Aischylos is one example. Thanks to these and the other extant plays (over thirty tragedies have survived intact), we can still be unnerved by the horror, and be moved to tears by the pity, of the explorations of the human condition to which this art form gave expression.

Satyr play: In satyr play the representation of myth is strikingly different. Satyrs are wild, lewd, snub-nosed followers of Dionysos who are usually depicted with the ears and tails of horses. Cowardly and grotesque, they overturn the *status quo*, bursting in upon mythological narratives and reducing them to burlesque or farce. Unfortunately only two examples have survived more or less intact: Sophokles' *Trackers* and the *Cyclops* of Euripides. The flavour of the latter play – a reworking of the episode in which Odysseus outwits the one-eyed giant Cyclops – is given by a brief dialogue between the satyrs' old leader Silenos and the drunken and ominously frisky monster. Such is the effect on the Cyclops of the wine which Odysseus has given him that he mistakes the satyrs for the lovely Graces, and Silenos for Zeus' boy-love Ganymede:

Cyclops The Graces are tempting me! That's enough! With this Ganymede I'll get better relief than with the Graces! And anyway, I prefer boys to females.
Silenos Am I Zeus' little Ganymede, Cyclops?
Cyclops You are, by Zeus! The boy I stole from the land of Dardanos!
Silenos I'm done for, lads. Dreadful things await me.

Comedy: Comic drama shows us a number of different faces in antiquity, from the riotously imaginative fantasies of 'Old Comedy' – whose most famous exponent was Aristophanes – to the more measured intricacies of plot and character to be found in the plays of Menander. So far as we can tell from surviving texts, the world of mythology impinges little on the theatre of Menander. But in Aristophanes, and in the many vase paintings apparently inspired by Old Comedy, we find traditional myths exploited, and turned upside down and inside out, for comic effect. Sometimes the intention is parodic, as when, in Aristophanes'

Laurence Olivier as Oedipus, in a 1945 production of the great Sophoklean tragedy Oedipus Tyrannos.

(Above) The satyr play, in which Dionysos' grotesque and sex-obsessed followers played a central role, evoked on a wine cup (c. 500–480 BC); Dionysos plays the lyre.

(Below) A common theme in Greek comedies is that of fantastic transformation. Here a vase-painter has depicted an actor dressed up as a cock.

Pentheus, who denied the divinity of the irresistible newcomer to the ranks of the Olympian gods. The only traces of grim humour here reside in Dionysos' sadistic toying with his victim, who is eventually torn limb from limb by his own mother and her sisters.

Written myths

Many of the performative contexts which we have just reviewed continued throughout antiquity to provide frameworks for oral mythological narration. To take an obvious example: one aspect of the extraordinary expansion of Greek culture in the wake of the conquests of Alexander the Great consisted in the building of *poleis*, 'cities'; within each *polis* the theatre was one of the most characteristic constructions; and with these theatres went the dramas represented in them, dramas whose original Athenian focus did not inhibit the subsequent, centuries-long, panhellenic popularity of the medium. But alongside such oral-performative contexts there began to develop more specifically literary settings for the retelling of the traditional stories. Signs of this process can be detected already in the Archaic period, but it gained momentum in Hellenistic times, particularly in the culturally intense atmosphere of the hellenized Egyptian city of Alexandria.

We may distinguish three main ways in which material from the world of mythology was subjected to such literary reworking. First, we have many examples of texts which, although composed in the same genres as earlier, orally performed myth-narrations, seem to have been primarily designed as texts-to-be-read. An instance would be the *Argonautica* ('Expedition of the Argonauts'), the four-book epic poem composed in the 3rd century BC by Apollonios of Rhodes. The metre (dactylic hexameters), many features of the language, and numerous aspects of the plot, demonstrate that this intricate poem was a deliberate renewal of Homer's *Iliad* and *Odyssey*, aimed at a cultured and literate public which could appreciate not only the echoes of Homer, but also the countless, subtle divergences from the path which that great predecessor had trodden. There are also many similarities to and differences from the work of other poets who had handled the story of Jason and Medea before Apollonios, notably Pindar (in his 4th *Pythian Ode*) and Euripides (in his tragedy *Medea*). This complex process of allusion is described by some modern literary critics as 'intertextuality'.

Secondly, we can trace the emergence of what seem to be entirely new genres of written mythological narrative. Once more, a decisive role was played by hellenized Alexandria. Two works may be taken as exemplifying the development to which we are referring. In his *Metamorphoses*, Antoninus Liberalis (probably 2nd century AD) retells in

Women at the Thesmophoria, Euripides' tragic version of a myth concerning the hero Telephos is mercilessly sent up. At other times there is no such specific allusion: it is just that mythological figures, whether heroic or divine, cheerfully rub shoulders with individuals drawn from contemporary Athenian life. A typical example is Aristophanes' exuberant and lyrical play *Birds*, in which two ordinary Athenians, fed up with life in their home city, set out to find a better future in Cloud-cuckooland; along the way they meet Tereus, who used to be a figure from mythology but, because of the unspeakable crimes he committed, was changed into a bird – in fact, into a hoopoe (see p. 154).

Our brief look at the three contrasting dramatic genres demonstrates once more that the world of Greek mythology is not closed or fixed or dominated by an orthodoxy, but mobile and fluid, responsive to the varying demands of context. Nowhere is this clearer than in the juxtaposition of two portrayals of Dionysos at the end of the 5th century. In Aristophanes' *Frogs* (405 BC) the god appears in cowardly and absurd guise, as he makes his riotously funny way down to Hades on his quest to bring the poet Euripides back up to the world of the living. Few of those whom he meets treat Dionysos with much respect ('Sit here, Fatty! … And stop fooling about!' bawls Charon, ferryman of the dead). Yet in Euripides' own *Bacchae* – staged soon after the poet's death, and thus separated from *Frogs* by just a few months – Dionysos is the terrifying punisher of the hapless King

succinct prose the outlines of tales in which mortals and gods underwent miraculous transformation. Antoninus' collection lacks the literary exuberance and virtuosity which characterizes the greatest reteller of such stories, namely the Roman poetic genius Ovid; but it does illustrate the fact that, at the periods when Antoninus and his Hellenistic sources were writing, there were reading publics keen to revisit the ancient tales of metamorphosis. Equally spare and unelaborate is the compilation which has come down to us under the name of the *Library of Mythology* attributed to one Apollodoros (date uncertain: some scholars have suggested 2nd century BC, others more plausibly 2nd century AD). This time there is no detectable thematic basis to the selection, as there was in the case of Antoninus' tales of transformation: Apollodoros relates, in bare outline, a narrative which indeed purports to be 'the complete world of Greek mythology'! For all its lack of pretension to literary quality, Apollodoros' compendium still repays re-reading, not least because its repeated signalling of the variant versions of any particular story reminds us of the cardinal fact that there was no one, single, orthodox way of retelling a given mythical episode.

A third type of text is perhaps the most significant of all, in terms of what it reveals about the location of myths within Greek culture. The authors of such texts do not so much retell myths as implicitly or explicitly explore the boundaries of 'the mythical', especially in opposition to a category such as 'the verifiable'; this opposition is sometimes expressed as a contrast between *muthos* – whence our term 'myth' – and *logos*, a term whose meanings extend from 'word' and 'story' to 'reason'. Some of the most spectacular works of imaginative and intellectual brilliance to have survived from classical antiquity conduct precisely this kind of boundary exploration. These works are conventionally assigned to the categories of 'history' and 'philosophy'.

Historians

To illustrate the various kinds of approach to 'the mythical' which historians could adopt, we may cite two of the very greatest: Herodotos and

(Above) The spectacular theatre of Segesta in western Sicily seen from the air. Its magnificent situation provided the backdrop for plays by the great tragedians and comedians of ancient Greece.

(Below) In the Hellenistic period the kings of Pergamon in Asia Minor aspired to outdo the cultural achievements of Athens and Alexandria. The theatre at Pergamon is perfectly designed to fit the curving slope of the citadel.

Thucydides. The project which Herodotos (5th century BC) sets himself in his *Enquiries* is to narrate, and to explain the causes of, the Greco-Persian Wars, fought in the first quarter of the 5th century BC. As part of the background to these violent events, Herodotos refers to earlier episodes, set in the time of myth, when Greeks and those whom they called 'barbarians' (i.e. non-Greek-speakers) came into conflict. What is important, and utterly typical of the way in which most Greeks viewed accounts of their mythical past, is that Herodotos follows a double strategy: on the one hand, he includes mythology within the evidence which a historian should evaluate; on the other hand, he subjects mythology to constant scrutiny from the point of view of its verifiability and plausibility. At the very beginning of his account, for instance, he mentions certain mythical heroines who were abducted by one side or the other – Io by Phoenicians (i.e. 'barbarians'), Europa by Greeks, then Medea by Greeks, and Helen by the 'barbarian' Paris. Herodotos presents such individual acts as forerunners of the later Greco-Persian wars. The myths are neither dismissed out of hand as 'mere' stories, nor regarded as repositories of a sacred and untouchable truth. They are simply more grist to the historian's mill. Herodotos implies that he accepts the historicity of these heroes and heroines, but passes in silence over some of the more extravagant details of their stories – such as Zeus' metamorphosis into a bull in order to abduct Europa.

These antique portrait heads give majestic – albeit idealized – form to four of Greece's greatest intellects.
From top left to bottom right: the historians Herodotos and Thucydides, and the philosophers Plato and Aristotle.

Tales of gods and heroes occupy but a tiny part of the historical narrative of Herodotos' great successor, Thucydides (second half of 5th century BC), who recorded and attempted to make sense of the Peloponnesian War. But in the early part of the narrative, where Thucydides uses 'ancient history' in order to show how much greater the Peloponnesian War was than any previous conflict, he does, for once, look back to mythology. Even more decisively than Herodotos had done, he examines his data with an eagle eye on its plausibility. Indeed, in his practice as a historian Thucydides claims explicitly to reject *to muthodes* ('the mythical', 'the story-like'): 'it may well be that my history will seem less easy to listen to because of the absence in it of *to muthodes*' – a barely disguised dig at Herodotos.

Yet even Thucydides accepts without demur the historicity of the Trojan War; it is just that, careful historian as he is, he subjects some of the claims made in the Homeric poems to the sceptical judgment of *Realpolitik* ('It was, I am inclined to think, because Agamemnon was the most powerful ruler of his day that he was able to assemble the expedition, and not so much because the suitors of Helen had bound themselves by the oaths which they had sworn to Tyndareos'). Once again, myths are neither dismissed as pure fiction, nor accepted as unchallengeable gospel.

Philosophers

Just as historians conducted a dialogue with the world of mythology, so too did those we call 'philosophers'. One common approach to the history of ancient Greek philosophy has been to present it as the story of a select group of intellectual pioneers who wrestled with, and progressively worked towards overthrowing, the mythico-religious environment within which they and their fellows were living. The first of these pioneers are known collectively as 'Presocratics' – individual speculative thinkers, from a variety of different *poleis* in the Greek world, active in the 6th and early 5th centuries BC (hence the name: 'before Sokrates'). One such thinker is Xenophanes, in whose reported opinion the gods of Homer and Hesiod were immoral, 'stealing and committing adultery and deceiving each other'. More radically, Xenophanes argued that not just certain kinds of all-too-human divine behaviour, but the very nature of these anthropomorphic gods, must be called into question, if one reflects that humans formulate their ideas of gods in their own (human) image – Egyptian gods being snub-nosed and black, Thracian gods having blue eyes and red hair. An even more impressive voice raised against traditional mythology (according to this same story of pioneers) is that of Plato (5th/4th century BC), who also railed against the immoralities of the divinities depicted by Homer and Hesiod, setting against such unworthy tales a more exalted and more absolute conception of divinity, to which one might hope to gain access through the power of dialectical argument. Ultimately there came Aristotle (4th century BC), whose intellectual priorities of empirical observation and logical argumentation could find no room for the fantasies of poets and other purveyors of tales.

This story is a misleading simplification. It is certainly the case that a series of brilliant thinkers – amongst them, to be sure, the Presocratics, Plato and Aristotle – did define central aspects of their intellectual positions in opposition to the traditional myths. However, first, these innovative intellectual strategies had little discernible impact on more widely held, socially pervasive attitudes towards stories of gods and heroes – these speculations were, that is to say, by and large unrepresentative. Secondly, these very thinkers were, to varying degrees, themselves intellectually implicated in the assumptions underlying the traditional tales. Many of the beliefs of such Presocratic philosophers as Empedokles and Pythagoras might with as much justice be described as 'mystical' or 'magical' as 'philosophical' ('I walk amongst you all an immortal god', wrote Empedokles, 'no longer a mortal'). Plato, for his part, was well aware of the contribution which stories, *muthoi*, could make towards the quest for truth, provided one remembered that such stories were not in themselves absolutely true. Such is the spirit in which he relates the 'myth of Er' at the end of his dialogue *The Republic*: this myth, speculating as it does on the fates of various types of mortal after death – and on the way in which the souls of the deceased could choose the sort of life into which they were to be reborn – ventures into territory inaccessible to the more orthodox procedures of Platonic dialectical argumentation. Er allegedly came to life again on his funeral pyre, and proceeded to relate the experiences which he had had in the Other World.

As for Aristotle, it is true that his writings on science and logic defer even less to mythology than do the investigations of Thucydides. Nevertheless, Aristotle concedes that the evidence of myth-tellers may from time to time need to be taken into account: indeed, given the Aristotelian belief that history is cyclic, the writings of the *muthologoi*, 'myth-tellers', may preserve a record of earlier explanations of which the contemporary scientist/philosopher needs to be aware. And we should remember too that even an Aristotle listened to tales as a child, handled all manner of mythologically decorated vessels, learned Homer at school, and went to the theatre, composing, in due course, the most influential single treatise ever written about the genre, namely *Poetics*, in which his brilliant analysis of tragedy turns on the role within it of the plot – which in Greek is designated by that astonishingly versatile term, *muthos*.

Plato Attacks Traditional Mythology

In this extract from the *Republic*, Sokrates and his interlocutor Adeimantos discuss how undesirable it would be if some of the traditional tales about the gods were to be told in the ideal city:

Sokrates First of all, it appears, we ought to supervise the myth-tellers, making sure that only noble stories are selected, while the rest are rejected. We shall persuade nurses and mothers to relate the selected stories to their children, so moulding them spiritually rather than corporally. Of the stories told at present, we must reject the majority.

Adeimantos Which stories do you mean?

Sokrates In the greater myths we shall be able to see the lesser also; for the form and effect of the greater and lesser should be identical, don't you think?

Adeimantos Yes, I do. But I don't know what these 'greater' myths are that you're referring to.

Sokrates The ones which Hesiod, Homer and the other poets used to tell us. For these people, I suppose, used to – and still do – compose false stories and relate them to mankind.

Adeimantos Which stories? And what objection do you have to them?

Sokrates An objection which must be lodged emphatically at the outset, especially if the false tale is also an ugly one.

Adeimantos How do you mean?

Sokrates I mean when a story-teller makes a bad likeness of the nature of the gods and heroes, like a painter making an inaccurate representation.

Adeimantos That's certainly something one ought to object to. But exactly what kinds of things are we talking about?

Sokrates Well, on the most important subject concerning the most important individuals, there was the ugly tale narrating the deeds which Hesiod ascribed to Ouranos, and the vengeance taken by Kronos upon him. As for the things which Kronos did and suffered at the hands of his son, even supposing they were true, these matters should not, I think, be carelessly related to those who are young and lacking in judgment. Rather, they should be passed over in silence; or, if they must be told, they should be communicated to a very few people in the context of secret mysteries, at a rite involving the sacrifice not just of a pig, but of an animal both large and difficult to procure. That way, such stories will be heard by the fewest people possible.

Adeimantos These stories are certainly tricky to deal with.

Sokrates And they should not, Adeimantos, be told in our city.

The Platonic Sokrates goes on to rule out as unsuitable the myth of the Battle of the Gods and Giants, as well as all kinds of other feuds between divinities. A wonderful storyteller himself, Plato is only too well aware of the power, for good or ill, of imaginative narratives about divine and heroic exploits.

Stories of the Beginning

The quest for origins is universal. Just as individuals will seek to establish a sense of their own rootedness by tracing their ancestry, so social groups, communities, and even whole civilizations legitimize and authenticate their place in the scheme of things by making claims about where they came from. One of the most effective ways of staking such claims is through myths; for a myth can seem to ground a claim to legitimacy in the natural order of things, tracing the merely contingent present back to a beginning in a more authoritative and 'definitive' era. But it is not just the social order of whose origin myths speak. They also reach back to the origin of the human race, and of the cosmos itself.

The Greeks told many stories about beginnings. Some stories narrated the origins of particular cities or social groups; some the origins of humanity ('anthropogony'); some took a further step backwards, to ask about the origins of the gods ('theogony') or of the universe itself ('cosmogony'). All these kinds of myths will be discussed in this chapter. We begin with myths which explore the ultimate question: how did the cosmos originate?

Aphrodite rises from the sea-foam, born from the severed genitals of the sky-god Ouranos. The extraordinary sensuality of the drapery has made this marble relief into an icon of female beauty (the 'Ludovisi Throne'; perhaps part of an altar, mid-5th century BC).

II Myths of Origin

Cosmogony

Accounts of the origin and development of the universe can be found in many cultures throughout the world; and our contemporary, 'scientific' world has its own way of telling such stories through cosmological theory. Like the peoples of other cultures, the ancient Greeks told their own tales about the beginnings of all that is. Such tales do not bulk large within the whole corpus of Greek mythology, which devotes more attention to the deeds of divinities and heroes in the already constituted world. But occasionally speculation does reach back to the ultimate beginning. A striking example is found in one of the earliest surviving Greek literary works.

Hesiod's *Theogony*

To profess to know about the ultimate beginning represents a claim to more-than-everyday knowledge. In ancient Greece, poets – inspired by the Muses – were one group who might stake such a claim. The earliest surviving example of Greek cosmogonical speculation is Hesiod's poem *Theogony* (8th/7th century BC). Its themes are violent strife, desire, and the ultimate victory of the Olympian divinities under the sovereignty of Zeus, who is regarded as still holding sway in the poet's own day. We shall examine this complex narrative in some detail.

At the beginning of everything there was Chaos; this does not mean 'Disorder', but rather 'Chasm', in the sense of a dark, gaping space. Afterwards came Gaia ('Earth') and Eros ('Sexual Love'), the principle whose existence is a prerequisite for all the subsequent acts of procreation by which the cosmos gradually became populated. From these three (with the possible addition, according to one reading of Hesiod's text, of Tartaros, a grim and

Genealogy of the Gods

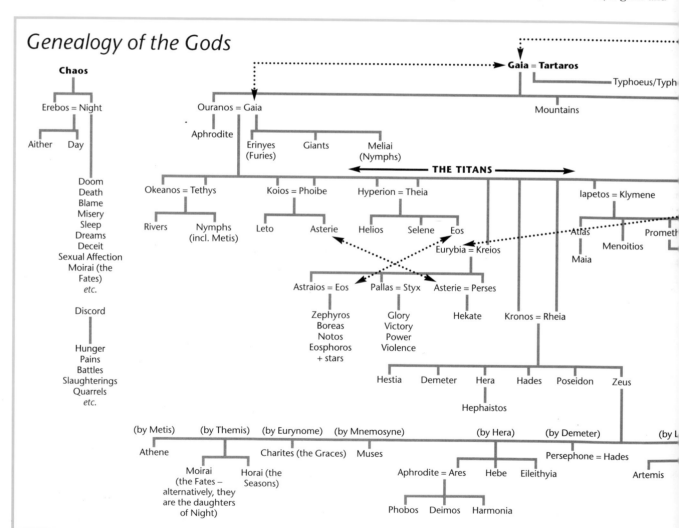

terrifying region below the Earth) there originated all that exists.

Next there came into being more of the spatial and temporal features which define the world. Chaos generated Erebos (a dark, infernal realm similar to Tartaros) and Night who, after union with Erebos, produced Aither (something between 'Light' and 'Air') and Day. Gaia produced, without union, Ouranos ('Sky'), who would be a kind of permanent, matching covering for her; out of herself she also brought forth Mountains and Pontos ('Sea'). More significant from the point of view of the later development of the story are Gaia's children by Ouranos. These included a race of divinities known as the Titans, amongst whom were Okeanos (i.e. Ocean, the river which encircles the world) and Kronos, youngest and most devious of Gaia's offspring, as well as the mighty one-eyed Cyclopes, forgers of the thunderbolt, and the three monstrous Hundred-Handers, each with fifty heads and one hundred arms springing from his shoulders.

Okeanos was the great river that flowed around the earth, and also the source of all fresh waters. In his human form as a bearded old man, Okeanos became a particularly familiar image in Roman times. This illustration is from the centre of a large silver salver from the Mildenhall treasure, 4th century AD.

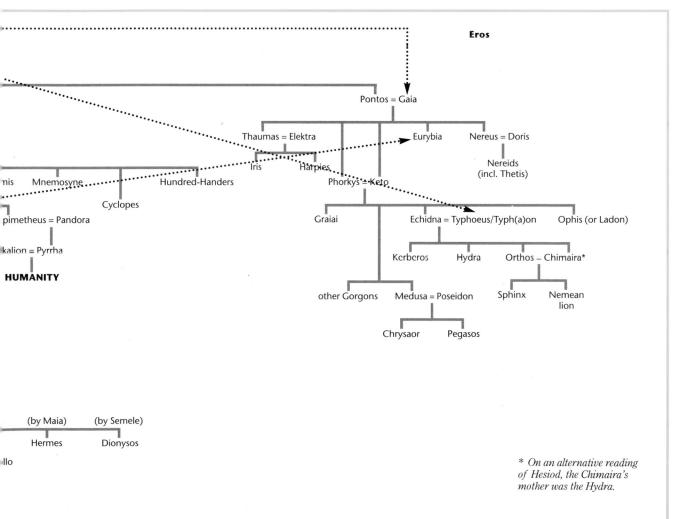

* On an alternative reading of Hesiod, the Chimaira's mother was the Hydra.

The gods' succession

The scene is now set for one of the poem's central themes: a violent struggle for succession. Gods do not voluntarily surrender power, nor does that power diminish with age. They are thus locked into a seemingly unwinnable war with their divine offspring: the immovable against the irresistible. However, the *Theogony* narrative shows that older deities can be circumvented by younger ones, provided the latter show enough ingenuity and daring. So it was with Ouranos and Kronos.

Ouranos sought to prevent his offspring by Gaia from emerging into the light: he hid them away in a recess of Gaia/Earth as each was born. This act of blocking is a counterpart to another aspect of Ouranos' behaviour, namely his desire for unremitting intercourse with Gaia – which is another way of saying that, in the time 'before', Earth and Heaven were an indissoluble whole.

It took an act of calculated, horrific violence on the part of one of Ouranos' sons to alter this situation. As Ouranos spread himself once more in the act of intercourse, Kronos sprang out of hiding and cut off his father's genitals with a sickle made of adamant (an unimaginably strong substance); the act of separation was sealed as Kronos hurled the severed genitals away. In spite of Kronos' act, Ouranos' ability to procreate was not yet quite exhausted. The prodigious fertility of the combined semen-and-blood could not fail to generate new life. Wherever drops fell from the cast-away flesh, they inseminated Gaia: this is how the Furies (Erinyes), Giants and Nymphs (the Meliai) came into being. As for the genitals themselves, they created the goddess Aphrodite, who distilled in her own nature the sexuality implicit in the manner of her conception.

Hesiod's *Theogony*: genealogy

The separation of Ouranos and Gaia inaugurated a definitive change: henceforth, the imprisoned Titans could emerge to wield their power and to produce their own progeny. Before reaching that culminating part of his narrative, however, Hesiod fills in another part of the genealogical matrix, by listing the offspring (and their offspring) of two of his primeval beings, Night and Pontos/Sea. In the case of both sets of descendants a clear 'mythical logic' is at work.

Amongst Night's grim progeny were Doom, Death, Blame and Misery (because the night is gloomy); Sleep and Dreams and Deceit and Sexual Affection (because they belong at night); the Fates (because one's fate is accomplished at death, which also belongs to Night); and Discord, who in her turn generated such ineluctable aspects of existence as Hunger, Pains, Battles, Slaughterings and Quarrels.

From Pontos/Sea descend many of the creatures, lovely or monstrous, that populate the world, especially its waters. One of Pontos' sons, Nereus, the righteous Old Man of the Sea, fathered fifty lovely sea-nymphs in union with Doris, a daughter of Okeanos. Thaumas ('Marvellous'), another son, enjoyed a similar liaison with Elektra; among his children were the wind-swift Harpies and Iris, divine messenger and goddess of the rainbow. A third son of Pontos, Phorkys, lay with his own sister Keto ('Sea Monster'), and together they generated a troop of monstrous creatures: the Graiai (women old already at birth), the Gorgons, and probably also (the text is uncertain) cave-dwelling Echidna, nymph above the waist and serpent below it; Echidna in her turn would count among her descendants the Chimaira and the Sphinx; for it is a regular pattern within Greek mythological

The Birth of Aphrodite

About [the genitals] a white foam grew from the immortal flesh, and in it a girl formed. First she approached holy Kythera; then from there she came to sea-girt Cyprus. And out stepped a modest and beautiful goddess, and the grass began to grow all round beneath her slender feet. Gods and men call her Aphrodite, because she was formed in foam [*aphros*], and Kythereia, because she approached Kythera, and Cyprus-born, because she was born in wave-washed Cyprus, and laughter-loving [*philommeides*], because she appeared out of genitals [*medea*]. Eros and fair Desire attended her birth and accompanied her as she went to join the family of gods. And this has been her allotted province from the beginning among men and immortal gods: the whisperings of girls; smiles; deceptions; sweet pleasure, intimacy, and tenderness.

(from Hesiod's *Theogony*)

The skill of the sculptor of the 'Ludovisi Throne' (see pp. 42–43) brings out Aphrodite's sweet desirability.

genealogy that a monstrous liaison will generate a monstrous progeny.

The narrative now renews contact with the Titans – that is, with the descendants of Ouranos and Gaia. Okeanos, the river that surrounds all, lay with his sister-Titan Tethys: their offspring were rivers great and small, and the nymphs, said to number 3000. Hesiod's catalogue of the names of some of them illustrates the kind of incantatory magic which a 'mere' list can work on a hearer:

Peitho and Admete, Ianthe and Elektra,
Doris, Prymno, and godlike Ourania,
Hippo, Klymene, Rhodeia, and Kallirhoe,
Zeuxo, Klytia, Idyuia, and Pasithoe,
Plexaura and Galaxaura, and lovely Dione,
Melobosis, Thoe, and fair Polydora…

By no means all these nymphs have a perceptible connection with water (see pp. 184–85). One who does is Styx, the stream whose waters take on fearsome powers under the regime of Zeus; she it is by whom the gods swear their oaths (see pp. 208–9).

Hesiod's *Theogony*: the birth of Zeus

The Titans inhabited a time which was both 'before' and transitional – a time when the world's physical framework was still being created. Thus when two Titans, Theia and Hyperion, lay together, their children were Helios ('Sun'), Selene ('Moon'), and Eos ('Dawn'); in her turn Eos gave birth to the winds and stars. Two other pairs of Titans bring the Hesiodic narrative to the brink of the Olympian era. The offspring of Phoebe and Koios is Leto, soon to bear Apollo and Artemis. More significant still is the union of Rheia and Kronos, which heralds the next stage in the cosmic-dynastic struggle for succession.

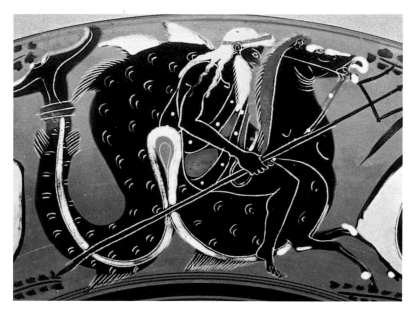

To Kronos Rheia bore Hestia ('Hearth'), Demeter, Hera, Hades, Poseidon and, finally, Zeus. Whereas Ouranos had tried to block succession by thrusting his offspring back into Gaia, Kronos' tactic was to swallow his children whole: since he could not kill immortal beings, he ingested them, having learned from Ouranos and Gaia to fear overthrow at the hands of his own child. In her grief at seeing her successive newborns disappear, Rheia sought the advice of her parents – the same Ouranos and Gaia. On their suggestion she took herself to Crete when she was about to bear Zeus, her youngest. In a cave – Hesiod locates it at Lyktos, but other sources speak of Mount Dikte or Mount Ida – she bore her son. To fool the voracious

The old sea-god Nereus, son of Pontos, moves about his domain mounted on a 'hippocamp', a marvellous, hybrid creature of the deep. Attic cup, c. 520 BC.

Mount Ida (mod. Mount Psiloritis) in Crete was one of the places where tradition located the birth of Zeus. At 2,500 m (8200 ft) in height it is one of the most dramatic features of the Cretan landscape.

even the strongest'). Defeated at last, the Titans were confined in Tartaros; once more, the notion of imprisonment replaces that of killing, for immortals cannot die. Even now Zeus' power was under threat, this time from the monstrous Typhoeus, Gaia's child by the grim Tartaros (who is a person as well as a place):

Out of his shoulders there emerged a hundred terrifying snake-heads with black tongues licking, and the eyes in the strange heads flashed fire under the brows; and there were voices in all the monstrous heads, emitting every kind of inexpressible sound.

Typhoeus too eventually succumbed to the thunderbolt, to be imprisoned in Tartaros (or, in some accounts, under Mount Etna).

In a final genealogical section Hesiod outlines the dynastic marriages by which Zeus consolidated his rule. His first wife was Metis ('Crafty Intelligence'). When Zeus learnt that the son whom she would bear after her firstborn Athene would rule over gods and men, he took the by now obvious step of *swallowing* his wife, which meant that the soon-to-be-born Athene would be born from Zeus himself (in fact, born out of the top of his head, split open with an axe wielded by, according to different versions, Hephaistos or Prometheus). Succession was now definitively blocked, and the liaisons which Zeus contracted henceforth would produce children who would generally act in support of, rather than in opposition to, the broad framework of his rule. From Themis ('Due Order') he produced the three lovely Horai ('the Seasons)', by name Eunomia ('Lawfulness'), Dike ('Right') and Eirene ('Peace'), and also the three Moirai ('Fates'), namely Klotho, Lachesis and Atropos; by Eurynome, an Oceanid, he had Charites ('the Graces'): Aglaia, Euphrosyne and Thaleia; the Muses came from Zeus' dalliance with Mnemosyne ('Memory').

Other unions led to the arrival of major new Olympian divinities: Apollo and Artemis (from Leto), Ares (from Hera), Hermes (from Maia, daughter of Iapetos' son Atlas). Hephaistos would emerge out of Hera alone as a kind of tit-for-tat for Zeus-born Athene (though the Homeric version gives Hephaistos' parents as, less anomalously, Zeus and Hera together). As for Dionysos, his perceived role as a late-comer is expressed by the fact that his mother is Semele, a mortal – which raises the issue of human beings (see pp. 53; 54).

The establishment of Zeus' power is now complete. There is no suggestion that his is a temporary regime: in this conception of the state of the world (and Hesiod's view is here typical of that expressed by most Greeks), no 'twilight of the gods' is envisaged, on the pattern of the Norse idea of Ragnarök (the day of the destruction of the world, when the great god Odin would be swallowed up by the terrifying wolf Fenrir). In the Hesiodic scheme, Zeus' is the sovereignty, and Zeus' it will remain.

One of the most striking ancient representations of the Kronos myth is this marble relief (2nd century AD). Rheia offers the wrapped stone to Kronos – who believes the wrapping to contain his baby son Zeus. The figures' calm expressions belie the savagery surrounding this episode: Kronos devoured his children one by one in order to prevent them from usurping his power.

Kronos, she wrapped a stone in swaddling clothes; Kronos duly devoured this 'child' too. Soon Zeus' force grew. He made Kronos vomit up everything that he had swallowed: first the stone (which Zeus placed at Delphi 'to be a monument in time to come, and an object of wonder for mortal men'), then the children.

Hesiod's *Theogony*: the power of Zeus

The remainder of the *Theogony* details the means by which Zeus definitively established his power. First he outwitted Prometheus, son of the Titan Iapetos (see pp. 54–56). Then, with the formidable Hundred-Handers as his allies, Zeus led the Olympians against the Titans in a battle of truly cosmic proportions: 'the indescribable flame reached the holy sky, and the brilliant glare of the thunderbolt and the lightning dazzled the eyes of

(Left) The birth of Athene from the head of Zeus (black-figure vase, 6th century BC). The warrior goddess is armed, ready to take her place among the assembled Olympians. Perched on Zeus' throne is an owl, the inscrutable symbol of Athene and Athens.

Other versions of cosmogony and theogony

Hesiod's account of first beginnings is the earliest and most detailed to survive, and was regarded, later in antiquity, as particularly influential. But it was not considered to be uniquely authoritative. There were numerous variants, some supplementing Hesiod and some diverging from him quite considerably.

Aphrodite: As a small but significant example of divergence we may take the parentage of Aphrodite. According to Homer's *Iliad* she was born, not from the severed genitals of Ouranos, but by a more orthodox route: her parents were Zeus and the goddess Dione, a little-known figure for whom our most extensive evidence relates to her role as Zeus' consort at the oracle of Dodona in Epeiros. Homer's genealogy thus shifts the emphasis away from Aphrodite-as-cosmic-principle to Aphrodite-as-anthropomorphic-deity. Indeed the Homeric Aphrodite is all too human: when wounded in the hand by the mortal hero Diomedes, *this* Aphrodite rushes from the battlefield to be comforted by her mother, like a child who has hurt herself in the playground.

Typhoeus/Typh(a)on: Another divergence from the Hesiodic account concerns Zeus' monstrous adversary Typhoeus, whom other sources refer to as Typhon or Typhaon. Amongst the various versions of his parentage is one which relates that he was produced by Hera alone, as a counterpart to Zeus-born Athene. In the mythographic *Library* ascribed to Apollodoros, and in one of the metamorphosis stories compiled by Antoninus Liberalis, we find preserved a fascinating account of Typhon's

struggles with the Olympians. In this version, the gods take flight to Egypt, transforming themselves into animals to avoid detection (the Greeks' perception of the Egyptians as believers in 'animal gods' doubtless plays a role in this story). In hand-to-hand combat with Zeus Typhon cuts through his adversary's tendons, and then carries him back to his cave-lair in Cilicia (southern Asia Minor). After recovering his tendons – which Typhon had hidden in a bearskin – and thus regaining his strength, Zeus at last overcomes his foe, for good measure hurling Mount Etna at him and pinioning him beneath it.

The *Homeric Hymns*

In other cases we find mythological accounts which do not so much diverge from Hesiod as supplement him. Prime examples here are stories of the births of some of the principal Olympians, as narrated for instance in the so-called *Homeric Hymns*. Each of these compositions (ascribed in antiquity to Homer, though their authorship is unknown) celebrates the origins and exploits of a single deity; the hymns may well have been intended for performance at a festival for the god or goddess concerned.

Apollo: Many slightly differing tales circulated about the birth of Apollo and his twin sister Artemis. The earliest and best-known version is that in the *Homeric Hymn to Delian Apollo*. For a long time the goddess Leto roamed Greece in search of a place to give birth. But her search was in vain, since the wrath of jealous Hera pursued her as it pursued so many of Zeus' other lovers: each place in turn rejected the distressed mother-to-be. But at last

According to one version of the mythological tradition, the parents of Aphrodite were Zeus and Dione. The divine couple were worshipped at Dodona in Epeiros, where this coin depicting the pair was struck (late 3rd century BC).

the humble, low-lying Cycladic island of Delos agreed to accept her, persuaded by Leto's promise that it would soon be the home of a glorious shrine to Apollo. According to a version related in the *Hymn to Delos* by Kallimachos (3rd century BC), Delos' reward for accepting Leto was that the isle, which had hitherto floated about in the sea, would henceforth be fixed for ever. Leto's sufferings were not yet at an end, however: for nine days and nine nights Hera contrived to keep the goddess of childbirth, Eileithyia, in ignorance of Leto's plight. But eventually Eileithyia reached Delos, and Apollo was born: 'so she cast her arms around a palm tree and knelt in the soft meadow; and the earth smiled beneath her. The child leaped out into the light, and all the goddesses raised a cry.' (According to Apollodoros' account, Apollo's twin sister Artemis was born first, and then acted as midwife for the birth of her brother.) Ever afterwards Apollo was linked as intimately with lowly Delos as he was with the peaks and chasms of Delphi.

Hermes: Apollo's brother Hermes is another Olympian whose origins are celebrated at length in a *Homeric Hymn*. Son of Zeus and the nymph Maia, he was born in a cave on Mount Kyllene in Arcadia. Having arrived in the world at dawn, by noon he was up to his characteristic tricks. He found a tortoise waddling along outside his cave, and in a trice had scooped out its flesh from the shell; with the addition of reeds, a stretched ox-hide, and strings made of sheep-gut, it became the first lyre. But as evening drew on, Hermes grew tired of his musical

toy. With miraculous speed he made his way to Pieria in northeastern Greece, where Apollo's cattle were pasturing. He stole fifty of them; to confuse pursuers he made the beasts walk backwards, and disguised his own footprints by wearing sandals plaited from twigs. In this way Hermes, the master

of opposites, blended forward and backward – and also babyhood and adulthood, for his return to the cave coincided with a reversion to the state of infancy. However, in spite of the trickster's wiles, Apollo traced his property to the thief's lair; under Zeus' dispensation, the rift between brother and

Mount Kyllene in Arcadia, legendary birthplace of Hermes. Like all Greek mountains, Kyllene was regarded as a place of wildness, where sacred and uncanny things might happen at any time.

Stories from Greek mythology were imaginatively retold in Etruria. On this Etruscan water-jar (c. 530 BC), baby Hermes sleeps – or pretends to – while Apollo remonstrates with Hermes' mother Maia over the theft of his cattle. The identity of the man on the far right is unknown; perhaps it is Maia's husband. The cattle, concealed in a cave, are visible proof of Hermes' guilt.

51

The Orphic Alternative

Renowned though Hesiod's narrative was, it was by no means the only account of 'first beginnings' in circulation. A very different narrative, embracing anthropogony as well as cosmogony, was ascribed to the legendary poet Orpheus. Until recently our knowledge of so-called 'Orphic poetry' relied mainly on extensive quotations by later Neoplatonist writers, who noted many anticipations of their own philosophy in these poems; but a new development took place in 1962 in the Macedonian town of Derveni, with the discovery of a fragmentary papyrus containing part of a 4th-century BC commentary on an Orphic theogony. The consequences of this find are still being assimilated; indeed, a definitive scholarly edition of the papyrus is still awaited. But what is clear is that, already in the early Hellenistic period and probably long before that, a non-Hesiodic view of the development of the cosmos was being narrated.

The Orphic narrative of origins differs from the Hesiodic in two major ways. First, it ascribes a fundamental role in creation to a divine figure who preceded not only Ouranos but even Night. This figure is referred to sometimes as Protogonos ('First Born'), sometimes as Phanes ('The One who Makes to Appear' or 'The One who Appears'), sometimes under other names (Eros, Bromios, Erikepaios, Metis, Zeus), as befits one who incorporates all existence within himself. What of the origin of First Born himself? According to our later sources, Time created a cosmic egg, from which First Born emerged, winged and bisexual – containing implicit within him all that would follow.

The second difference from the Hesiodic narrative is more radical. According to the Orphic theogony, Zeus' rule was succeeded by that of his son Dionysos, the product of a union between Zeus and his own daughter Persephone. Urged on by a jealous Hera, the Titans cooked and devoured the baby Dionysos; in return, Zeus struck the Titans with his thunderbolt. At this point theogony becomes anthropogony, for it was from the soot of the incinerated Titans that humanity was formed. As for Dionysos, he was destined to be born again, regenerated by Zeus thanks to the fact that the baby's heart had been preserved by the Titans.

This last episode in the Orphic theogony combines the genesis of humanity with the death and rebirth of Dionysos. In so doing, it dovetails with certain rites linked with the name of Orpheus. Individual practitioners known as *Orpheotelestai* ('Initiators of Orpheus'), and groups who participated in 'mystery' cults in honour of Dionysos, were concerned with 'eschatology', that is, beliefs in the Afterlife. In order to maximize his or her chances of a successful transition to the world of the dead, a person needed to go through certain procedures, some of which were specified in ritual formulae inscribed onto thin leaves of gold, buried with the deceased. From leaves which have survived from sites in southern Italy (see p. 212) and in Thessaly, it seems that Dionysos could be thought of as a potent intercessor on behalf of the dead, since (following the Orphic genealogy), he might be able to persuade his mother Persephone, Queen of the Dead.

Understanding Orphic beliefs continues to pose problems. Some scholars used to believe that there was actually an 'Orphic religion', in virtual opposition to the 'normal' religion of the *polis*. Such a view is regarded as less tenable today. What is undeniable is that the existence of distinctively 'Orphic myths' provides yet one more instance of the richness and plurality of the Greek mythological network.

The Derveni Papyrus, which preserves unique evidence about ancient cosmogonical views.

brother was healed, as Hermes' gift of the lyre to Apollo was reciprocated by Hermes' taking over of the patronage of herds.

Dionysos

The latest arrival amongst the Olympians was generally reckoned to be Dionysos, whose birth is recorded by Apollodoros:

As for Semele [a mortal], Zeus fell in love with her, and lay with her without Hera's knowledge. Now Zeus had agreed to do whatever Semele asked, and, as the result of a deception by Hera, she asked him to come to her just as he had come when he was wooing Hera. Unable to refuse, Zeus came to her bedchamber in a chariot, complete with lightning and thunder, and hurled a thunderbolt. Semele expired from terror, but Zeus snatched her six-month abortive child from the fire, and sewed it into his thigh... When the due time arrived, Zeus brought Dionysos to birth by undoing the stitches, and handed him over to Hermes...

As yet another product of an extramarital liaison on the part of Zeus, Dionysos could hardly expect to evade Hera's jealousy. When Hermes gave the baby to Semele's sister Ino and her husband Athamas to bring up as a girl – Dionysos' career as a boundary-crosser began early – Hera afflicted the couple with madness, in which state they murdered two of their own sons. But the offspring of Zeus could not be so easily eradicated. Zeus first rescued his little son by transforming him into a kid, and then had Hermes entrust him into the care of nymphs, who lived at a specially holy place called Nysa, located by various sources in different but equally 'remote' regions, including Ethiopia, Arabia and Scythia. An alternative foster-parent of baby Dionysos was Silenos, the elderly and ugly leader of the satyrs.

The Giants

Another episode in divine 'prehistory' for which we have to look beyond Hesiod concerns the Battle of the Gods and the Giants. Generated by the blood of castrated Ouranos where it dripped upon Gaia, the monstrous brood of Giants contested the Olympians' power, as had the Titans before them. Some accounts depict the Giants as huge and shaggy-haired, hurling such typically 'uncivilized' projectiles as rocks and trees. Other sources, including several visual representations, portray them as formidable warriors with more orthodox armour and weaponry. Their base was Pallene/Phlegrai, the most westerly of the three prongs of the Chalkidike peninsula. The Giants were as mighty as their names were resonant: Pallas, Porphyrion, Alkyoneus, Enkelados. But the Olympians triumphed in the end, thanks to the thunderbolts of Zeus, the arrows of his son Herakles, and some remarkable virtuosity by Athene: she flayed Pallas, used his resilient skin as a shield (adopting his name for good measure), and despatched Enkelados by throwing the island of Sicily at him.

(Above) When Zeus sewed the unborn Dionysos into his thigh after annihilating the baby's mother Semele with a thunderbolt, he was acknowledging his paternity in a very intimate way. Here a south Italian vase-painter (c. 400 BC) represents Dionysos' re-emergence into the world to take his place amongst the Olympians.

(Left) As befits a god who belongs 'outside', Dionysos is entrusted for his upbringing to divinities of the wild world of nature. Here Hermes – identifiable by the wings on his helmet and boots – hands the infant to Papposilenos, a kind of arch-satyr. Attic vase, c. 430 BC.

Origins of Humanity

In some of the accounts we have looked at so far, mortals put in an occasional, sometimes almost incidental appearance. It is now time to focus on the Greek myths which deal specifically with the beginnings of humankind. These myths are quite few in number, and often buried in texts whose main thrust lies elsewhere: we shall look in vain for a canonical equivalent of the biblical Old Testament Genesis story. Indeed, in keeping with the local differentiation which is so deeply characteristic of Greek mythology, we are more likely to hear about, for instance, the first Argive, or the first Arcadian, than we are to hear about the first man or woman. Nevertheless, from time to time Greek myth-tellers did speculate about humanity's generic origins.

The Five Races

One way of conceiving the human past makes it the product of leaps between a series of typologically different breeds, the differences being symbolized by a set of contrasts between metals. This conception has strong parallels in the thought of other ancient civilizations, especially Zoroastrianism; and it was to enjoy a profoundly influential afterlife in the form of the widespread belief in a decline from a paradisiacal 'Golden Age'.

In the version narrated by Hesiod in his *Works and Days*, the series began when the gods created a Golden Race. These beings knew neither toil nor old age; life consisted of feasting; death came like sleep. It was a perfect existence, and it took place under the sovereignty of Kronos – which shows that, in spite of those gruesome tales of pre-Olympian castration and swallowing, one way of imagining 'the time before Zeus' was as a lovely idyll.

In time the Golden Race passed away, turning into benign spirits who watch over the earth. Their successors, again made by the gods, were the Race of Silver, an inferior and rather immature breed:

For a hundred years a child would be reared by his careful mother, playing childishly at home, a big baby; but after reaching adolescence and the full measure of youthful prime, they lived only a short time, and in sorrow, because of their witlessness. For they could not keep from wrongful aggression against each other, nor would they serve the immortals, nor sacrifice on the sacred altars of the Blessed Ones, as is proper for human beings wherever they dwell.

By this time the universe was ruled by Zeus, who angrily put an end to the Silver Race.

Third came the Race of Bronze, whom Zeus created out of ash-trees. The strength of the ash makes it suitable for spear-shafts: this was a warrior Race which devoted itself to the works of Ares the war-god. In Hesiod's version they were not themselves *of* bronze (in other versions they were), but their armour, houses and tools certainly were made from that metal. There was no need for the gods to intervene to put an end to their aggression: the Men of Bronze exterminated themselves through their relentless fighting.

The logic of the metallic series is now interrupted, since the next Race created by Zeus is that of Heroes, mighty mortals who fought and died at Thebes and Troy. In many ways they resembled the Bronze Race, but they won much glory, and a few of them were even said to have been rewarded with a post-mortem existence in the Isles of the Blessed, somewhere at the edge of the world beside Okeanos. What a contrast with what follows: the Race of Iron. This is our world, the world of the present. Toil and misery are our lot; and it will get worse. In the future there will be lack of respect, impiety, and every sort of villainy.

Prometheus and fire

Side by side with this story of decline – and not necessarily integrated with it in a seamless whole – we find another set of traditions which link human origins with the Titan Prometheus ('Forethought'), son of Iapetos and the Oceanid Klymene. How exactly Prometheus fitted into the story of anthropogony was, however, a matter of debate. Apollodoros mentions in passing that Prometheus fashioned humans from water and earth, and this story, although not found in our extant sources before the 4th century BC, may have been much older, and certainly spread widely: the traveller Pausanias, visiting the small community of Panopeus in Phokis, saw two rocks which were alleged to smell like human flesh, and which were said to be the remains of the clay out of which Prometheus had fabricated the human race. Much commoner, however, was the variant which made Prometheus the champion, rather than the creator, of humanity. According to the Titan himself, speaking in Aischylos' play *Prometheus Bound*, he had bestowed upon human beings every skill, from arithmetic to navigation to medicine to prophecy. But one gift above all marked him out as humanity's benefactor: fire.

Hesiod famously relates how, when Zeus had hidden fire from mortals, Prometheus stole it and conveyed it to them in a hollow fennel-stalk. With fire humans could practise the ritual which, beyond all other rituals, made them, in Greek eyes, human: animal sacrifice. Here, too, Prometheus played a role as originator. At Mekone (said to be an ancient name for the city of Sikyon, near Corinth in the northeastern Peloponnese) Prometheus practised a

The sculptor of this Roman sarcophagus has portrayed Prometheus as a workman creating mini-humans. The scene is supervised by Athene, herself supreme in craftsmanship.

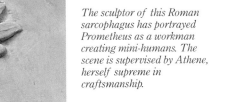

(Below) Prometheus the creator, fashioning a human figure which uncannily resembles his own, beard included. Hellenistic gemstone.

deception which proved to be not only disastrous for himself, but also decisively aetiological for humanity. He laid out before Zeus two portions of food, one of which would henceforth be that of the gods, the other that of mortals: either a succulent dish of meat and offal, unappealingly covered with an ox paunch; or a heap of bones, cunningly made to look tasty thanks to an overlay of fat. With the complex logic which Greek myths often exhibit, Zeus *both* saw through the trick *and* made the choice which would go against the gods' good. From that day forward, the division of the sacrificial spoils has remained fixed: the bones are burned for the gods, but the choicest meat and fat stay with mortals.

The consequences of Prometheus' recklessness were dire, both for him and for the humanity he championed. For the erring Titan, Zeus devised a torture both agonizing and long-lasting. As the Aischylean tragedy *Prometheus Bound* vividly dramatizes, the blacksmith god Hephaistos, accompanied by Kratos ('Power') and Bia ('Violence'), was instructed to clamp Prometheus to a remote crag in

(Left) Prometheus, hands painfully bound behind his head, is at the mercy of the eagle, whose beak is fixed into his body. Etruscan gem, 5th century BC.

(Below) The long nightmare draws to an end. Herakles launches a volley of arrows towards the eagle, as Prometheus looks helplessly on, tied to or impaled upon a stake. Attic vase, mid-6th century BC.

the Caucasus with fetters that none could undo. There, each day for a near-eternity, he would be visited by a monstrous eagle which would peck out the lobes of his liver (a part of the anatomy which Greeks regarded as the site of strong passions). Each night the liver would re-grow, enabling the torment to repeat itself down the millennia, until at last the fruit of Zeus' own loins should bring release: the eagle would fall to one of Herakles' arrows.

Pandora

For humanity, the results of Promethean defiance were even more far-reaching. Once more the agent was Hephaistos, master of immortal technology. Much as Prometheus did in other myths, so Hephaistos too used earth to mould a living creature. Just like the twin portions which Prometheus had offered to Zeus, this creature too had a deceptive exterior; but unpleasantness lay within. This was the first woman, the closest Greek mythology came

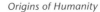

(Left) Pandora, sometimes
called Anesidora, stands
looking out towards the
viewer: she is ready to descend
upon humanity. To the left
and right of her on this vase-
painting (mid-5th century BC)
are various Olympian deities:
Zeus, Poseidon, Iris, Ares and
Hermes.

to an 'Eve'. Each of the Olympians gave her a gift: hence her name, Pandora ('Allgift'). Prometheus had anticipated that Zeus might devise trouble for mortals, and advised his unheeding brother Epimetheus ('Afterthought') to beware of unsolicited presents. He was too late. Hermes, divine go-between, brought Pandora to humanity, and Epimetheus accepted her with open arms. What happens next 'explains' the presence of woe in the world. However, at least in some of its tellings,

this myth is as perplexing as it is memorable.

The phrase 'Pandora's Box' has become proverbial (thanks to the Renaissance scholar Erasmus), but, in our Greek sources, what the first woman

(Right) Pandora, 1869, by
Dante Gabriel Rossetti.
Already escaping from
Pandora's box are the world's
evils – here envisaged in the
form of a smoky vapour
which surrounds the woman
responsible for their release.

brings with her is not a box, but a *pithos* – a very large storage jar, of the kind that archaeological excavations have frequently brought to light. Pandora's crucial action is to open her jar, allowing what was formerly within it to escape into the world – with the sole exception of Elpis ('Hope' or 'Expectation'). But what exactly does the jar contain? And what does the 'escape' signify? According to one of antiquity's lesser-known writers, Babrios (a 2nd-century AD teller of fables), the jar originally contained *good things*; when the lid was removed, all these goods escaped from humanity's grasp, with the lone exception of Hope – which is all we have left to console us. Hesiod, though, tells a very different story. In his version, the jar originally contained any number of *evils*: their escape meant that they roamed the world for humans to encounter, while only Hope was left behind. But does that amount to saying that humans do have Hope (because it is still at their disposal, in the storage jar), or that they do not (because, unlike the evils, it has not flown out into the world)? The myth of Pandora perfectly illustrates several key characteristics of Greek myths: their capacity to intrigue, to engage, and sometimes to baffle, and their power to generate fresh and sometimes mutually contradictory variants.

The Flood

Many traditions have exploited the theme of a great Flood, from the Ancient Mesopotamian *Epic of Gilgamesh* (in which the sole survivor was Ut-napishtim), to the Hebrew Bible (Noah), to many native American stories. Greek accounts, too, record the occurrence of a primeval Flood, which had the effect of eradicating the humans who had existed hitherto, and of regenerating a new breed from which all subsequent humans are descended.

The survivors of the Flood are named (by Apollodoros, among others) as Deukalion and his wife Pyrrha. The genealogy of this pair – Deukalion is the son of Prometheus, and Pyrrha is the daughter of Epimetheus and Pandora – seems

to imply that they are seen as 'doubles' of Prometheus and Pandora. Indeed one way of interpreting Deukalion's role is as analogous to that of Prometheus: like the Titan, he succeeds in circumventing the will of Zeus by championing humanity. According to Apollodoros, Zeus wanted to eliminate the Race of Bronze (a motif paralleled in Near Eastern accounts, including Genesis), and so flooded the earth with a deluge (Hesiod's Bronze Race had, of course, saved Zeus the trouble, by wiping themselves out). On the advice of his father Prometheus, Deukalion built a chest and climbed into it with Pyrrha. The waters rose, but the chest floated on; after nine days and nine nights it came ashore on Mount Parnassos, above Delphi. Interestingly, in a variant preserved by Aristotle the Flood is said to have occurred in the area 'round Dodona and the river Acheloös'; could it be that the two influential oracles at Delphi and Dodona competed with each other in making claims about which was the oldest inhabited part of Greece?

Unlike his father, Deukalion prudently sacrificed to Zeus, who reciprocated by granting him a favour: to populate the earth. As Apollodoros puts it: 'On Zeus' instructions, he picked up stones and threw them over his head; and the stones that Deukalion threw became men, and those that Pyrrha threw became women.' All over Greece the flood waters receded, leaving their trace in collective belief: within the precinct of the temple of Olympian Zeus in Athens the traveller Pausanias was shown a broad cleft in the earth, which, people said, was where the water ran away after the Flood. For Greece it was a new beginning. Among the descendants of the people-of-stone were many of the greatest heroes and heroines of Greek mythology.

Mount Parnassos, where the 'ark' of Deukalion and his wife Pyrrha finally came to rest. Even in this land of spectacular panoramas, few sights are more breathtaking than this one: truly a place for a new beginning.

Local Origins

Ants and snakes

The pluralism which characterizes so many aspects of Greek civilization is reflected also in its myths of origin. Much more interest was expressed in the origins of individual communities than in those of the entire human race.

One pattern of such tales was to explain how this or that region or city was not only ancient, but also in some way naturally embedded in the ground where its people lived. A good example is provided by the myth of origin of a community which does not, on the whole, feature prominently in our knowledge of ancient Greece: the island of Aigina, situated between Attica and the Argolid region. The story went that the first inhabitant of the island was Aiakos, son of Zeus and the nymph Aigina, homonym of the island itself: Aiakos could not have been more 'rooted' than that. But he was lonely, for there were no other human beings apart from himself. Out of pity, Zeus changed all the Aiginetan ants (*murmekes*) into humans, who became known as 'Myrmidons'. They were to have a glorious history as warriors: Aiakos' son Peleus became in his turn the father of Achilles, mighty leader of the Myrmidons – who had by then migrated northwards to Phthia in southern Thessaly – in the

Trojan War. Aiakos, for his part, would be honoured alongside Minos and Rhadamanthus as one of the judges of the souls of the dead, as befitted one whom Pindar called 'the best of men on earth'. Even on this point, however, we may note the ineradicable pluralism of Greek mythology: in the irresistibly comic vision realized by Aristophanes in the *Frogs*, Aiakos is portrayed as a kind of over-the-top stage villain, revelling in the cruelty to which his role as Hades' doorkeeper entitles him.

Ants – the original, prehuman form of the Myrmidons – live in the ground; and so do snakes. A common mythological way of expressing rootedness – and also sacredness, since snakes were felt to have a numinous quality which associated them with the more-than-human – was to link the ancestry of a community with a serpent. Kekrops, one of the earliest kings of Athens, was imagined as having the upper body of a human, but the tail of a snake. He was a perfect embodiment of autochthony (Apollodoros says explicitly that Kekrops was earth-born), and, by his ambivalent form, mediator of the dichotomy between nature and culture. Through his binary shape, Kekrops expressed the idea of humanity's growth out of animality. He was said to have made a number of important innovations in the Athenians' way of sacrificing to the gods, and also to have introduced the institution of marriage.

Theban beginnings

A more decisive and violent way of imagining human development depicted it as an aggressive overcoming of animality – the human equivalent of Zeus' defeat of Typhon, and, as we shall see later

This vase (south Italian, 4th century BC) depicts a scene in Hades, with Aiakos standing between Triptolemos and Rhadamanthus, both of whom had roles as judges of the dead.

(p. 73), of Apollo's defeat of the serpent Python when the god seized control of the Delphic oracle. The complex foundation myth of Thebes graphically illustrates the point.

The legendary founder of Thebes was Kadmos, one of the sons of Agenor the king of Phoenicia. When Kadmos' sister Europa was abducted by Zeus, Agenor sent his sons out into the world to search for her. Kadmos' travels brought him to Greece, where he consulted the Delphic oracle. Kadmos was by no means the only enquirer to whom the Delphic priestess gave an unanticipated answer: in his case, the instruction he received was to follow a distinctively-marked cow and to found a city where it lay down to rest. Finding and following the cow, Kadmos came at last to the site of the future Thebes, in Boiotia. Since the best way of expressing gratitude to the gods was to sacrifice the cow to them, and since sacrifice required not just fire but also purificatory water, Kadmos sought water from a nearby spring. But Greek springs were sacred (see pp. 188–89), and this one belonged to the god Ares; a monstrous serpent lay there as its menacing guardian. Kadmos slew the serpent, and on the instructions of the goddess Athene sowed its teeth in the earth. Up sprang armed warriors ready for combat; but, once more prompted by Athene, Kadmos threw a stone in the midst of his adversaries. In their consternation they attacked and killed each other – all but five of them, who became the ancestors of later Thebans, under the name of the 'Spartoi' ('Sown Men').

Thus far, the Thebans' origins were complex enough: myth presented them as originating both from outside Greece (from Kadmos the Phoenician)

and from deep within it (those earthborn ancestors, deriving from an 'autochthonous' snake). But the complexity is even greater than that. When Kadmos took a wife, the favour of the gods smiled upon him: he was permitted to marry Harmonia, daughter of Ares and Aphrodite. Their wedding was blessed by the presence of the gods, and their union produced five children. Thanks to intermarriage between the Sown Men and the descendants of Kadmos and Harmonia, the population of Thebes could be said to have grown from the combined seeds of animality, humanity and divinity.

Not even the illustrious Kadmos lived a life unblemished by sorrow: what mortal did? The fates of his four daughters were as unhappy as they were various: Semele was struck by a thunderbolt when she begged to see her lover Zeus in all his pomp; Ino killed her own child when maddened by Hera; Autonoe and Agaue were the mothers of Aktaion and Pentheus respectively, each of whom died a horrible death for opposing the gods. A descendant of Kadmos' one son, Polydoros, was Oedipus, whose own visit to Delphi was to precipitate the revelation of ills beyond imagining.

The last episode in the tale of Thebes' origins returns us, in a manner of speaking, to where we started. For Kadmos and Harmonia were metamorphosed into snakes, and were, like some other heroes, preserved from death in a perpetual existence in the Elysian Fields. Their humanity had passed away, leaving a distinctive mixture of the animal and the divine.

(Below) As various divinities look on from above, Kadmos prepares to hurl a stone at the snake guarding Ares' spring. To the right of the snake is a figure, perhaps personifying the city of Thebes, or the spring itself. South Italian vase, c. 330 BC.

(Left) The mythical Athenian king Kekrops, whose earthborn quality is expressed by his partially snaky form, is here seen in the company of Athene. Between them is an olive tree, symbol of Athene and Athens alike. Attic vase, end of 5th century BC.

Bringers of Culture

Mount Lykaion, in a remote region of Arcadia. This is the place where, it was said, Lykaon was transformed into a wolf for his wickedness.

Phoroneus, Pelasgos and civilization

We have already seen how the Titan Prometheus was credited with introducing not only fire, but also various skills and practices which the Greeks regarded as necessary for human culture (see pp. 54–55). But Prometheus was far from being the only such mythological culture-bringer. As befits the fundamental pluralism of the Greeks' mental universe, it is no surprise to find that different regions, indeed different cities, had their own views about who brought the wherewithal for social life.

The culture-hero of the Peloponnesian city of Argos was, Pausanias tells us, Phoroneus. Few traditions have survived about him, but it is clear that he, no less than Aiakos and Kekrops, was felt to be embedded in his native territory: his father was the local Argive river-god Inachos. Phoroneus was the local equivalent of Prometheus, the bringer of fire (the Argives kept a 'fire of Phoroneus' burning in his honour) and the introducer of that

basic quality of human social development, the art of living together in a *polis* ('city', 'citizen state').

The Arcadians, however, had a story just as good. To the rest of the Greeks, Arcadia was a backwater, but to the Arcadians themselves, Arcadia had its own narrative of the arrival of civilization. At the beginning, they said, there was Pelasgos, aboriginal inhabitant of the country. (Typifying the Greeks' willingness to turn the eye of common sense upon their myths, Pausanias comments that 'it seems likely that there were other people with Pelasgos and not just himself alone, or else whom could he have ruled over?') Pelasgos began the process of socialization, teaching people to build huts, to wear sheep-skins, and to give up eating leaves, grasses

Triptolemos is one of several mortals to whom Greek myths sometimes assigned a special role after death: in his case, as one of the judges of the dead. But his main province was agricultural fertility. On this Hellenistic gem, he holds a plough in one hand, and a poppy and ears of corn in the other.

and roots in favour of acorns. Pelasgos' son Lykaon took the process of acculturation further: he founded the city of Lykosoura and introduced athletic competitions in honour of Zeus. But progress is fraught with danger. Lykaon made a massive mistake when he sacrificed a human child on Zeus' altar on Mount Lykaion, and was turned into a wolf as punishment (see pp. 88–89). Eventually, though, Arcadian culture resumed its forward momentum when Arkas, Lykaon's grandson, introduced a further set of markers of civilization: the cultivation of crops; bread-making; spinning and weaving.

The innovations ascribed to these culture-heroes of the Argives and Arcadians, not to mention the gifts bestowed by Prometheus, illustrate a characteristic pattern, sometimes known as that of the 'first finder': an object or practice deemed in some way typical of or vital to human social life is attributed to a named individual from the mythological past. Sometimes the invention derives from the ingenuity of the gods, like the lyre which Hermes made from tortoiseshell and sheep gut, or the *aulos* (oboe-like double pipe) which Athene made (and then rejected because blowing it made her look ugly) – Hermes and Athene being, of all the deities, especially linked with the notion of cleverness. Other inventions were seen as the product of merely mortal intelligence, albeit of a high order of sophistication: in this respect no one surpassed Daidalos (see p. 92), among whose brilliant feats was said to have been the first creation of the 'walking pose' for figurative statues. Important as such innovations were felt to be for a 'cultivated' existence, they could hardly compare with the gift brought to mortals by Demeter's mortal protégé Triptolemos, who distributed corn, and the arts of its cultivation, to humankind.

Colonies

(Opposite) At over 3,300 m (10,800 ft) high, Mount Etna (ancient Greek form: Aitna) is Europe's highest active volcano. It was active too in antiquity: its constant stream of smoke and lava was believed to derive from Zeus' monstrous foe Typhon, vanquished but still wrathful, imprisoned for eternity under the volcano.

Especially during the Archaic period, but also before and long after it, Greeks exported their civilization to other areas of the Mediterranean world through the establishing of new *poleis* (cities). The whole enterprise of founding these new communities was shot through with ritual procedures, from the standard, preliminary consultation of an oracle (very frequently that of Apollo at Delphi), to the significant role played by seers in the inauguration of the new community, to the transference of sacred fire from the hearth of the mother-city to the equivalent location in the daughter community. But alongside ritual, mythology too functioned as a means of affirming a continuity of cultural experience from mother-city to new foundation. Just as the cities of the Greek homeland grounded their claims to antiquity and cultural priority in the network of mythological narrative, so too 'second-order' foundations – often referred to as 'colonies' – were woven into the same set of tales. Here, then, is yet another kind of origin for which mythology provided legitimation.

One example of such legitimation is associated with the 5th century BC foundation of the Sicilian city of Aitna. This was indeed a fresh beginning, inaugurated by the despot Hieron when he established a new community to be ruled over by his son. Weaving a celebration of this event into a poem (*Pythian* 1) about Hieron's Pythian chariot victory in the year 470, Pindar establishes an intricate set of parallels between, on the one hand, Hieron's act of foundation – which is presented as imposing the values of firm government and bountiful rule

upon a raw and untamed landscape – and, on the other hand, Zeus' primordial overwhelming of his hundred-headed adversary Typhon. This adversary, although pinioned for all time beneath Mount Aitna (i.e. Etna), retains the terrible power to pour forth 'pure streams of unapproachable fire from the hidden places within', as Pindar puts it. The poem's mythological imagery enforces not only a sense of the remarkable achievement which Aitna's foundation is held to represent, but also a sense of the fragility of any human claim to be able definitively to tame this unpredictable landscape.

For a further example of the way in which myth-tellers shaped perceptions of colonial foundation, we may think back for a moment to the tale of the foundation of Thebes, with its narrative of the cow which guided Kadmos, and the overcoming of the serpent of Ares, before the new city could be established. Thebes is, so to speak, a 'first-order' foundation – in the heart of mainland Greece itself. But literally dozens of narratives about colonial foundation much further afield use the same story-patterns. Cows feature regularly as guides, but other animals which guide founders to the sites of their future settlements include crows, dogs, doves, eagles, foxes, rats and seals. As for the symbolic overcoming of a beastly adversary, snakes – those typical 'indigenous' inhabitants of the soil – appear very frequently; but we hear of many other animals also. Byzas, founder of Byzantium, had to overcome a bull; Seleucus Nicator (a 4th/3rd century BC Seleucid ruler in the post-Alexander Hellenistic East) killed a boar which sprang out at him, and used its blood to trace out the perimeter of the new city of Laodicea in northern Syria.

Throughout antiquity, Greek myths provided a language in which to confer legitimacy through the invoking of the notion of origin. Any new foundation needed all the help it could get, practical as well as symbolic, to shore it up against potential foes. To this end, the rich symbolic treasury of the mythological network was exploited to the full.

The Sicilian city of Kamarina was a colony of Syracuse; Syracuse itself had been settled by Greeks from Corinth. The citizens of both Kamarina and Syracuse used myths to express their cities' identities. The silver coin illustrated here (415–405 BC) comes from Kamarina. One side (left) shows Athene driving a chariot, with the winged figure of Nike ('Victory') holding a crown above her; the other side (right) portrays Herakles, unmistakable in his lionskin.

Divinities of Myth and Cult

Throughout classical antiquity, from one end of the Greek world to another, the gods who dwelt on Mount Olympos were the recipients of worship. Through sacrifices, votive offerings, prayers, oaths, curses and incantations, mortals involved their gods in every conceivable human activity, from politics to love-making, from warfare to burial, from athletic competition to the public performance of drama and music. No neat separation can therefore be made between 'religion' and 'society': each pervaded the other.

What were the distinctive contributions made by cult and myth to the Greeks' perceptions of the sacred?

Cult tended to focus on specific features of divine power, singling out the particular quality in virtue of which a god was being invoked: Zeus Horkios ('of oaths'), Poseidon Hippios ('of horses'), Athene Poliouchos ('holder of the citadel'), and so forth. Moreover, different localities highlighted quite different characteristics of a given divinity. On the evidence of cult alone, therefore, it is impossible to speak of a single, homogeneous Greek religion.

In mythological narratives, by contrast – and here one thinks first, as so often, of the Homeric and Hesiodic poems – we may detect a tendency to articulate the discrete behaviours of ritual into something approaching an interrelated system, depicting a shared and sometimes even 'Panhellenic' view of divine power and action. Still, the degree of internal coherence in this system should not be exaggerated: one should never underestimate the pluralism of Greek culture. Just as rituals varied from place to place and from historical period to historical period, so did the ways in which different myth-tellers portrayed those mighty figures of the imagination, the Olympian divinities.

Dionysos reclines by the side of his bride Ariadne, a mortal woman raised to the condition of unageing divinity so that she might be the god's lovely consort for ever. From a large bronze krater *(c. 330 BC) found at Derveni near Thessaloniki (see ill. on p. 83).*

III   The Olympians: Power, Honour, Sexuality

Powers and Spheres of Influence

Zeus

Related as he is, etymologically speaking, to other Indo-European sky gods (compare Indic Dyaus pitar, Roman Diespiter/Jupiter), Zeus has at the centre of his being a configuration of what we would describe as 'natural phenomena': not only sky, but also weather, storm, lightning, and thunderbolt. Already in Homer, one of the god's epithets is *nephelegereta*, 'marshaller of clouds'. When Semele, a mortal who caught Zeus' roving eye, begged her lover to appear to her in his full glory, he was obliged to do so as Lord of Lightning, with predictably fatal results. Countless images portray Zeus with thunderbolt in hand.

This terrifying power translates into various other kinds of supremacy. First, there is domination by sheer physical strength. Again we may turn to the *Iliad*, in a passage where Zeus boasts of his awesome superiority even to the other Olympians:

Let down out of the sky a cord of gold; take hold of it
all you who are gods and all who are goddesses, yet not
   even so could you drag down Zeus from the sky to the
   ground, not
Zeus the high lord of counsel, though you tried until you
   grew weary.
Yet whenever I might strongly be minded to pull you,
I could drag you up, earth and all and sea and all
   with you,
then tie the golden rope about a peak of Olympos
and make it fast, so that all should dangle in mid air.
So much stronger am I than the gods, and stronger
   than mortals.

To supremacy by brute force we may add supremacy through sovereignty. Zeus' symbolic equivalent in the animal world is the eagle, lord of birds; another of the god's attributes is the sceptre, which confers authority upon human rulers. Yet the sovereignty of mere mortals pales beside that of Zeus, whose will is enacted with a nod of the head.

For another aspect of Zeus' dominion we must look to the context of the family. An epithet consistently bestowed upon Zeus is 'father of gods and men'. As regards the generality of mankind, this paternity is metaphorical; but many of the gods were quite literally his children. He stood at the head of the family of the Olympians – an unruly family, though, and one whose members were

One of the symbols of Zeus' authority is the eagle, mightiest of birds, as depicted on this Lakonian cup, c. 560 BC. Zeus himself is bearded, long-haired, enthroned, and clad in an elaborate cloak.

Greek Divinities and their Principal Attributes

divinity	spheres of activity	attributes
Zeus	sky, weather; numerous aspects of social life, including hospitality, supplication, oaths; 'father of gods and mortals'	thunderbolt, eagle, sceptre
Hera	consort of Zeus; consumed by jealousy at his serial infidelity; supports the integrity of marriage	often a sceptre or crown; peacock
Poseidon	sea; earthquake; the raw energy of the horse and the bull	trident; typically surrounded by sea-creatures
Hades	lord of the Underworld	his cap confers invisibility on the wearer; H. is represented as a regal, sceptre-bearing figure in spite of his 'hateful' role
Aphrodite	sex, love	aphrodisiac girdle; doves, sparrows
Demeter	corn and the fertility of the land; in conjunction with her daughter Persephone, patroness of the Eleusinian Mystery cult	often carries a torch or corn
Artemis	hunting; wild animals; helper of women in childbirth	bow and arrows
Apollo	music; divination and prophecy; purification; healing; in later antiquity, identified with the Sun	bow and arrows; lyre; laurel
Athene	craftsmanship, esp. in wood; cunning; warfare, for example as used in defence of the citizen body	helmet and spear; snake-fringed cape (*aegis*) bearing image of Gorgon; owl
Ares	the fury of war	helmet, spear, shield
Hephaistos	physical infirmity (lameness) combined with brilliant virtuosity as an artisan; especially skilled at metalwork, whence his association with fire	axe, forging tongs, anvil
Persephone	bride of Hades and so Queen of Underworld; worshipped, along with her mother Demeter, in the Eleusinian Mysteries	corn and fruit as the symbols of growth
Hestia	(fire of) hearth	
Hermes	divine intermediary; messenger; guide of souls of dead to Hades; bringer of fertility to flocks	herald's staff (*kerukeion*); winged boots/sandals; broad-brimmed hat
Dionysos	ecstasy; the madness of intoxication; wine; exuberance and danger of animal and vegetable nature	ivy; vines; panther; the *thyrsos* – a wand of fennel bound at the end with ivy
Pan	god of lonely, rustic wildness; induces 'panic'	hybrid, half-goat, half-human form
Priapos	god of sexual arousal	endowed with large and permanent erection
Eros	sexual desire	bow and arrows

quite capable of challenging, if only for a time, the authority of their head. Modelled as it was on an institution of human society, the concept of the divine family was an image (unlike, for instance, the notion of god-as-thunderbolt) which brought the gods' behaviour at least partly within the framework of the comprehensible.

How far Zeus' authority can be said to be *moral* is a very complex question. On the one hand, myth (for instance, Hesiodic myth) depicts him as father of Dike ('Right') and consort of Themis ('Due Order'); he is also represented as the punisher of oath-breakers (as Zeus Horkios) and of those who reject suppliants (as Zeus Hikesios). On the other hand,

(Above) Every four years representatives from all over the Greek world assembled in Elis to celebrate the Olympic Games. The Games were held in honour of Zeus, whose head adorns this coin (4th century BC) struck in Elis.

(Below) The ruins of Zeus' great temple at Olympia (c. 470 BC). The temple was a treasure-house of mythology: the metopes represented the twelve Labours of Herakles; among the sculptured reliefs on the pediments were the preliminaries to the chariot race between Pelops and Oinomaos; inside the temple was Pheidias' world-renowned statue of Zeus, which alas no longer survives.

Zeus' own conduct places him well beyond the norms of *human* morality – witness his incest with his sister Hera, and his serial adultery. There is a tension at the heart of the portrayal of the father of the gods, for he can be thought of as simultaneously the source of right and the source of everything.

No less difficult than the question of Zeus' morality is the question of the limits of his power. Here is a prime example of the effect which the pluralism of Greek mythology can have. Some of our texts speak of the perfection and completeness of Zeus. Amongst these texts is the remarkable *Hymn* by the Stoic Kleanthes (4th/3rd century BC), who elevates Zeus to a kind of universal principle:

This entire cosmos which moves round the earth follows where you lead it, and is willingly mastered by you… Nothing happens in the world without you, god, neither in the divine air of the sky, nor in the sea, except for that which evil men do in their folly.

But other texts depict Zeus as emphatically within, rather than above, the causality of events. Again it is the *Iliad*, the location of so many of the strands of later Greek belief, which touches on the central issues. In a pivotal and deeply moving scene, Zeus looks down upon the impending death of one of his own sons, the Trojan warrior Sarpedon. Zeus could in theory intervene to save him, even though this would overturn what is 'allotted'; but, as Hera is

quick to point out, by doing so he would arouse the implacable hostility of the other gods. So even Zeus must bow to the inevitable:

So she spoke, nor did the father of gods and men disobey her;
but he wept tears of blood that poured to the ground, honouring
his beloved son, whom Patroklos was presently
to kill, by generous Troy and far from the land of his fathers.

Hera

As the sister and consort of Zeus, the great goddess Hera was worshipped at sanctuaries throughout the Greek world. Especially renowned were one temple on the island of Samos and another between Argos and Mycenae; but she also had major shrines at Olympia, at Perachora near Corinth, and at south Italian sites such as Croton, Paestum and Foce del Sele. The progression which typifies Hera's rites in these sanctuaries is the transition from virgin to bride. In some localities, cults celebrated her as Parthenos ('Maiden'); elsewhere it was her presiding over the institution of marriage (e.g. as Zugia, 'She who Unites') which concentrated the worshipper's attention; in still other places she was worshipped under both aspects, as in the Boiotian city of Plataea, where she had, Pausanias reports, two statues, one as Numpheuomene ('Bride') and one as Teleia ('Consummated').

The temple of Hera at Olympia (c. 600 BC), the oldest temple in the sacred precinct. It was dwarfed by the later temple of Zeus.

Given the prominence and geographical spread of Hera's sanctuaries, it is somewhat paradoxical that Hera's place in mythology is relatively subordinate, being dominated, in virtually every respect, by her role as consort of Zeus. Occasionally her myths hark back to her pre-nuptial days, such as the time when Zeus wooed her in the form of a cuckoo. But much more often her mythology dwells on a related but more sombre theme: her vindictiveness towards Zeus' lovers and their children. Her pursuit of the pregnant goddess Leto continued relentlessly throughout the length and breadth of the Greek world, until at last the humble island of Delos was willing to accept the anguished mother-to-be, soon to give birth to the glorious children Apollo and Artemis. When Io, Hera's own mortal priestess at Argos, found favour with Zeus, Hera's spite took an ingenious form: transformed into a cow, Io wandered from land to land, driven mad by the stinging of the fly which the queen of the gods sent against her. Zeus' liaison with another mortal, Semele, provoked Hera to equal fury. First Hera tricked her rival into precipitating her own death by asking to see her lover in the shattering fullness of his cosmic power. Then she turned her attention to Dionysos, Semele's son by Zeus. She drove him mad, and caused two mortals (Athamas and his wife Ino) who had dared to nurse the infant god, to murder their own children in fits of insanity.

The list of Hera's vendettas could be considerably dwelt upon; but they pale beside her all-consuming hatred for Herakles, Zeus' son by yet another of his mortal lovers, Alkmene. When Alkmene was about to be delivered, Zeus proclaimed before the gods (*Iliad* Book 19) that the honour of ruling over Mycenae was to be the birthright of that descendant of his own who was about to be born. It was Herakles for whom Zeus believed he was predicting glory. But he reckoned without the intervention of Hera. For there was another child soon to be born in the Peloponnese, namely Eurystheus, who, as grandson of another of Zeus' sons – Perseus – would also qualify as 'a descendant of Zeus'. Hera persuaded the Eileithyiai (goddesses of childbirth) to block Alkmene's delivery until Eurystheus' mother had been prematurely delivered. Thereafter, Hera never relented in her persecution of Herakles – whose name, with supreme irony, meant 'Glory of Hera'. Subject as he was to the domination of the inferior and cowardly hero Eurystheus, Herakles nevertheless completed astonishing exploits; but at the height of his powers he was driven insane by Hera, so that he slaughtered his own wife and children (see p. 122).

(see p. 122).

The 'sacred marriage' of Zeus and Hera is evoked on this metope (Temple E, Selinus, Sicily; c. 470 BC). By gripping Hera's wrist Zeus seems to be trying to prevent her from veiling herself. His languid pose may be a hint at his amorous intentions.

Hera's cults and myths turn predominantly upon the theme of marriage, but with contrasting emphases. Whereas her cults stress the fundamental necessity of this socio-psychological transition, the myths explore the reverse side of the picture – what happens when fulfilment gives way to the bitterness of rejection. But not the least of the paradoxes concerning the great queen of Olympos is that her triumphs were only temporary. Even Herakles, whom she thwarted and humiliated at every turn, succeeded at last in joining the company of the gods on Olympos.

Poseidon

When Kronos' inheritance was divided, his sons received the portions which would locate and shape their powers for ever afterwards. Zeus took the sky, Hades the Underworld; to Poseidon was allotted the sea. The Mediterranean in general, and the Aegean in particular, was and is two-faced: mirror-smooth one day, tempestuous the next. Correspondingly, the sovereignty of Poseidon was imagined as expressing itself both through serene authority and through raw, explosive violence. Nowhere is this latter capacity more graphically described than in Homer's *Odyssey*, where Poseidon, in revenge for Odysseus' blinding of the Cyclops (Poseidon's son), uses every weapon in his armoury to impede the homecoming of Odysseus to Ithaca:

So he spoke, and drew the clouds together, in his hands
    gripping
the trident, and stirred up the sea, and urged on all the
    stormblasts
of all the winds together, and swathed earth and sea alike
in cloud. Night sprang from heaven. East Wind and
    South Wind
clashed together, and the bitter blown West Wind
and the North Wind born in the bright air rolled up
    a heavy sea.

(Below) This image of the trident-wielding Poseidon is from a coin, c. 530 BC, of the city of Poseidonia (Paestum, southeast of Naples). The inscription 'POS' represents the beginning of the name of both the city and the god.

As symbol of his stormy energy Poseidon wields the trident, used by fisherfolk to spear their prey, but by the god of the deep to raise havoc among the waves.

Although Poseidon's power centres on the sea, on land too he stirs up the turbulence of nature. He is Ennosigaios, 'Shaker of the Earth', prone to punishing his foes by breaking up the ground where they stand. Such activity is by no means confined to the 'long ago': Thucydides records that it was to Poseidon that people attributed the catastrophic Spartan earthquake of 464 BC.

The third form of natural energy represented and released by Poseidon is that of animals. He is linked especially closely with the horse, through the cult of Poseidon Hippios. Several myths express this proximity in graphically sexual terms. For example, according to a story associated with Thessaly and Athens, it was when the god's semen spurted onto a rock that the first horse was

conceived. Another myth with a similar implication derives from Arcadia: when Demeter turned herself into a mare in order to avoid the attentions of Poseidon, his metamorphosis into a stallion enabled him to fulfil his desire.

For a terrifying dramatization of how Poseidon's power expresses itself through the raw energy of beasts, we need look no further than Euripides' tragedy *Hippolytos*. The eponymous hero, cursed by his own father Theseus (who mistakenly believes him to have violated the honour of Phaidra, Theseus' wife and Hippolytos' stepmother), is being forced into exile. As his chariot drives along the seashore, a monstrous bull manifests itself from the ocean, driving Hippolytos' horses into a frenzy which precipitates a fatal crash. The curse whose invocation called the bull into existence was granted to Theseus by Poseidon (who in this version of the myth is Theseus' father). The congruence of foaming sea and awesome beast epitomizes Poseidon's placing within the Greeks' world of the sacred.

Demeter

As the goddess associated with corn, Demeter symbolizes the source of the bread which formed the Greeks' staple diet. Although the notion of 'fertility goddess' has been extensively overused in the study of ancient religions, in Demeter's case the phrase has some degree of justification. At the Thesmophoria, her main and widespread festival, the women of a given community practised an annual autumn (i.e. pre-sowing-time) rite whose explicit function was to promote the success of the following year's harvest: piglets were thrown into pits, their decayed remains were recovered and placed upon altars, and 'it is believed,' (reports the

ancient commentator who is our chief source) 'that anyone who takes of this and scatters it with seed will have a good harvest.'

But Demeter is concerned with more than corn and fertility. She is also a mother – in fact, arguably the most powerful image of a mother in the whole of Greek mythology. One myth above all expresses the essence of how the goddess was imagined by the Greeks: the tale of her reaction to the abduction of her daughter Persephone by Hades, god of the Underworld. In the *Homeric Hymn to Demeter*, a poem that probably dates from the Archaic period, we have a rich narrative of Demeter's grief and its partial assuaging. After wandering the world in search of her daughter, she comes at last to Eleusis, between Athens and Megara. Disguised as an old woman, Demeter receives hospitality from King Keleos and his family. She is even granted the privilege of nursing Demophon, the baby son of Keleos and his wife Metaneira. In gratitude for her treatment, Demeter secretly sets about conferring immortality on Demophon by anointing him with the divine substance ambrosia and holding him in the hearth so as to purge his mortality by fire. In the logic of Greek myth, however, the boundary between god and mortal is hard to cross. Discovered in the act by the horrified and uncomprehending Metaneira, Demeter reveals her divine identity and commands the Eleusinians to build her a great temple. When Demeter, still grieving for her daughter, withdraws into this shrine, all fertility disappears from the earth along with her. It is left to Zeus to avert disaster by requiring Hades to restore Persephone to her mother, though for only a part of the year: since the god of death has induced his bride to eat the seed of a pomegranate, she is bound to return to him each year for four months (six, in some versions), when fertility once more abandons the earth.

Apollo

The embodiment of youthful masculine beauty, Apollo (son of Zeus and Leto) has often been taken to represent 'the Greek ideal'. Yet he is simply *a*, not *the*, Greek god. Like all the other divinities he has his own specific provinces of activity which differentiate him from his fellow Olympians. He is especially linked with music, healing, purification and prophecy; in later Greek thought he is also associated with the Sun.

Two locations form the centres for Apolline cult and its related mythology: Delos and Delphi. The island of Delos, at the hub of the Cyclades, was from at least the 8th century BC the site of cults to Apollo, his sister Artemis, and their mother Leto; correspondingly, as we have already seen, a myth narrated how, when every other place had rejected Leto's pleas, little Delos alone braved the fury of Hera and accepted the forlorn mother-to-be. Equally strong was Apollo's connection with Delphi, the oracular shrine wonderfully situated just below Mount Parnassos. The oracle's foundation-myth told of Apollo's overcoming of a monstrous snake whose corpse then putrified, thereby lending an epithet to 'Pythian Apollo' and to the 'Pythian Games' held at Delphi in Apollo's honour (*puthein* in Greek means 'to cause something to rot').

One connecting thread running through many of Apollo's divine powers is harmonious order. This quality is self-evidently present in the god's patronage of music, especially the music of the lyre: Greeks drew a contrast between the soothing Apolline lyre and what were perceived to be the

(Left) Regal authority combined with power over vegetative growth: these are the impressions of Demeter created by the painter of this Corinthian plate (5th century BC). In the goddess' right hand is a torch, in her left, poppies and corn ears; in front of her – perhaps on an altar – there is a pomegranate.

The link between Apollo and the taut string could express itself in violence (bow and arrows) or, as here, in the harmony of the lyre. Attic vase, c. 430–420 BC.

Temple of Apollo, Delphi. Through the voice of his priestess, the Pythia, Apollo spoke oracles in response to human enquirers. But human minds are fallible: the god's message was always liable to misinterpretation.

more exotic and ecstatic forms of music associated with Dionysos. (This is one area where the opposition between Apollo and Dionysos, so prominent in the work of the philosopher Friedrich Nietzsche (see pp. 235–36), finds some justification in the ancient sources.) Another kind of harmony is that of a healthy body, and here too Apollo played a role in his capacity as healer, that is, as restorer of the disorder brought about by illness; the god's son Asklepios was the prototypical doctor. A third context in which the restoration of order may operate, according to Greek belief, is that of the purification which redresses a state of religious

'pollution'. The offering of this kind of fresh start was another of Apollo's provinces. Most famously, it was to the Delphic oracle that Orestes came as a polluted outcast after having murdered his mother Clytemnestra. Even in defiance of the Furies, who legitimately pursued everyone guilty of shedding kin-blood, Apollo defended Orestes, enabling him ultimately to escape from the mesh of blood-guilt in which he had become entangled (a tale brilliantly staged in the third play of Aischylos' *Oresteia* trilogy).

Since knowledge may be regarded as a form of order, it might be felt that Apollo's patronage of

*Apollo, on the east frieze of
the Parthenon, Athens (mid-
5th century BC) He is flanked
by Poseidon and Artemis.
This exquisite sculpture helps
to explain why the name of
Apollo has become
synonymous with an idealized
male beauty*

benevolent or non-violent in a way that Zeus and
Poseidon, say, were not. On the contrary: Apollo's
slaying of the Pythian snake typified the manner in
which his power might sometimes manifest itself.
As Zeus brandished the thunderbolt and Poseidon
the trident, so Apollo too held an aggressive
weapon as his iconographical signature: a bow,
which he was well capable of using to defend his
honour and his interests. When his priest Chryses
was dishonoured by the Greeks at Troy, the god
reacted with lethal fury, striding down from
Olympos (according to the *Iliad*) 'like night', and
shooting plague-bearing arrows at man and beast
alike; the obverse of the capacity to heal was the
capacity to destroy with disease. This attack is
the more terrifying because it is inflicted from a
distance: a group of linguistically related epithets
by which Apollo is regularly described may be
translated as 'he who shoots from afar'. Whether he
acts with benevolence or with aggression, there is
always something distant about Apollo.

Artemis

If we attempt to draw a profile of Apollo's sister
Artemis on the basis of her place in religious practice, the closest we come to a unifying schema is the
notion of 'transition to adulthood'. For young
people of both sexes, sanctuaries of the goddess
provided the focus for rites of passage, ranging
from the initiation ceremonies for young Spartan
men at the shrine of Artemis Orthia, to rituals performed for Artemis by young girls as 'bears' at

prophecy is one more respect in which the god
represents the capacity to control and harmonize
experience. However, one of the most insistent
themes in the whole of Greek mythology – above
all, in the mythology explored in tragedy – is the
impossibility for humans to anticipate the future
with accuracy. When a mortal – be it Oedipus or
anyone else – consults an oracle, the voice of the
god is relayed indirectly, through fallible human
interpreters. One of Apollo's epithets is 'Loxias',
which may be translated as 'he who talks obliquely'.

The stress on order and harmony should not
be taken to imply that Apollo was somehow

Brauron in Attica. A related form of transition in which Artemis was deemed to play a role was childbirth: in several places she was identified with the goddess Eileithyia, whose specific province this was. Some scholars press the notion of 'transition' still further by relating it to the tendency for some of Artemis' sanctuaries to be located in liminal places such as marshes or the sea shore. That would, in turn, chime in with another feature of the symbolism of Artemis' worship, namely 'wildness'. As is hinted at by the imagery of bears, Artemis was regarded as the mistress of wild animals; indeed at the festival of Artemis Laphria in Patrai (mod. Patras, on the north coast of the Peloponnese), a remarkable ceremony took place in which a virgin priestess, riding in a deer-drawn chariot, presided over a holocaust sacrifice of wild beasts.

The myths in which Artemis figures both reflect and refract these motifs. When Homer in the *Odyssey* seeks to evoke the virginal beauty of the young princess Nausikaa, he compares her to the peerless divine huntress Artemis,

This Archaic image of Artemis – the handle of a bronze water-jar from Sparta, c. 600 BC – characteristically locates her at the centre of a group of wild animals.

who showers arrows, moves on the mountains
either along Taygetos or on high-towering
Erymanthos, delighting in boars and swift deer…

Artemis loves the beasts of the wild, yet like her brother Apollo she carries a bow: she will hunt those same beasts, and her aim is unerring. An analogous paradox occurs in the poignant story of Iphigeneia, the virgin daughter of Agamemnon (commander of the Greek expedition against Troy). When Agamemnon offends Artemis – according to one version, he boasts that he is a better hunter than she – the goddess demands the sacrifice of Iphigeneia in recompense. The protectress of young girls will not flinch from demanding their death if her own divine honour is threatened; though in one version of the myth the goddess relents at the last moment, whisking Iphigeneia away to safety and replacing her with a sacrificial deer.

The key notions of transition and adolescence, as well as the connection with animals, find echoes in the recurrent narratives in which Artemis is accompanied by young, unmarried hunters, both male and, in stark contrast to the practice of real life, female. These hunters – males such as Hippolytos, Orion and Aktaion, females such as Kallisto – fall under the patronage of the virgin huntress because they have not, as she has not, made the transition to full sexual life within marriage; socially speaking, they still belong 'in the wild'. However, Artemis' relationship to virginity is far from unambiguous. As is suggested by the fact that one of her roles in cult is as goddess of childbirth, she is by no means hermetically sealed off from sexuality. Her virginity is dangerously fragile: although never actually violated, it is constantly under implied threat.

Myths express this fragility in two ways. First, the goddess' young hunter-companions often find their attachment to the group compromised by sexuality. Kallisto, for example, was a devotee of Artemis, but was raped by Zeus (who had deviously taken the form of Artemis); according to one of several versions of her punishment, she was shot by Artemis herself. Another favourite companion was the mighty hunter Orion, but he too fell from grace because of a sexual liaison, either the rape of a maiden or an affair with Eos, goddess of the Dawn; in one version of the story it was Artemis who engineered his death, by sending a giant scorpion to kill him.

In yet another variant of the Orion story, Artemis herself was sexually attracted to Orion; this time it was Apollo who intervened to kill the rash transgressor. This points to a second way in which mythology highlights the fragility of Artemis' virginity, with tales in which it is not Artemis' companions, but she herself, who comes uncomfortably close to a sexual liaison. The nature of Aktaion's offence against the goddess is variously reported: either he lusted after her, or, more mildly, he unwittingly came across her and her companion nymphs bathing in a mountain spring. Either way, Aktaion's infringement of Artemis'

(Left) The death of Aktaion, as Artemis looks on. Aktaion's own hounds tear him apart, believing him to be a stag; the metamorphosis is alluded to through the deerskin slung around his shoulders. Metope from Temple E at Selinus, Sicily, c. 460 BC.

(Right) The erection displayed by 'herms' such as this is a marker of power as well as sexuality.

divine space was enough to condemn him: metamorphosed into a stag, he was ripped apart by his own hounds. The giants Otos and Ephialtes made a similarly fatal mistake by trying to win the hands of Artemis and Hera respectively. It was Artemis who effected their downfall. She turned herself into a deer and ran between them: each hurled a javelin, missing the deer, but killing his fellow giant.

Hermes

The son of Zeus and the nymph Maia, Hermes became quite literally a household word to the Greeks through his characteristic sculpted image, a four-sided pillar with a bust on the top and an erect phallus projecting from the front. Rigid and potent, such 'herms' were found in many types of situation – in the city, in the country, at crossroads – but the most typical location was as a boundary-marker outside the threshold of an ordinary Greek house. When conspirators mutilated the herms in the city of Athens on the eve of the departure of the mighty military expedition to Sicily in 415 BC, the event was held to forbode disaster – not surprisingly since, as sacred markers delimiting one man's territory from another, herms articulated the most basic structure of the city-state.

Hermes' mythology both contrasts with and complements the iconography of the herm. On the one hand, the mythological Hermes is a god of movement, of travel, of deft alternation between opposed states – quintessentially mobile, as against the herm's fixity. On the other hand, the mythological Hermes is – as the form and location of the herm imply – a god of fertility (especially that of flocks and herds) and a god of boundaries.

Three episodes from Homeric epic exemplify contexts in which Hermes oscillates between opposites. First, in the final Book of the *Iliad* the disguised god guides Priam, aged king of Troy, from his beleaguered city to the Greek camp, in order to ransom the corpse of his beloved son Hektor; Hermes, that is, operates in 'no man's land'. The second episode occurs in Book 5 of the *Odyssey*, when Hermes flies down from Olympos bearing a message for Kalypso, the goddess who dwells on an island at the end of the earth. Since he is capable of spanning sky and land, mountain and sea, Hermes is the perfect courier. Finally, near the end of the same poem, when those suitors who schemed to usurp Odysseus' home and marry his wife have been slaughtered by the returned hero, then:

Hermes of Kyllene summoned the souls of the suitors
to come forth, and in his hands he was holding the
beautiful
golden staff, with which he bewitches the eyes of those
mortals
whom he would bewitch, or wakes again the sleepers.
Moving
them on with this, he drove them along, and they
followed, gibbering.

Life and death; sleep and waking; Olympos and the Underworld: Hermes' favourite role is to move between such polarities.

This ability has been with him since the very day of his birth on Arcadian Mount Kyllene. As we learn from the delicious *Homeric Hymn to Hermes*, the resourceful newborn, child of Zeus and the nymph Maia, celebrates his arrival into the world with a spot of cattle-rustling; the victim is his own half-brother Apollo. With his mission accomplished, the young god withdraws to his base, passing through the keyhole of his shelter: the ultimate example of controlling a boundary.

Hermes' province, then, is theft, guile, craft. He lacks the capacity for brute force which typifies some of the other Olympians: his trademark symbol, a staff, is not an aggressive weapon. He it is who recommends that Odysseus use the plant *moly* as an antidote in order to circumvent the potions of the enchantress Circe; he it is who, before slaying the many-eyed Argos (deputed by Hera to watch over Zeus' lover Io), first lulls his eyes to sleep one by one, again preferring a trick to unmediated violence.

One last role is worth stressing. In his capacity as messenger and conveyor, Hermes regularly acts as a facilitator for the actions of the other gods. When Hera, Athene and Aphrodite need guiding down to Mount Ida for the Judgment of Paris (see p. 132), Hermes is the one to take them there; when Persephone returns from the Underworld to rejoin her mother Demeter, who else but Hermes shall guide her steps? But one man's servant is another man's lackey. Prometheus, in Aischylos' *Prometheus Bound*, voices one of the bitterest condemnations of one god by another when he reviles Hermes for doing the bidding of Zeus, the new tyrant in heaven.

Aphrodite

As a rule it is misleadingly reductivist to ascribe one epithet to a Greek divinity; but in the case of Aphrodite the description 'goddess of sexuality' hits the mark. About her genealogy sources disagree. In Homer's *Iliad* she is the child of Zeus and the goddess Dione, with no mention of the gory Hesiodic tale of her birth from the severed genitals of Ouranos. There are also different versions of her relationship to the other divine embodiment of sexual love, Eros: the Hesiodic account places Eros at the very beginning of the cosmos, with Aphrodite arriving later; but other myth-tellers, such as Apollonios of Rhodes, cast Eros as an eternal child, the spoilt and (with his unerring, aphrodisiac arrows) dangerous offspring of Aphrodite herself. Common to all the variants, however, is the perception of Aphrodite as incarnation of *ta aphrodisia*, the sexual act.

This quality dominates Aphrodite's many cults, whether at her major sanctuaries at Paphos and Amathus on the southern coast of Cyprus (whence her regular epithet Kypris, 'The Cyprian') or elsewhere. Amongst her appellations are Porne ('Prostitute') and Hetaira ('Sexual Companion'). But we should not infer that Aphrodite was there by marginalized in relation to civic life. On the contrary, in several localities religious practice stressed her social centrality, for example in the context of marriage cults, or as the embodiment of civic concord in virtue of the epithet Pandemos ('Of the Whole People').

Several myths express the irresistible power which Aphrodite could exercise in the most intimate of emotional settings. The most famous such tale has become known as the Judgment of Paris. When Hera, Athene and Aphrodite quarrelled over who was the most beautiful, they delegated the decision to a mere mortal: Paris, son of King Priam of Troy. With a choice of bribes before him – power from Hera, victory from Athene, and from Aphrodite the love of the world's most lovely woman – the decision was a foregone conclusion: Aphrodite took the prize, and Paris took Helen, thus precipitating the Trojan War.

Although married to the lame smith Hephaistos, Aphrodite was notorious for her amorous liaison with Ares: as Demodokos' song in the *Odyssey* recounts, the adulterous pair were once locked in each other's arms when the poor cuckold decided to take his revenge, binding them fast in a net of magical craftsmanship. Not even Zeus was immune to the goddess' charms. Aphrodite's girdle, worn next to her breasts, contained an overwhelming allure which, at a pivotal moment in the *Iliad*, was borrowed by Hera to help her to seduce her husband, so as to divert him from his master-plan on the battlefield.

But it was not in Zeus' nature to allow himself or the other gods to be manipulated by Aphrodite without riposte. On one occasion he determined to demonstrate that she too could be a victim of desire. As the *Homeric Hymn to Aphrodite* narrates, Zeus made her demean herself by falling in love with a mortal shepherd. His name was Anchises, and he tended his beasts on Mount Ida, near Troy. First the goddess withdrew to her shrine at Paphos, bathing and then anointing herself with perfumes of inexpressible sweetness. Then, disguised as a mortal, she came to Anchises. The fruit of their lovemaking would be Aineias, one of the few Trojans to escape from his city's destruction at the hands of the Greeks. As for Anchises himself, when he awoke to see the goddess in her true form, she warned him never to reveal what had happened. But in myth such prohibitions are made to be broken, and this duly happened: one day Anchises got drunk, and blurted out his secret. Because he had now intolerably diminished Aphrodite's honour, punishment was inevitable. According to different versions, Zeus either blinded or lamed him, so reaffirming the limits which no mortal could transgress with impunity.

Athene

Child of Zeus and Metis ('Crafty Intelligence'), wise, resourceful and valiant, Athene was the virgin warrior who sprang fully armed from the head of Zeus. Her military trademarks were the helmet, the spear, and above all the 'aegis', the tasselled goatskin which she wore about her shoulders; on it was set the grim image of the Gorgon, instiller of panic.

Unlike Apollo, who acted 'from afar', Athene was felt to be 'close', especially to heroes whom she favoured. Already in the Homeric poems it was Athene who stood beside Achilles and Odysseus. When Achilles' quarrel with Agamemnon threatened to turn into a deadly duel, thus compromising the Greek war-effort, Athene tugged Achilles by the hair to restrain him. As for Odysseus, Athene repeatedly assisted him on his wanderings back home to Ithaca, by turns praising and chiding the shrewd protégé with whom she shared so many characteristics.

Athene was 'close' not only to individual heroes but also to communities, in her capacity as Polias ('Goddess of the Citadel'). Sometimes the very fate of a city hung upon her presence: only when her talismanic statue, the Palladion, was stolen from Troy by Diomedes and Odysseus, could the city fall to its besiegers. The principal temples of Argos, Sparta and Lindos (on Rhodes) were dedicated to her, as was, most famously of all, the resplendent Parthenon on the Athenian Acropolis; indeed Athene may have taken her name from the city of Athens. Even if, as some scholars argue, the process of naming was the other way around – with Athens being named after its patron deity – the link between city and goddess was intimate: her sacred

(Left) Athene strides into battle, spear and shield at the ready. Coin from Alexandria, c. 315–310 BC.

Athene's temple at Lindos, on the island of Rhodes, stands on a sheer cliff above the sea. Built in the Doric style, it dates from the 4th century BC.

bird, the owl, is a typical image on Athenian coinage. As for the aetiology of Athene's connection with Athens, mythology supplied an answer. Once, Athene and Poseidon vied for the role of pre-eminent deity in the city. Whereas Poseidon's trident struck a source of sea-water from the bare rock of the Acropolis, Athene's gift, which duly earned her the victory, was at once more sustaining and more economically useful: a cultivated olive tree.

In fact cultivation – the process of bringing the natural into the realm of human productivity – is a key notion for understanding Athene. She watches over the woman who works wool; she is at the elbow of the carpenter who turns raw timber into a seaworthy vessel, such as the *Argo*, or into a one-off creation such as the Trojan Horse; she inspires the trainer of horses and the builder of chariots. The polarity between nature and culture, and the related polarity between raw and cooked – oppositions which many anthropologists have seen as fundamental to the ways in which humans think about the world – are of central relevance to the special powers exercised by the goddess. What shocked her into abandoning her support for one of her favourites, the hero Tydeus, was when she saw him devouring the brains of an enemy raw.

For all her willingness to be 'close', her wrath could be devastating. When Arachne boasted that she could outweave Athene, the rash girl underwent metamorphosis into a spider; when the young

hunter Teiresias saw the virgin goddess bathing naked, blindness was the penalty she exacted; when, during the sack of Troy, Aias the son of Oileus (often called 'the lesser Aias' to distinguish him from Aias the son of Telamon) raped the prophetess Cassandra at the very altar of Athene, his reckless act prompted the goddess to side with Poseidon in wrecking the Greek fleet on its homeward voyage. The two last-mentioned stories imply a distancing of the goddess from sexuality, and this is a theme which runs through many of the myths in which she figures. Her virginity remains intact; her divine persona combines masculinity and femininity in an idiosyncratic yet never grotesque way.

One myth which stresses both the goddess' resilient virginity and her closeness to Athens is that which narrates her erotic pursuit by Hephaistos. The lame smith-god had split Zeus' skull open with his axe in order to bring Athene into the world; but his interest in her did not end with her birth. One day, sexually aroused, he pursued her, but it all ended, as things so often did for Hephaistos, in anticlimax: he spilled his semen on her thigh. Athene wiped it off with a bit of wool, which she then cast aside on to the ground. Where it fell, the earth conceived, subsequently bringing forth a child who would be one of Athens' earliest kings: Erechtheus, sometimes called Erichthonios. Manifold and steadfast was the bond between the goddess and the city which she so ardently championed.

Dionysos and his followers

No literary portrayal of a Greek divinity equals Euripides' tragedy *Bacchae* for sheer, mesmerizing power. The plot centres on the Theban king Pentheus, who refuses to acknowledge a wonder-working 'Stranger' newly arrived from the east. The entire community is disrupted when the Stranger induces the city's women to abandon their homes and worship a new god, Dionysos, on the nearby mountain of Kithairon. Leading the women are Ino, Autonoe and Agaue (Pentheus' mother), the three sisters of Dionysos' mother Semele; Dionysos has driven them mad because they denied that the father of Semele's child was in fact Zeus himself. The Stranger – none other than Dionysos – inflicts horrible revenge when Agaue tears her son limb from limb in an orgy of uncomprehending violence.

Virtually all of Dionysos' principal mythological characteristics are encapsulated in *Bacchae*. The madness which he brings is collective rather than individual, a fact symbolized by the groups of devotees who surround him (in *Bacchae* these are his 'maenads', raving women); he is linked with a state of 'ecstasy', which literally means 'standing outside oneself'; he is the kind of god who, by virtue of his subversiveness, first provokes resistance and then crushes it without remorse; amongst

his symbols are the intoxicating grape and the evergreen and burgeoning ivy. He is, in short, inexpressibly delightful but formidably dangerous.

All these characteristics are depicted in other myths about Dionysos; we shall take each characteristic in turn.

Collective worship: Two groups of followers attend the god. His female adherents, the maenads, figure in many literary narratives and countless visual representations. A maenad's typical pose – head tossed back in ecstatic abandon – matches the wildness of her garb, with a spotted fawnskin slung around her neck, and sometimes a snake to bind her hair or girdle her dress. Dionysiac closeness to nature is expressed by the frequent depiction of maenads holding wild animals, or even tearing them limb from limb in the rite known as *sparagmos*. Less fearsome than maenads, with a grotesqueness verging on the absurd, were Dionysos' male devotees, the satyrs. Their form, unlike that of the maenads, physically incorporated a closeness to the animal world, since their predominant anthropomorphism was enlivened by traits belonging to horses or (especially in representations from later antiquity) goats. They habitually pursued nymphs or maenads, but their advances were often rebuffed – perhaps unsurprisingly, as

(Below left) Dionysos' capacity to identify himself with animal nature sometimes expresses itself as terrifying savagery. Here he dismembers a deer with uncanny ease. Attic vase, c. 490–470 BC.

(Below right) Two groups of Dionysos' adherents, the maenads and the satyrs, sometimes come into close proximity, thanks to the urgent desires of the satyrs. The Dionysiac atmosphere of this image on an Attic cup (c. 490 BC) is evident from the wild animal being wielded by the maenad, and by the characteristic 'wand', the thyrsos.

81

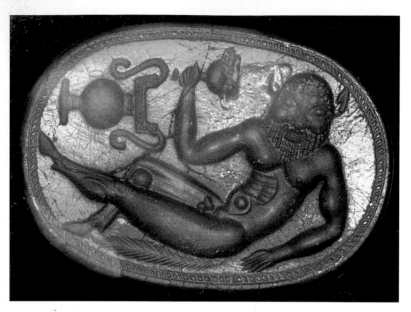

unfamiliar liquid, thought he had poisoned them instead of just making them tipsy – and they murdered him. Where vine and ivy are present together, Dionysos is present too. Some Etruscan pirates, having rashly taken the god captive, found their ship sprouting with the tendrils of these two plants. Astonished – and terrified by the wild beasts which also manifested themselves on deck – the hapless pirates dived overboard, miraculously changing into dolphins as they did so.

Danger and delight: Many Dionysiac myths speak of the god's dangerousness: humans crossed him at their peril. But his presence also brought sweetness and comfort. When Theseus carried off the Cretan princess Ariadne, he abandoned her on the island of Naxos. Borne on a chariot drawn by exotic wild beasts, Dionysos arrived to rescue her, and to give rise to one of the most spectacular and gracious of all surviving ancient artworks, the Derveni *krater*, on which the god and his new bride recline in luxuriant splendour.

Ares and Hephaistos

Two other gods, though quite different from each other in their spheres of influence, shared the indignity of being regularly disparaged by their fellow

their uneven mixture of partial baldness and exaggerated hairiness may not have been to everyone's taste. Ugliest of all was Silenos, the old man who was said to be their leader, and whose near-permanent inebriation symbolized the satyrs' addiction to one of the central Dionysiac pleasures.

Standing outside: Dionysiac ecstasy is mirrored in several tales which present the god as coming from 'outside'. This is apparently not a matter of historical memory (from Linear B tablets we have evidence for the presence of the god's cult in Greece at least as far back as the 13th century BC). Rather, it is a question of the god's alienness being symbolically represented as a 'belonging outside'. Thus it was that, according to mythology, Dionysos was driven mad by the jealous Hera (since he was the product of Zeus' adultery with Semele), and then wandered through a variety of non-Greek lands, from Egypt to India, until he came back at length to Greece.

Resistance and its overcoming: Several myths recount the resistance which Dionysos provoked. The daughters of Proitos, king of Tiryns, were driven out of their minds and homes when they failed to acknowledge Dionysos. Worse still was the fate of one of the daughters of Minyas, founder-ruler of Orchomenos. She and her sisters preferred weaving in honour of Athene to worshipping Dionysos; just like Agaue, she tore her own son to pieces. As for the Thracian king Lykourgos, his persecution of Dionysos led to (depending on the variant) madness, blinding, or rending by wild beasts.

Dionysiac vegetation: The intoxicating vine and the irrepressible ivy are the Dionysiac plants *par excellence.* The gift of the vine cut both ways: when the god bestowed it upon the Attic peasant Ikarios, the man's neighbours, with whom he had shared the

divinities. Ares was disliked because of what he stood for: the unrestrained cruelty of war. His own father Zeus called him, in the *Iliad*, 'most hateful to me of all the gods who hold Olympos'. Though usually regarded as equivalent to the Roman god Mars, Ares was far less central to the Greek pantheon than Mars was at Rome (see p. 218). He was said to come from Thrace – which was, in the eyes of some Greeks from elsewhere, a barely half-civilized place. It was to Thrace that he withdrew after making adulterous love to Aphrodite behind the back of her husband Hephaistos. The adulterers met on a regular basis, producing four children: Phobos ('Fear'), Deimos ('Terror'), Harmonia ('Harmony') and (according to a variant different from that preserved by Hesiod) Eros ('Sexual Love').

(Above) One of the glories of the Thessaloniki Museum, the large (height 91 cm/36 in) bronze krater *(mixing bowl) from nearby Derveni gleams with idealized mythological figures. Watched over by two relief heads of Herakles decorating the volutes, the imagery on the body of the vase has as its focus the union of Dionysos and his bride Ariadne. (See ill. on p. 66–67.)*

(Left) The interior of Exekias' famous cup (c. 530 BC) depicts Dionysos' transformation of pirates into dolphins, as punishment for kidnapping him. The scene is a virtuoso demonstration of metamorphosis: the mast becomes a vine, while the hull assumes the form of a dolphin.

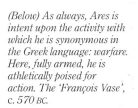

(Below) As always, Ares is intent upon the activity with which he is synonymous in the Greek language: warfare. Here, fully armed, he is athletically poised for action. The 'François Vase', c. 570 BC.

The painter of this vase (c. 560 BC) has depicted a juvenile-looking Hephaistos riding on an ithyphallic donkey. Off-picture to the right is Dionysos, who is leading Hephaistos back up to Olympos. At the top left is a jaunty satyr.

mythological genealogy, an unorthodox method of conception produced an imperfect offspring – she hurled him out of Olympos in disgust. His revenge was intricate rather than violent, for he sent her a golden throne which held her with invisible bindings. In the end Dionysos made him drunk and led him back up to Olympos on a donkey; after that, he agreed to free his mother.

The theme of 'casting out from Olympos' recurs a second time. When Zeus took his quarrel with Hera to terrifying lengths by hanging her from the mountain with anvils weighting her feet, Hephaistos sided with his mother. For his pains, Zeus hurled him as far as the smith's 'own' island of Lemnos. Even so, he gamely scaled Olympos once more to rejoin the company of the immortals. Though he continued to be a butt of their rough humour, he earned their respect too, thanks to his unrivalled mastery of the arts of metal and fire.

Lesser divinities: Hekate, Hestia, Pan

Hekate's role in mythological narrative is relatively modest. Her links with the sinister powers of the Underworld are exemplified in a memorable scene from Apollonios' *Argonautica*, when Jason, on the advice of Hekate's priestess Medea, summons the goddess to lend him her aid. Hekate's associations with night, with howling dogs, and with the no man's land of crossroads, all stress the infernal and uncanny nature of her divine persona. Yet, as usual, it is unwise to generalize too confidently about what 'the Greeks' thought about a given religious phenomenon. In his *Theogony*, Hesiod utters a remarkable, almost personal paean to Hekate, praising her in lavish terms as helpmeet of kings, granter of victory, and bringer of prosperity. In our picture of Greek mythology, there must always be room for local and even idiosyncratic variations.

The first two inherited their father's traits, the second two their mother's – as if the contrast between the parents was so stark that their offspring could not be a blend of each.

Hephaistos, the divine smith, was, like Ares, marked as an outsider: doubly so. First, he was associated with the north Aegean island of Lemnos, populated (as inscriptional evidence suggests) by non-Greek-speakers until well into the Archaic period. Secondly, he was lame. According to one version, Hera bore him alone, apart from Zeus; but – since, as so often in the logic of

Jason Summons Hekate

In the course of his narrative of the Argonautic expedition, Apollonios of Rhodes relates these eerie preliminaries to Jason's contest with the fire-breathing bulls. Under instructions from Medea, the hero invokes the help of the dread goddess Hekate:

In the distance the sun was sinking beneath the dark earth, beyond the furthest peaks of the western Ethiopians, and Night was placing the yoke upon her horses; beside the ship's ropes the heroes prepared their beds. Not Jason, however. As soon as the bright stars of Helike, the Bear, had slipped down, and the air was perfectly still through the heavens, he went to an empty place, like a furtive thief, with everything he needed, which he had prepared in advance during the day. Argos [the son of Phrixos] had fetched him a ewe and milk taken from a flock, but the rest he took from the ship itself. When he found a place set apart from men's paths, open to the skies in the midst of pure water-meadows, he first of all bathed his tender body in the holy river as ritual demanded, and then dressed

in the dark robe which Lemnian Hypsipyle once gave to him, to remind him of their sweet love-making. After this he dug a trench a cubit long in the earth and made a heap of cut wood; then he slit the sheep's throat over the pit and stretched its body over the fire in accordance with the rite. He lit the wood by putting in fire at the bottom, and poured out over it a mingled libation, calling upon Brimo Hekate to assist him in the contest. Having summoned her, he retreated. Hearing the call, the dread goddess came from the furthest depths to accept the sacrifices of the son of Aison. Around her head was a garland of terrible snakes entwined with oak-branches, and her torches flashed out a blinding brightness; all around her was the piercing bark of hellish dogs. All the fields trembled at her approach; the marsh-dwelling nymphs of the river who dance around that meadow of the Amarantian Phasis screamed aloud. The son of Aison was seized by fear, but even so he did not turn around as his feet carried him back to find his companions; already early-born Dawn was scattering her light as she rose above the snowy Caucasus.

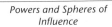

(Left) To Greeks and Romans alike Pan was a god of the 'outside': unnerving and potentially dangerous. Anyone who came across the god unawares might be afflicted with 'panic'. Pan's closest associates were the nymphs, with whom he shared many cults, especially in caves. Roman Imperial gold statuette.

Vesta, though Hestia lacks the social prominence lent to Vesta by her guardians at Rome, the Vestal Virgins (see p. 218); as often, the notion of Greek and Roman 'equivalent' deities can be more misleading than helpful.

Implicit in the nature of Greek divinity is the capacity to transcend anthropomorphism. For many of the gods, this capacity manifests itself in self-transformation, for example into the shape of an animal. But with Pan, this mixing of human and animal form constitutes, as in the case of satyrs, not a fleeting metamorphosis but a permanent, hybrid condition: part human, part goat. His promiscuity is all-embracing: no nymph is safe from him, but shepherd boys, and even animals from the flock, need to keep a wary eye too. Pan roams the solitary wilds between communities; Arcadia, regarded by Greeks from other regions as rough and pre-civilized, is the area most associated with him, but his worship spread throughout the Greek world. Indeed his name ('All') was sometimes taken to betoken a universal divine force. However, his typical image is more modest in scope: horned, goat-footed, and, in the brief interludes between sexual escapades, peacefully occupied in playing the reed pipes.

The Muses

Because many of our sources for Greek mythology are composed by poets, it is not surprising that the Muses, those traditional inspirers of poetic performance, receive regular acclaim. 'Untiring flows the sweet voice from their lips,' sings Hesiod, 'and the house of their father Zeus the loud-thunderer rejoices at the lily-like voice of the goddesses as it spreads abroad; the peaks of snowy Olympos and the homes of the immortals resound.' They were the daughters of Zeus and Mnemosyne

Equally modest in her mythological role is Hestia, goddess of the hearth. In fact, 'of the hearth' is misleading – she *is* the hearth, the sacred fire at the focus of every home and every community. (The ancient Greek language knows no distinction between 'capital' and 'small' letters: the word *hestia* means both 'hearth' and 'the goddess Hestia'.) She is a virgin: the sexual act would have polluted the purity of her fiery essence. Her role is to be central and fixed; indeed the French scholar Jean-Pierre Vernant has convincingly identified a significant contrast-cum-complementarity between Hestia and Hermes, the god of mobility and exchange. But another significant contrast is with Hephaistos. While he represents fire in its dynamic aspect – productively, as in the forge, or aggressively, as in the elemental conflict between himself and a river-god in Book 21 of the *Iliad* – Hestia is the undying focus, the element necessary for the act of sacrifice. In this she partly resembles her Roman 'equivalent'

The Muses and Their Functions

Daughters of Zeus and Mnemosyne ('Memory'), the Muses are principally associated with various aspects of the charming power of artistic expression. Ancient accounts of them vary in many details: in earlier texts they were not thought of as nine in number, even though this size of grouping has become canonical. Their functions vary, too. Here is one possible list of their 'provinces':

Erato	lyric poetry
Euterpe	the playing of the *aulos* (double pipe)
Kalliope	epic poetry
Kleio	history
Melpomene	tragedy
Ourania	astronomy
Poly(hy)mnia	hymns, or, later, (Roman) pantomime
Terpsichore	choral dance
Thaleia	comedy

('Memory'): Kleio, Euterpe, Thaleia, Melpomene, Terpsichore, Erato, Poly(hy)mnia, Ourania, Kalliope. In later antiquity they were assigned particular genres: history to Kleio, tragedy to Melpomene, and so on. Though associated with song, dance and celebration, they were still capable of the wrath which characterized every divinity. When the bard Thamyris rashly claimed to be able to out-sing and out-play them, they blinded him, taking away his poetic skills into the bargain. No less decisive was their reaction to provocation by the nine daughters of King Pieros, a ruler in Macedonia: when challenged to a musical contest by these silly girls, the Muses first won, and then, according to one variant, turned their opponents into magpies.

The Fates

Unlike, for example, their 'equivalents' the Norns in the mythology of northern Europe, the Fates (Moirai, from the word for 'portion' or 'share') figure only rarely in Greek mythology. Usually the causation of narrated mythical events is presented as a product of the interweaving of the purposes of the gods and the more-or-less free choices of human agents.

Just occasionally, though, another agency comes into play, namely partnership of the three Fates: Klotho ('She who Spins'), Lachesis ('Disposer of Lots') and Atropos ('She who May Not be Turned'). The symbolism underlying these names is that of the spinning, measuring and cutting of a woollen thread, a thread to whose length there corresponds the duration of a mortal's life. Since this triple process takes place at birth, there is, in theory, no scope for subsequent renegotiation: what's cut is cut. That certainly applies to the hero Meleager. 'When he was seven days

old,' reports Apollodoros, 'it is said that the Moirai appeared and announced that Meleager would die when the log burning on the fire should be completely consumed.' His horrified mother Althaia snatched the log and hid it away. But one day, in a fit of anger with her son (who had quarrelled with and slain her brothers), Althaia rekindled the log, bringing to pass the fulfilment of the Fates' prediction.

However – typically of a mythology which loves to conduct thought experiments – several stories explore possibilities for circumventing that which is allotted. We have already come across the instance in the *Iliad* where Zeus maintains that, although he could prolong the destiny of his son Sarpedon, on balance he chooses not to, so as to avoid enraging the other gods.

No less intriguing is the situation in Euripides' play *Alkestis*. In gratitude for his hospitable treatment at the hands of the mortal Admetos, Apollo induces the Fates to prolong Admetos' life, by the simple expedient of getting them drunk. The prolongation is conditional upon Admetos' finding a substitute who will undertake to die instead of him; it is the emotional traumas consequent on this substitution which form the basis of Euripides' complex and poignant drama.

The Furies

Altogether more active than the Fates are the Furies (Erinyes). Sometimes they were thought of as a numerous collectivity, though later writers represent them as a triad whose names were Alekto ('Relentless'), Megaira ('She who Bears a Grudge') and Tisiphone ('Avenger of Bloodshed'). They were thought of as primeval – certainly 'older' than the Olympians. But they survived into the era of the Olympians, precisely because

(Right) The death of Meleager. The Moirai (Fates) told Meleager's mother that he would die when a firebrand was burnt up completely. She preserved it, but one day angrily rekindled it – so fulfilling the Fates' prophecy. Relief from a Roman sarcophagus, 2nd–3rd century AD.

(Below) This bronze statuette (c. 400 BC) from near Mount Vesuvius, Campania, may represent an Erinys ('Fury') or the Etruscan Underworld demon Vanth. Either way the wings, and the serpents coiled around the arms, convey a sense of unearthly power.

the power which they embodied had not been superseded. They were automatically called into action each time an act of murder took place, particularly the murder of an individual related by blood to his or her killer. According to one variant, they were conceived when the drops of blood from Ouranos' severed genitals fell upon the earth. Their looks were repulsive: snuffling and barking like dogs, they had snakes in their hair and foul liquid dripping from their eyes. Yet they were not evil. They had a vital job to do, namely to hound the perpetrators of violent human transgressions.

As we have already suggested, one of the functions of Greek mythology was to set up thought experiments: what if…? Especially in the tragedies, these thought experiments centred on dilemmas of an apparently insoluble kind. A classic case occurs in Aischylos' *Oresteia* trilogy, in the latter part of which the Furies are at the centre of the action. When Orestes kills his mother Clytemnestra, he is pursued by the Furies; yet his almost unthinkable action of committing matricide has been precipitated by Clytemnestra's treacherous murder of her husband, Orestes' father Agamemnon. Are the Furies still right to persecute Orestes? In the end, the dilemma reaches a kind of resolution at Athens, under the wise guidance of Athene herself: Orestes is acquitted, but the Furies, so far from being dishonoured, retain their rights, and are granted a place of privileged worship at the centre of Athens (see pp. 184–85). These 'old' deities were still needed even under the new dispensation of the Olympians.

Honour and Boundaries

In describing the powers and spheres of activity ascribed to the various Greek divinities, we have from time to time come across conflicts of interest and boundary disputes. We now focus directly on this theme, both in so far as it touches on relations between one god and another, and also, most particularly, in connection with relationships between divinities and mortals.

On their own territory, the gods are supreme: no one except Hephaistos can undo the invisible fastenings with which the adulterers Ares and Aphrodite are bound; not even Zeus can resist the charms of the girdle of Aphrodite when Hera puts it on. The problems arise at the margins, on the boundaries, when there are choices to be made, and when a divinity's honour is therefore at stake. The story of Hippolytos illustrates the point.

Hippolytos

Hippolytos is a young mortal who prefers hunting and virginity to the pursuits over which Aphrodite holds sway. As a devotee of Artemis *exclusively*, by implication he belittles the goddess of sexual love. Divinities never brook dishonour to themselves; Aphrodite is no exception. In Euripides' tragedy *Hippolytos* – the basis for Racine's great drama *Phèdre* and many later adaptations – Aphrodite avenges the slight by causing Hippolytos' stepmother Phaidra to fall in love with her stepson. When the horrified Hippolytos rejects her, Phaidra hangs herself, but not before writing a suicide note incriminating Hippolytos (see p. 129). Ignorant of the true course of events, Hippolytos' father Theseus curses his son, and the curse duly leads to Hippolytos' death. Though the play's final scene portrays the tender parting between Artemis and her dying protégé, the abiding impression left by the play is that of Aphrodite's ruthless vengeance. The only thing more chilling than that is Artemis' vow to inflict a comparable punishment, as soon as she gets the chance, on one of Aphrodite's own favourites.

Lykaon

A particularly significant kind of boundary transgression which the gods intervene to rectify is that involving an attempt by a mortal to deceive the gods themselves into transgressing. A graphic example is the tale of Lykaon, one of the earliest mythical inhabitants of Arcadia. There are several variants, but a common thread is the attempt, either by Lykaon or his sons, to deceive Zeus into eating a meal consisting of the flesh of a cooked human child. This was a wicked perversion of the hospitality which should have bound host to guest, and it led Zeus to inflict an exemplary retribution, variously specified as the death by thunderbolt of Lykaon's sons, the sending of a great flood, or the transforming of Lykaon into the symbolically appropriate form of a wolf. This tale provides a plausible case of the symbiosis of a myth with a

Theseus mistakenly believes that his son Hippolytos has forced himself upon Theseus' wife Phaidra. Theseus' curse calls up a monstrous bull from the sea (bottom of picture) which, together with a Fury (right), maddens the horses drawing Hippolytos' chariot. South Italian vase, 4th century BC.

ritual. On Mount Lykaion in Arcadia, a cult was practised in which one of the participants, having (really or symbolically) partaken of human flesh, was believed to leave human form and to become a wolf; if he were able to abstain from human flesh for nine years, he would resume human form once more. Some of the details of the rite – the man in question stripped and then swam across a pool, before leaving the community – suggest that we have here an echo of an initiation ritual, which might at some date have involved a whole age-cohort as opposed to just one individual. The eerie ceremony on this remote mountain would thus have marked the prelude to a period spent in the wilds by a group of young Arcadian men; after the expiry of this period they would have returned to the community, no longer as wolfish outsiders, but as fully-fledged citizens.

Tantalos

A similar type of transgression to that of Lykaon – although it resulted in a different punishment – was that perpetrated by Tantalos, king of Sipylos (in the region of Lydia, north of Ephesos). Tantalos' privileged position as a son of Zeus enabled him to dine with the gods; but he abused it. According to one version, he served the gods a cooked human child, namely his own son Pelops (whose shoulder was absentmindedly consumed by Demeter, grieving for Persephone); alternatively, Tantalos revealed the gods' secrets, to which his intimacy with them made him privy; or else he passed on to mortals the divine food and drink – ambrosia and nectar – to which he had access. The second and third of these transgressions clearly involve infringing the boundary which should separate gods from mortals, while the first resembles the catastrophic rupture of hospitality found also in the Lykaon story. The punishment devised by Zeus was eternal: in the Underworld Tantalos stood in a pool which drained whenever he tried to reach for water. As for food, he was no luckier:

Over his head trees with lofty leaves had fruit like a
    shower descending,
pear trees and pomegranate trees and apple trees with
    fruit shining,
and figs that were sweet and olives ripened well, but each
    time
the old man would straighten up and reach with his
    hands for them,
the wind would toss them away toward the
    overshadowing clouds.

Sisyphos and Ixion

Two other mortals endured everlasting suffering in the Underworld, confirming that what really goaded the gods into intervening in human affairs was any threat to their own honour, honour which depended in part upon proper maintenance of the boundary between themselves and mortals.

Sisyphos, mythical founder of the city of Corinth, was condemned to spend the Afterlife rolling a boulder up a hill, only to see it roll back again to the bottom just as he neared the top. His transgression had been to call into question the fundamental difference between gods and mortals: that mortals die, whereas gods do not. He had tried to elide this distinction by using two tricks. First, he bound and thus incapacitated Thanatos, god of Death. Secondly, he instructed his wife not to perform burial rites for him, thus cheating Hades of his due. When Hades allowed him to return to life to rectify the situation, he did so – but did not bother to go back down again until he had reached a ripe old age.

The career of a third exemplary sinner perfectly illustrates what it was in mortal conduct that attracted divine wrath. King Ixion of Thessaly committed the first kin-murder. Zeus, however, far from chastising him, actually purified him from his crime. It was only when Ixion took the catastrophic further step of trying to rape Hera – the ultimate invasion of divine space – that his fate was sealed. All he managed to impregnate was a cloud, fashioned by Zeus in Hera's likeness; the product of this bizarre liaison was Kentauros, first of the Centaurs. As for Ixion, the Afterlife was to hold no joy for him,

Ixion's eternal punishment for his attempted sexual assault upon Hera. Furies look on as he lies helpless, bound with snakes to a wheel. South Italian vase, 4th century BC.

for he was fastened upon a wheel, to be whirled everlastingly through the air.

Competing with the gods

The variety of ways in which mortals could challenge or defy the gods was matched by the severity and ingenuity of the punishments meted out to them. 'Sacrilege avenged' is a common theme; a vivid example is the myth of Erysichthon, a rash mortal whose story was told by Kallimachos in one of his hymns, and later elaborated by Ovid. Erysichthon's wicked destruction of the trees in a grove sacred to Demeter was punished when the goddess of corn sent upon him a terrible hunger, which ended only when he devoured his own body.

Another recurrent pattern is that of the unwisely undertaken competition with the gods. One day the Phrygian satyr Marsyas found the *aulos* (double pipe) which its inventor Athene had discarded, because it made her look ugly when she puffed out her cheeks to blow it. Marsyas was ugly already and so didn't care; he challenged Apollo to a musical contest, pipe versus lyre. When the lyre-player managed a feat which was quite beyond the pipe-player – playing the instrument upside down – Apollo took advantage of the terms of the bet, which had been that the victor could do what he liked with the vanquished. The god suspended the

(Below) Titian, The Flaying of Marsyas, *c. 1570–76. Of all the punishments inflicted by the Olympians on those who challenged their authority, that meted out to Marsyas is the most grisly. Suspended upside down from a tree, the satyr waits to be skinned alive, while Apollo (probably) provides musical accompaniment.*

presumptuous satyr from a pine tree and skinned him alive, an image which would recur disturbingly in post-classical visual art.

If challenging Apollo was rash, challenging Zeus was the height of folly; yet that was what Salmoneus did. This king of a city in Elis (in the western Peloponnese) claimed to be Zeus himself, imitating the lightning by hurling torches into the sky, and making thunder by dragging bronze kettles behind his chariot. Zeus' thunderbolt wiped

out both Salmoneus and his people. This was a case where Zeus stepped in to vindicate his own personal honour. But on another occasion, in an altogether more complex myth, Zeus intervened to maintain the general integrity of the divide between gods and humans. Apollo's son Asklepios was a great healer, but one day he took his medical prowess too far, by raising a corpse to life. Zeus' thunderbolt restored the status quo, blasting doctor and patient simultaneously. But the story did not end there,

either in myth or in cult. In myth, Apollo retaliated by killing the Cyclopes, who made the lethal thunderbolt for Zeus (and Apollo in his turn would have to pay a price, doing penance as a servant to a mortal, Admetos). As for cult, the enduring value of Asklepios' medical skill was reflected in his worship throughout the Greek world. The magnificent theatre at Epidauros lies adjacent to a huge sanctuary to Asklepios, as impressive, in extent if not in state of preservation, as the theatre itself.

Modern visitors to Epidauros marvel at the magnificent theatre (see p. 36); so did their ancient counterparts. Epidauros attracted countless visitors to the sanctuary of the healer god Asklepios (above). The sick would sleep in a designated area, hoping to be granted a healing dream, and to leave next morning cured.

(Right) In artistic as well as literary sources, Greece has left us few accounts of the Daidalos and Ikaros myth. But from Rome we have this fine relief (2nd century AD), showing us the father carefully working on his son's wings.

(Below) Pieter Bruegel the Elder, Landscape with the Fall of Icarus, *c. 1567. Deliberately sidelined in the painter's vision, the fallen youth is in the process of disappearing from view, while the everyday concerns of herdsmen and ploughmen remain entirely unaffected.*

Daidalos and Ikaros

In comparison to its extensive influence on later art and literature, the myth of Ikaros has survived in only sparse accounts from Greek antiquity. But it clearly constitutes another instance of the destruction of a mortal who quite literally came too close to the gods. Ikaros' father was Daidalos, a mythical master-craftsman linked with locations as diverse as Crete, Athens and Sicily, and credited with inventing everything from King Minos' Cretan Labyrinth to the 'walking' (i.e. lifelike) pose in monumental statues. It is in fact on the Labyrinth that the most poignant part of his story is concentrated. When the Athenian hero Theseus came to Crete to slay the Minotaur, he and Ariadne – Minos' daughter, with whom Theseus fell in love – sought Daidalos' help in order to escape from the maze. Daidalos gave them a thread to unwind behind them and thereby retrace their way out; Minos retaliated by imprisoning Daidalos and Ikaros in the Labyrinth. Resourceful as always, Daidalos constructed wings for the two of them, and they soared out of Minos' clutches. But when Ikaros ignored his father's warning not to fly too close to the sun, the heat melted the wax with which the wings were fixed, and the boy plunged to his death.

The Labyrinth becomes an emblem of Knossos on this coin, c. 350–300 BC. Some visitors to the 'labyrinthine' remains of the palace complex at Knossos have detected in them an 'origin' for Minos' mythical maze.

Phaethon

Although less explicit than the tales of Asklepios or Salmoneus, the Ikaros myth too cautions mortals against coming too close to the gods. It also counsels sons against thinking they know better than their fathers. The same moral is present in a tale which is virtually a 'double' of the Ikaros story, namely that of Phaethon, son of the Sun god Helios. The boy's reckless driving of his father's chariot threatened the world with destruction, until Zeus put an end to his career with the ineluctable thunderbolt. (Our evidence for this dramatic tale is meagre in extant Greek sources; the Roman poet Ovid provides the earliest detailed account.)

Teiresias

As a final illustration of how myths explored the boundaries between mortals and immortals, and of how the gods jealously defended their territory, we may cite the myth of Teiresias. Teiresias was one of the most renowned seers in Greece; he figures in many myths based in Thebes, for example the story of Oedipus. Like many a mortal with a more-than-human skill, he also had a compensating physical defect – as if to bring him down to a level which posed no threat to divine supremacy. Teiresias' defect was blindness.

There were several different accounts of how he lost his sight.

(1) Some, including the poet Kallimachos, said that he accidentally saw Athene bathing at a mountain spring. Why, then, did his death not follow immediately, as it had for Aktaion when he saw Artemis naked? What subtly differentiates the two myths is the fact that Teiresias' mother, the nymph Chariklo, was Athene's dear companion, and interceded on her son's behalf. Athene could not rescind the punishment of blinding – the Greek gods are never seen as omnipotent – but granted him the compensating gift of prophecy, especially the capacity to understand the language of birdsong.

(2) In the view of other myth-tellers, the gods blinded Teiresias because he divulged the gods' secrets to mortals. This makes him a kind of Prometheus or even Tantalos figure; the implication is that, in this variant, his special powers preceded his blindness.

(3) Even more intricate is a third explanation for his blindness. Teiresias was once in the kind of landscape where mortals typically encountered divinities: a mountain (Arcadian Kyllene). He saw two snakes copulating, and struck them with his staff. This must have counted as a crime (perhaps because the act they were engaged in 'belonged' to Aphrodite, or because the snakes were themselves sacred); at any rate, Teiresias suffered what, in Greek terms, counted as a diminution: he was transformed into a woman. Some time later he saw the same pair of copulating snakes, and regained his masculinity. These two acts of boundary-crossing made Teiresias uniquely qualified to judge a tricky dispute between Zeus and Hera, about whether males or females enjoyed the act of sex more. Teiresias, who had experienced both possibilities, said women enjoyed it nine times more than men. This answer won the argument for Zeus, so Hera blinded the hapless Teiresias. (As when Paris was invited to judge the beauty of three goddesses, the honour of being consulted by quarrelling divinities was a mixed blessing.) By way of compensation, Zeus rewarded Teiresias with the gift of prophecy, so that the notion of balance (power versus defect) occurs once more, as it does in other versions. However, one motif which is unique to this version is that the secrets betrayed are those not of the gods but of women. The Teiresias myth embodies some of the recurring concerns of Greek mythology, and also the richness of narrative variation which typifies it.

Divine Sexuality

One of the most striking ways in which the gods' awesome power expressed itself was through sex. Their potency and fertility were unfailing: even such a risible failure as Hephaistos' ejaculation onto Athene's thigh led to the birth of a child. Collectively the gods embraced a whole gamut of proclivities, from heterosexual sex (instances beyond number) to brother-sister incest (Zeus and Hera) to same-sex liaisons (Zeus and Ganymede, Apollo and Hyakinthos) to bestiality (Pan amid the flocks), to the dimensions and variations implicit in the figures of Priapos (a god of rustic promiscuity, endowed with a gigantic phallus) and Hermaphroditos (a child of Hermes and Aphrodite, whose bisexuality consisted of having a fused male/female body complete with both sets of genitals), not forgetting the virginity successfully defended by Athene, Artemis and Hestia.

Sexual activity was an area in which the gods overshadowed even the most vigorous of mortals. Frequently, however, myths told of sexual liaisons across the divine/mortal boundary; and these liaisons are, in a variety of ways, extremely revealing of the Greeks' perceptions of divinity. Of course, for a divinity to engage in the act of love with a mortal was to court inevitable sadness, since humans, bound to die sooner or later, lived on a time-scale quite different from that enjoyed by immortals. To this we must add another complicating factor – indeed, a double standard – in terms of gender. For female divinities, sex with a mortal might entail potential dishonour as well as long-term unhappiness; for male divinities, loss of status was not a part of the equation.

Goddesses with mortal men

Aphrodite: Aphrodite's brief fling with Anchises (see p. 78) provides one model for the relationship between a goddess and her mortal lover: physical bliss is soon clouded by Aphrodite's shame, and by the risk, which naturally becomes reality, that Anchises may blurt out what happened (once more the theme of 'revealing the gods' secrets'), and so draw down divine wrath upon himself. An even more poignant tale links Aphrodite with another young mortal, Adonis. There were varying accounts of his genealogy, but one of them made him the child of an incestuous union between a king (of Cyprus or Assyria, or another 'eastern' land) and his own daughter. Adonis was thus the distillation of a peculiarly concentrated kind of sexuality –

not unlike Aphrodite herself. At any rate, Aphrodite was passionately attracted to the youth, and gave herself to him. It could not last; he was gored to death by a wild boar. The goddess' extravagant grief is explored in *Lament for Adonis*, a poem as brief and intense as the affair itself, composed by the Hellenistic writer Bion; the poet's home was Smyrna, the city which shared its name with Adonis' mother (alternatively called Myrrha).

Thetis: Was there an alternative, for a goddess, to these all-too-brief encounters? Another model did seem to offer hope of greater permanence: *marriage* to a mortal. Such was the eventual fate of the sea-nymph Thetis. At first she was wooed by Zeus and Poseidon, but they backed off when they learned of

(Right) A remarkable combination of male and female characteristics is captured in this Hellenistic bronze figurine of Hermaphroditos. The upper part of the robe falls from the left shoulder, to reveal a female breast; the lower part of the robe is raised, to display male genitals.

At all events, the union of goddess with mortal formed an unstable pairing. Thetis strove to bridge the gap by making their child, Achilles, immortal; the method is variously described as involving fire, anointing with ambrosia, or (in a late variant, enshrined in post-classical tradition) dipping into the river Styx. But Peleus intervened to stop the process, being unable, mortal that he was, to comprehend what was happening. Part of the magnificent pathos of Homer's *Iliad* resides in the situation of Thetis. Estranged now from Peleus,

(Below) To try to escape her mortal suitor Peleus, the goddess Thetis transforms herself into different and alarming shapes. Here she becomes a lion; the artist has represented both goddess and animal simultaneously. Melian relief, c. 460 BC.

(Left) The decoration on this Hellenistic bronze mirror probably represents Aphrodite leaning over her doomed lover Adonis (his boots suggest that he is a hunter).

a prophecy that Thetis' son was destined to be greater than his father. That cleared the way for Peleus, heroic but still a mere mortal. Like several other sea deities, Thetis had the power of serial self-transformation, which she used in order to resist Peleus' ardour; but at last she gave in. The wedding was held on Mount Pelion, and the Olympians came along as guests. Perhaps it was symbolically appropriate that on this occasion Eris, goddess of discord, threw the apple marked 'For the Fairest' between Hera, Athene and Aphrodite, so bringing about the Judgment of Paris, and the Trojan War.

Aphrodite's Lament for Adonis

The cult of Adonis came to the Greek world from the Near East, via Syria and Palestine. In this extract from the *Lament for Adonis* by the Hellenistic poet Bion, the language is as unrestrained as the grief which it expresses. It is hard to think of a more anguished evocation of the gulf between divinity and mortality.

When she saw, when she noticed Adonis' unstaunchable wound, when she saw the crimson blood upon his wasting thigh, she spread wide her arms and lamented:

'Stay, Adonis, stay, ill-fated Adonis, so I may hold you for the last time, embrace you, and mingle my lips with yours. Awake, Adonis, for a little, kiss me one last time; kiss me as long as the kiss has life, till your spirit passes into my mouth, and your breath flows into my liver, so that I may suck your sweet love-charm and drink up your passion; I shall keep

that kiss as if it were Adonis himself, since you, unlucky one, are leaving me. You leave on a long journey, Adonis; you go to Acheron, to a hateful, savage king; but I live on in my grief, and I, a wretched goddess, cannot follow you. Take my husband, Persephone, for you are much more powerful than I: everything fair flows downwards to you, but I am utterly wretched, my sorrow has no cure; I mourn Adonis, my dead Adonis; and you I shun.

'O my thrice-desired lover, you die; my longing has flown away like a dream. Kythereia is widowed; in my house the Loves lie idle, while my girdle of desire is no more. Rash Adonis, why did you go hunting? Lovely as you are, why did you furiously pit yourself against a wild beast?'

Such was the lament of the Cyprian goddess. Answering her, the Loves cried:

'Alas for Kythereia! Lovely Adonis is dead.'

she has returned to her former existence at the bottom of the sea, yet is repeatedly drawn to the land, and to the world of humans, by the anguished imploring of her doomed and vulnerable son Achilles.

Harmonia: Another goddess who married a mortal was Harmonia, daughter of Ares and Aphrodite. Her husband was Kadmos, founder of Thebes; but the union was not entirely happy. As in the case of Peleus and Thetis, the gods registered their approval by attending the ceremony; but trouble lay in store. One of the wedding gifts to Harmonia was a necklace, which in later generations was to exercise a baneful influence on those who possessed it (see p. 166).

As for Kadmos and Harmonia, most of their children were destined to live lives touched by conspicuous grief, notably Ino (driven mad), Semele (struck by a thunderbolt), and Autonoe and Agaue (mothers of the doomed Aktaion and Pentheus). In the end, Kadmos and Harmonia did receive the reward of an eternal life together, albeit a transformed one: they dwelt in the Elysian Fields as a pair of snakes. From slaying the serpent sacred to Ares before the foundation of Thebes, Kadmos had come full circle.

Eos and Selene: Pervading these tales is a combined sense of the obstacles impeding a goddess/mortal union, and the ingenuity deployed to overcome those obstacles. The goddess who worked most concertedly to achieve a long-term relationship with a mortal was Eos, the Dawn. But in her case, too, success was only partial. Her desire for the young Kephalos (offspring of the union between Hermes and a daughter of Kekrops) was either successfully consummated when she carried him off to Olympos, or thwarted by the enduring love between him and his wife Prokris. Eos also loved the mighty hunter Orion, but the gods brought about his violent death.

Most revealing of all, and notable for its mingling of genuine pathos with worldly-wise realism, is the myth of Eos and Tithonos. The handsome son of Laomedon king of Troy, Tithonos was carried off by Eos, who begged Zeus to make him immortal. Zeus' nod confirmed the promise, but Eos had been too hasty: she had forgotten to ask that Tithonos be granted eternal *youth*. The *Homeric Hymn to Aphrodite* spells out the sequel:

> But when hateful old age completely oppressed him, and he could neither move nor lift his limbs, this seemed to her in her heart the best plan: she put him in a room and closed the shining doors. There he babbles ceaselessly, but has no more vigour at all, such as once he had in his supple limbs.

According to another version, Tithonos was transformed into a cicada, to chatter away invisibly all his days. Either way, the passion was gone – which is why Dawn rises so early.

Perhaps only one goddess was truly fortunate in her mortal lover. Selene, goddess of the Moon, loved a young man named Endymion. Beautiful he certainly was, but wise also. When asked by Zeus what boon he would like, he asked to be able to sleep for all eternity, and, what is more, to sleep without ageing. And so each night the Moon joyfully came to Endymion where he lay, in a cave on Mount Latmos in Caria (southwest Asia Minor).

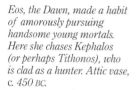

Eos, the Dawn, made a habit of amorously pursuing handsome young mortals. Here she chases Kephalos (or perhaps Tithonos), who is clad as a hunter. Attic vase, c. 450 BC.

Zeus' Mortal Lovers and Their Offspring

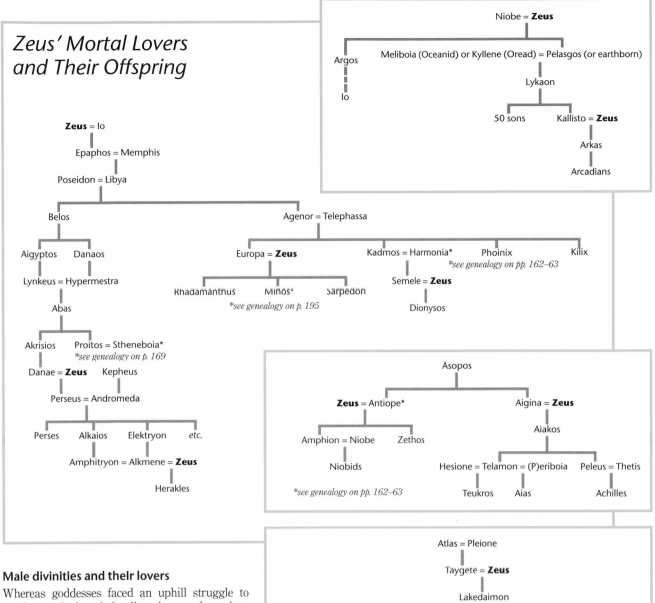

Niobe = Zeus
- Argos
  - Io
- Meliboia (Oceanid) or Kyllene (Oread) = Pelasgos (or earthborn)
  - Lykaon
    - 50 sons
    - Kallisto = **Zeus**
      - Arkas
        - Arcadians

Zeus = Io
- Epaphos = Memphis
  - Poseidon = Libya
    - Belos
      - Aigyptos
      - Danaos
        - Lynkeus = Hypermestra
          - Abas
            - Akrisios
              - Danae = **Zeus**
                - Perseus = Andromeda (Kepheus)
                  - Perses
                  - Alkaios
                  - Elektryon
                  - *etc.*
                    - Amphitryon = Alkmene = **Zeus**
                      - Herakles
            - Proitos = Stheneboia*
              *see genealogy on p. 169
    - Agenor = Telephassa
      - Europa = **Zeus**
        - Rhadamanthus
        - Minos*
        - Sarpedon
          *see genealogy on p. 195
      - Kadmos = Harmonia*
        - Semele = **Zeus**
          - Dionysos
        *see genealogy on pp. 162–63
      - Phoinix
      - Kilix

Asopos
- **Zeus** = Antiope*
  - Amphion = Niobe
    - Niobids
  - Zethos
    *see genealogy on pp. 162–63
- Aigina = **Zeus**
  - Aiakos
    - Hesione = Telamon = (P)eriboia
      - Teukros
      - Aias
    - Peleus = Thetis
      - Achilles

Atlas = Pleione
- Taygete = **Zeus**
  - Lakedaimon
    - **Zeus** = Leda = Tyndareos
      - Helen
      - Polydeukes
      - Kastor
      - Clytemnestra

parentage of all four variously reported

Male divinities and their lovers

Whereas goddesses faced an uphill struggle to continue enjoying their all-too-human favourites, their male counterparts took their pleasure where they liked, and suffered few emotional traumas as a result; the traumas were for their lovers to cope with. We shall focus on Zeus and Apollo, the progenitors, through their affairs with mortals, of most of the leading heroes and heroines of Greek mythology.

The loves of Zeus

Europa: One lover who emerged relatively unscathed from her seduction by Zeus was the Phoenician maiden Europa. Having spied her while she was picking blooms in a seaside meadow, Zeus trickily transformed himself into a handsome bull. Its effect on her emotions was immediate: 'and she caressed him,' recounts the Hellenistic poet Moschos in his sensual poem *Europa*, 'and gently with her hands wiped the abundant foam from his mouth, and kissed the bull.' Innocently she climbed onto the beast's compliant back; when the animal promptly sped off across the sea, it was too late to protest. They made landfall in Crete, where Europa

Leda's encounter with Zeus in the form of a swan was to enjoy a long artistic history. Among the more physically intimate examples is this 2nd-century AD marble relief from Brauron in Attica.

Zeus') – that is, Kastor and Polydeukes – and Clytemnestra. The form in which he visited Alkmene was, more cunningly, that of her own husband. Not surprisingly, there was doubt about the children's paternity, but the logic of divine power entailed that the mightier son, Herakles, had been sired by Zeus, while the feebler, Iphikles, owed his conception to Amphitryon, a mere mortal.

Danae and Antiope: When the women whom Zeus seduced were unmarried, their fathers tended to take a sceptical view of what had allegedly happened. Akrisios, king of Argos, was one such father. Having received an oracle that the child to be born to his daughter Danae would kill him, he confined her in a bronze prison. But Zeus, in the form of golden rain, penetrated the prison and then the prisoner; in due time she bore Perseus, destined to be a mighty hero. However, as any uncomprehending mortal would, Akrisios refused to believe that it was Zeus who had fathered the child, so again he locked his daughter away, this time with her baby, in an ark which he cast adrift on the sea; a fragment by the Archaic lyric poet Simonides wonderfully evokes the isolation and tenderness of the scene. (For Perseus' career see pp. 104–5.) Two lesser heroes, Amphion and Zethos, were the twin boys born when Antiope was raped by Zeus in the form of a satyr; like Danae, she too was thrown out of the house by her father, the river-god Asopos (for the further adventures of Amphion and Zethos see pp. 156–57).

Io: Thanks to their heroic children, Danae and Antiope in the end achieved rehabilitation after their tribulations. The same would be true of another victim of divine lust, Io, though the sufferings she endured along the way were unimaginable. She was assailed on every side: first she received mysterious approaches from Zeus; then she was banished from her home by her father, the river-god Inachos; finally she was persecuted by Hera, in whose Argive temple she had been serving as priestess. To cap it all, she was turned into a cow, either vindictively by Hera, or by Zeus himself to try to disguise her from Hera's wifely suspicions.

Hera, however, would not be fooled, and set the hundred-eyed Argos to watch over the 'cow'. Even when Zeus' henchman Hermes slew the watcher, Hera was not to be outdone: she sent a stinging fly to madden the bovine maiden and to drive her wandering throughout the world. Only when she reached Egypt – endowed, here as often in Greek myth, with a positive quality – did she find peace: Zeus changed her back into human shape, and mated with her in the gentlest possible way, just by touching her. Her child Epaphos ('Child of Touch') was ancestor to Danaos, who would make the return journey from Egypt to Argos and found a dynasty there.

was to bear Zeus three sons: Minos, Rhadamanthus and Sarpedon. The myth is doubly aetiological. First, it explains the etymology of 'Europe', to which the maiden-no-longer lent her name. (Significantly, the originator of the term 'Europe' was Phoenician; it is notable that early Greek myths usually make little of the distinction between between 'Greek' and 'barbarian', until the Greco-Persian Wars in the early 5th century BC sharpened the Greeks' awareness of politico-ethnic difference.) Secondly, the myth constructs an origin for the link between Crete and bulls, an association established not only in other myths such as that of the Minotaur, but also in evidence from the archaeological record. (For more on Crete see pp. 194–99.)

Leda and Alkmene: The irruption of amorous Zeus into a family's domestic life always produced complications, especially if the object of his ardour was married. This was true of Leda (married to the Spartan king Tyndareos) and Alkmene (wife of Perseus' grandson Amphitryon). To Leda, Zeus appeared in the guise of a swan; according to variants, she hatched either one or two eggs, the children being Helen, the Dioskouroi ('Children of

Kallisto: In numerous Greek myths concerning a god's interaction with humans, metamorphosis plays a part, either because a divinity adopts a 'mediating' shape in order to make his presence amongst humans less overpoweringly direct (contrast Semele's fatal encounter with an 'unmediated' Zeus), or because, after a divinity's intervention, one or more of the humans has been so drastically 'destabilized' that they can no longer retain their original form. Zeus' seduction of Kallisto exemplifies both motifs. She was a nymph, or a daughter of the Arcadian king Lykaon. Either way – since Arcadia was perceived by non-Arcadians as uncivilized – she was from 'the wilds'; hence myths represented her as a devotee of Artemis. In order to unite with her, Zeus took the form either of Apollo

Danae and Baby Perseus Adrift in a Chest

The works of the ancient Greek lyric poets, with the exception of Pindar and to a lesser extent Bacchylides, have survived in pitifully small fragments. Often the reasons for survival are highly idiosyncratic. The extract which follows, part of a poem by Simonides (6th/5th century BC), was quoted by an ancient writer on literary style (Dionysios of Halikarnassos, a contemporary of Augustus, 1st century BC) who wanted to demonstrate how difficult it could be to identify the metre of a lyric poem if the words were written out as prose. In spite of such an unusual motive for preservation, these few lines by Simonides constitute an unusually touching evocation of the human implications of a heroic myth.

…when in the elaborately wrought chest
the wind blowing
and the turbulent sea
brought her low with terror,
with wetted cheeks she placed her loving arm
around Perseus, and spoke:
'My child, what trouble I have.
But you sleep, slumbering in your tender way,
in this horrible vessel, bronze-riveted,
shining in the night,
as you lie in the black gloom.
Of the deep spray of the passing wave
over your hair,
and of the wind's voice,
you take no heed, as you lie wrapped
in your purple covering: a lovely face.
If danger were danger to you,
you would be turning your delicate ear to my words.
But I tell you: sleep, my baby,
and let the sea sleep, and let
our measureless trouble sleep.
From you, Father Zeus,
may there be some change of will;
but if this prayer of mine is too bold, or unjust:
forgive me.'

or of Artemis herself. Wishing to escape Hera's notice, Zeus changed Kallisto into a bear, an animal which was at home in the landscape where Artemis roamed. With a vengefulness typical of the way in which intra-Olympian rivalries were conducted, Hera then tricked Artemis herself into shooting her ursine former companion; alternatively, in a variant in keeping with Artemis' divine role, the virgin huntress herself shot Kallisto for yielding up her virginity. The outcome is doubly typical: the child of the union would be a founder of a dynasty, namely Arkas, ancestor of the Arcadians; as for Kallisto, she was removed yet one stage further away from humanity – but towards immortal celebrity – when she was changed into the constellation of the Bear.

Ganymede: One erotic exploit by Zeus which entailed relatively few problems for those involved was his abduction of the young Trojan prince Ganymede; either in his own person, or changing himself into an eagle, the king of the gods plucked Ganymede from earth to be the gods' nectar-pourer on Olympos, as well as his own 'catamite' (cf. Etruscan *catmite*, Latin *catamitus*, a passive partner). Within Greek society, there was widespread social acceptance of same-sex relationships when one of the partners was reckoned to be (e.g. in age or status) 'superior' and the other 'inferior' (see pp. 174–75); so, to the extent that it reflected real-life custom, Zeus' passion for Ganymede raised none of the moral issues attendant on, for example, the act of adultery, which threatened the integrity of the

husband's household. Though the boy's mortal family were bound to grieve for his loss, they were comforted by the assurance that he would be granted not only immortality but also (unlike poor Tithonos, p. 96) eternal youth.

The loves of Apollo

Cassandra: The mortal objects of Apollo's sexual advances fared little better than did the favourites of Zeus. The tribulations of two of Apollo's victims are explored extensively in Greek tragedy.

Cassandra, like Ganymede, belonged to the Trojan royal house, though, as a daughter of Priam, she was of a later generation than Zeus' favourite. When Apollo made a bargain with her – that he would grant her second sight if she would yield her virginity to him – she accepted the boon but then rashly broke her promise. Apollo's gift could not be rescinded, but he added a qualification: that no one would ever believe Cassandra. Before and during the Trojan War, her prophecies of doom fell on deaf ears. Her ill fortune never deserted her: raped by Aias son of Oileus at Troy, she was allotted as concubine to Troy's conqueror Agamemnon. Like him, she died in Mycenae, slain by his vengeful wife Clytemnestra.

Kreousa: Kreousa ('Queen') is the name of several mythical heroines. The Kreousa whom Apollo seduced came from Athens. Her anguish is portrayed in Euripides' play *Ion*, named after the son whom she bore to her seducer. Kreousa later married a mortal, but the two of them had no children; so, like many an ordinary Greek couple (as archaeological evidence from Dodona confirms; see below), the pair consulted an oracle about their prospects for having a family. As it happened, the oracle they chose – Delphi – had as one of its temple-servants none other than Ion, who had been surreptitiously conveyed there as a newborn by Hermes. After an intricate series of misunderstandings, mother and son are reunited; but the play's tone is more bitter than sweet. Apollo never appears in person, and his rape of Kreousa remains inescapably shameful.

(Below left) When Zeus, in the form of a majestic eagle, swooped on the Trojan prince Ganymede and carried him up to Olympos, the boy's response could be imagined in various ways. Here he seems to react with trust, even sensuous abandon. Bronze mirror cover, c. 360 BC.

(Below right) Archaeological evidence from Dodona, such as this lead 'tablet' (c. 500 BC), confirms that Greeks might consult an oracle at a time of personal anxiety. In this case a man named Hermon asks which god he should pray to in order to have 'useful children' by his wife. Similar anxieties about childlessness are explored, in more extreme form, in Euripides' play Ion.

When Troy's conqueror, Agamemnon, took Priam's daughter Cassandra as his slave-concubine, the reaction of Agamemnon's wife Clytemnestra was bound to be explosive. On this Attic cup (late 5th century BC) Cassandra has fled to an altar (presumably Apollo's, suggested by the laurel, his sacred tree). But Clytemnestra, to whom myth-tellers often attribute a man-like aggression, is about to finish off her rival with an axe.

(Below) The tender embrace of two mythical lovers, Hyakinthos and the winged West Wind Zephyros, in an image of intense physicality. Attic cup, c. 490 BC.

Koronis: All the tales we have reviewed so far, about both Zeus and Apollo, confirm that resistance to a god's advances was perilous. Even if the girl had submitted to sex, the danger did not pass. So it was with Koronis, who came from Thessaly. Apollo united with her, and she conceived the son who would be Asklepios, the great healer. But when she preferred her mortal lover, Ischys, to Apollo, the god (or his sister Artemis) slew the injudicious girl, along with all her innocent neighbours.

Hyakinthos: Apollo was every bit as catholic in his tastes as Zeus. Foremost among the youths he courted was Hyakinthos. So beautiful was the boy that others yearned for him too – for example, the West Wind Zephyros. What Hyakinthos shared with Apollo was a love of sport and exercise; for the Greeks who told the myths, too, the gymnasium was an ideal spot for homoerotic encounters. But myths refract life as well as reflect it, and the pattern of the Hyakinthos story follows a familiar course, via pathetic death to metamorphosis: accidentally, Apollo caused his beloved's death with a discus throw (see pp. 176–77). But the boy lived on in another form – as the lily-like flower which the Greeks called *hyakinthos*. The world which surrounded the myth-tellers was – so at least the stories implied – filled with transformed mortals whose lives had been overturned by their encounters with divinity.

Extraordinary Mortals

Mythical narratives involving divinities gained added resonance, as we have seen, from the fact that those same divinities were the object of cult. In the same way, 'heroes' and 'heroines' played a continuing role within the communities of those who told the myths. From the Archaic period onwards, there were cults – complete with sacrifices according to detailed, ritual prescriptions – to 'heroic' individuals, that is to say, to a class of exceptional mortals who were believed to have lived in the time of myth, and whose deeds and sufferings marked them out as especially memorable. The focus of the cult of a heroine or hero was usually the place where they were said to have been buried, since this site was regarded as concentrating the power which the individual in question was thought to be still capable of exercising; not to pay them respect might invoke their dangerous wrath.

The company of the heroes/heroines was not static: in the course of recorded Greek history, various individuals were 'heroized' after death. But there was nevertheless a considerable overlap between the recipients of hero-cult and the figures who, in the traditional mythological narratives, acted and suffered so unforgettably, in paradigmatic exploration of the potentialities of human experience, for good and evil, in triumph and in catastrophe. This chapter and the next examine some of the individual and collective exploits which the Greek myth-tellers ascribed to these remarkable figures.

The Wooden Horse, attributed to the craftsman Epeios. The enormous wheeled hollow horse, drawn by the Trojans into their own city, concealed ranks of armed Greeks: some can be seen peering out through portholes and handing out armour, while others are already outside, ready for battle. Clay relief pithos, Mykonos, c. 670 BC.

IV Heroic Exploits

Perseus

(Right) The fixed,
nightmarish gaze of the
Gorgon stares out from this
6th-century BC gold plaque.

(Below) Baby Perseus looks
up imploringly at his mother
from the chest in which he
has already been confined.
Danae's father Akrisios
extends his hand in a gesture
of authority: he is presumably
ordering Danae to climb in
alongside her son. Attic vase,
c. 480–470 BC.

Patterns of adventure

What characterizes the heroic mortals of Greek mythology is not any virtue which they may have – one should therefore avoid any analogy with 'saints' – but rather the conspicuousness and sometimes outrageousness of what they do and suffer. They test the limits of human potential, attaining the heights of success, and plumbing the depths of disaster. This is what makes them worth remembering, worth singing about.

In the present chapter we are going to look at myths in which two story-patterns insistently recur. The first is the *quest*, the arduous journey, often undertaken with a group of like-minded companions, to bring back a precious prize, such as the Golden Fleece, or Helen of Troy. The second story-pattern is the *combat* with terrifying and often monstrous opponents, whose manner of fighting stretches the ingenuity or strength of the hero to the limit. These combats are invariably of such import that the gods too are drawn into the action; it is therefore impossible to make a hard-and-fast distinction between 'heroic myths' and 'divine myths'.

Given Greek assumptions about the contrasting social roles of males and females, it will come as no surprise that it is males who carry out most of the quests and combats; females more often figure as the objects of quests, or as helpers. It is only when we come to focus, in the next chapter, on the context of the family that heroines will come into far greater prominence. Nevertheless even in the present chapter we shall sometimes come across women whose role in mythological exploits is active, whether they be such atypical figures as the huntress Atalanta, or women whose lives are so drastically affected by the heroes' deeds that they too are driven to act.

Perseus' adventure

Like many a hero in other traditions – from Romulus and Remus to Moses and Jesus Christ – Perseus had to survive persecution and humiliation in his earliest days. His mother Danae, having been seduced by Zeus, was, through the anger of her father Akrisios, set adrift in a chest, along with her baby son; for Akrisios had learned from an oracle that he would be killed by Danae's child. From the coast of the Argolid the sea current carried mother and baby

southeastwards to the island of Seriphos, where Diktys ('Net Man') fished them up. Diktys' brother Polydektes, the local ruler, fell in love with Danae – an ominous development, for his name ('All-Receiver') was one of a group of epithets applied to Hades in order to connote his indiscriminate 'hospitality'; it is as if, after surviving seduction by Zeus, Danae was, in the symbolism of myth, now being pursued by his even more terrifying brother, the god of death. At any rate, Polydektes in due course schemed to get rid of the now grown-up Perseus, who was an obstacle to his desires. He lured the young man into agreeing to fetch the head of Medusa, one of the monstrous Gorgons.

The Gorgons lived by Ocean, i.e. at the edge of the world. Their heads were fringed with serpents; they had boars' tusks, bronze hands, and wings of gold; and they literally petrified anyone who looked at them. With the help of Hermes, Athene and, under compulsion, the repulsive Graiai (three crones who shared a single eye and a single tooth between them), Perseus amassed the wherewithal for the task: an unbreakable sickle, a pouch, winged sandals, and a cap of invisibility. By looking at Medusa's reflection in a shield, Perseus managed to avoid her direct and lethal stare; he cut off her head with the sickle, put it into the pouch, and eluded the other Gorgons by donning the cap of invisibility.

The hero's flight back to Seriphos included a stop-over in Ethiopia, where he saved Andromeda, the daughter of King Kepheus; the girl had been chained to a rock as an offering to a sea-monster which was threatening the land, but Perseus despatched the beast and took Andromeda as his bride back to Greece. And it was in Greece that his fate came full circle. First, on Seriphos, he used the Gorgon's head to petrify Polydektes, who was still oppressing Danae. Then he took a further step towards the restoration of normality by relinquishing his special instruments of power, giving sandals, pouch and cap to Hermes, and the Gorgon's head to Athene. There remained Akrisios, Danae's father, who still feared the death which the oracle had predicted for him. He was right to be afraid: involuntarily, Perseus killed him with a discus throw in an athletic competition. In spite of this, and although Perseus' career was not free from hardship, that which his myth narrates is essentially the overcoming of obstacles and the restoration of order. The many heroic descendants of Perseus and Andromeda would include Herakles, the mightiest hero of them all.

On a wall-painting from Pompeii, Perseus frees Andromeda from the sea monster. The painting may be based on a 4th-century BC original by the Greek artist Nikias. In any case, the Roman image creates its own impression of grace and romance.

(Below) Perseus speeds away, having decapitated Medusa; Athene looks on. The Gorgon's head lies securely in Perseus' pouch, he holds the sickle with which he did the deed. Many have detected humour here, as the normally belligerent Athene holds up her skirt daintily between thumb and forefinger. Attic vase, c. 460 BC.

Meleager, Atalanta and the Kalydonian Boar

The exploits of Meleager are on a more human scale than those of Perseus. His story illustrates not so much the magnificence of the human condition as its limitations and fragility, when faced with the power of the gods and the inevitability of fate.

Meleager's home was Kalydon, a place in Aitolia which figures only sporadically in the events of Greek history. When Meleager's father Oineus, king of Kalydon, failed to sacrifice to Artemis – a lapse which set the tone for his family's subsequent fortunes – the goddess riposted by sending a fearsome boar to ravage the territory. Meleager, together with a band of stalwart companions, managed to kill the beast; but the events which followed took an acrimonious and ultimately tragic turn. There were quarrels over who should keep the prized hide of the boar, and Meleager fought and killed the brothers of his mother Althaia. As for his own death, we have already come across the poignant tale of the

It was in the hill-country near Kalydon, just north of the Gulf of Corinth at its western end, that mythology located the lair of the mighty boar slain by Meleager and his band of heroic companions.

fatal log which Althaia angrily burned in order to seal her son's fate: the hero's prowess is undermined by domestic strife (see p. 86).

Alongside Meleager – indeed, far more colourful than he – we must mention the figure of Atalanta, another participant in the Boar Hunt. Atalanta was a kind of human equivalent of Artemis, except that at last, unlike the goddess, she did surrender her virginity. As a child she was abandoned by her father in the wilds; he had wanted a male child. However, a she-bear suckled her, and she grew up to resemble her foster-mother in temperament. When she

The ferocious Kalydonian
boar is opposed by ranks of
heroic hunters. In front of
the beast are Meleager and
Peleus, followed by Melanion
and the light-skinned
Atalanta. Also represented
are hunting dogs, several of
whom are given expressive
names such as Methepon
('Chaser'), Ormenos
('Leaper') and Marpsas
('Grabber'). The 'François
Vase', c. 570 BC.

reached marriageable age, she challenged her suitors to outrun her; failure meant their death. One suitor, Melanion (sometimes called Hippomenes), cunningly defeated her by dropping before her a number of golden apples given to him by Aphrodite; Atalanta stooped and Melanion conquered. However, everything about Atalanta suggested that she could not be confined within the institution of marriage; and so it proved. When she and Melanion were out hunting, they chanced upon a sanctuary of Zeus, where, in flagrant disregard for religious propriety, they made love. As punishment they were turned into lions, so that Atalanta rejoined the wild state to which she had belonged since her earliest nurturing. Her myth explores a tension central to Greek perceptions of gender ideology, namely that, although there is an aspect of women which is 'wild' (and must therefore be tamed by men), there can be no compatibility between, on the one hand, the role of wife-and-mother, and, on the other, the activities of hunting and warfare. The Atalanta myth spells out the implications of the question, 'What would it be like if a woman *did* live out her potential wildness?'

One of Atalanta's 'masculine' skills was wrestling. She had a famous bout with Peleus, shown on this Attic vase (c. 500 BC).

Jason, the Argonauts and Medea

In 1922 the anthropologist Bronislaw Malinowski published his classic ethnographical account of 'native enterprise and adventure in the Archipelagoes of Melanesian New Guinea', *Argonauts of the Western Pacific*. His metaphor exploited the resonances of one of the most celebrated exploits in Greek mythology. Jason's quest for the Golden Fleece originated, like several other mythical quests, in a crisis of destabilization, which the quest was designed to rectify. In this case, one destabilizing factor was the disputed dynastic succession in the Thessalian city of Iolkos: for reasons which are not entirely clear (although some form of intrafamilial rift was presumably at work) King Kretheus had been succeeded not by his son Aison (Jason's father), but by Aison's half-brother Pelias. To this

factor is added the by now familiar motif of an oracle received by Pelias warning him to beware of a stranger: in this case, a stranger wearing only one sandal. When the young Jason presented himself to Pelias having just lost a sandal as he was crossing a river, Pelias' understandable reaction was to send the young man away on an impossible mission.

Retrieving the Fleece meant bringing back to Greece a talismanic treasure located in the far-off Black Sea kingdom of Colchis. The Fleece had once belonged to a magical, flying ram, which figured in the fortunes of another branch of Kretheus' family. Kretheus' brother Athamas married twice; his second wife, Ino, persecuted her predecessor as well as the two children of the first marriage. Since Greek myths tended to render social tensions more 'visible' by making them extreme, it is no surprise that the persecution of the children, whose names were Phrixos and Helle, should escalate into an attempt on their lives, engineered by Ino. They only escaped being sacrificed by their own father when the magic ram, courtesy of Hermes the divine conveyor, carried them out of harm's way on its golden back. Alas, poor Helle fell into the stretch of water named thereafter Hellespont ('Helle's Sea'); but

Genealogy of Jason

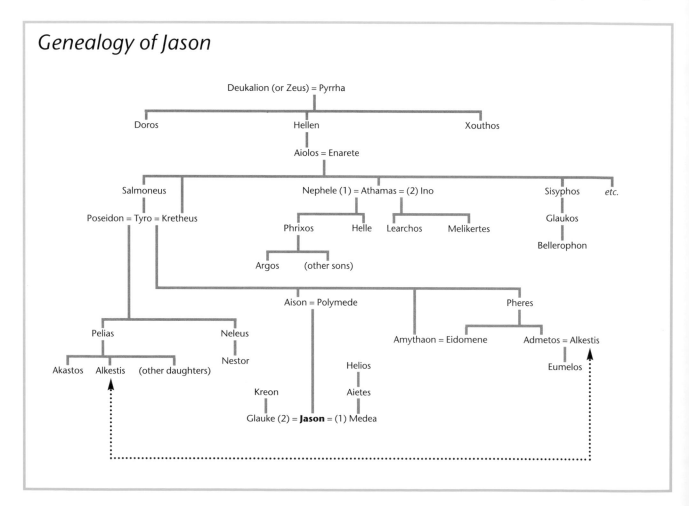

Phrixos clung on. The ram touched down in Colchis, a land at the world's edge, ruled over by Aietes, the son of the Sun God. Since sacrifice was a ritual aimed at securing proper communication between humans and gods, it was logical that the god-sent ram should forthwith be sacrificed by Phrixos, as a way of 'returning' it to the gods. But the Fleece stayed, for the time being, with Aietes in Colchis.

The *Argo* and its crew

Unlike Meleager, Jason was faced with a challenge which took him far away into the unknown. The same was true of Perseus, but, unlike Perseus, Jason could not count on aerial transportation. He needed a ship, and his vessel, the *Argo*, lies at the heart of Apollonios of Rhodes' great epic about the quest for the Fleece, from its building, crewing and departure, to its return to home port in the last lines of the poem. Through its very construction the *Argo* expressed the involvement of the gods in Jason's adventure, for one of its timbers came from the sacred oak tree of Zeus' oracle at Dodona. And just as the god of Dodona 'spoke' his oracles through the sound of the rustling oak leaves, so the *Argo*'s timber had the power of prophetic utterance.

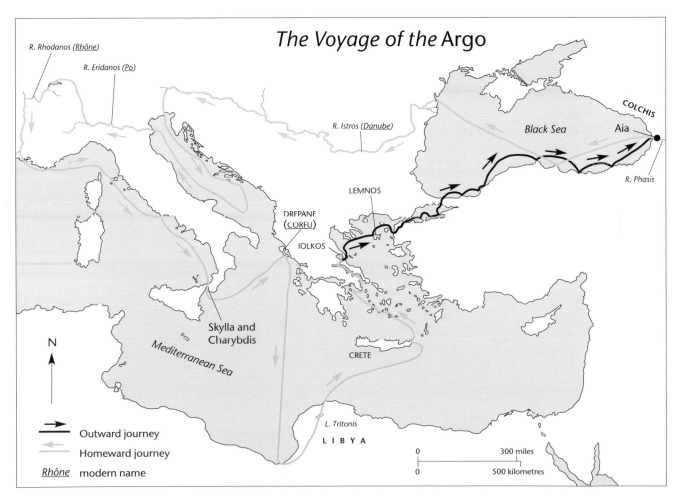

The Voyage of the Argo

R. Rhodanos (<u>Rhône</u>)

R. Eridanos (<u>Po</u>)

R. Istros (<u>Danube</u>)

Black Sea

COLCHIS

Aia

R. Phasis

LEMNOS

DREPANE (<u>CORFU</u>)

IOLKOS

Skylla and Charybdis

Mediterranean Sea

CRETE

N

L. Tritonis

LIBYA

→ Outward journey
→ Homeward journey
<u>Rhône</u> modern name

0   300 miles
0   500 kilometres

When Herakles' young
companion Hylas is abducted
by an amorous water-nymph,
the episode leads to Herakles'
withdrawal from the
expedition of the Argo.
In François Gérard's Hylas
and the Nymph, c. 1826, the
impression created is one of
luxuriant sensuality.

The ship's crew consisted of most of the greatest heroes from the generation before the Trojan War: Orpheus, Telamon, Peleus, Herakles, and the twins Kastor and Polydeukes, together with many lesser-known but still valorous fighters. As the *Argo* left Pagasai harbour (on the coast of Thessaly) and headed north, from the summit of Mount Pelion the benevolent Centaur Cheiron, who had advised Jason in the hero's youth and was now tending baby Achilles, bade the expedition farewell. Cheiron's guidance enabled these and other heroes to progress from the rawness of childhood to the socialization which they needed in order to co-operate with other warriors. Part horse, part human, the Centaur inhabits a form which symbolically combines the two poles – uncivilized/civilized – between which the developing hero has to travel.

The outward journey

The Argonauts' first significant landfall was the northeastern Aegean island of Lemnos. The episode which unfolds there is fascinating not only in terms of the development of the mythical narrative, but also as an illustration of how a myth may be seen as corresponding to a ritual. The island at which the all-male crew of *Argo* put in was populated entirely by women: when their husbands had turned away from them in favour of slave-girls

from the Thracian mainland, the Lemnian wives had taken murderous revenge, not only upon their husbands and the slave-girls, but also upon the rest of the male population of Lemnos. The Argonauts lay with the lonely widows, following Jason's example – his choice naturally being the queen of the Lemnians, Hypsipyle. Corresponding to this tale was a ritual practised on the island, whereby once a year every fire was extinguished, to be rekindled from 'new' fire brought from across the sea.

Although they had fulfilled their regenerative role, the Argonauts showed no sign of wanting to leave Lemnos; but Herakles shamed them into departing when he reminded them of the true purpose of their quest. The presence of mighty Herakles on board was not, however, to last much longer. Having passed through 'Helle's Sea' into the Propontis (the area between the Hellespont and the entrance to the Black Sea), the Argonauts went ashore in the land of the Mysians. Herakles had a young squire, Hylas, who set out into the country-side to find a spring, so as to draw water. But all Greek springs were sacred, and springs in mythology are prime locations for encounters with the more-than-human (see p. 188–89). When Hylas did find a spring, its nymph was entranced by Hylas' good looks, and she drew him down beneath the water into her embrace. Learning that Hylas had gone missing, Herakles reacted with passionate anguish ('sweat poured down over his temples, and within his innards the dark blood boiled', sang Apollonios), so as to leave little doubt about the homoerotic intensity of his relationship with Hylas. When the *Argo* sailed on, Herakles remained behind, putting his fruitless quest for the boy before the collective enterprise of the expedition.

As the voyage proceeded eastwards, the Argonauts' encounters with the sacred became still more dramatic. An example is their meeting with the blind seer Phineus. In Apollonios' version, his affliction had come about because he had, through his prophetic insight, revealed the gods' secrets to mortals. Though he had retained his powers of prophecy, those powers afforded him little comfort, since the succulent morsels brought as gifts by those who wanted to consult him were rendered inedible by the Harpies, a pack of foul, bird-like creatures who compounded Phineus' punishment of blindness by pouring a repellent stench over his food. When the Argonauts arrived, however, the starving and emaciated Phineus realized that his deliverers were at hand. It had, he knew, been decreed by the gods that two of the Argonauts, Kalais and Zetes, sons of Boreas (the North Wind) and brothers of Phineus' first wife Kleopatra, would chase the Harpies away from him for ever; and so it turned out.

It is worth adding – as yet another confirmation of the intricate variation-within-similarity characteristic of Greek mythology – that, according to a completely different version, it was the Argonauts themselves who blinded Phineus, to pay him back for blinding the sons he had had by Kleopatra. That act of cruelty by Phineus, motivated by the hostility of his second wife towards the first family, is a reminder that there are countless overlaps between heroic exploits (our focus in this chapter) and myths of the family (the subject of the next).

Thanks to Phineus' advice the Argonauts contrived to negotiate the dreaded Clashing Rocks at the entrance to the Black Sea, and continued sailing along its southern shore. So far had they ventured that at one point they caught sight of the very eagle which daily flew to tear out Prometheus' endlessly self-regenerating liver; they even heard the tortured Titan's screams.

At last the Argonauts put ashore in Colchis. Aietes' reaction to their arrival mirrored the response of Pelias when confronted by the young Jason: he sent him out to perform an 'impossible' task. If he wanted to win the Golden Fleece, Jason must first yoke two bronze-hooved, fire-breathing bulls, plough with them, and sow the furrows with the teeth of a serpent – the one slain by Kadmos when he founded Thebes (Athene had given half of the teeth to Aietes). As with the teeth sown by Kadmos, they would bear an unconventional harvest: armed warriors. Alone, Jason would have

List of Argonauts

Different myth-tellers give rather different versions of the *Argo*'s heroic crew. Below is a list drawn from Apollonios' epic poem *Argonautica*:

Admetos	Jason
Aithalides	Kalais
Akastos	Kanthos
Amphidamas	Kastor
Amphion	Kepheus
Ankaios (of Arcadia)	Klytios
Ankaios (of Samos)	Koronos
Areios	Laokoön
Argos	Leodokos
Asterion	Lynkeus
Asterios	Meleager
Augeias	Menoitios
Boutes	Mopsos
Echion	Nauplios
Erginos	Oileus
Erybotes	Orpheus
Euphemos	Palaimonios
Eurydamas	Peleus
Eurytion	Periklymenos
Erytos	Phaleros
Herakles	Phleias
Hylas	Polydeukes
Idas	Polyphemos
Idmon	Talaos
Iphiklos (of Aitolia)	Telamon
Iphiklos (of Thessaly)	Tiphys
Iphitos (of Euboia)	Zetes
Iphitos (of Phokis)	

The heroic figures on this Etruscan *krater, c. 300–275* BC, *have plausibly been identified as Argonauts.*

had no chance of accomplishing these tasks; but he had the support of Athene and Hera. The plan they devised relied on the fact that Aietes had a daughter, Medea, who was a priestess of Hekate, and hence versed in the charms, chants and drugs which lay within Hekate's sphere. Athene and Hera persuaded Aphrodite to bribe her spoilt son Eros, who then shot Medea with his love-arrow. Medea was seized with a desperate and uncontrollable passion for Jason.

Thanks to her witchcraft, Medea rendered Jason temporarily invulnerable; the bulls were yoked, the teeth were sown, the armed men were defeated. The final act in the drama was completed when Medea lulled to sleep the serpent which guarded the Fleece, enabling her beloved to remove the talismanic treasure. Medea now had no choice: like many Greek myths, this one portrays a girl's rejection of her father in favour of her lover/husband. Indeed no rupture could have been more decisive than Medea's. Having sailed away with the fleeing Argonauts, she lured her pursuing brother Apsyrtos into an ambush – and turned her eyes aside while Jason slew him. This, in the version as told by Apollonios, was bad enough; but, according to a variant, it was Medea herself who butchered Apsyrtos, scattering his dismembered corpse into the sea so that the Colchians, her father Aietes included, would have to delay their pursuit so as to recover the sad remains.

The return of the *Argo*

The *Argo*'s homeward voyage to Greece is extraordinary for its complexity, and for the way it contrasts totally with the outward journey. Some of the complexity is literary rather than mythological. This is because our richest account, that by Apollonios, was composed some five hundred years after the narrative of Odysseus' wanderings as told in the Homeric *Odyssey*. Thus, although in 'mythological time' the *Argo*'s voyage preceded that of Odysseus, Apollonios is able to weave into his tale encounters between the Argonauts and some of the most celebrated of Odysseus' adversaries and helpers, such as Skylla and Charybdis, Circe, and the Sirens, as well as Arete and Alkinoos, queen and king of the Phaeacians (see p. 143). But Jason's return outstripped even that of Odysseus in its geographical idiosyncrasy. The *Argo*'s route out of the Black Sea took it westwards down the Istros (Danube) and thus out (so it was believed) into the northern Adriatic. Borne southwards by wind and tide, the vessel was driven onto the North African coast, rejoining the sea only after the crew had carried it for twelve days and twelve nights through the desert.

With the *Argo* already back in Aegean waters, an encounter with one last outlandish creature underlines just how uncannily lethal was the young woman whom Jason was bringing home as his bride. The giant Talos, last survivor of the Race of Bronze, inhabited the island of Crete. (Unlike Hesiod's account of the Races of Gold, Silver, Bronze and Iron, Apollonios' picture of Talos is of a creature *made* of metal, rather than one who used it

Under the watchful eye of Medea, Jason, naked and heroic, seizes the Golden Fleece. The snake which guards it has been disabled by Medea's magic; the apple she is holding was presumably drugged. Roman marble sarcophagus, AD 130–160.

or was symbolized by it.) Talos was almost invulnerable, but he had a weak point in his ankle, since the life-blood of this metal man flowed at that point through a vein covered only by a thin membrane. When Talos hurled great crags at their vessel, the Argonauts could think of no recourse; it was then that Medea stepped in. She overpowered Talos simply by staring at him, directing malevolent glances into his eyes and causing him to stumble, so that he fatally grazed his ankle at the only spot where his life could be threatened.

Nothing now could hinder the *Argo*'s safe return to its home port – which is the point at which Apollonios' *Argonautica* ends. But other sources take up the narrative thread. While Jason was safely off the map, Pelias had cleared away some remaining dynastic obstacles by bringing about the deaths of Aison (Jason's father) and of other members of his family too. But the return of Jason, with Medea, spelled the end of Pelias' career. Medea demonstrated her magical powers by cutting up and boiling a ram, which then emerged whole and rejuvenated from the cauldron; she then tricked Pelias' daughters into thinking they could perform the same service for their father. When all that happened was that he died a ghastly death – chopped up and boiled, but unrejuvenated – Jason and Medea escaped from Iolkos and fled to Corinth. Here Medea maintained her track record of being at the heart of the disruption of families. As Euripides unforgettably dramatized the story in his tragedy *Medea*, Jason decided to put Medea aside and to marry instead the daughter of Kreon, king of Corinth. In an act of hideous revenge

Medea sent the girl (named as Glauke in some sources) a poisoned robe whose fiery venom ate her flesh, together with that of her father as he tried to rescue her. Killing her own children so as to inflict further pain on Jason (although variants say it was others, for example the Corinthians, who killed them), she escaped to Athens (see p. 127) in a conveyance lent to her by her grandfather, the Sun god: a chariot drawn by flying serpents.

(Above left) Talos, the bronze giant, collapses after Medea's magical attack on him, symbolized by her potion-container; a tear falls from his right eye. His arms are held by two of the Argonauts, Kastor and Polydeukes. Are they supporting him out of compassion, or pinioning him like torturers' accomplices? The image appears on a famous Attic vase (c. 400 BC) in Ruvo di Puglia, southern Italy.

(Above right) Medea's miraculous rejuvenation of a sheep into a lamb is designed to impress Pelias (seated left) and his daughters. Soon Pelias himself will undergo what he thinks will be rejuvenation – but actually he will meet a gruesome death, boiled alive in the cauldron. Attic water-jar, c. 510 BC.

(Left) Having taken revenge on Jason by murdering their children, Medea escapes from the consequences of her deeds on a serpent-borne chariot. The 'oriental' headgear and costume point to her 'outlandishness'; the rays emphasize the connection with her grandfather, Helios the Sun god. South Italian krater, c. 400 BC.

Herakles

As we saw in discussing the mythology of Hera (pp. 70–72), the exploits and sufferings of the greatest Greek hero are bound up with the persecution which he endured at Hera's hands. Herakles (whom the Romans knew as Hercules) was the product of Zeus' affair with Alkmene, and so incurred the jealousy of Zeus' divine consort. But even as an infant Herakles showed his mettle: when Hera sent a pair of giant snakes into the cradle, the baby promptly strangled them. Most of Herakles' subsequent career is prefigured in this episode: persecution by Hera, combat with wild beasts, resistance through brute force rather than guile.

Herakles was a hugely popular character in Greek mythology. His exploits appear on countless visual images, from vase-paintings to sculptures to coins to gemstones. Yet in our written sources he is a much more complex figure than the predominantly action-oriented images might suggest. Whereas some myth-tellers, for instance the praise-poet Pindar, celebrate him as a straightforward model for athletic prowess, for the tragedians he is a person afflicted by catastrophe even at moments of ostensible triumph, while the writers of comedies present him as a figure of broad farce, with appetites both diverse and gross. In short Herakles is deeply paradoxical: the author of extraordinary feats of physical effort, he is nevertheless repeatedly made subservient to those weaker than he is, and is capable of inflicting violence upon his own family no less than upon the monstrous animals with whom his Labours confront him. As a hero, he is both typical and untypical. Like all heroes, he pushes at the limits of humanity, yet he does so to a degree and in ways which no other hero can match: his exploits take him to the ends of the earth, down to Hades, and eventually up to Olympos. This narrative ubiquity is echoed by the fact that, uniquely for a hero, he has no grave, and hence no localized, and thus delimited, place of cult. Wherever help was needed, one could call out for Herakles.

The hero's adolescence followed the path which his exploits in the cradle had anticipated. Although he had the best of lyre-instructors – Linos, brother of Orpheus – Herakles' tendency to lash out got the better of him: when Linos not only criticized him for (according to one source) 'sluggishness of soul', but also hit him, the uncontrollable pupil brained his teacher with the lyre (although he was acquitted on a plea of self-defence). A little later, another part of Herakles' nature came to the fore when, while a guest of Thespios, the king of Thespiae in Boiotia, he successively bedded every one of the king's fifty daughters. These were the first of the innumerable women with whom the hero coupled; some he even

The already muscular baby Herakles comes to grips with the snakes which Hera has sent against him. Silver coin minted in Kyzikos, on the shore of the Propontis (just east of the Hellespont), c. 390 BC.

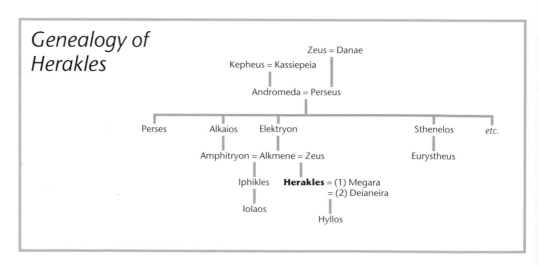

Genealogy of Herakles

Zeus = Danae

Kepheus = Kassiepeia

Andromeda = Perseus

Perses | Alkaios | Elektryon | Sthenelos | *etc.*

Amphitryon = Alkmene = Zeus

Eurystheus

Iphikles

Herakles = (1) Megara
= (2) Deianeira

Iolaos

Hyllos

married, and all bore him children, yet his perpetual rootlessness formed the background – as it did in the case of Medea – to a series of disasters in everything which related to his family life.

Herakles' mortal 'father' Amphitryon – whose shape Zeus had assumed when he came to Alkmene – was no more settled than his 'son'. After involuntarily killing Alkmene's father Elektryon (involuntary homicide is a common mythical motif, since it conveniently motivates the transference of a hero from one city to another), Amphitryon was obliged to seek refuge with Kreon, king of Thebes; to seal the bond, Herakles married Kreon's daughter Megara. But Hera's jealousy was not to be gainsaid: she caused Herakles to go mad, and to kill his wife and children. In expiation, Herakles was required to serve a man weaker than he – Eurystheus, ruler of all the Argolid including Tiryns and Mycenae – by performing a series of Labours according to Eurystheus' instructions. As usual, there are variants: according to Euripides' play *The Madness of Herakles*, the Labours preceded the madness, an affliction with which Hera, with supreme vindictiveness, crushed Herakles at the summit of his success (see p. 122). In the account of the Labours which follows, we shall broadly follow the order of events preserved in Apollodoros' *Library of Mythology*.

The Labours of Herakles

The **first Labour** took Herakles just a few miles northwest of Mycenae to Nemea, where he overcame an invulnerable lion by throttling it; the pelt of this beast would thereafter provide his characteristic clothing, a marker of wildness to match the

mighty club which, alongside his bow, was his preferred weapon. The **second Labour** was also local: he had to exterminate the monstrous watersnake ('hydra') which lived near the marshy settlement of Lerna. The hydra had numerous heads (nine and fifty are among the figures men-

(Below) Herakles' combat with the Nemean lion is a phenomenally popular motif in ancient art. One of the many thousands of surviving images is this intaglio dating from the Hellenistic period.

The Labours of Herakles

As usual, the details vary somewhat from account to account. On the far right is the list and ordering of Herakles' Labours as given in Apollodoros' *Library of Mythology*. Numbers correspond to those on the maps; the Peloponnese is shown (right) as a boxed inset within the whole Mediterranean region (below).

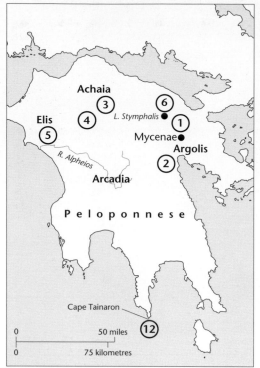

exploit	location
1 fetch hide of lion	Nemea (Argolid)
2 kill hydra	Lerna (Argolid)
3 capture hind	Keryneia (between Argolid and Achaia)
4 capture boar	Mt Erymanthos (Arcadia)
5 clean Augeian stables	Elis (west Peloponnese)
6 drive away birds	Lake Stymphalis (Arcadia)
7 capture bull	Crete
8 capture man-eating mares	kingdom of Diomedes (Thrace)
9 bring back belt of the Amazon Hippolyte	land of the Amazons; sometimes located in N. Asia Minor
10 rustle the cattle of Geryon	in the Far West
11 pick apples of the Hesperides	perhaps in the Far West, or the Far North
12 fetch the infernal dog Kerberos	Hades

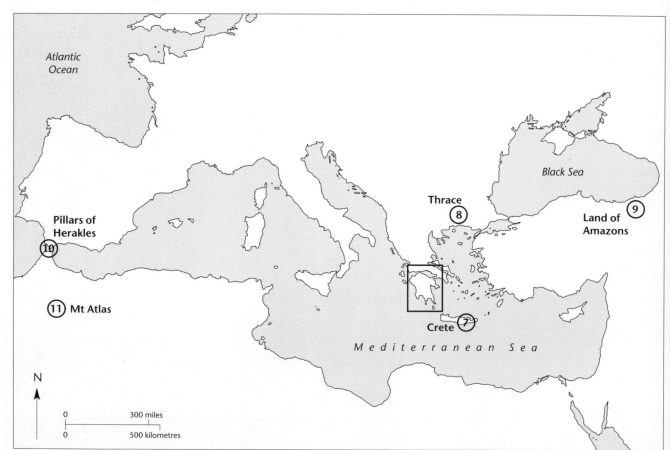

(Below) The Centaur's double character, between nature and culture, expressed in a silver head and torso, perhaps one of a pair of handles of a dish (Greek, 2nd century BC). The dishevelled hair is wreathed with vine-leaves, suggesting Dionysiac abandon. The plektrum in the right hand indicates the playing of a stringed instrument.

tioned), with one of the heads being immortal and the rest self-regenerating, such that two grew where before there had been only one. However, the hero cut off the mortal heads, after which his helper, Iolaos the son of his half-brother Iphikles, cauterized the stumps; Herakles then finished off the immortal head by severing it and burying it under a boulder. As with the lion, so with the hydra, Herakles adopted one of the characteristics of his former adversary: he slit open the body, and dipped the tips of his arrows into its death-bringing gall.

Like all heroes and heroines, Herakles operated within a narrative landscape in which divinities were liable to intervene at any moment. When, therefore, for his **third Labour**, he was ordered by Eurystheus to bring back the Keryneian hind, a golden-horned doe sacred to Artemis, he dared not risk killing the animal; instead he pursued it for a year until it was exhausted. With this exploit Herakles moved further afield, westwards into the Peloponnese; the same region formed the backdrop to his fourth Labour, the capture of a fearsome boar which lived near Mount Erymanthos in Arcadia.

On his way to this mountain, Herakles encountered a group of beings with whom he had much in common: the Centaurs. Wild, unruly and unpredictable, they had a semi-equine, semi-human form which mirrored their equivocal position on the edge of culture. Their character, too, was ambivalent: on the one hand there was benignity, on the other, a crude animality which often exploded into violence. Foremost among the benign Centaurs was Cheiron, tutor to some of the most renowned heroes including Achilles, Asklepios and Jason. Another kindly Centaur was Pholos, and he it was who entertained Herakles during his hunt for the Erymanthian boar. As a clear marker of difference – and an example of how empirical categories such as 'raw' and 'cooked' play a considerable part in Greek thought and experience – Pholos offered Herakles roast meat, but ate his own portion uncooked. When Herakles, never the perfect guest, demanded wine, the bouquet

attracted Centaurs from far and wide. Their lust for strong drink turned to violence; in the ensuing fracas, Herakles pursued them until they sought refuge with Cheiron, whom Herakles accidentally shot with an arrow. The wound was incurable, but, since Cheiron was immortal, it seemed he was

(Below) As the supposed founder of the original Olympic Games, Herakles was the perfect choice of subject for the twelve marble metopes at the front and rear of the temple of Zeus at Olympia. This drawing offers a conjectural restoration of six of the Labours.

destined to suffer for ever. However, in order to be permitted to die, he struck a deal with Zeus, effecting some kind of exchange with Prometheus – perhaps (though the story is extremely enigmatic) agreeing to take Prometheus' sufferings down with him into the Underworld.

By comparison with his adventures with the Centaurs, Herakles' capture of the Erymanthian boar (the **fourth Labour**) was straightforward; when the hero arrived back in Tiryns carrying the animal,

Eurystheus timorously hid in a large storage jar – an image which artists loved to reproduce. Yet still Eurystheus issued his commands about further Labours. The fifth and sixth were again based in the Peloponnese. To cleanse the dung-clogged stables of Augeias king of Elis (the **fifth Labour**), Herakles cunningly diverted the courses of the rivers Alpheios and Peneios so that they ran through the yard; this show of acumen, not usually the hero's forte, is symbolized by the guiding presence of Athene on the only extant representation of this Labour, a metope from the temple of Zeus at Olympia, a site which lies adjacent to the river Alpheios (six drawings based on metopes from the temple are reproduced on the left). Moving north, Herakles cleared away another infestation, this time of birds, from the Stymphalian lake in Arcadia (the **sixth Labour**). Once more it was Athene's presence of mind which proved decisive. She lent him some bronze castanets, whose din startled the birds; Herakles' bow and lethal arrows did the rest.

As Eurystheus' exasperation with Herakles' successes increased, so did the distance which the hero was obliged to cover. After overpowering a mighty bull in Crete and conveying it to Mycenae (the **seventh Labour**), Herakles next had to travel north to Thrace. There he captured the fearsome man-eating mares belonging to King Diomedes (the **eighth Labour**), and brought them back to Eurystheus as proof of his exploit. Crete and Thrace could be seen as the southern and northern limits of

(Above) Lake Stymphalis in
the northeastern Peloponnese,
the reedy and marshy home of
the birds which Herakles was
ordered to eradicate as the
sixth of his Labours.

To destroy the Stymphalian
birds, Herakles forsakes his
club and bow for a more
appropriate weapon: a sling.
Attic vase, c. 550 BC.

the Greek homeland. But the scope of Eurystheus' demands did not stop there. The **ninth Labour** required Herakles to bring back to Mycenae the belt of Hippolyte, queen of the Amazons, a mythical people believed to inhabit the northeast of Asia Minor. Their society resorted to men for the purposes of procreation only; female children were raised, males left to die. The Amazons' lifestyle made them a kind of collective equivalent of Artemis, but with one crucial difference: they were mortal. Herakles slew Hippolyte and stole her belt.

The **tenth Labour** was the most outlandish yet. Herakles had to fetch the cattle of the three-bodied monster Geryon, who lived by the stream of Ocean. To get there Herakles had to pass the boundary between Europe and Africa, where, in order to mark his journey, he erected two pillars, sometimes 'identified', in real-world terms, as the headlands on either side of the Straits of Gibraltar. From there Herakles had to cross the mighty Ocean, which he did in the golden cup which the Sun god himself used. Having slain Geryon and taken his cattle, he ferried them back in the Sun's cup.

The **eleventh Labour** – the picking of the golden apples of the Hesperides on Mount Atlas – was to take Herakles once more to the world's end. The precise location of this exploit varies between the far west ('Hesperides' means '[Nymphs] of the Evening') and the far north (the Hyperboreans, the people in whose land the apples were to be found, bore a name meaning 'Dwellers beyond the north wind'); at all events, Herakles travelled prodigious distances in order to get there. On the way he over-

which Athene took back from Herakles and restored to the nymphs. It applied with even more force to Kerberos, multi-headed dog of the Underworld, who fulfilled the vital role of guarding that gloomy realm against those who would enter or leave it without permission. The fetching of Kerberos (the **twelfth Labour**) was the last and direst of the twelve Labours. Herakles descended to the Underworld via a cave at Tainaron, which lies at the tip of the middle promontory of the Peloponnese (mod. Mani). (Modern visitors to the fabulously intricate network of water-filled underground caverns at nearby Pirgos Dirou may be forgiven for imagining, as they are punted along in the chilly gloom, a certain continuity of experience with the souls of the dead in Charon's boat.) Overcoming Kerberos by sheer brute strength, Herakles dragged him up to the light of day, showed him to a terrified, pot-bound Eurystheus, and then returned the monstrous dog to his lawful abode in Hades.

The loves of Herakles

The obverse of Herakles' crushingly successful use of violence against fearsome adversaries was his propensity for serial disaster in his relationships with women. One example already referred to, an example which we know best from Euripides' tragedy *The Madness of Herakles*, was his marriage to **Megara**, daughter of King Kreon of Thebes. Returning home in glory after accomplishing his Labours, the hero found his family being oppressed by the city's despotic usurper Lykos ('Wolf'). Herakles had no trouble in killing Lykos,

(Opposite above) Herakles grasps the neck of one of the man-eating mares of Diomedes. The gruesome remains of the animal's last meal – a human head and arm – can be seen protruding from its mouth. Attic vase, c. 510 BC.

(Opposite below) In this battle between Greeks and Amazons, the female warrior whose arm Herakles holds is Andromache (which means 'Male Battle'). Attic vase, c. 575–550 BC.

(Left) One of Herakles' more unusual opponents was the triple-bodied Geryon, whose two-headed dog Orthros (or Orthos) made him an even more formidable foe. On this Chalkidian vase (c. 540 BC) the dog lies dead, as Herakles' arrows fly towards Geryon.

(Below) Kerberos' faces wear puzzled expressions as Herakles, having put aside his club, prepares to pat the dog before putting a chain around its necks. Attic vase, late 6th century BC.

came Antaios, a mighty wrestler who drew his strength from the Earth (Herakles lifted him up and so was able to crush him); he slew the inhospitable Egyptian ruler Bousiris, who used to sacrifice strangers on the altar of Zeus; and he shot the eagle that was devouring Prometheus' liver. Even for Herakles, though, theft of the Hesperides' apples was a difficult task, for they were guarded by an immortal serpent. According to one version, the hero sought the help of Atlas, the Titan who had to hold up the sky for all time. Herakles offered to shoulder this burden temporarily while Atlas fetched the apples; but, when Atlas returned with the fruit, he was none too keen to relinquish his new-found freedom. However, the Titan did agree to take up his burden for just a few moments longer, so that Herakles could go to get a cushion. But instead Herakles strode off, bearing the apples, in the direction of Mycenae, while Atlas had the whole of eternity to regret his gullibility.

The only way Eurystheus could test Herakles fully was with adversaries who had something of the superhuman about them. The corollary was that whatever Herakles brought back with him might be in some way sacred, and so have to be surrendered to the gods. This applied to the Hesperides' fruit,

121

but in his moment of triumph was sent mad by the ever-vindictive Hera, acting through her agent the goddess Lyssa (literally 'Wolf Rabies'). He slaughtered his wife and children, and was only prevented from taking the ultimate step of killing his mortal 'father' Amphitryon when Athene intervened, striking him senseless by hurling a boulder at him. Yet eventually, thanks to the friendship of Theseus, Herakles was rescued from the pit of depression, and from the state of ritual pollution into which he had fallen. Theseus offered him the prospect of new hope in yet another new home: Athens.

Another episode in Herakles' career – an intricate sequence of events which led to his final downfall – involves his relationships with three women: Iole, Omphale and Deianeira. Having heard that King Eurytos of Oichalia (which some ancient sources located on the island of Euboia) had offered the hand of his daughter **Iole** to anyone who could defeat him in archery, Herakles accepted the challenge, and of course won. But Eurytos refused to keep his side of the bargain, being afraid that, if Herakles had children by Iole, he might again go mad and slaughter them. For the moment, uncharacteristically, Herakles did not pursue the matter; but his involvement with Eurytos' family was far from over. In a fit of madness – a condition from which he seems always to be only a hair's breadth away – he slew Eurytos' son Iphitos, hurling him from the walls of Tiryns when the young man had come to see him on an innocent errand. Stained once more by murder pollution, Herakles consulted the Delphic oracle, but was turned away by the oracle's priestess precisely because he was polluted. When Herakles reacted angrily by seizing the oracular tripod and wrestling with Apollo himself over its possession, the fact that the only immediate consequence was Zeus' hurling of a thunderbolt *between*

the two of them – rather than (as in the case of Asklepios) *at* the guilty party – illustrates just how unique was Herakles' standing.

But he remained polluted. To overcome this, he was required to undergo a period of marginalization as the slave of **Omphale**, queen of Lydia. With the slate eventually wiped clean, the hero could resume his exploits in the world of action, journeying now to Kalydon, in western Greece just north of the Gulf of Corinth; there he out-wrestled the river god Acheloös, a rival suitor for the hand of the king's daughter **Deianeira**. Herakles had, as usual, no fixed abode, and so with his new bride he moved on to the next place where he was offered lodging: Trachis, near the deep inlet opposite the northwestern cape of Euboia. On his way eastwards from Kalydon to Trachis, he and Deianeira had to cross the river Euenos, where an encounter with the Centaur Nessos planted the seeds of Herakles' final destruction. Nessos acted as ferryman, but used the crossing to attempt to rape Deianeira. When Herakles shot him with an arrow steeped in the poison of the Lernaean hydra, the dying Centaur craftily whispered to Deianeira that she should preserve the blood from his wound, to use it, if the need ever arose, as – so Nessos said – a love charm.

Never at rest, Herakles felt bound to avenge every slight. From Trachis he crossed to Oichalia, determined to settle his score with Eurytos. As so often in his career, war went hand in hand with sexual aggression: he sacked Oichalia, and abducted the king's daughter Iole to be his new wife.

The death of Herakles

The reaction of Deianeira was – as depicted in Sophokles' tragedy *Women of Trachis* – to smear a robe with the Centaur's so-called love charm and to send it as a gift to Herakles. But the 'charm' turned out to be a deadly, torturing poison, reminiscent of that used by Medea to murder Glauke; racked with pain, Herakles begged his son Hyllos to take him out to neighbouring Mount Oita, to die on a funeral pyre. What happened next typifies the polarities between which Herakles constantly lurched. As the pyre was burning – ignited by the Argonaut Poias, who happened to be passing by, and whom his former shipmate rewarded by bequeathing to him his infallible bow and arrows – Herakles was miraculously raised up to Olympos, where he was said to have made the transition to immortality, and to enjoy the favours of yet another female, **Hebe** goddess of youth.

But not every narrative of the hero's end gave him such an unambiguous future. The *Odyssey's* account of the Underworld describes Odysseus' encounter with the 'double' of Herakles, although Herakles himself is regarded as being on Olympos. Such a post-mortem bifurcation, extraordinarily unusual in the context of Greek beliefs about the Afterlife, expresses both the uniqueness of

Herakles and the deep-rooted polarities which his nature exemplifies.

Heraklids, Dorians and genealogical politics

What makes Herakles' descendants ('the Heraklids') unusual compared with the offspring of other major heroes is that they have a collective destiny. This derives from the continuing persecutions which they endured at the hands of Eurystheus, who did not relent even after the demise of his chief adversary. He pursued the Heraklids to Athens, whose people refused to surrender them; in this story, as in so many other stories filtered through a myth-telling tradition centred on Athens, the city is depicted as the haven of the oppressed. After the death of Eurystheus, the Heraklids 'returned' to the Peloponnese; that is, they claimed what they saw as their territorial birthright. This first 'return' was abortive, since the occurrence of a plague led to the revelation that the true 'return' was not yet destined to happen. But in due course the Heraklids, and their allies the Dorians (descendants of Deukalion through his son Hellen), settled the principal Peloponnesian regions of Argos, Messene and Sparta.

The preceding narrative raises fascinating although extremely problematic issues about the relationship between mythological tradition and the events of Greek history. The 'Dorian invasion' was for long understood to be a real historical occurrence, representing the conquest of a 'pre-Dorian' population by a force of outsiders – a process of which stories of 'the return of the Heraklids' were alleged to be a reflection. It is, however, very hard to find corroborative archaeological material to establish when, or indeed whether, such an invasion even took place. But what is not in doubt is the way in which Greek myth-tellers manipulated tradition in order to make political points, especially in the crucible of polarized 5th century politics, when there came about a heightened awareness of differences between states styling themselves as 'Dorian' (notably Sparta) or 'Ionian' (notably Athens). The intrinsic malleability of mythology lent itself perfectly to ethnic self-assertion – nowhere more graphically than in Euripides' play *Ion*. In that work – produced in Athens in the midst of the war between Athens and Sparta, perhaps around 410 BC – Ion, ancestor of the Ionians, is the son of Apollo and Kreousa, an Athenian princess and daughter of the 'autochthonous' King Erechtheus; by contrast, Doros, the ancestor of the Dorians, is merely the son of Kreousa and *another mortal*, an Athenian king named Xouthos. All this differs sharply from other versions, in which Doros is Xouthos' brother, and his elder brother at that. There can be no clearer illustration of the fact that the present constantly rewrote the mythological past in its own image.

Herakles' ultimate, chariot-borne transition to Olympos is the final step in a career which has taken him into some of the most extreme situations – depths and heights – which art and poetry can imagine. Here Nike, goddess of Victory, drives the chariot, with the beardless Herakles, club in hand, as her passenger. Attic vase, c. 400 BC.

Theseus and the Heroic Athenian Past

Kekrops and the birth of Theseus

Several 'Dorian' communities looked back to a group, the Heraklids, who owed their territorial claims to sheer martial prowess as exemplified in a successful invasion. Athenians, by contrast, prided themselves on the claim of autochthony: aboriginal occupation of the same land. Their first king, Kekrops, was allegedly born from the earth, an origin embodied in his half-human, half-serpent form. His successors, Kranaos and Amphiktyon, were also said to have been earth-born, as was the next in line, Erichthonios, conceived when the semen of Hephaistos (ejaculated in a vain attempt to rape Athene) impregnated the ground. Erichthonios too was associated with a snake, or in some versions even had partially or completely a snake's form; but gradually the Athenian royal lineage took on an exclusively human shape. That was true of the greatest of Kekrops' descendants: Theseus.

Theseus was born at a time when the Athenian royal succession was in a state of uncertainty, being divided between four brothers. One of these,

Aigeus, was uncertain about his personal future also, since neither his first nor his second wife had given him children. He therefore consulted an oracle, as any anxious Greek might have done (at the oracle of Dodona archaeologists have excavated numerous lead strips, 'tablets' recording real-life questions put by ordinary people anxious about childlessness; see p. 100). The inscrutable reply of the Delphic prophetess urged Aigeus not to undo 'the protruding foot of the wineskin' until he had returned to Athens. When he passed through Troizen (in the Argolid), his shrewd host Pittheus understood the oracle to refer to the act of sex (taking 'protruding foot of wineskin' to mean 'penis'); wishing to link his own family dynastically with Athens, Pittheus ensured that Aigeus got drunk and slept with Pittheus' daughter Aithra. In due course she gave birth to Theseus. However, the birth of many heroes was cloaked in mystery; and so it was with Theseus also. On the same night as Aigeus lay with Aithra, Poseidon lay with her too. Thus the ambiguity of Herakles' parentage was replicated in that of Theseus: anything worthy of the great Peloponnesian hero was worthy of the hero of Athens too.

Before Aigeus returned to Athens, he left instructions with Aithra that, if she bore him a male child, she was to bring up the boy without revealing to him his father's identity; then, when the growing lad was strong enough to move the great boulder beneath which Aigeus had placed a sword and a

Genealogy of the Mythical Kings of Athens

It cannot be emphasized enough that there is a built-in fluidity about any Greek genealogical table relating to mythology: to construct a table is to give an impression of fixity, yet genealogies were in fact the subject of constant 'negotiation' by interested parties. Claims and counter-claims were particularly likely to arise in relation to the genealogies of specific cities, or specific families within those cities. This family tree of Athens' mythical rulers is broadly taken from Apollodoros' *Library*. According to Apollodoros, the first kings were in this order: Kekrops I (earthborn), Kranaos (earthborn), Amphiktyon (not in this genealogy; either earthborn or a son of Deukalion), Erichthonios, Pandion I, Erechtheus, Kekrops II, Pandion II. After the death of Pandion II, a dynastic feud led eventually to the taking of power by Aigeus.

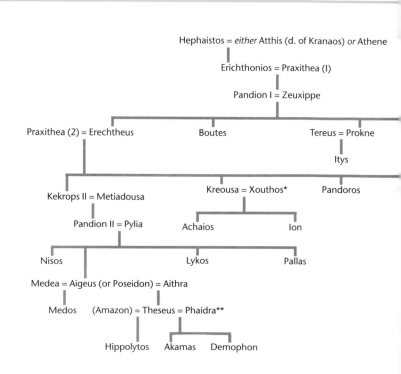

pair of sandals, Aithra was to send her son to Athens with these tokens. Ancient visitors to Troizen were shown the 'very rock' described in the story; just the same happens to modern visitors, who are shown a rock on the path from Troizen to Hermione. Like their ancient counterparts, such visitors are encouraged to read the landscape in terms shaped by mythology.

(Left) Ge/Gaia ('Earth') hands the 'earth-born' child Erichthonios up to Athene, whose expression displays a tenderness rare in representations of the warrior goddess. Hermes watches from above; so does an owl with an olive branch – twin symbols of the city of Athens. Attic vase, end of 5th century BC.

(Right) When Theseus reached adulthood in the city of Troizen, he moved a mighty rock and so discovered the sword and sandals which his father Aigeus had left there. Immediately Theseus set off for Athens, where Aigeus recognized the sword, and welcomed Theseus as his son. Attic vase, c. 470 BC.

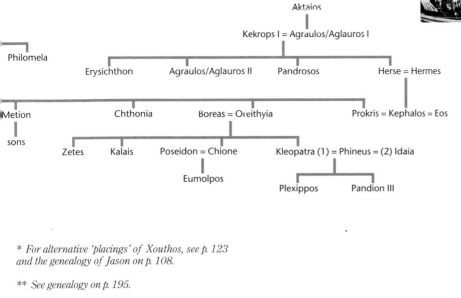

* For alternative 'placings' of Xouthos, see p. 123 and the genealogy of Jason on p. 108.

** See genealogy on p. 195.

Theseus comes of age

Aithra's child was indeed male: when Theseus had grown to adulthood, he duly moved the stone, claimed the tokens, and set out for Athens. En route he ruthlessly despatched a series of aggressive malefactors who were blocking the road. His method was to turn against them their own mode of aggression. Sinis ('Destroyer') compelled travellers to bend a pine tree down to the ground, and then looked on while they were catapulted into the air; or else, he tied them to a pair of adjacent, bent pines

Theseus' Exploits En Route for Athens

location	exploit
1 Epidauros	kills Periphetes, a son of Hephaistos who used an iron club to murder travellers
2 Isthmus of Corinth	kills Sinis the Pine-Bender
3 Krommyon	kills the monstrous sow called Phaia, alleged by some to be offspring of Echidna and Typhon
4 Skeironian rocks	hurls the bandit Skeiron into the sea, to be devoured by a giant turtle
5 Eleusis	kills Kerkyon in a wrestling bout
6 near Eleusis	kills Polypemon/Prokroustes by fitting him to one of his own beds

*(Left) Sinis the Pine-Bender
is about to be killed by the
method which he used to kill
others. Theseus pulls down a
pine branch, to which he will
soon attach his adversary.
Attic cup, c. 490 BC.*

tales liked to envisage their local hero. There is an instructive difference between these exploits of Theseus and the Heraklean Labours: Theseus' retributions are more measured, showing little capacity for uncontrollable violence; there is a marked contrast, for instance, with Herakles' brutal killing of his lyre-teacher Linos.

Theseus' arrival in Athens

Aigeus' Athenian household, at which Theseus now presented himself, contained the volatile personality of Medea, whom Aigeus had married after her flight from Corinth (see p. 113). Having borne Aigeus a son (Medos), she saw the arrival of Theseus – whose identity she recognized but Aigeus did not – as a threat to her own position and that of her child. She duly attempted to poison the incomer, but in the nick of time his father recognized his sword and saved him. Medea was driven out on yet another stage in her wanderings; eventually she returned to Colchis, where she restored her father Aietes to the throne after he had been driven from power.

Theseus' arrival in Athens coincided with a military-political crisis. Androgeos, son of the Cretan king Minos, had been killed on a visit to Athens; one version had it that, having proved himself superior to all-comers in athletic competition, the young Cretan prince had been sent out by Aigeus to confront the lethal 'bull of Marathon' (a beast which Theseus would later kill). Minos was said to have great power thanks to a mighty navy; given the fact that, from the Archaic period onwards, real-world Cretan power was insignificant compared with that of states such as Sparta, Athens and Thebes, Minos' mythical thalassocracy has often been reckoned to represent a folk memory of the glory days of Bronze Age ('Minoan') Crete (see p. 198). At any rate, Minos attempted to seek revenge for Androgeos' demise by attacking Athens. When force failed, the grieving Minos prayed to his father Zeus, who afflicted the Athenians with famine and disease. On seeking the advice of an oracle, the Athenians were instructed to offer Minos whatever satisfaction he demanded; and so it was that Athens had to send a regular tribute of seven youths and seven maidens to Crete, where they would be devoured by the Minotaur, the semi-human, semi-bovine monster which inhabited the Labyrinth (see p. 196).

Theseus and the Minotaur

Minos had not reckoned with Theseus' valour, nor with the capacity of the females of the Cretan royal line (including Europa, Pasiphae and Phaidra) to yearn for the attractions of a stranger – or of the strange. When Theseus valiantly volunteered to join the next party of youths destined to be the Minotaur's tributary meal, what saved him was the love of Minos' daughter Ariadne. On Daidalos'

and watched the victims be ripped apart as the trees sprang to the vertical. Theseus did the same to him. The bandit Skeiron, who dwelt in towering cliffs on the coast of the Megarid, made passers-by wash his feet; while they did so, he would kick them down into the sea, to be devoured by a giant turtle. Theseus meted out to Skeiron the same treatment. The next target was Polypemon ('Much Woe'), also called Prokroustes ('He who Beats Out'), whose ruse was to offer travellers a bed for the night. But he actually had two beds, which he required his guests to correspond to exactly: he gave short people the long one (beating them out to the proper length with hammers) and tall people the short one (cutting them to size with a saw). As usual Theseus made the punishment fit the crime, for he adapted Prokroustes to the length of his own bed. Theseus was apparently already a paragon of justice – which is how the Athenians who recounted these

*The painter who decorated the
inside of this Attic cup (c. 480
BC) chose the moment just
before the Minotaur's death.
With one hand gripping a
horn, Theseus is about to hack
or saw off the beast's head.*

advice she told Theseus to unwind a thread
attached to the entrance of the maze, so as to be able
to retrace his steps once he had killed the Minotaur.
Having broken definitively with her father by this
act, Ariadne fled with her lover. In preferring
Theseus to Minos she was, in a sense, simply doing
what any ordinary Greek bride did when she left her
father's home for her husband's; but Ariadne's
choice takes on the highly charged and exaggerated
profile characteristic of mythology.

The sequel, certainly, was far from ordinary.
When the pair stopped off at Naxos on the way
from Crete to Athens, they were destined to go no
further together; for Theseus abandoned his bride.
Our sources suggest a range of motivations, not
all of which present the hero as blameworthy (e.g.
divine compulsion). Ariadne's reputation was re-
deemed when an even greater lover, Dionysos, made
her his own. As for Theseus, this second return to
Athens was to seal conclusively his passage to
adulthood; for it caused the death of his father.
Although Theseus had promised to hoist white sails

if his mission had been successful, he absentmindedly left the vessel's original black sails in place.
Aigeus imagined the worst, and threw himself to
his death from the heights of the Acropolis.

Theseus the King

Theseus now took over the kingship. One of his
policies illustrates how myth-tellers saw him as a
quintessentially political figure. Through the act of
'synoecism' ('dwelling together'), Theseus was said
to have combined the numerous small villages of
Attica into a single state, with Athens at its head;
this was a creative move (utterly unlike most of the
deeds ascribed to Herakles). Whether or not there
ever was a real individual named Theseus who
played a political (or any other) role in Athens, the
crucial point is that here we have, as so often, a
mythical narrative which isolates a fundamental
feature of the present and sets its genesis back
into the time of myth. Some scholars have sought
to explain the increased frequency with which
Theseus appears in visual art from the end of the

6th century BC onwards, citing the attempts of the democratic reformer Kleisthenes to marshal mythical precedents for his policy of concentrating and consolidating Athenian power. Greek myths are only ostensibly about the past: they are much more revealing about the changing present.

Amazons, Centaurs and abductions

Alongside his unique role as a political *exemplum*, Theseus retained a more typically heroic profile as a doer of mighty deeds and as a locus of domestic disruption. Three exploits will illustrate his great deeds. First there was his campaign, shoulder to shoulder with Herakles, against the Amazons, the race of warrior women. In revenge for Theseus' abduction of one of their number, the Amazons laid siege to the Acropolis itself; however, Theseus' army managed to defeat them – it would have been mythically unthinkable for so 'unnatural' a tribe to have achieved final victory over male heroes.

Secondly, Theseus and his stalwart companion Peirithoös confronted another monstrous brood: the Centaurs. When Peirithoös married Hippodameia ('Horse Tamer'), her semi-human, semi-equine kinfolk were invited to the wedding. Unfortunately, their closeness to raw nature expressed itself – as it had done in the case of the Centaurs whom Herakles had encountered in the Peloponnese – in a drastic weakness for wine; under its influence they went so far as to try to rape the bride (echoes here of Nessos' attempted rape of Deianeira). Theseus and Peirithoös victoriously defended civilized values against such conduct.

The final challenge took Theseus and Peirithoös to the infernal destination which Herakles had reached on his last Labour. Their project was something between a foolhardy dare and a crazy assault on morality and the divine order. It involved the abduction of two females: Helen, then aged twelve, and Persephone, who, being the wife of Hades, was about as far off-limits as any female could be. Theseus took Helen for himself (though her brothers Kastor and Polydeukes soon recaptured her), and then descended to the Underworld to try to seize Persephone for Peirithoös. No action could so clearly emphasize that Theseus' status as moral paragon was in some respects severely compromised: he was behaving almost as badly as Ixion, the archetypal sinner who would have assaulted Hera and who had fathered, amongst others, none other than Peirithoös. At any rate, when Theseus and Peirithoös were entertained by Hades, the god of death cunningly induced them to sit in the Chair of Lethe ('Forgetfulness'), whose rock (according to one version) grew into their flesh, so rendering escape impossible. Theseus was eventually freed by Herakles, but Peirithoös remained seated for ever. Like his father Ixion, eternally tormented in the Afterlife, Peirithoös would embody the dire consequences of infringing a goddess' honour.

Theseus and Phaidra

From heroic deeds to domestic disruption: once more, we need to look to Theseus' love-hate relationship with Crete. To heal the enmity between the two peoples, he was offered the hand of Phaidra, daughter of Minos and the ill-fated Pasiphae. True to her mother's inclinations (Pasiphae had mated with a bull and given birth to the Minotaur; see p. 196), Phaidra lusted after what was forbidden. In Phaidra's case, the object of her passion was her stepson, Hippolytos (Theseus had fathered him upon the Amazon whom he had abducted). When her advances were rejected, Phaidra hanged herself, but in a suicide note falsely accused Hippolytos of rape. Theseus was furious at what he took to be a betrayal by his stepson, and intemperately invoked one of the curses which his 'father' Poseidon had granted him. As the messenger narrates in Euripides' terrifying tragedy *Hippolytos* (see pp. 72, 88), a monstrous bull appeared from the sea, wrecking the young man's chariot and so perhaps causing his nominal destiny: according to one interpretation, the name 'Hippolytos' means 'torn apart by horses'.

After Theseus

Many Greek heroes died unremarkable deaths: ordinariness could touch even the greatest. Theseus was driven out of Athens in a dynastic dispute, to be ignominiously killed on the island of Skyros (off the coast of Thessaly), where he had sought refuge. But his influence, above all in Athens, was only just beginning. In the 470s BC the Athenian politician Kimon claimed to have discovered the hero's bones on Skyros, and ceremonially transferred them to Athens.

Earlier we gave our working definition of a myth as 'a socially powerful traditional story'; in Athens the social power of Theseus, as a distillation of the city's idealized self-representation, came to exceed by far that of any other mythical figure. In contrast to his morally ambiguous role in relation to Ariadne, Helen and Hippolytos, we may set his generosity and nobility as depicted in two other episodes: he extended to the blood-polluted Herakles the hand of friendship and the prospect of asylum, and he welcomed into Athens an even more horrifically polluted outcast, the self-blinded transgressor Oedipus (cf. Sophokles' *Oedipus at Colonus*). In the tough world of 5th century interstate politics, Athens often asserted her interests with ruthless brutality; but in the figure of Theseus Athenian myth-tellers found an emblem of the values for which their city ideally wished to be known. As Theseus himself proudly asserted, in words put into his mouth by Euripides in the tragedy *Suppliant Women*:

By my many noble deeds
I have displayed this characteristic to the Greeks:
always to be a punisher of wickedness.

The Trojan War

One heroic adventure stands out beyond all others in Greek mythology: the expedition of the Greeks against the Trojans. Its memorableness for ancient and modern audiences alike is partly due to the fact that two supreme poems, Homer's *Iliad* and *Odyssey*, are devoted to events during and after this expedition; in addition, countless images and numerous narratives, including many tragedies, deal with the same theme. A quite different aspect of the appeal of the Trojan War lies in the seemingly inexhaustible enthusiasm of the modern public for asking whether mythical events 'really happened', an enthusiasm fuelled by remarkable archaeological efforts to uncover the 'real' Troy (see pp. 200–5). However, such real-world oriented investigations, for all their fascination, run the risk of making the complexities and subtleties of the ancient narratives subservient to questions about historical and material evidence. The account which follows tries to give full weight to those complexities and subtleties, since the Trojan War was a backdrop against which Greeks explored every manner of intellectual and emotional issue, from free-will and human responsibility, to honour, shame and guilt, to relationships between humans and gods and between males and females – all this under the fearsome pressure of warfare.

The founding of Troy

Unlike the land of the Colchians to which the Argonauts journeyed, the city of Troy (also known as Ilios or Ilion) was not seen by Greeks as a place of intrinsic strangeness and magic. The mythical Trojans were grounded in the same genealogical soil, and followed the same religious and social customs, as the inhabitants of the Greek mainland and islands. The first founder of a settlement in the Troad was Zeus' son Dardanos; his foundation, 'Dardania', lay in the foothills of Mount Ida, where he was said to have come ashore after the Flood, sailing southeastwards on an inflated wineskin from his home on the island of Samothrace. His grandson Tros named the region 'Troia'. As if to consolidate the land's proximity to the gods, Zeus' ever-vigilant eye fell upon one of Tros' sons, Ganymede, whom he took up to Olympos to be his steward/sexual companion (see pp. 100, 176). It fell to another of Tros' sons, Ilos, to found the city which would be known as Ilios/Ilion; in a story-pattern almost exactly replicating that of Kadmos at Thebes, Ilos obeyed the instruction of an oracle by following a cow to the place where it first lay down to rest, and founded his city at that spot. Although Greek myths often carry the message that oracular responses can be misleading, nothing in the tale of Ilos' foundation suggests that the settlement of Ilion/Troy was against the gods' wishes.

A critical moment in the building of any city, real or imaginary, is the construction of its walls. This

The most probable site of Troy, at Hisarlik in the northwest of modern Turkey, was initially excavated by Frank Calvert in the 1860s; in the early 1870s the German Heinrich Schliemann identified the site from his reading of Homer's Iliad.

Genealogy of Trojan Royal Family

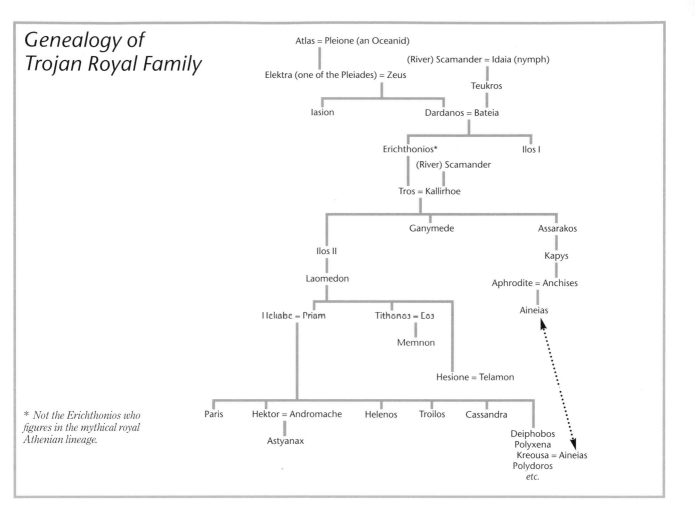

Atlas = Pleione (an Oceanid)

Elektra (one of the Pleiades) = Zeus

(River) Scamander = Idaia (nymph)

Teukros

Iasion

Dardanos = Bateia

Erichthonios*

Ilos I

(River) Scamander

Tros = Kallirhoe

Ganymede

Assarakos

Ilos II

Kapys

Laomedon

Aphrodite = Anchises

Aineias

Hekabe = Priam

Tithonos = Eos

Memnon

Hesione = Telamon

Paris   Hektor = Andromache   Helenos   Troilos   Cassandra

Astyanax

Deiphobos
Polyxena
Kreousa = Aineias
Polydoros
etc.

** Not the Erichthonios who
figures in the mythical royal
Athenian lineage.*

---

act calls for special skill: when the walls of Thebes were built, Amphion, Orpheus-like, used his magical lyre to charm the stones to move into place. It may also entail special peril: in a tradition about the founding of Rome, Romulus murdered his brother Remus when the latter jumped disparagingly over Romulus' still-incomplete wall. The construction of Troy's walls was such a significant event that Ilos' son Laomedon was able to enlist the aid of two divinities, Apollo and Poseidon, as builders. But Laomedon made the kind of mistake which many myths show to be disastrous: he broke his contract with the gods. When Apollo and Poseidon received no wages, they sent, respectively, a plague and a sea-monster. Laomedon followed the advice of an oracle and offered up his daughter Hesione to the monster by way of appeasement. However, Herakles, passing by en route from his Labour with the Amazons, agreed to rescue her, provided Laomedon would give him a reward, namely the wonderful mares which Zeus had given to Tros as recompense for the loss of Ganymede (as so often, a Greek myth implies the importance of 'right balance'). Unfortunately, Laomedon had learned nothing, for

he reneged on his agreement. The hero duly sacked the newly built city and slew Laomedon, giving Hesione as bride to Telamon, his companion in arms and the future father of the great warrior Aias.

Priam's Troy

The kingdom was now taken over by Laomedon's son Priam, during whose reign the gods' involvement in Troy's fate reached its shattering climax. One day, Priam's queen Hekabe (Hecuba, in Latinized form) dreamed she would give birth to a fire-brand which would ignite the city. At the time Hekabe was pregnant; the ominous dream prompted her and Priam to send the newborn baby boy to be exposed to die on nearby Mount Ida. But in the mythology of Greece (and of many other peoples) stories abound of exposed children who return to fulfil their fateful destinies. This is exactly what happened to baby Paris (also called 'Alexandros', i.e. 'Warder-off of Men'). Having been suckled by a she-bear and raised by the servant charged with killing him (another analogy with Romulus and Remus), Paris grew to adulthood as a herdsman on the mountain slopes. Then one day he entered

(Above) Hera, Aphrodite and Athene have come to Mount Ida, where Paris will judge their beauty. Hermes is their guide. Between Hermes (centre) and Paris (far right) is another female figure, whom some have wanted to identify as Eris, goddess of discord. Attic container for unguents, 570–560 BC.

and won an athletic competition in Troy. Because he was apparently an intrusive, unknown outsider, his victory aroused the wrath of the defeated competitors, including another of Priam's sons, Deiphobos, who tried to kill him. But the logic of myth dictated that Paris' identity should be revealed just in time; and he was joyfully welcomed back into the family.

The Judgment of Paris

Symbolically, of course, Paris was still the destructive firebrand, a role which he was about to play to

the full. While still a shepherd on Mount Ida, he was visited by the goddesses Hera, Athene and Aphrodite, who demanded that he make a judgment about their relative beauty; for Eris, goddess of discord, had thrown between them an apple inscribed 'For the Fairest' (see p. 95). In post-classical tradition 'The Judgment of Paris' has been one of the richest of all themes deriving from Greek mythology. For mortals, deciding between divinities was impossible and usually catastrophic, since all divinities had their indispensable functions; but Paris' decision was at least displaced from the goddesses themselves, since it turned on a choice between the three bribes which they offered: power (Hera), victory in war (Athene), or the hand of Helen, the world's loveliest woman (Aphrodite). Paris' decision to opt for Helen/Aphrodite reflected his own personality, which myth-tellers often represented as vain and superficial – both attractive and susceptible to attractiveness. Also implicated in his choice was transgression: for Helen was another man's wife.

Helen, the child of Zeus and Leda, was married to Menelaos, king of Sparta. Why would she desert him for another man, and so court the extreme opprobrium, and worse, which awaited any Greek woman who committed adultery? (Real-world Greek laws authorized a wronged husband to kill – or, in the law code of Locri in southern Italy, to blind – a man whom he caught in adultery; the erring wife was to be divorced and barred from participation in public sacrifice.) Throughout Greek myth-telling, from epic to lyric to tragedy to philosophical prose

(Above) Helen was conceived when her mother Leda was approached by Zeus in the form of a swan. This unusual sculpture (5th century BC) shows Helen about to emerge from her broken eggshell.

analyses of motivation, competing explanations were given of why Helen was unfaithful. She was a wicked woman; she succumbed to the irresistible power of persuasion; she was abducted by force; or she was compelled by Aphrodite. More intriguing than any of these options was a version which by-passed altogether her elopement with Paris: according to this story (found for example in Euripides' play *Helen*), what went to Troy with Paris was a mere phantom, whereas the real Helen, chaste and faithful, was spirited away to Egypt to await rescue by Menelaos. As so often in Greek mythology, motivation is variable; much more stable is the underlying structure of events. In the present case, what is constant is the unleashing of war in retaliation for the perceived breaking of a basic moral rule: for Paris had been a guest in Menelaos' house (albeit in Menelaos' absence), and had repaid this hospitality with gross betrayal.

Before Helen's marriage, such was her beauty that all the greatest heroes had sought her hand. To neutralize in advance the wrath of the disappointed suitors, Helen's mortal 'father' Tyndareos obliged them all to swear an oath to aid whoever should be the lucky man, in the event of any future threat to the marriage. After Helen's scandalous elopement, Menelaos turned to his more powerful brother, Agamemnon king of Mycenae, who put together an expeditionary force requiring of all the oath-takers that they be as good as their word. Some of the participants were the sons of Argonauts: for example, Aias and Teukros were the sons of Telamon; Philoktetes, the son of Poias; and Achilles, the son of Peleus. But the sense of collective endeavour which bonded together the crew of the *Argo* was never matched among the numerous and varied contingents of Greeks who went to Troy.

The Trojan expedition

There was reluctance on the part of some participants from the outset. The Ithacan Odysseus, said by some to be the son not of Laertes king of Ithaca, but of the notorious trickster Sisyphos, used all his guile to try to escape the call-up. When Palamedes, an envoy from the Greek high command, came to recruit him, the hero feigned madness by yoking a horse with an ox and sowing the earth with salt instead of seed. But Palamedes saw through the deception, and compelled Odysseus to reveal his sanity when the life of his young son Telemachos was in danger. Odysseus wished to avoid the expedition because of an oracle, which had predicted his twenty-year absence from home in the event of his going to Troy.

Another prediction threatened to block the participation of Achilles, greatest of all the warriors. Achilles' divine mother Thetis knew he was fated to die if he went to Troy, so she sent him to be brought up, disguised as a girl, on the isle of Skyros. But Odysseus, who was by now part of the Greek force,

exposed the ruse by setting before Achilles and his girl companions both women's clothing and men's weapons. When Achilles instinctively concentrated on the shield and spear, his disguise was unmasked.

Omens and sacrifice

At all periods of ancient Greek history, the inception of a military campaign was marked by religious observances such as sacrifice; it was also a time around which other forms of interaction with the sacred tended to cluster, such as omens, prophecies and oracles. When, for example, the Athenian expedition to Sicily was about to set off in 415 BC, several unusual events – including the desecration of nearly all the stone images of Hermes in the city – were felt to set an ominous tone for this ultimately disastrous campaign. The mythical expedition to Troy began with a whole series of such ominous events, as well as with delays and false starts. At every stage in these complex and hesitant preliminaries it seemed that the gods were involved, an indication of the magnitude of the undertaking and perhaps also of its overall moral ambiguity.

The Greek army and fleet assembled at Aulis, on the northeastern coast of Boiotia opposite Euboia. Immediately there was a false start, which took the Greeks not to the Troad but to neighbouring Mysia, which they sacked in the mistaken belief that it was Troy. When they reassembled at Aulis, there was a much more serious delay, for the fleet was

(Above) The seduction of Helen by Paris was presided over by Aphrodite and her son Eros. On this relief (a copy of a 4th-century BC original) the goddess has her arm around Helen, while the winged Eros, with a parallel gesture of persuasive intimacy, rests a hand on Paris' shoulder. Seated above is Peitho, goddess of Persuasion, symbolizing the process which is unfolding in this scene.

(Opposite, below left) The 'Judgment of Paris' was an enormously popular literary and artistic theme in the Middle Ages. This illustration is taken from a 15th-century illuminated manuscript of The Trojan War, *a poem by Konrad of Würzburg, who wrote in the 13th century. A kneeling Paris presents the Apple of Discord to Aphrodite/Venus, whose expression is, to say the least, enigmatic.*

Greek Contingents at Troy

	region	leaders	ships
1	Boiotia	Peneleos, Leitos, Arkesilaos, Prothoenor, Klonios	50
2	Aspledon, Orchomenos	Askalaphos, Ialmenos	30
3	Phokis	Schedios, Epistrophos	40
4	Lokris	Aias, son of Oileus	40
5	Euboia	Elephenor	40
6	Athens	Menestheus	50
7	Salamis	Aias, son of Telamon	12
8	Argos, Tiryns, adjacent cities	Diomedes, Sthenelos, Euryalos	80
9	Mycenae, Corinth, N coast of Peloponnese	Agamemnon	100
10	Lakedaimon (Sparta)	Menelaos	60
11	Pylos and W Peloponnese	Nestor	90
12	Arcadia	Agapenor	60
13	Elis	Amphimachos, Thalpios, Diores, Polyxeinos	40
14	Doulichion	Meges	40
15	Ithaca, nearby islands	Odysseus	12
16	Aitolia	Thoas	40
17	Crete	Idomeneus, Meriones	80
18	Rhodes	Tlepolemos, son of Herakles	9
19	Syme	Nireus	3
20	Kos, nearby islands	Pheidippos, Antiphos	30
21	Pelasgian Argos (region of NE Greece)	Achilles	50
22	Thessaly (N of Euboia)	Protesilaos, then Podarkes	40
23	Pherai	Eumelos, son of Admetos and Alkestis	11
24	Thessaly (Meliboia, etc.)	Philoktetes, then Medon	7
25	Thessaly (Trikke, etc.)	Podaleirios and Machaon, sons of Asklepios	30
26	Thessaly (Ormenion, etc.)	Eurypylos	40
27	Thessaly (Argissa, etc.)	Polypoites, Leonteus	40
28	NW Greece	Gouneus	22
29	Magnesia	Prothoös	40

blocked in port by adverse winds sent by Artemis. Different myth-tellers allege different motivations for her anger, but a common version is her resentment towards Agamemnon for boasting that his hunting prowess was superior to her own. A more intriguing account is that given in Aischylos' play *Agamemnon*, where the motivation for her wrath is fundamentally obscure – a perspective which tragedy often advances about the human condition.

The only way out of the impasse at Aulis was for Agamemnon to sacrifice his daughter Iphigeneia to Artemis, in a horrific perversion of the everyday ritual of animal (but never human) sacrifice which was a central feature of Greek social life. Agamemnon's act enabled the expedition to continue, but it also inaugurated a sequence of brutal revenge killings within his own household – another illustration of the seamless connection in Greek mythology between heroic exploits and domestic catastrophes. The episode also illustrates the inexhaustible capacity for difference-within-sameness evinced by Greek myths. For there was one version (see p. 76) in which Artemis intervened, at the very instant of sacrifice, to substitute a deer for Iphigeneia, after which the maiden was miraculously transported to the Black Sea to become the goddess' priestess. The more usual version, however, was bleaker and less escapist, an appropriately cruel inauguration of a conflict in which so much blood would be spilled.

So the fleet sailed; but two more 'hesitations' were in store. First, when the Greeks put in to an island in the northeast Aegean – Tenedos, according to some – Philoktetes was bitten in the foot by a sacred serpent; bearing in mind what the logic of myth has to say about divine/human relations, it is not surprising to learn that Philoktetes had allegedly been guilty of a previous transgression against the gods, although, as usual, accounts differ over what the precise offence was. At any rate, the wound festered and stank, so that the army, represented by Odysseus, put Philoktetes ashore on the nearby island of Lemnos, with nothing but his miraculously unerring bow to help him survive. The second 'hesitation' involved a last-ditch attempt to negotiate: an embassy, led by Menelaos and Odysseus, was sent to ask the Trojans to return Helen. The overture was rejected; the Greeks landed; the killing began.

Piecing together a continuous narrative of the whole of the ensuing ten-year campaign is an impossible exercise. What we can do, though – relying on our main source, the Homeric *Iliad*, as well as on retellings in other genres and media, especially tragedy and vase painting – is to home in on the specific events which myth-tellers regarded as worth remembering. These retellings create a drama of peace as well as war, of fragility as well as prowess, of universal as well as local significance.

The *Iliad*

After nine years of fighting, there have been many instances of valour on both sides; but the issue is no closer to a resolution. Then in the tenth year there occurs a sequence of episodes which demonstrates, thanks to Homer's monumental narrative, just how profound are the implications, for gods as well as mortals, of this squabble over an unfaithful wife.

Agamemnon has a concubine, the daughter of a priest of Apollo. When her father protests to the god, Apollo intervenes by sending a plague upon the Greeks. Agamemnon has no choice but to give up the girl; however, to repair the damage to his honour, he takes for himself a captive slave-girl who has been allotted to Achilles. Now it is Achilles whose honour is damaged. He thinks at first of killing Agamemnon on the spot, but Athene intervenes to stop him. Instead Achilles withdraws to his tent to brood, in the company of his dear companion Patroklos.

Several consequences flow from his refusal to fight. First, the onus of battle is now borne by the other Greeks, who successively pit their courage against that of the Trojans: Menelaos, Diomedes, Odysseus, Aias the son of Telamon, Agamemnon himself. Secondly, Achilles turns, in his isolation, to his mother, the sea-nymph Thetis, who successfully implores Zeus to grant temporary victory to the Trojans in order to make the Greeks recognize the worth of her absent son. Indeed few things are more moving, in this wonderful poem of pathos and anger, than the tender interchanges between the

Artists by no means always follow the version of a myth given by Homer (or any other poet, for that matter). In the Iliad *Agamemnon sends his two heralds to lead away Achilles' slave-girl Briseis and bring her to Agamemnon's tent. But in this image (Attic cup, early 5th century BC) Agamemnon himself has taken Briseis by the wrist. They are followed by Talthybios (one of the heralds) and Diomedes.*

Achilles, on the left, is about to kill Hektor, who is in a state of collapse. To the left and right of them, though not visible in this picture, are Athene, who is urging Achilles on, and Apollo, who has abandoned Hektor and is walking away. Attic vase, c. 490 BC.

At the climax of the Iliad, *Priam visits Achilles to ransom the body of his son Hektor. As Homer presents it, the relationship between Priam and Achilles is full of anguish, pathos, tension and latent anger. In this later artistic depiction, by contrast, the protagonists appear restrained and dignified. Silver cup, 1st century AD; found in the grave of a local chieftain at Hoby in Denmark.*

mortal son and the divine mother, whose super-human foresight reveals to her only too clearly the imminence of her son's death.

The third consequence of Achilles' withdrawal – a withdrawal in which he obstinately persists even in the face of lavish reparations by Agamemnon – is his loss of Patroklos. Seeing the Trojans already setting the first of the Greek ships alight, Achilles allows his friend to go into battle in his (Achilles') armour. But Patroklos is a lesser man, and falls beneath the spear of Priam's son Hektor, bulwark of the city. Patroklos' death at last undams Achilles' resistance; acting not for the Greek cause, but to assuage his own vengeful grief, he returns to the fray, slays Hektor, and drags the corpse behind his chariot in order to disfigure it. It is only through the gods' intervention that the corpse remains undefiled; for the Trojans too are dear to the gods of Olympos.

The brutality of war now gives way, in the *Iliad*'s narrative, to two scenes of public, ritualized formality, which frame an intervening, private scene of unique and shattering intensity. First there is the ceremonial of Patroklos' cremation, celebrated with an extended series of athletic competitions in which the best of the Greeks vie with each other for honour, with a zeal no less vigorous than that which they display in combating the Trojans. In absolute contrast, the focus switches to the privacy of

Achilles' quarters, to which Priam, aided by the mediator-god Hermes, makes his way in secret in order to ransom Hektor's corpse. This is a meeting of unbearable tension, because the rules for this unprecedented encounter have to be improvised by the two protagonists. What allows Achilles to calm his rage just enough to let Priam take back Hektor's body is a sense of the underlying, common humanity which links foes in this and every war. Most particularly, Priam reminds Achilles of his own father Peleus, far away in Greece:

So [Priam] spoke, and stirred in Achilles a passion of grieving
for his own father. He took the old man's hand and pushed him
gently away, and the two remembered, as Priam sat huddled
at the feet of Achilles and wept loud for manslaughtering Hektor,
and Achilles wept for his own father, and then again for Patroklos.

There follows the second scene of public ritual, the funeral of Hektor back in Troy. The climax of this ceremony, at once orderly and agonized, consists of the successive lamentations of the three women to whom Hektor had been especially dear: his wife Andromache, his mother Hekabe, and Helen, the lonely outsider whose unique perspective enables her to testify to Hektor's matchless generosity of spirit, even to one like her, towards whom he might have had every reason to feel spite. So ends the epic – but not the war; for once Hektor has been buried, the fighting will start once more.

What makes the *Iliad* the greatest of all mythological narratives is its unflinching confrontation of the grim brutality of war, while still conveying a sense both of the respect and affection which humans can show each other, and of the world of peaceful activities within which warfare is merely one factor. The action is played out at the divine as well as the human level, and the gods too suffer, at least within the brief time-scale represented by the events of the poem. But it is the heroes whose deeds and sufferings stand out in sharpest relief, etched against the background of the inevitable limitations of mortality.

To the Fall of Troy

For the series of episodes between the death of Hektor and the capture of Troy, we rely principally on non-epic sources. Several of these episodes centre on Achilles. His combat with the Amazon warrior Penthesileia, with whom he fell in love even as she lay dying from his spear-thrust, and the duel in which he slew Memnon, child of the Dawn and leader of the Ethiopians, are the prelude to his final, fatal encounter before the gates of Troy. In his infancy his divine mother Thetis had sought to make him invulnerable by passing him through

which surviving hero was the bravest, and hence most worthy to inherit Achilles' arms? Various myth-tellers give different accounts of how the choice was said to have been made, including by consultation of Trojan prisoners to discover who had done them most harm, or by a vote taken among the Greeks. But the outcome is always the same: there is a two-man contest between Aias and Odysseus, which Odysseus wins. The tragic sequel is explored by Sophokles in his drama *Aias*. In a fit of rage at what he sees as this slur on his honour, Aias attempts to murder Agamemnon, Menelaos and Odysseus. But the goddess Athene, ever solicitous for the Greek cause, deludes Aias' mind so that he kills, not men, but some sheep penned in the camp. His loss of face being thus compounded, Aias sees no alternative to suicide: he falls upon the sword which Hektor had once given him, in an exchange of gifts between respected foes. Yet the last word rests with Odysseus, who successfully persuades a reluctant Agamemnon to allow burial to the 'traitor' Aias, on the grounds that, as Odysseus puts it, 'I too shall come to that need': that is, every mortal will one day need the hand of another to bury him.

The mythological stage is now set for the endgame; but how will the city fall? Just as prophecies and other interactions with the sacred proliferate at the start of the campaign, so do they also at its climax. The Greek seer Kalchas foresees some of the many conditions which are necessary for Troy's capture, but he also realizes that, since his own insight, like that of any mortal, is incomplete, it has to be supplemented by the predictive powers of the Trojan seer Helenos. The Greeks thus seize Helenos and force him to tell what he knows. A complex set of preconditions for the fall of

purging fire and smearing him with ambrosia, the gods' magical food ('ambrosia' means 'immortal'), or else, in a version surviving only from late antiquity, by dipping him in the waters of the river Styx. Only his ankle, by which she held him, remained unprotected, and it was into this spot that Apollo guided the lethal arrow shot by Paris.

Achilles' death precipitated another feud among the Greek leaders; for a central motif of the expedition to Troy is the Greeks' rivalry for honour amongst themselves. The issue this time was:

(Left) Love and death on the plain of Troy. Even as Achilles thrusts his spear into the neck of the Amazon warrior Penthesileia, the eyes of the two combatants meet. According to the myth, this was the fleeting instant at which the two fell in love. Attic vase, c. 530 BC.

(Below left) By placing a pebble onto one or other pile, the Greek warriors indicated whether they thought Odysseus or Aias deserved to be awarded the armour of the dead Achilles. Athene's gesture shows that Odysseus, on the far left, has won; he raises his arms excitedly. Just off picture to the right is Aias, who is covering his head in shame. Attic cup, early 5th century BC.

(Below right) When Aias failed to be awarded Achilles' armour, he tried unsuccessfully to murder the Greek commanders. Now, overcome with shame, he prepares for suicide: he will throw himself on his sword, a gift from Hektor. On this Attic vase (c. 460 BC) Aias may be cursing his enemies, or begging his friends to take proper care of his corpse.

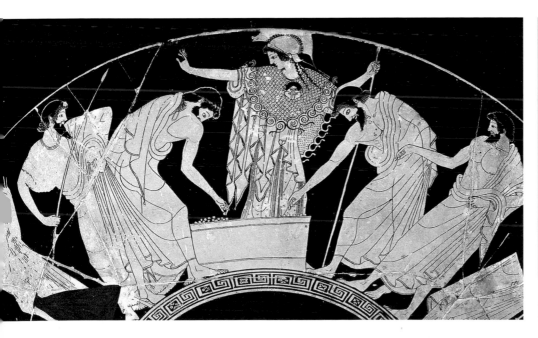

137

(Opposite, above left) Apollo's priest Laokoön and his two sons, killed by sea-serpents. Perhaps 1st century BC, but the dating of this famous sculpture is controversial.

(Below) The deadly work of the 'crew' of the Wooden Horse in progress, in the background. French book illumination, 15th century, from Le recoeil des histoires de Troyes, *by Raoul Lefèvre.*

Troy emerges, including the following: the bow of Herakles, now in the possession of Philoktetes, must be brought to Troy, with or without the acquiescence/presence of Philoktetes himself (our fullest account of the 'persuasion' of the ailing outcast is in the eponymous Sophoklean play); Achilles' son Neoptolemos ('New War') must also be brought to Troy; the Palladion, a talismanic image, must be stolen from the Trojans, because otherwise the city will be impregnable. The achieving of all these objectives is ascribed by most myth-tellers to Odysseus, since, with the passing of Achilles, sheer force defers in importance to the mixture of guile and persuasion which the trickster hero embodies.

The Wooden Horse

The ultimate stratagem to effect Troy's capture is the Wooden Horse. That this becomes, in post-classical tradition, the best-known detail of the entire Trojan saga is due not to any Greek author (for extant Greek accounts of the episode are surprisingly sparse) but to the Roman poet Virgil, who incorporated a stunning evocation of the fall of Troy in his *Aeneid*. There is irony in the fact that the Trojans should be outwitted by the ruse of a huge, hollow effigy of a horse, since in the *Iliad* one of the epithets regularly applied to the Trojans is 'tamers of horses' – indeed, the very last word of the poem is *hippodamoio*, 'tamer of horses', applied to the dead Hektor. At any rate, it is through the Wooden Horse that Troy's defences are to be breached. On the advice of Odysseus or Athene, a craftsman named Epeios makes the deceptive animal, whose exterior belies the ranks of armed men concealed within. Leaving this image behind, complete with its carved inscription, 'For their return home, a thank offering to Athene from the Greeks', the fleet sails away – but only as far as Tenedos.

As the dénouement approaches, so does the intensity of the gods' involvement. First Cassandra, Priam's daughter, urges the destruction of the false gift, but of course is not believed, thanks to Apollo's curse (see p. 100). Then the priest Laokoön echoes Cassandra's view; but Apollo sends two sea-serpents to devour his children (and, according to some accounts, Laokoön himself). All agree that this is an omen, but it is interpreted, as omens usually are, in the light of the observers' various expectations, either as a confirmation of Laokoön's impiety or as an anticipation of Troy's imminent fall. One last hurdle remains to be overcome by the Greek force, as the ever-untrustworthy Helen circles the horse, imitating the voices of the wives of the Greek heroes. Once more it is Odysseus who is equal to the test, as he stops the mouth of one soldier who is about to call out in reply to his 'wife'.

Having hauled the horse into the city, the heedless Trojans sleep. What follows lays the basis for the next several stages in the unrolling of this sequence of myths. Countless Trojan men are slain, except for a fortunate few, such as Aineias ('Aeneas' in Latin), who escapes to find a future in Latium in Italy, and Antenor, who had been conciliatory on the occasion of the embassy to Troy of Menelaos and Odysseus, and who was variously said to have founded Kyrene in Libya, or settlements on the sites of Venice and Padua. Otherwise virtually the only Trojans left alive in the city are women and children. The widows are allotted as slave concubines to their Greek captors, an act which stores up trouble for the future (especially in the case of Cassandra's assignment to Agamemnon).

The Greek victory is also marked by acts of signal cruelty and impiety, directed in particular at the surviving members of the Trojan royal family. Hektor's infant son Astyanax is hurled from the ramparts to his death, in callous mockery of his name ('Lord of the City'). Priam's daughter

Polyxena is sacrificed at the behest of the ghost of Achilles, who demands her death as a tribute to his honour. As for Cassandra, she is raped by Aias, the son of Oileus, as she clings for sanctuary to an image of Athene; no less ghastly is the slaughter of Cassandra's father Priam, by Achilles' son Neoptolemos, upon the altar of Zeus. Such intolerable dishonour to a divinity will bear bitter fruit, in the form of divine intervention to shatter the Greeks' homecoming.

The Greeks return home

The English word 'nostalgia' has acquired a romantic patina, but its Greek semantic roots have, in combination, a harsher edge: *nostos* means 'return journey', and *algos* means 'pain'. Painful indeed were the returns of most of the Greek expeditionary force. Aias son of Oileus, violator of Cassandra, had his ship struck by Zeus' thunderbolt, and was then destroyed by Poseidon's trident. Many others less culpable than he were also shipwrecked, misled by a beacon treacherously lit by Nauplios at the southern tip of Euboia (he was avenging the death of his son Palamedes, who had seen through Odysseus' attempt to avoid the call-up, and whose death Odysseus had then contrived).

Even those who were not killed wandered far and wide. Some never made it back to Greece, instead founding new settlements far from their homeland: Diomedes and Philoktetes, for example, were said to have settled in southern Italy. Through such stories, Greek colonial foundations laid claim to connections with the motherland; mythical genealogy was a powerful mental tool for recognizing but also managing differences between peoples, by incorporating those differences into a structured lineage of related identities.

Nor was life uncomplicated for the Greeks who did reach home. Menelaos was shipwrecked by a storm which drove him to Egypt; his eventual return to Sparta brought him an uneasy life at home with Helen. Agamemnon's return to Mycenae was to be even more dramatic (see p. 151). But the most famous *nostos* of all was that of Odysseus. His awe-inspiring journey back to Ithaca was in some ways

(Above) Achilles' son Neoptolemos drives his sword into the throat of Polyxena, youngest daughter of Priam. Her death had been demanded by the ghost of Achilles, onto whose tomb spurts the blood of the dying maiden. Attic vase, c. 560 BC.

(Below) The Death of Priam, c. 1787–90, a plaster relief by the Italian neoclassical sculptor Antonio Canova.

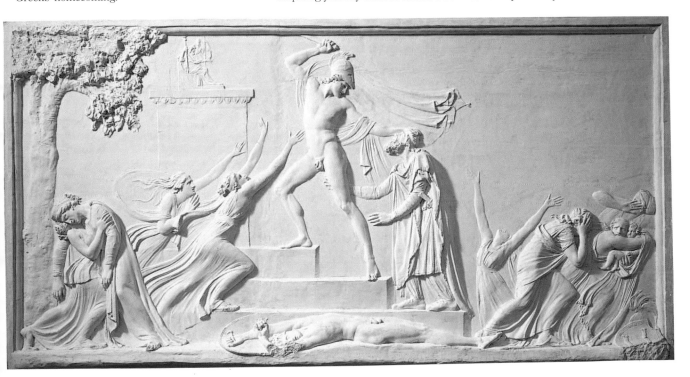

comparable with the voyage of the *Argo*, yet differed from it in crucial respects: its focus was not a vessel, but an individual man, and the objective was not a far-off, golden treasure, but simply the prize of going home.

The *Odyssey*

The narrative of Odysseus' return is known to posterity thanks above all to the second monumental poem attributed to Homer: the *Odyssey*. Although scholars have analysed countless similarities and differences between the *Iliad* and the *Odyssey*, the one point which concerns us here involves temporality. In brief: the narrative chronology of the *Odyssey* is far more intricate than that of the *Iliad*. When the *Odyssey* opens, its hero is nearly at the end of his wanderings. He is being detained by the enchantress Kalypso on her island; when, after several years, the gods persuade her to let him depart, he undertakes the penultimate stage of his voyage, to the land of the Phaeacians. It is only now – in Books 9 to 12 (out of a total of 24 Books) – that the narrative reverts to the first part of Odysseus' travels, beginning with the sack of Troy. Once that tale is told (in Odysseus' own words), the Phaeacians convey him to his home in Ithaca. The poem's chronology is complex, enabling an elaborate series of thematic cross-references to be set up; in the interests of clarity of exposition our own reconstruction of Odysseus' *nostos* will follow the 'actual' chronology of events.

After leaving Troy, Odysseus and his ships sail northwestwards. They put in first at Ismaros in Thrace, home of the Kikonian people. Odysseus' behaviour here replicates his actions at Troy: the city is sacked, many of the male inhabitants are killed, and their wives and goods are shared out among the victors. At least Odysseus avoids the costly mistake which Agamemnon made at Troy, for he spares Maron, Apollo's priest, who in gratitude presents him with a wonderfully sweet red wine; this gift will soon save Odysseus' life. But on balance the stay at Ismaros heralds the disasters which will beset this *nostos*. Odysseus' imprudent companions linger too long in order to enjoy themselves, so giving the Kikonians time to regroup. In the end Odysseus and his men effect their escape, but only after losing many of their number in battle.

A return to Ithaca from the Aegean entails rounding the southern Peloponnese and then heading north. But homecoming is not to be so simple. Zeus sends a tempest; then, off Cape Maleia, adverse currents sweep the ships out of the known world. After nine days – a recurring 'punctuation mark' in the *Odyssey*, marking the time between major landfalls – they reach the country of the Lotus Eaters. On Odysseus' journeyings, one of the most important markers of cultural difference is food. To eat 'the honey-sweet fruit of the lotus' – and not, therefore, to follow the normal Greek ways of 'bread-eating men' – leads one to forget one's *nostos*; Odysseus has to use force on those of his men who have tasted this exotic food, in order to drag them back into the ships, and towards the future.

Polyphemos

Next, a more aggressive adversary awaits: Polyphemos, the one-eyed giant whose preferred diet is raw human flesh. He belongs to the race of the Cyclopes, who dwell, each apart from the others, in mountain caverns, occupying themselves with the deceptively tranquil life of herding. If food is one central concern of the *Odyssey*, another is hospitality: more specifically, the treatment of strangers, suppliants and beggars by the communities in whose midst they present themselves. Instead of offering the new arrivals food and shelter, as he should have done, before presuming to enquire about their identity, Polyphemos immediately greets them with the abrupt question, 'Strangers, who are you?' Odysseus' reply shrewdly omits his own name; he pretends that his ship has been destroyed (in fact, when Odysseus went inland to spy out the country, he left many of his shipmates on the shore). Polyphemos' gleeful response is to snatch up some of Odysseus' men, dash out their brains on the floor of his cave, and devour them; he then blocks the Greeks' exit from the cave with a mighty boulder.

Odysseus uses several ruses to prepare his escape. To begin with, he assures Polyphemos that his name is Outis ('Nobody'). Then he gets the Cyclops drunk with Maron's sweet wine. Next he organizes his men to put out the giant's eye with a heated and sharpened olive-wood stake. When Polyphemos' fellow-Cyclopes approach to ask why he is crying out in pain, he replies, 'Nobody (i.e. Outis) is killing me'; at which they let him alone, assuming his illness to be of the mind rather than the body. Finally – for the cave-mouth is still blocked by the boulder – Odysseus and his men sling themselves beneath the sheep which the Cyclops keeps in his cave. When he lets the animals out to pasture, the giant feels the back of each to check for escapers – but does not have the wit to check under their bellies. Before sailing away, Odysseus cannot resist calling out his real name to Polyphemos – thus giving the giant the opportunity to beg his father Poseidon to load further hardships upon his puny adversary for the rest of his *nostos*. But Odysseus too has his influential backers. From this point on, his journey is poised between the aggressive rage of the mighty sea-god and the defensive aid of Athene, who stands beside him now, as she did at Troy.

Aiolos

The episode of the Kikonians illustrates the contrast between the wariness of Odysseus and the imprudence of his men. The same contrast recurs to even more destructive effect in the next stage of the

journey, the visit to the floating isle of Aiolos, god of the winds. This island is a kind of ordered paradise, where the moral rules are idiosyncratic: Aiolos' six sons are married to his six daughters. Corresponding to this geometrically perfect domestic equilibrium is its meteorological equivalent: Aiolos has power over all the winds from every direction. Having entertained Odysseus hospitably, Aiolos gives him a bag containing all the winds, to enable him to control his own passage home. But Odysseus' men cannot restrain their curiosity: believing the bag to contain treasure, they open it. The winds burst out and blow the ships back to Aiolos' kingdom; but this time the Greeks receive a sour welcome. Aiolos infers that the gods must be against Odysseus, and brusquely sends him on his way.

Circe

The inexorable reduction in Odysseus' circumstances continues with the next encounter, that with the giant Laistrygonians; all the ships are lost except that of Odysseus himself. He and his crew sail on, to an island every bit as extraordinary as that of Aiolos. On it there dwells the goddess Circe, whose name means 'Hawk'; and indeed, although she is human in form, her home is a place of metamorphosis. When some of Odysseus' men go to investigate the sign of smoke rising in the middle of a forest, they find a secluded house around which can be seen tame lions and wolves meekly moving about. These were formerly humans, but were

transformed by Circe's magic, which she now uses to change Odysseus' men to swine. Just one escapes to tell the tale; Odysseus sets out to free the rest. On his way he meets Hermes, in the likeness of a young man. As an antidote to Circe's powers the god gives Odysseus a marvellous plant, *moly*, black-rooted, with flowers of milky white. Since antiquity, countless scholars have tried to identify it, perhaps forgetting that it is a magic plant, and hence, like the ambrosia and nectar consumed by divinities, not a part of the everyday experience of mere mortals.

When Odysseus reaches Circe's house, she welcomes him with a potion, strikes him with a wand, and orders him to the sty to join his 'men'. But thanks to *moly*, Odysseus' shape remains human. Circe then urges Odysseus to make love with her, which he does, but only after (again on Hermes' instructions) making her swear an oath that she intends him no harm. Recognizing that she has met her match, Circe transforms Odysseus' men back to human form, and her island too undergoes a kind of symbolic metamorphosis, becoming a paradise in which the Greeks feast without care for a whole year. Yet their *nostos* has not quite been forgotten; at last they sail onward once more, aiming for an ultimate destination, less perfect but more real.

Odysseus visits the Underworld

Now comes the supreme test, at a port of call from which only such heroes as Herakles and Theseus have emerged unscathed. At the limit of the world, Odysseus and his men disembark and walk to a spot which Circe had described: the edge of the Underworld. By performing an animal sacrifice, Odysseus summons up the ghosts of the dead, who are attracted by the blood. Among the first is the blind seer Teiresias, who reveals experiences which still lie in store for Odysseus. Then, in a scene full of pathos, Odysseus converses with the ghost of his mother Antikleia, who died of grief as she pined for her absent son. She reassures Odysseus that his wife Penelope, his son Telemachos, and his father

(Above right) Polyphemos' favourite ram provides Odysseus with the means of escape from the giant's cave: the wily hero has hidden himself underneath the animal. Bronze relief, c. 550–500 BC.

(Above left) The blinding of the Cyclops Polyphemos: Odysseus, aided by his men, pushes a long pole into the giant's eye. The cup which Polyphemos is holding recalls the detail which made this attack possible: he has been made drunk by the wine which Odysseus gave him as a present. Vase from Eleusis, c. 670 BC.

The key to this image is in the bottom left-hand corner: the head of the blind prophet Teiresias is emerging from the Underworld. Odysseus, sitting on a rock, has just summoned Teiresias' ghost by sacrificing a ram. South Italian vase, early 4th century BC.

The birdlike Sirens fail to lure Odysseus' sailors to their death, since Odysseus alone (who is tied to the mast) can hear their fatally enticing voices. Below the ship's sail, one of the Sirens has thrown herself off a cliff – perhaps because the safe passage of Odysseus' vessel marks a defeat for the Sirens' power. Attic vase, c. 450 BC.

Laertes are all still alive, though in a poor state: Penelope weeps incessantly, while aged Laertes ekes out a pitifully squalid existence.

Next there is a stark reminder of the Trojan campaign, as the ghost of Agamemnon relates the gruesome outcome of his own *nostos* (see p. 151). Achilles, too, is there; he would, he tells Odysseus, rather work as the humblest labourer in the world of the living than be king of the gloomy realm of the dead. What has not changed is Achilles' concern, utterly typical of Greek heroes, for the reputation of his son Neoptolemos; when he hears from Odysseus about the young man's prowess in fighting, Achilles strides away in pride. Bound up with the heroic concern for reputation, of course, are the tensions and resentments which accompany failure. Such feelings underlie the next of Odysseus' encounters, that with the shade of Aias the son of Telamon.

Even in death Aias stands apart, still burning with hatred at his failure to be awarded Achilles' arms. Odysseus' compliments and expressions of regret have no effect: Aias stalks off into the darkness, without uttering a single word.

During his brush with the kingdom of Hades Odysseus catches sight of many others of the famous dead, but at last even he loses his nerve, undermined by a 'green fear' that Persephone might unleash a terrible monster against him. He returns to Circe's isle, but this time just for one day; perhaps – the poet may be suggesting – the hero's longing for Ithaca has been sharpened by what he has learned in the Underworld.

The Sirens; Skylla and Charybdis

In confirmation of the pattern which represents most of the Greeks' nightmare-figures as feminine, Odysseus' next adversaries on leaving Circe are the Sirens and the paired destroyers Skylla and Charybdis. The Sirens, depicted by post-Homeric sources as women above the waist and birds below it, are beautiful but lethal, for their hypnotically mesmerizing songs lure unsuspecting sailors to banish all thoughts of *nostos*, and to remain lethargically with the Sirens until death. On Circe's advice, Odysseus stops the ears of his comrades with wax, but leaves his own hearing unimpaired, in keeping with his insatiable curiosity to test his experience to the very limits. He orders his men to bind him to the mast, and to turn deaf ears to his pleas to be released when the Sirens begin their singing.

Equally dangerous, but without the Sirens' compensating allure, are Skylla and Charybdis, joint guardians of a precipitous and turbulent channel. They offer seafarers a choice of horrible deaths. Skylla is a cave-dwelling flesh-eater with twelve feet and six necks, each neck topped by a ghastly head; from her lair halfway up a cliff she springs out to seize and devour her wretched victims. Charybdis is a whirlpool whose sucking down and vomiting up no vessel can survive. Once again it is Circe's advice which enables Odysseus to come through the ordeal. As she had urged him to do, he sets course to avoid Charybdis, and, by deft steering and hard rowing, manages to get past Skylla, though with six of his comrades lost in the process.

Helios; Kalypso

Homer's narrative consistently alerts us to differences between Odysseus and his crew: from the outset, this is an individual *nostos*, not a collective one. The next episode places a conclusive seal upon this individuality. Odysseus' ship puts in to Thrinakia, an island belonging to the Sun god. Odysseus' men are starving, but Circe has warned that on no account should Helios' sacred cattle be eaten. When his crew disobediently slaughter and cook some of the beasts, the transgressive nature of their act manifests itself hideously, since the meat

bellows as if the animals were still alive. Little wonder that, as soon as the vessel puts to sea, Zeus' thunderbolt smashes it to oblivion. Odysseus alone survives, riding on the keel and the mast lashed together until, after the customary, symbolic interval of nine days, he comes ashore on Kalypso's island.

If Circe ('Hawk') had threatened to metamorphose Odysseus, Kalypso ('Concealer') proposes to excise him altogether from the narrative of his return, by detaining him for ever by her side. She even offers to make him immortal and ageless (thus going one step beyond Eos' gift to the immortal but senile Tithonos); but what a goddess can never provide is the solid reality of a mortal's home and family. Not that, at first, Odysseus declines the sexual delight that Kalypso can offer him; but in time his memories of Ithaca intensify. On his own he cannot break free, but at Athene's prompting – this is the moment at which the *Odyssey*'s intricate narrative begins – Zeus sends Hermes to persuade Kalypso to let her lover go. Practically as well as intellectually 'crafty', Odysseus constructs a raft, and sets out. However, there is one last deferral of the *nostos*: Poseidon, his thirst for vengeance unslaked, smashes the raft in a vicious storm. Alone, and half-dead with exhaustion, Odysseus manages to swim to a new shore.

Nausikaa

The island of Scheria, home of the Phaeacians, poses the greatest threat to Odysseus' return to Ithaca, because it most closely approximates to a place where Odysseus might settle down. The first Phaeacian whom he encounters – naked and caked with sea salt as he is – has the freshness, energy and exuberant beauty of the goddess Artemis herself: it is Nausikaa, daughter of Alkinoos and Arete, the king and queen of the Phaeacians. Not only is she lovely, but also thoughtful beyond her years: a younger version of Penelope. It may be a subtle piece of Homeric psychology when, near the end of the *Odyssey*, the returned Odysseus, reminiscing with his wife, mentions both Circe and Kalypso, but says not a word about Nausikaa. At any rate, Scheria has much to offer Odysseus: lavish hospitality; an audience avid to hear him sing of his adventures; the opportunity to show his athletic prowess in competition with the pick of the Phaeacians. There is even a bard, the blind Demodokos, whose lay about the Trojan Horse shows that Odysseus has become part of a myth in his own lifetime.

Yet Phaeacia is not Ithaca. Its people's characteristic occupation is seafaring (almost all the personal names, including Nausikaa's, relate to the sea or ships), yet this restless mobility cannot quite rival the poorer but more stable ruggedness of Odysseus' homeland. In the end the Phaeacians accept Odysseus' desire to leave, and convey him to Ithaca, suffering one last stroke of Poseidon's wrath for their pains, as the god turns their ship to stone (so that their mobility is for once replaced by stability) on its return journey.

Odysseus' return

The hero's arrival in Ithaca, secret and anonymous, prefigures his overall strategy for recovering his name and family. He proceeds with stealth, telling a whole series of false tales about his identity, warily attempting to discover who has been loyal and who not. In time he reveals himself to his son Telemachos and to the faithful goatherd Eumaios, but for the moment the only other individual in the know is Athene, his constant ally, cajoling, mocking, warning. As for Penelope, her loyalty seems rock-solid, but her position is in fact delicate. She is beset by suitors, who act on the assumption that Odysseus is dead. Were he in fact to be dead, the suitors' cause would be legitimate; but the *manner* of their suit would still be disgraceful, for they have installed themselves in Odysseus' palace and are eating and carousing there with no respect for their absent host; once more, the consumption of food is a significant marker of moral difference.

By presenting himself as a beggar, Odysseus gains admission to the household, and is even able

Skylla, shown in the lower half of the coin. Above she is a woman; further down she becomes two dogs; below that, she is a sea-snake. The Straits of Messina, between Sicily and the toe of Italy, were one traditional location for Skylla and the monstrous whirlpool Charybdis. Silver coin, late 5th century BC, Akragas (mod. Agrigento), Sicily.

(Below) Odysseus in disguise, half-crouching before his grieving wife Penelope, before she recognizes him. Terracotta relief, Melos, 5th century BC.

to converse at length with Penelope, to whom, however, he does not disclose himself. But he does assure her that Odysseus is nearby. While Penelope asserts that she does not believe this, there follows a remarkable decision on her part. She announces a contest: whoever strings Odysseus' formidable bow, and with it shoots an arrow through twelve axe-heads in a line, shall have her hand in (re-)marriage. Her motivation is unclear; generations of scholars have pored over the text of the *Odyssey* at this point, but the poem intriguingly leaves the issue open. At any rate, only the unknown beggar has the strength and skill to win the contest. Not only that: he reveals his identity, and takes bloody revenge on the suitors.

Neither Odysseus' vengeance, nor his profoundly moving reunions with his wife and father, are the end of the story. One of the most insistently recurring motifs which structure Greek mythology is the law-like regularity with which violent deeds beget violent reactions. The suitors have fathers and brothers: potential avengers. A battle ensues between those on Odysseus' side and those who would avenge the dead suitors. Where will it all end? The ending is arbitrary: Zeus' warning thunderbolt draws a line under the action. But the absence of narrative closure (as modern literary critics put it) leaves the way open for accounts of the sequel.

After the *Odyssey*

There is an intriguing group of tales which speculate about what happened to Odysseus and his family, tales whose thrust could hardly be predicted on the basis of the *Odyssey*. According to one such tale, Odysseus and Circe had a son, Telegonos ('Born Far Away'), who came to Ithaca in search of his father, but accidentally killed him. In an extraordinary and, on the face of it, emotionally implausible tying up of dynastic loose ends, Telegonos was said to have married Penelope, and Telemachos Circe.

More thought-provoking is a tradition according to which Penelope was seduced by one or other of the suitors, a variant which is a mirror-image of the 'alternative' Helen story, which reinvented her as a faithful wife who never went to Troy at all. Just how strong might be the slant put on myths by local

The Reunion of Odysseus and Penelope

The final proof which convinces Penelope that the stranger in her house is indeed Odysseus concerns their marriage bed. Odysseus alone knows its secret: that he had himself constructed it around the bole of an olive tree growing in the courtyard. When

Odysseus reveals his knowledge of this detail, Penelope is persuaded at last.

The simile with which the passage ends recalls the moment when, earlier in the *Odyssey*, the shipwrecked, salt-caked and exhausted Odysseus had come ashore in the land of the Phaeacians, to be chastely rescued by the princess Nausikaa. Now, back in Ithaca, Odysseus has a more enduring homecoming.

So he spoke, and her knees and the heart within her went slack
as she recognized the clear proofs that Odysseus had given;
but then she burst into tears and ran straight to him, throwing
her arms around the neck of Odysseus, and kissed his head, saying:
'Do not be angry with me, Odysseus, since, beyond other men,
you have the most understanding. The gods granted us misery,
in jealousy over the thought that we two, always together,
should enjoy our youth, and then come to the threshold of old age.
Then do not now be angry with me nor blame me, because
I did not greet you, as I do now, at first when I saw you.
For always the spirit deep in my own heart was fearful
that some one of mortal men would come my way and deceive me
with words. For there are many who scheme for wicked advantage.
For neither would the daughter born to Zeus, Helen of Argos,
have lain in love with an outlander from another country,
if she had known that the warlike sons of the Achaeans would
bring her
home again to the beloved land of her fathers.
It was a god who stirred her to do the shameful thing she

did, and never before had she had in her heart this terrible
wildness, out of which came suffering to us also.
But now, since you have given me accurate proof describing
our bed, which no other mortal man beside has ever seen,
but only you and I, and there is one serving woman,
Aktor's daughter, whom my father gave me when I came here,
who used to guard the doors for us in our well-built chamber;
so you persuade my heart, though it has been very stubborn.'

She spoke, and still more roused in him the passion for weeping.
He wept as he held his lovely wife, whose thoughts were virtuous.
And as when the land appears welcome to men who are swimming,
after Poseidon has smashed their strong-built ship on the open
water, pounding it with the weight of wind and the heavy
seas, and only a few escape the grey water landward
by swimming, with a thick scurf of salt coated upon them,
and gladly they set foot on the shore, escaping the evil;
so welcome was her husband to her as she looked upon him,
and she could not let him go from the embrace of her white arms.

tradition is demonstrated by an Arcadian legend which turned Penelope – sent away by Odysseus on the grounds of her adultery – into the lover of Hermes, by whom she became the mother of, of all creatures, the goatish god Pan.

As for the later career of Odysseus himself, we know of a number of variants (including that in which he died at the hands of his son Telegonos). Most myth-tellers agreed that Odysseus, ever the wanderer, left home once more and remarried on the mainland of northwest Greece, either in Thesprotia or Aitolia. But the *Odyssey* suggests another possibility. Teiresias predicts that Odysseus must go on a long journey inland, carrying an oar, to a place where people mistake the oar for a winnowing fan;

in other words, he must reverse his destiny, which has hitherto been dominated by the sea. At this inland spot he must placate Poseidon with a sacrifice, whereupon he may return to Ithaca. The prophecy concludes with the prediction that Odysseus will suffer a gentle death 'from the sea'. We do not know how the prophecy worked out in detail, but there is a symbolic neatness about it: from the moment that he feigned madness by sowing the ground *with salt*, Odysseus' fate has been inseparable from the element where Poseidon holds sway.

Odysseus is not a 'typical' hero; there is no such thing. His individual trademark is crafty intelligence. This lends to him, from the moral perspective, a certain ambiguity, since his ability to deceive can be interpreted positively, as enabling the overthrow of oppressive brute force, or negatively, as exalting shifty persuasiveness over forthright honesty. Indeed under the Athenian democracy of the late 5th century, a period when certain radical-democratic politicians were portrayed by their enemies as 'demagogues', Odysseus frequently appeared (for instance in Sophokles' tragedy *Philoktetes*) in this 'shifty' role. Yet side-by-side with his characterization as demagogue there survived the more complex image of the hero of the *Odyssey*: wily, courageous, reluctant to trust others, unfaithful yet devoted to his wife, insatiable in his testing of the limits of civilization through his exploration of the unknown.

Odysseus brought to warfare some of the reflectiveness and thoughtfulness characteristic of his patron deity Athene. On this cheek-piece from a helmet (c. 400 BC), the hero seems especially preoccupied; some interpreters have seen this as an illustration of the Homeric episode in which a pensive Odysseus gazes out over the sea, longing to be free from his confinement on Kalypso's isle.

Norms and Disruption

The present chapter focuses on a number of mythical lineages whose members, by their actions and sufferings, illustrate the bonds which unite families, and the tensions which tear them apart. What happens to the individuals in those families is 'exemplary', in the sense that it shows, albeit to an exaggerated degree, the kinds of pressures that may affect ordinary human beings in their everyday lives. For example, the House of Pelops and the House of Laios, which include such figures as Clytemnestra, Orestes, Oedipus and Antigone, provide extreme paradigms for crises in relationships between parents and children. Myths about these same individuals – and other myths, such as those involving Tereus and Prokne, Orpheus and Eurydice, Admetos and Alkestis – explore another central family relationship, that between husband and wife. Since throughout the world, despite innumerable variations, the family remains *the* fundamental feature of social organization, the durability of Greek myths is self-explanatory, since subsequent generations have been able to recognize and engage with the emotional world within which these astonishing events unfold.

But not every human relationship, in antiquity or today, can be circumscribed within the framework of male–female unions leading to the production of children. Same-sex partnerships are also part of the spectrum of human affective behaviour – and they received subtle and varied exploration in Greek mythology. Especially in view of the distinctive pattern exhibited by such relationships in ancient Greece, they will play a significant role in the story which this chapter will tell.

A family drama raised to an extraordinary level of brutality. Orestes' sword pierces the heart of his mother Clytemnestra, as her lover Aigisthos runs away in terror. Panel of a relief on a bronze tripod from Olympia, c. 570 BC.

The House of Pelops

Myrtilos, Oinomaos'
treacherous charioteer
(bottom right), has been
bribed to tamper with his
master's chariot; on this
south Italian vase (c. 350 BC)
he is shown holding one of
the wheels. Naked and heroic,
the seated Pelops has devised
this plot in order to defeat
Oinomaos in a chariot race,
so winning the right to marry
his daughter Hippodameia
(probably standing at the
far left).

Competing for honour and power

Several interwoven themes will occupy us in this
chapter. The first is *honour*. The desire to maintain
and enhance one's honour applies just as much to
the domestic sphere as to that of adventure and
warfare: shame occasioned by loss of honour drives
Phaidra to suicide, and Oedipus to another form of
self-harm (pp. 129, 165).

Connected to honour is the theme of *sexual
jealousy*. For a man, this may be indistinguishable
from a sense of diminished honour; for a woman,
it overlaps with a feeling of powerlessness, if she
perceives herself to be in danger of replacement by
a new, especially a younger, woman. Already we
have looked at the calamitous outcomes precipitated by the jealousy of Medea towards Jason
and of Deianeira towards Herakles; in the

present chapter we shall touch on the jealousy of
Clytemnestra towards Agamemnon.

A third theme, associated with both of the preceding two, is *power*. As we shall see, the struggles
between contending pairs of brothers (Atreus and
Thyestes, pp. 150–51; Eteokles and Polyneikes,
pp. 166–67) are played out in a way which takes
them far beyond mere sibling rivalry, since what is
at stake is also sovereignty over a kingdom.

A common emphasis in Greek myths, above all
those retold in tragedy, is the conflict between
strong but incompatible claims upon an individual
– or *competing claims*. While in everyday Greek life
these claims did not often result in disaster, in
myths more drastic outcomes prevail. Some of
these dilemmas are: (1) the conflict, for a child,
between the irreconcilable demands of its parents
(this is the dilemma of Orestes, pp. 152–53);
(2) the conflict between the claims of, on the one
hand, blood kin, and, on the other, one's wider
allegiance to the *polis* (this is an aspect of
Antigone's dilemma, p. 168); (3) the conflict, for a
woman, between the claims of her father and
those of her husband or lover (Ariadne and Medea
experience this, pp. 128, 112, as does Pelops' wife
Hippodameia, p. 149).

Finally, amid all this emphasis on conflict, we
must not forget that myths also celebrate the
strength of bonds between humans, whether
between lovers/spouses or between kin. Given that
myth-tellers love to explore extreme cases, it will
come as no surprise that these bonds are tested in
conditions of extraordinary difficulty, such as
the death of a spouse (for example, in the stories
of Protesilaos and Laodamia, p. 170, Admetos
and Alkestis, pp. 170–71, Orpheus and Eurydice,
pp. 171–73), or the strain imposed on the sibling
relationship in a situation of extreme violence.

The House of Pelops

Tantalos, ruler of Lydia, was one of the transgressors punished in exemplary fashion in the
Underworld (see p. 89); yet his crime implied, paradoxically, his proximity to the gods. He had been
honoured with the right to dine with the Olympians,
but abused this privilege in a manner both ghastly
and imprudent: he killed his own son Pelops, boiled
him, and served him up as the main dish. Although
the gods could not abolish historical fact, they
could, at least in this case, bring the dead back to
life. In his reconstituted form the boy was even more
handsome than before, although he did have a pros-
thetic shoulder made out of ivory, to replace the one
inadvertently eaten by grief-stricken Demeter,
whose thoughts were concentrated on the abduction
of her daughter Persephone.

Readers of Plato's dialogues will be familiar with
the cultural pattern according to which adolescent
Greek males bonded with older men in temporary
homoerotic relationships. It is misleading to

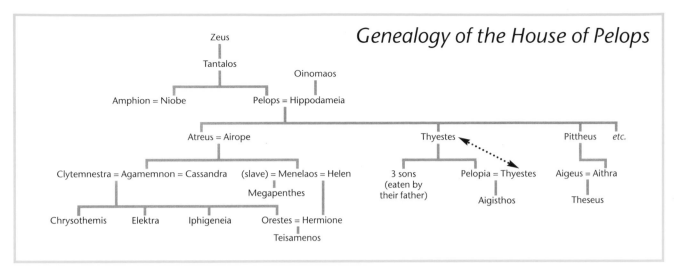

Zeus
Tantalos
Oinomaos
Amphion = Niobe   Pelops = Hippodameia
Atreus = Airope   Thyestes   Pittheus *etc.*
Clytemnestra = Agamemnon = Cassandra   (slave) = Menelaos = Helen   3 sons (eaten by their father)   Pelopia = Thyestes   Aigeus = Aithra
Megapenthes   Aigisthos   Theseus
Chrysothemis   Elektra   Iphigeneia   Orestes = Hermione
Teisamenos

describe such couples as 'homosexual', if that term is meant to designate a person whose sexual orientation is same-sex *for life*. In Greek society the normal assumption would have been that the younger partner would, in a later phase of his life, go on to marry and reproduce (see p. 174). Precisely such a two-stage development underlies the story of Pelops. As a youth of outstanding beauty he caught the eye of Poseidon (just as Ganymede had attracted Zeus). But as he grew up, Pelops' thoughts veered towards marriage, a direction which also involved him in a geographical move. Tantalos' kingdom of Lydia was, in the world of Greek mythology, deemed to be a part of a network of regions within a very broadly conceived area of Greek cultural influence. It was only to be expected, therefore, that Pelops should have been drawn to the heart of the southern Greek mainland in search of a bride.

The woman he sought was Hippodameia, daughter of Oinomaos king of Pisa (in the western Peloponnesian district of Elis). Her relationship with her father was an exaggeration of the normally close bond between father and daughter: one variant went so far as to portray their relationship as incestuous, whereas a 'weaker' variant had it that Oinomaos feared an oracle which predicted that he would die at the hands of his son-in-law. Either way, Oinomaos aimed to block the inevitable. He challenged each of his daughter's suitors to a chariot race, in which victory to Oinomaos would mean death to the suitor, though victory to the suitor would entitle him to marry Hippodameia.

Now Oinomaos, like Pelops, was close to the gods, and had been presented by Ares with a magnificent team of horses. In the face of such opposition, Pelops' only recourse was deception. He suborned Oinomaos' charioteer Myrtilos, who agreed to tamper with the axle-pins in his master's chariot wheels. Oinomaos duly crashed, and with his dying breath cursed Myrtilos. The charioteer's end was not slow in coming. Pursuing his career of deceit,

he turned against Pelops by attempting to rape Hippodameia; in response, Pelops hurled him into the sea, but not before Myrtilos had, in his turn, cursed Pelops and his descendants, a curse which would be worked out in the next phase of violence to afflict this unfortunate lineage.

For the moment, however, Pelops' power was supreme. It had been consolidated by a chariot victory, an image with double resonance. First, it dramatically magnified the imagery of the normal Greek wedding ceremony, in which the groom led/dragged the bride on to a cart or chariot, so as to convey her from her father's house to his own. Secondly, it affirmed the link between Pelops and the Olympic Games, which were held in Elean territory.

Pelops and Hippodameia being pursued by Oinomaos and Myrtilos. The scene is one of love yet also impending violence: the hovering figure of Eros symbolizes the love between Pelops and Hippodameia; but the spear which Hippodameia is brandishing expresses her hostility to her father. South Italian vase, c. 330 BC.

Pelops himself had a major shrine at Olympia, and was said by Pausanias to be 'revered by the Eleans as much more than the other heroes at Olympia as Zeus is revered more than the other gods.' As a final seal upon his sovereignty, he lent his name to the Peloponnese ('Pelops' Island').

Pittheus, Atreus and Thyestes

The three most renowned sons of Pelops and Hippodameia were Pittheus, Atreus and Thyestes. Of these, only Pittheus enjoyed the kind of good fortune of which his father could be proud. Pittheus' rule over the east Peloponnesian city of Troizen was celebrated for fairness and wisdom, some of which he transmitted to his grandson Theseus, whom he raised jointly with the boy's mother (Pittheus' daughter Aithra) until Theseus left to seek his father in Athens (see p. 126). But if Pittheus displayed the positive aspects of sovereignty, his brothers Atreus and Thyestes embodied the negative. Their bitter enmity expressed itself in ways which utterly distorted family relationships, and sowed the seeds of further violent disruption in the next two generations.

After the death of Herakles' persecutor Eurystheus, rule over Mycenae was to devolve, according to the prediction of an oracle, upon a descendant of Pelops. But would it be Atreus or Thyestes? In this crisis, as in the story of the *Argo*, the indicator of talismanic authority was a golden fleece. Once Atreus had made a vow to sacrifice the finest lamb in his flock to Artemis; however, when a golden lamb miraculously appeared, he cheated the goddess by concealing the marvellous beast when he had killed it, sacrificing to the goddess an ordinary beast in its stead. Breaking a bargain with a divinity is a sure path to ruin; and so it proved. Atreus' wife Airope was conducting an adulterous affair with Thyestes, to whom she revealed the secret of the lamb – which he then stole. When Thyestes persuaded Atreus to agree that rule over Mycenae should fall to whichever brother possessed a golden lamb, Thyestes' deception enabled him to take the throne.

But the balance of power between the brothers was permanently precarious, and liable to collapse into dissension. (According to a variant of the lamb episode, it had been Hermes, father of Myrtilos, who had sent the marvellous animal, in order to provoke acrimony amongst Pelops' descendants.) Zeus now intervened – as in the days of Tantalos, the gods remained, for good or ill, closely involved in the family's affairs – to urge Atreus to propose a counter-bargain with Thyestes, a bargain whose basis was even more miraculous than that relating to the lamb. The understanding was that Atreus would be king if the Sun temporarily reversed its course so as to set in the east – which it naturally then did, under Zeus' influence.

Although Atreus now held the reins of public power, Thyestes' adultery with Airope still gave him a domestic advantage over his brother. But when Atreus found out, his revenge harked back to the hideous precedent set by Tantalos. Summoning Thyestes to a meal which would ostensibly seal a fraternal reconciliation, Atreus served up to their father the minced and boiled body-parts of Thyestes' own children. In the gruesome symbolism of myth, Thyestes' coming-too-close to his brother's wife was punished by a coming-too-close to his own offspring. The scene would hang over the subsequent history of the house like a foul-smelling pall of smoke. Speaking in Aischylos' tragedy *Agamemnon* (the first play of the *Oresteia*), the visionary prophetess Cassandra sensed the still-active presence of the murdered children:

Do you see these young ones, sitting by the house,
looking like the shapes of dreams?
Children slain by their own kindred,
with their hands full of meat, their own flesh as food,
entrails and innards, a pitiable burden to carry,
clear to behold: food their father tasted.

Agamemnon and Menelaos

The central motif of the house's saga now shifts from sovereignty to vengeance. Thyestes' transgressive proximity to that from which he should have remained distant took a new twist when, in response to an oracle which predicted how his avenger would come into being, he fathered a son, Aigisthos, upon his own daughter Pelopia. It was this Aigisthos who killed Atreus, restoring the kingdom of Mycenae to Thyestes; Thyestes then banished Atreus' two sons, Agamemnon and Menelaos, in case they should threaten his reassumption of power.

Thyestes' story ends in anti-climax, in contrast to the hideous events which went before. He was removed from power by the Spartan king Tyndareos, whose daughters, Clytemnestra and Helen, were married to Agamemnon and Menelaos respectively. This quartet now inherited two motivations signally displayed by Atreus and Thyestes, namely the inclination to transgression and the drive for vengeance. In addition, the experiences of this new generation, especially as explored in the tragedies of Aischylos, Sophokles and Euripides, illustrate two additional themes: the seemingly ineluctable manner in which the past shapes the future, like a net from whose mesh one can never be free; and the crushing burden of guilt which threatens to drag down, and even drive insane, the successful avenger.

The brothers Agamemnon and Menelaos were not locked into the kind of mutual hatred which estranged Atreus from Thyestes. It was their marriages, and not sibling rivalry, which undermined their households. During Agamemnon's absence at Troy, Clytemnestra took Aigisthos as her lover. Various versions attribute different motives to her, including grief-stricken anger at Agamemnon's sacrifice of their child Iphigeneia, or a transgressive desire to warm a cold bed; and when Agamemnon returned from Troy with Cassandra as his concubine, the situation was made worse still. The outcome was a grim parody of the appropriate welcome for a victorious conqueror, for Clytemnestra and/or Aigisthos (sources ascribe the deed variously to one or both of them) murdered the defenceless Agamemnon. According to one account, he was slain in his bath, in the act of symbolically cleansing himself from the accumulation of ten years of bloodshed at Troy.

Bloodshed – the story of Pelops' lineage affirms it at every turn – begets more bloodshed. After Agamemnon's murder, his son Orestes was sent far away from Mycenae to minimize the risk of his assuming the role of avenger; by contrast, Orestes'

One of the recurring motifs in Aischylos' Oresteia trilogy is that of the 'net' of the past, from which the characters cannot break free. Agamemnon himself was 'netted' when Clytemnestra entangled him in a robe as he stepped out of the bath. In this image (Attic vase, c. 470 BC) the leading role in the murder is taken by Aigisthos, Clytemnestra's lover. His sword has already struck once, as the wound in Agamemnon's body reveals. The gesticulating figure to the right may be Agamemnon's daughter Elektra.

Orestes slays his mother Clytemnestra. Having wounded her already in the breast, Orestes now prepares to strike the fatal second blow. Silver seal (end of 5th century BC).

sister Elektra stayed at home, powerless and burning with rancour. Grown to adolescence, Orestes returned, and with Elektra carried out the expected vengeance-killing of Aigisthos, compounded by the almost unthinkable matricide of Clytemnestra. The extreme nature of the myth's narrative pushes us ever further, until we can no longer imagine where it will all end.

It was to be anticipated that Orestes would be pursued to the brink of insanity by the repulsive Erinyes ('Furies'), the deities who incite the avenging of blood murder (see pp. 86–87). Yet from another angle Orestes was doing the right, indeed the only thing he could: avenging his father. As his wanderings unfold, certain narrative details spell out the anomaly and ambiguity of his condition. He can argue that, through the passage of time and as a result of ritual purifications, he is no longer polluted by his crimes; and yet the Furies continue to hound him as one who is still tainted. He can be accepted as a guest in Athens; and yet no one will talk to him, for fear of becoming tainted themselves. And when, as represented in the third play of the *Oresteia*, a special Athenian court is consti-

tuted in order to evaluate this extraordinary case, the jury of twelve men is evenly divided about whether to condemn or acquit, so that it takes the unique voice of Athene to resolve the matter. She intervenes to find a one-off solution: being herself born from Zeus alone, she promotes the father's parental role over the mother's, and casts her vote in favour of acquittal. Potentially such an outcome might have drawn the Furies' vengeance upon Athens, but Athene's combination of strength with tact persuades the dread goddesses to accept a revered place within the city. *Ad hoc* though this verdict may be, it allows all the protagonists to emerge with honour, an even more important outcome, in this culture of 'saving face', than the nice apportioning of justice.

'Just' or not, this conclusion to the bloodshed within the Pelopid family does re-impose order. The same is true if we follow through the variant of the story according to which Iphigeneia is substituted with a deer instead of being sacrificed at Aulis. As the episode is retold by Euripides in his play *Iphigeneia in Tauris*, Orestes and Iphigeneia are reunited in a far-off country, but both at last return to their Greek homeland. The failed *nostos* (return)

Athene Persuades the Furies

In *Eumenides*, the third play of Aischylos' *Oresteia* trilogy, the acquittal of Orestes risks bringing dishonour upon his unsuccessful accusers, the Furies. The future of Athens – where the acquittal took place – is thus balanced on a knife edge, since the Furies seem bent on unleashing their anger upon the Athenians by sending a blight upon the city. But Athene's persuasion triumphs over wrath and venom, so turning the Erinyes ('Furies') into the Eumenides ('Kindly Ones'). (In this extract, the Furies are referred to in the singular, because one goddess speaks on behalf of all her sisters.)

Furies	That I should suffer this! Ah! That I, with my primordial wisdom, should dwell in this land dishonoured and loathed! Ah! I breathe forth all anger and wrath against you! Ah! Woe! What pain penetrates my ribs! O mother Night, the irresistible tricks of the gods have robbed me of my ancient privileges, and made me of no account.
Athene	I shall not tire of speaking blessings to you, that you may never say that you, an elder goddess, were cast out dishonoured from this land by me, a younger divinity, and this city's mortal dwellers. If you hold sacred the mighty power of Persuasion - the honeyed enchantment of my tongue - then you will stay. But if you decline to do so, then you would not rightly launch your anger or wrath upon this city, nor send hurt upon its army. For you have the right to be a landholder here, being justly honoured for all time.
Furies	Goddess Athene, what dwelling do you say I shall have?
Athene	One free from all pain; accept it.
Furies	Suppose I do accept – what privilege awaits me?
Athene	That no home shall prosper without your aid.
Furies	Will you bring this about – that I shall have such power?
Athene	I shall grant good fortune to all who revere you.
Furies	And will you pledge me this for all time?
Athene	I am free not to promise what I shall not fulfil.
Furies	It seems you will enchant me; my rage abates.
Athene	And so, a dweller in this land, you will have us as your friends.

(Left) Apollo holds a piglet above Orestes' head: the god is about to use the animal's blood in a ritual of purification, to cleanse Orestes from the miasma *(pollution) of matricide. To the right stands Artemis, Apollo's sister. Partly visible to the left is one of the Erinyes (Furies) who have come to Delphi in pursuit of Orestes. South Italian vase, c. 390–380 BC.*

of Agamemnon prolongs the horrors of Tantalos, Atreus and Thyestes; Orestes, by contrast, after all his torment, at length reconnects with something of the past glory of Pelops.

Menelaos and Helen

In comparison with that of Agamemnon, the post-*nostos* history of Menelaos is uneventful indeed. Its details are inevitably inflected by the contrasting versions of Helen's story, regarding whether or not she 'really did' go to Troy (pp. 132–33). The most intriguing and nuanced account is that in the *Odyssey*. The reason why Menelaos and Helen figure at all in the narrative is that Odysseus' son Telemachos goes to Sparta early on in the epic (Book 4), in order to enquire about his father's whereabouts. At the moment of Telemachos' arrival, a double wedding feast is being celebrated, jointly for Hermione, the only child of Menelaos and Helen, and for Megapenthes, the son of Menelaos by a slave woman: Hermione is being sent to marry Achilles' son Neoptolemos, while Megapenthes is being betrothed to the daughter of a Spartan noble. There is rich symbolic appropriateness here: that Menelaos and Helen should have just one child, as if the affective bond between them could not sustain more offspring; and that Megapenthes ('Great Woe') should bear a name suggestive of Menelaos' domestic fortunes (one may compare the name of Dionysos' doomed adversary, Pentheus, 'Woe'). There is also irony: that there should be a wedding in progress in a house with such a troubled domestic past.

And yet, on the surface, domestic harmony has been re-established in Menelaos' household. The hospitality offered to Telemachos is exemplary, and Helen is the perfect hostess, 'looking like Artemis of the golden distaff' – not, for example, like sexy Aphrodite. However, if we look more closely, this apparent harmony masks latent unease. In order to make Telemachos feel honoured,

Menelaos and Helen recall some of Odysseus' exploits at Troy. Yet those exploits inevitably raise the delicate question of the role played at Troy by Helen, especially the episode in which she attempted to beguile the Greeks concealed within the Wooden Horse, by imitating the voices of their wives (p. 138). Surely these memories must sit uncomfortably with the reunited pairing of Menelaos and Helen? But no: for Helen has prepared the ground carefully:

Into the wine of which they were drinking she cast a drug
of heartsease, free of gall, to make one forget all sorrows,
and whoever had drunk it down once it had been mixed in
    the wine bowl,
for the day that he drank it would shed no tear down his
    cheeks,
not if his mother died and his father died, not if men
murdered a brother or a beloved son in his presence
with the bronze, and he with his own eyes saw it.

So this Odyssean Sparta is a place which in one important respect resembles both Circe's island and the Land of the Lotus Eaters. Helen's potions can blot out painful recollections; the link between past, present and future can be temporarily obliterated. Instead of coping with loss, Helen's guests are surreptitiously drugged into ignoring it.

By contrast with what went before, the end of the story of Menelaos and Helen has a degree of serenity about it. Both were said to have been made immortal; Helen certainly received worship as a goddess, especially in Sparta and its vicinity, and one variant had it that the two of them enjoyed a post-mortem existence in the (variously located) region known as Elysion (see p. 213). Among their descendants, too, there was a certain drawing together of strands, as if to heal some of the pain suffered by earlier members of the Pelopid dynasty. According to one variant, Hermione, the pair's daughter, married Orestes after the death of her first husband Neoptolemos, so that two branches of the family tree intertwined.

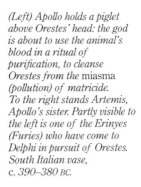

This Boiotian cup (c. 420 BC) offers a satirical view of two encounters occurring during the capture of Troy. At the far left is Cassandra, who has sought refuge from Aias (the son of Oileus) at an altar. To the right are a distracted Helen and a profoundly unheroic Menelaos, reunited after years of separation.

Tereus, Prokne and Philomela

Immortalization, such as that of Helen and Menelaos, was one way in which a hero(ine)'s continuing power after death could be imagined. Another way involved a different sort of change, in which the transfigured individual forsook human form for that of, for instance, an animal, a plant, a rock or a star. A graphic example is provided by the saga of Tereus, Prokne and Philomela, a tale of cruelty every bit as disturbing as that associated with Atreus and Thyestes.

The villain of the piece is Tereus, king of Thrace, a region which Greeks from further south tended to characterize as savage; corresponding to this 'wild' provenance was Tereus' genealogy as son of the uncontrollable war-god Ares. It was Tereus' own prowess in war which first involved him with Pandion, one of the mythical kings of Athens. In return for Tereus' military assistance, Pandion offered him his daughter Prokne in marriage, and in due course the couple had a son, Itys. But Tereus' transgressive character soon manifested itself, in a manner which heaped violence upon infidelity. He lusted after Prokne's sister Philomela, raped her, and hid her away; not only that but, in an act which the post-classical literary and artistic tradition would retell with a kind of horrified fascination, he cut out Philomela's tongue in an effort to silence her.

However, one of the family relationships to whose strength several Greek myths testify is that between sister and sister. Normally this was superseded by the marriage-bond, but, if the marriage went wrong, the sister–sister bond

Metamorphoses

Some Heroes and Heroines Transformed into Animals, Plants or Stones

Adonis	anemone (sprung from his blood)
Aktaion	stag
Arachne	spider
Atalanta and Melanion	lions
Daphne	laurel
Hekabe	bitch
Hyakinthos	*hyakinthos* (lily-like flower sprung from his blood)
Io	cow
Kadmos and Harmonia	snakes
Kallisto	bear
Keyx and Alkyone	tern and 'halcyon' (? kingfisher)
Kyknos	swan
Lykaon	wolf
Minyads, i.e. daughters of Minyas	night birds, or bats
Narkissos	narcissus flower
Niobe	rock
P(e)leides (women pursued by Orion)	doves, then stars
Philomela	swallow
pirates who oppose Dionysos	dolphins (see illustrations, pp. 19, 82)
Prokne	nightingale
Teiresias	woman; then back into man
Tereus	hoopoe
Tithonos	cicada
women who mourned Meleager	guinea-fowl (*meleagrides*)

(Left) *The rape and mutilation of Philomela by her sister's husband Tereus – one of the most brutal narratives in all Greek mythology – is rarely depicted; on this Attic cup (c. 490–480 BC), Prokne and Philomela prepare to kill Itys, son of Tereus and Prokne. Philomela – mute after Tereus cut out her tongue – expresses herself by animated gestures.*

resurfaced in all its power. The mute Philomela found a way to communicate with Prokne: by weaving a tapestry, she used images to narrate her violation. What happened next put the normal sequence of virginity–marriage–childbearing into reverse: setting sisterhood above both marriage and even motherhood, Prokne killed her own child Itys, dismembered his corpse, and fed it to her villainous husband.

The actions of Tereus and Prokne, and the sufferings of Philomela, put them beyond the merely human, into an 'exemplary' category, though not of course a category of exemplary *virtue*. Their deeds and sufferings were prolonged indefinitely, through metamorphosis into birds. Tereus became a hoopoe, whose cry of '*pou? pou?*' ('Where? Where?') eternally replicated his anguished question about the whereabouts of his son. Prokne became a nightingale, ceaselessly lamenting her lost Itys. The tongueless Philomela turned into a swallow, flitting and swooping in perpetual restlessness, with no melody to sing.

(Below) *The ferocious wildness of the dismemberment of Itys is powerfully conveyed in* The Banquet of Tereus *by Rubens (c. 1636–38). Clad as bacchic revellers, Prokne and Philomela confront Tereus with the evidence of the crime they have committed. Prokne has the boy's head in her arms; Tereus kicks over the table in horror – for the meal he has just eaten contained the cooked remains of his son.*

155

Antiope and Her Sons

(Below) Greek tragedy and Greek visual art may sometimes echo one another. Here the vase-painter's treatment of the Antiope myth seems to reflect a play by Euripides (which survives to us only in fragments). The twins Amphion and Zethos are taking vengeance on Lykos, while their mother Antiope (on the right) looks on. The Dionysiac context of this episode is hinted at by the pantherskin draped over the entrance to the cave. Sicilian vase, early 4th century BC.

The next complex of stories illustrates some of the characteristic ways in which relationships within a mythological family are shaped by the larger issue of humanity's interaction with the gods. At the centre of the drama is Antiope, one of countless mortal women sexually pursued by Zeus. Her situation partially resembles that of Io (see p. 98), in that the discovery of her pregnancy led her father Nykteus ('Night') to drive her away. Antiope's wanderings did not, however, lead, as Io's did, to metamorphosis, but to a temporary alleviation: from her Theban home she fled to Sikyon, where the king, Epopeus, married her. But her Theban origins reasserted themselves. Before Nykteus died – some said it was by suicide, from depression at his

daughter's behaviour – he ordered his brother Lykos ('Wolf') to exact due punishment from the erring Antiope. Having killed her husband, Lykos forcibly brought her back to Thebes, where he and his equally vindictive wife Dirke imprisoned her. Yet for a woman worthy of Zeus' bed this could not be the end of the story. She had borne him twins, Amphion and Zethos, but had been compelled by Lykos to abandon them in the wild. However, by a familiar mythical logic they had been discovered by a herdsman, who raised them himself. Their role on reaching manhood was to avenge Antiope's mistreatment: after freeing her, they killed Lykos, and brutally dispatched Dirke by binding her to a bull.

But this apparently 'complete' saga has several further twists. Dirke was to gain a kind of immortality, when she lent her name to the Theban stream into which Amphion and Zethos had tossed her corpse. Antiope, it might be thought, had earned an building the walls of Thebes, they each knew great personal sorrow. Amphion's wife was Niobe, who rashly boasted of her own fecundity compared with that of Leto, the mother of Apollo and Artemis; she was punished when the divine twins slaughtered every one of her many offspring, after which her depressive immobility caused her to solidify into a rock. Zethos too passed away in grief when his wife Thebe (who gave her name to the city) unwittingly brought about the death of their son. Death from sadness is a recurring theme in the story of this family.

(Left) Artemis and Apollo avenge their mother Leto after she has been insulted by Niobe's boasting. Some of the arrows have already found their mark, as the bodies of two of Niobe's children testify. The anonymous painter of this Attic vase (c. 450 BC) has been named the Niobid Painter, thanks to his powerful rendering of this example of divine vengeance.

(Right) This eloquent marble statue depicts one of the dying children of Niobe; she has been shot in the back. The statue was found in Rome; originally it may have formed part of the pediment of a classical Greek temple, though we do not know which one.

even more glorious memory, to match her blamelessness. Yet Greek myths rarely deal in unalloyed virtue. In Antiope's case, what clouded the sky was a circumstance connected with the murder of Dirke: when Amphion and Zethos had tied her to the bull, she had been on the point of doing the same to Antiope as an act of maenadic worship for Dionysos. No god could tolerate interference with his worship, and the niceties of Antiope's 'innocence' did not outweigh Dionysos' sense of grievance. So poor Antiope was persecuted by the god, who sent her wandering in madness – again her story echoes Io's – until another mortal (Phokos from Phokis, this time) took her in as his wife; when death eventually came to the couple they were, according to Pausanias, buried in the same grave.

As for Amphion and Zethos, their later history was no more unrelievedly joyful than was that of their mother. Although they had the honour of

157

Danaos and His Kin

The city of Argos was no more immune to family disruption than was any other location within the Greek mythological landscape. This becomes clear if we look at the deeds and sufferings of the descendants of Io, the Argive priestess pursued by Zeus. Io's child by her divine lover was Epaphos (see p. 98), who was born in Egypt, where Io's wanderings reached their term. The lineage which he founded illustrates how, in the world of mythological narrative, Greece was not hermetically sealed off from surrounding peoples, but was, rather, genealogically interfused with them. Epaphos' marriage to a daughter of the Nile established a definitive link with Egypt; their descendants included Libya (eponym of an area of north Africa) and her twin sons by Poseidon: Agenor, who became ruler of Phoenicia, and Belos, who remained in Egypt.

It was the sons of Belos who were to shift the focus of Io's descent back once more to the Greek homeland; and it was they who were to exemplify the theme of family disruption. Belos' sons were Danaos and Aigyptos. Like many another pair of royal mythological brothers, they quarrelled over power – in this case, over the sovereignty of Egypt. The preciseness of the balance between their respective claims expressed itself through the symmetry

of their families: Aigyptos had fifty sons, Danaos fifty daughters. Yet such symmetry was less exact than it might appear, for in any power struggle males were, in Greek perception, far superior to females. And so it came about that Danaos and his daughters fled from Egypt in the direction of Danaos' ancestral homeland of Argos. There Danaos took over power from its then ruler, an act confirmed by an ominous happening when a wolf (signifying 'dominant outsider') killed a bull (signifying 'leader of the resident population'). Thereafter, such was Danaos' authority that his name became applied not just to the people of Argos, but to Greek speakers more widely: 'Danaans' is one of the appellations used in Homeric poetry to designate the Greeks as a whole.

Aigyptos could not bear to let Danaos' power remain intact, even in far-away Greece. His fifty sons pursued their fifty cousins, bent on a collective marriage for which the girls had no inclination. In the 'extreme' language which Greek mythology favours, the outcome was an astonishing act of collective resistance: at their father's behest, Danaos' daughters slew their husbands on the wedding night. The exception was Hypermestra, who spared her husband Lynkeus in recognition of the respect which he had shown her. Here, then, is another thought experiment: should Hypermestra have disobeyed her father, or killed her husband? This dilemma seems to have been explored in the third play of a trilogy by Aischylos, in which (on one possible reconstruction of the fragmentary final play) the goddess Aphrodite may have intervened to sanction the conduct of Hypermestra, for the reason that, without the sexual union between married couples,

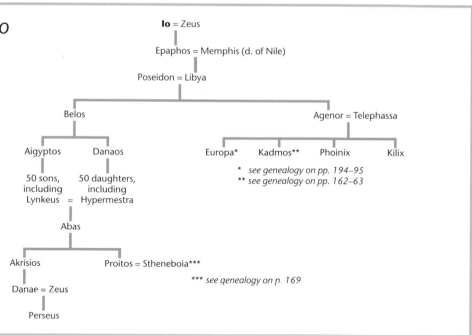

Descendants of Io

Io was variously said to be the daughter of Inachos (an Argive river), or of Iasos the son of Asopos (another local river), or of Peiren (a son of Argos – i.e. the eponymous embodiment of the city). Each of these variants expresses Io's rootedness in the local community.

Io = Zeus
Epaphos = Memphis (d. of Nile)
Poseidon = Libya
Belos — Agenor = Telephassa
Aigyptos — Danaos — Europa* — Kadmos** — Phoinix — Kilix
50 sons, including Lynkeus = 50 daughters, including Hypermestra
* see genealogy on pp. 194–95
** see genealogy on pp. 162–63
Abas
Akrisios — Proitos = Stheneboia***
*** see genealogy on p. 169
Danae = Zeus
Perseus

John William Waterhouse,
The Danaïdes, *1904. The
Danaids' eternal punishment
for murdering their husbands
is to pour water into a leaking
container in a fruitless
attempt to fill it. In spite of
their exertions they manage
to retain a languid beauty in
this painting.*

there can be no households and thus no future for humanity. At any rate, Lynkeus and Hypermestra were the future: their coruscating lineage would include both Perseus and Herakles.

What of the remainder of the Danaids? One of them, Amymone, was raped by Poseidon. As for the others, their apparent justification for their act of collective murder is thoroughly occluded by their posthumous fate. As their punishment in the Under-world, they were compelled perpetually to try to fill a leaking water-jar. Given that the drawing of water from the local spring was, alongside weaving and cooking, one of the typical duties expected of the Greek wife, the symbolism of the Danaids' punishment implies that the ultimate negation of wifehood – murder of one's husband – must be redressed by a ceaseless, albeit fruitless, effort to make good one's deficiency.

Proitos, Stheneboia and Bellerophon

The next instance of acute domestic upheaval involves several familiar themes: a quarrel between brothers, in this case twins; an attempted false accusation by a vindictive woman (reminiscent of the story of Phaidra and Hippolytos); a young hero sent away on a potentially fatal monster-slaying mission. What makes this tale unique is the addition of a magical creature: the flying horse Pegasos.

Lynkeus and Hypermestra had twin grandsons, Akrisios and Proitos. After the inevitable quarrelling – they were said to have been the inventors of shields – they reached an agreement whereby Akrisios should retain power in Argos, while Proitos took nearby Tiryns. Akrisios' misfortunes were determined from the moment when his daughter Danae caught the eye of Zeus (see p. 98). Proitos' family too was the focus of trouble. For one thing, his daughters offended a divinity (either Dionysos or Hera) and were punished with madness; but at least the sequel was less horrific than in the case of the daughters of Kadmos (see p. 61), since the girls' wits were eventually restored (though not without Proitos' eldest daughter having met her death).

If the problems unleashed by Proitos' daughters were of a directly religious nature, those provoked by his wife Stheneboia grew from an all-too-human emotional situation: unrequited love. The object of her affection was the young hero Bellerophon. Having committed involuntary homicide in his own community at Corinth, Bellerophon was accepted

The monstrously hybrid Chimaira was a popular motif in Etruscan art. This bronze sculpture, dating from the late 5th century BC, is a fine example. The goat has a wound in the upper part of its neck, perhaps inflicted by Bellerophon.

into the city of Tiryns, where Stheneboia conceived a passion for him. In a story-pattern parallel to that of the biblical tale of Potiphar's wife, Stheneboia reacted duplicitously to Bellerophon's rejection of her advances, by alleging to Proitos that it had been Bellerophon who had tried to seduce *her*. Proitos fought (alleged) deception with deception, for he dispatched Bellerophon to Lycia, to the court of Stheneboia's father Iobates, bearing a letter in which Proitos urged Iobates to put Bellerophon to death. Iobates responded with a tactic which echoed that employed by Pelias towards Jason, and by Eurystheus towards Herakles: he sent the unwelcome hero out on an apparently hopeless quest.

Bellerophon and the Chimaira

Bellerophon's adversary was the Chimaira, the equal of any monster confronted by Jason or even Herakles: usually imagined as lion at the front, serpent at the rear, and fire-breathing goat in the middle, it was a hideous hybrid whose parents were, appropriately enough, the monstrous pair Typhon and Echidna. But Bellerophon had a secret weapon in the form of the flying horse Pegasos, which enabled him successfully to complete this and other tasks which Iobates set him. Indeed, in recognition of the hero's prowess Iobates ignored the lethal provisions of Proitos' letter and offered

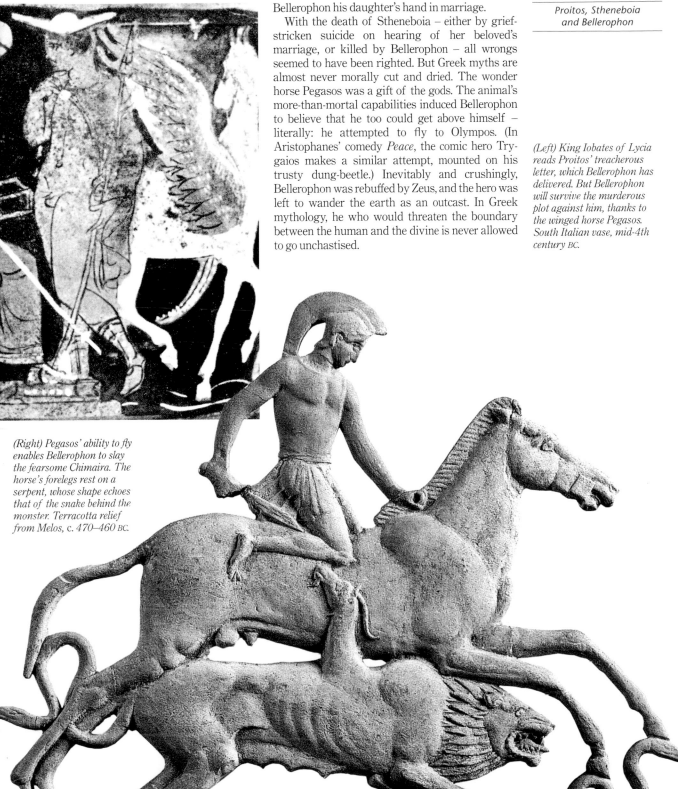

Bellerophon his daughter's hand in marriage.

With the death of Stheneboia – either by grief-stricken suicide on hearing of her beloved's marriage, or killed by Bellerophon – all wrongs seemed to have been righted. But Greek myths are almost never morally cut and dried. The wonder horse Pegasos was a gift of the gods. The animal's more-than-mortal capabilities induced Bellerophon to believe that he too could get above himself – literally: he attempted to fly to Olympos. (In Aristophanes' comedy *Peace*, the comic hero Trygaios makes a similar attempt, mounted on his trusty dung-beetle.) Inevitably and crushingly, Bellerophon was rebuffed by Zeus, and the hero was left to wander the earth as an outcast. In Greek mythology, he who would threaten the boundary between the human and the divine is never allowed to go unchastised.

(Left) King Iobates of Lycia reads Proitos' treacherous letter, which Bellerophon has delivered. But Bellerophon will survive the murderous plot against him, thanks to the winged horse Pegasos. South Italian vase, mid-4th century BC.

(Right) Pegasos' ability to fly enables Bellerophon to slay the fearsome Chimaira. The horse's forelegs rest on a serpent, whose shape echoes that of the snake behind the monster. Terracotta relief from Melos, c. 470–460 BC.

The House of Laios

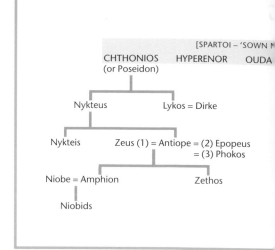

Only one lineage can compare with that of Pelops for the stark horror of the events with which myth-tellers associated it: the Royal House of Thebes. The great-grandson of Kadmos, the city's founder, was Laios, and it was with Laios that the grim sequence of transgressions began. At the home of Pelops, he had fallen in love with, and subsequently abducted to Thebes, the handsome illegitimate son of Pelops, a boy named Chrysippos ('Golden Horse').

This was represented by Greeks as the first act of pederastic abduction, and its catastrophic mytho-logical consequences suggest that, for all the toleration of pederasty in classical Greek culture, the practice could easily run into powerful social disapproval. Chrysippos was driven by shame to take his own life, as a result of which his enraged father laid a curse upon Laios. The outcome would be every bit as dire as the outcome of Myrtilos' malediction upon the house of Pelops.

An early episode in the history of the House of Laios is that of the abduction of Pelops' son, the young Chrysippos, by Laios. As the gods look on from above, Chrysippos holds out his hands to his distraught father. South Italian vase, c. 340–330 BC.

Consulting the oracles

A feature central to many Greek myths, and at the same time present as an active reality in Greek life, was the consultation of oracles. Our best evidence about the kinds of enquiries which were put to real-life oracles comes from the shrine of Zeus at Dodona (see p. 100); the questions reflect various types of anxiety and uncertainty,

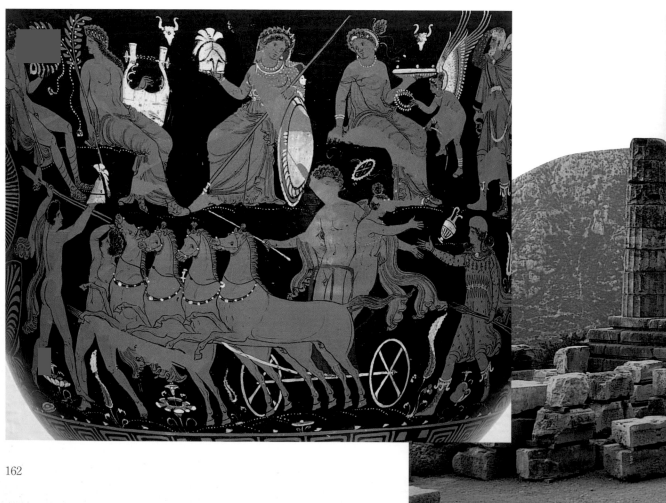

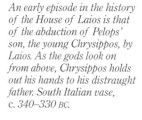

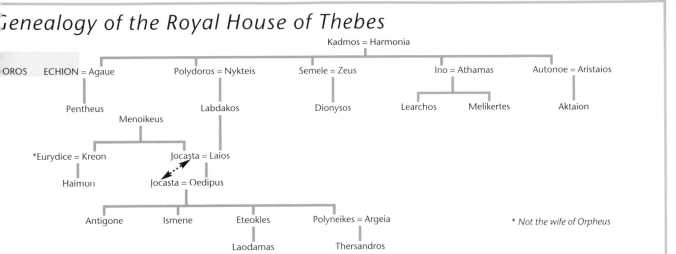

Genealogy of the Royal House of Thebes

Kadmos = Harmonia

OROS   ECHION = Agaue   Polydoros = Nykteis   Semele = Zeus   Ino = Athamas   Autonoe = Aristaios

Pentheus   Labdakos   Dionysos   Learchos   Melikertes   Aktaion

Menoikeus

*Eurydice = Kreon   Jocasta = Laios

Haimon   Jocasta = Oedipus

Antigone   Ismene   Eteokles   Polyneikes = Argeia   *Not the wife of Orpheus

Laodamas   Thersandros

---

whether on the part of individuals ('Will I have children by the wife to whom I am currently married?') or communities ('Does the bad weather which has been affecting us stem from religious pollution?').

However, the oracle which features most prominently in the Greek imagination is that of Delphi. Its high profile in mythology parallels its real-life importance; but in myths the Delphic oracle takes on a distinctive voice, magnifying and exaggerating what must have been a much more restricted aspect of real-life responses. This voice is typified by ambiguity, a quality which goes hand in hand with the eventual, relentless working out of mythical predictions in a catastrophic direction.

The temple of Apollo at Delphi, where Greeks might gain access to the mind of a god, through the Pythian oracle. But as the story of Oedipus demonstrates, a god's answers were always open to misinterpretation, given the fragility of human understanding.

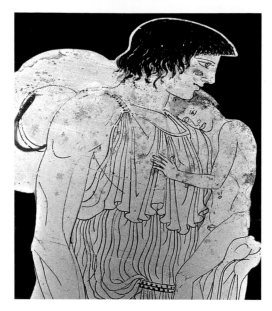

Oedipus

The saga of Laios and his child is articulated by several Delphic oracles, whose collective impact creates an overwhelming sense of the fragility of human aspiration in the face of forces beyond mortal understanding. The first oracle was that given to Laios and his wife Jocasta, who consulted Apollo's priestess because of an anxiety about childlessness – an anxiety replicated literally hundreds of times in the questions put to the oracle at Dodona (see p. 100). The god's reply was a grim one:

do not have a child; if you do, it will kill its father. Laios' past history did not augur well for his capacity to exercise restraint in sexual matters, and, sure enough, one day he drank too much and fathered a child upon Jocasta. Belatedly striving to elude the oracle's fulfilment, the couple pinned the baby's ankles together and gave it to a herdsman to expose on Mount Kithairon. But the herdsman – ironically, out of pity – saved the infant ('Oedipus', i.e. 'Swollen Foot') and handed it on to a fellow-herdsman. As it happened, this second herdsman kept the Corinthian royal flock; thus, as fortune would have it, the baby was brought up as the child of the hitherto childless Corinthian king and queen, Polybos and Merope.

One day, with Oedipus now grown to adulthood, someone casually insulted him for not being the true child of his ostensible parents. Now it was the anxious Oedipus' turn to seek counsel at Delphi. The reply was even more repugnant than that given to Laios and Jocasta, for it predicted that Oedipus would not only kill his father, but also lie with his mother. Given that, as far as Oedipus knew, his parents were Polybos and Merope, he determined at all costs not to return to Corinth.

What follows is perhaps the best-known story in all Greek mythology. On the road from Delphi Oedipus encountered an old man with his retinue, not knowing him to be Laios, his real father. The old man would not give way, so an incensed Oedipus slew him, together with all but one of his servants. Then Oedipus heard of a calamity which had befallen the nearby city of Thebes: the monstrous

Oedipus Uncovers the Truth

As the action of Sophokles' *Oedipus Tyrannos* reaches its horrifying dénouement, Oedipus' interrogation of the Theban shepherd brings to light the identity of the baby whom that shepherd had, once upon a time, saved from death on Mount Kithairon. Also on stage is the Corinthian herdsman to whom his Theban colleague had entrusted the fated baby. The jigsaw is nearly complete.

Oedipus	Where did you get the baby from? Was it your own, or someone else's?
Shepherd	It wasn't my own; someone gave it to me.
Oedipus	Which of these citizens gave it to you? From which household?
Shepherd	Master, do not, in the gods' name, do not ask me more!
Oedipus	You are a dead man if I have to ask this question again.
Shepherd	It was someone from the house of Laios.
Oedipus	A slave, or one of his own kin?
Shepherd	Ah! I am on the point of speaking something terrible.
Oedipus	And I on the point of hearing it. But I must hear.
Shepherd	It was said to be Laios' own child. But your wife within the house could best tell you how it was.
Oedipus	It was she who gave it to you?
Shepherd	It was, my lord.
Oedipus	With what intention?
Shepherd	That I might destroy it.
Oedipus	Its own poor mother wished this?
Shepherd	Yes: from fear of dire prophecies.
Oedipus	What prophecies?
Shepherd	It was said that the child would kill its parents.
Oedipus	Why then did you entrust it to this old man [i.e. the Corinthian herdsman]?
Shepherd	Out of pity, my lord: I believed he would take it away to another land, his own home. But in fact he saved it for complete disaster. For if you are who this man says you are, then ruin was your destiny at birth.
Oedipus	Ah! Ah! All comes out clearly. Light, may this be the last time I look upon you. I am revealed as born from those who should not have conceived me; as living with those with whom contact was impious; as killer of those whom it was wicked to kill.
Chorus	Alas for the generations of mortals: I count you as equal to nothingness. What man, what man gains more good fortune than a mere semblance, and after that semblance, a decline? Wretched Oedipus, taking your fate, your fate as an example, I call nothing in human existence happy.

Sphinx – part woman, part winged lion – was plaguing the citizens, by a method which distinguished her from some of the more brutally aggressive of Greek monsters. She challenged all passers-by to the ultimate intellectual contest: solve a riddle, or be devoured. What creature, she asked, goes on four feet, and on two, and on three? Oedipus, the most cerebral of the Greek heroes, solved the riddle. The answer: man, who crawls as an infant, walks erect in adulthood, and leans upon a stick in old age. By answering correctly, Oedipus put an end to the power of the Sphinx (who committed suicide). His reward was marriage to Jocasta, the recently widowed queen.

The marriage was fruitful, for Jocasta bore two sons, Eteokles and Polyneikes, and two daughters, Antigone and Ismene. But in time Thebes' prosperity was devastated by a fresh plague, this time one which blighted the fertility of people, animals and crops. In the logic of Greek myth, such things never happen without a cause; as usual, consultation of an oracle is the obvious expedient. The response: find the killer of Laios, who is at the root of the pollution. As head of the city, Oedipus ruthlessly uncovered the truth, the narration of this most profound of all detective stories is to be found in Sophokles' tragedy, *Oedipus Tyrannos* (often known under its Latin title, *Oedipus Rex*). In this play, finding himself to be both father-murderer and breeder of children from his own mother, Oedipus blinds himself; he cannot bear to kill himself, since that would bring him instantly face-to-face, in the Underworld, with both his parents – for Jocasta has committed suicide in the depths of her shame. The 'message' of Sophokles' play is not, it is worth emphasizing, the dull proposition, 'Fate rules everything', but something more complex: 'The ways of the gods are inscrutable; human beings do their best to understand and to cope; but even the best of them, such as Oedipus, are fragile and fallible.' Oedipus demonstrates his heroism not in the way that Herakles or Jason do, but through an unswerving drive to discover the truth.

Having travelled from Thebes to Mount Kithairon, from Mount Kithairon to Corinth, from Corinth to Delphi, and from Delphi to Thebes, Oedipus now took what proved to be his final journey: to Athens. Athenians loved to hear and tell myths about their own hospitality towards outcasts; the prime example of a mythical granter of asylum was Theseus. As he had once sheltered the polluted Herakles, so now he accepted the pariah Oedipus, whose self-blinded state would for ever testify to his extraordinary transgressions. But at last, on Athenian soil, Oedipus would find rest; he passed from this world by a mysterious death (recorded in Sophokles' drama *Oedipus at Colonus*), bequeathing to the Athenians a legacy of beneficial power which would reside in his tomb.

Eteokles and Polyneikes

To his own descendants, however, and to the entire city of Thebes, Oedipus' legacy was calamitous. Just before his death he had cursed his sons Eteokles and Polyneikes, who were trying to exploit for their own selfish ends the power which control over their father's grave would bring. The animosity between the feuding brothers soon erupted into outright war. It is typical of the narrative variability of Greek mythology that myth-tellers differed over which brother was the elder, and what kind of power-sharing arrangement they devised. But common to all accounts is the fact that Polyneikes ('Much Quarrelling') raised an army from outside Thebes in order to wrest sovereignty from Eteokles, whose name ('True Glory') rings hollow in the light of subsequent events.

Polyneikes sought help from the city of Argos, whose ruler Adrastos offered him not only military support but also the hand of his daughter. Seven champions, including Polyneikes and Adrastos, led

the army which marched on Thebes: one champion for each of Thebes' legendary seven gates. As we have seen before, the inception of a military campaign – in actual Greek practice as well as in stories – inevitably attracted religious observances designed to anticipate and, if possible, to influence the future.

In the present case, Amphiaraos, a seer, predicted his own death and that of all the champions except for Adrastos. His reluctance to take part was overcome by his wife Eriphyle (Adrastos' sister), whose role in this tale echoes the deceptiveness attributed to such females as Pandora, Medea, Clytemnestra and Deianeira. Polyneikes bribed her with the necklace of Harmonia, a Theban family treasure which had been fashioned by Hephaistos, and which Kadmos' bride had received from her husband as a fateful wedding gift. Susceptible to persuasion herself, Eriphyle wheedled her husband Amphiaraos, against his better judgment, into becoming a member of the Seven.

The capture of Thebes

The tale of the capture of Thebes incorporates, in more modest form, some of the motifs found in the saga of Troy. One such motif is that of the *necessary condition*, but this time it is a condition for the

The Seven Against Thebes, and Their Theban Opponents

These names are found in Aischylos' play *Seven Against Thebes*, in which each pair of champions fights at one of Thebes' legendary seven gates. In other versions of the story, the names of the champions vary somewhat; even the number seven is not sacrosanct.

attackers	defenders
Amphiaraos	Lasthenes
Eteoklos	Megareus
Hippomedon	Hyperbios
Kapaneus	Polyphontes
Parthenopaios	Aktor
Polyneikes	Eteokles
Tydeus	Melanippos

(Left) The motif of the 'fatal gift': Polyneikes bribes Eriphyle with a necklace, to induce her to persuade her husband Amphiaraos to take part in the expedition of the Seven against Thebes. Attic vase, mid-5th century BC.

(Below) Death was not the end for Amphiaraos. On a 4th-century BC marble relief from his shrine at Oropos (on the coast of Attica, opposite Euboia) he is shown as 'healer hero'. He tends the shoulder of Archinos, who dedicated the relief as thanksgiving for his cure. To the right, sleeping, Archinos dreams of a sacred serpent licking his injured shoulder.

salvation of a city rather than for its capture. Naturally it required a seer to recognize this condition. The great Theban diviner was Teiresias, who revealed that, if the city were to survive, the anger of the god Ares must first be appeased by the sacrifice of Menoikeus, the son of Jocasta's brother Kreon. (Ares was still smarting at Kadmos' slaying of his sacred snake, when Thebes was founded.) By his altruistic act of suicide, Menoikeus paved the way for the repulse of the invading force.

Heroic exploits were performed on both sides. It being in the nature of heroes to push up to and beyond limits, Tydeus, one of the Seven, was savage enough to devour the brains of one of his adversaries, whereupon a horrified Athene promptly withdrew the gift of immortality which she had been about to bestow upon Tydeus. One of the Seven who did achieve a kind of immortality was the reluctant seer Amphiaraos, who was swallowed up by the earth, chariot and all, to become after death a healing hero, thanks to the intervention of Zeus.

Antigone

What differentiated the siege of Thebes from that of Troy was that, basically, this was a civil war. The climax is the duel to the death between the two Theban brothers, Eteokles and Polyneikes, and

(Above) Tydeus was a favourite subject for Etruscan artists. An example is this gem (c. 450–400 BC) which vividly depicts the warrior's characteristically unbridled aggression.

An Etruscan bas-relief showing the combat between Eteokles and Polyneikes. 2nd century BC.

exposed corpse, in a symbolic act of burial. This classic, insoluble conflict of priorities was immortalized in Sophokles' tragedy *Antigone*, a work which would exert a massive influence on later European theatre. In Sophokles' telling of the myth, Antigone is entombed alive by Kreon, and then hangs herself; her betrothed, Kreon's son Haimon, stabs himself to death from grief, after spitting into his father's face in a vicious act of rejection. Although, on the advice of the seer Teiresias, Kreon rescinds his edict forbidding Polyneikes' burial, it is all too late: his wife Eurydice (not the wife of Orpheus) takes her own life, as the fortunes of the household disintegrate.

Alkmaion

Actions, Greek myths repeatedly emphasize, have consequences; and the consequences of Kreon's actions were bound to reverberate further. Since Kreon had forbidden the burial, not just of Polyneikes, but of all the Argive fallen, Adrastos, as sole survivor, sought help where he could find it – in Athens, which, under Theseus, figured in its usual virtuous role as helper of the distressed. Athenian intervention brought about the defeat of the Thebans, and the Argive dead were duly buried. Moreover, the relatives of the Argive slain – specifically their sons (the Epigonoi, 'Those Born After') – determined to avenge their fathers. Their leader was Alkmaion, offspring of the uneasy marriage of Amphiaraos and Eriphyle.

There is an exact homology between the entries of Amphiaraos and Alkmaion into their respective expeditions. It was Eriphyle who persuaded them both, having herself been bribed, first by Polyneikes with the gift of Harmonia's necklace, and now by Polyneikes' son, through the gift of another lethal family treasure, Harmonia's robe. The major difference between the two expeditions is

their mutual slaughter cancels the hatred which fuelled the campaign. However, as the end of the *Odyssey* graphically illustrates, the dead have surviving relatives through whom past griefs live on. In this case, the catalysts for the next stage of the action are two surviving members of the house of Laios: Oedipus' daughter Antigone, and Kreon, brother of Jocasta, and acting ruler of Thebes.

For Kreon, the well-being of the *polis* (city-state) must be placed before anything else, even – if the two come into conflict – before the claims of the *oikos* (household). Polyneikes' attack on his own *polis* thus represented, in Kreon's eyes, the ultimate act of treason, and Kreon punished it with the ultimate sanction: denial of burial to the traitor. Eteokles, by contrast, the defender of his city, received every honour in death. But Antigone, sister of both Polyneikes and Eteokles, could accept no such nice distinction between her brothers. Her choice was to put kin before all else. In defiance of Kreon's edict, she cast earth upon Polyneikes'

Tara Fitzgerald playing the title role in a production of Sophokles' great tragedy Antigone, *at the Old Vic Theatre, London, in 1999.*

Genealogy of Alkmaion

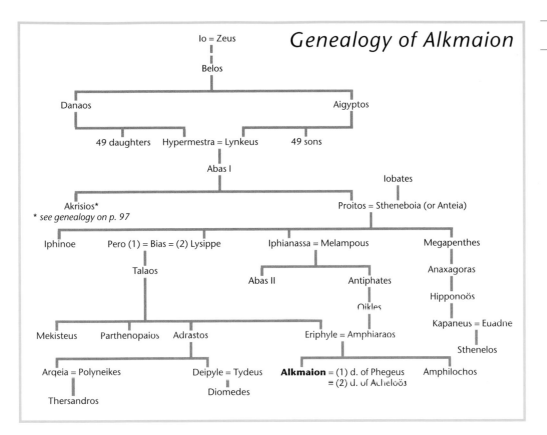

Io = Zeus

Belos

Danaos — Aigyptos

49 daughters — Hypermestra = Lynkeus — 49 sons

Abas I

Iobates

Akrisios*
* see genealogy on p. 97

Proitos = Stheneboia (or Anteia)

Iphinoe — Pero (1) = Bias = (2) Lysippe — Iphianassa = Melampous — Megapenthes

Talaos

Anaxagoras

Abas II — Antiphates

Hipponoös

Oikles

Kapaneus = Euadne

Mekisteus — Parthenopaios — Adrastos — Eriphyle = Amphiaraos

Sthenelos

Arqeia = Polyneikes — Deipyle = Tydeus — **Alkmaion** = (1) d. of Phegeus = (2) d. of Acheloös — Amphilochos

Thersandros

Diomedes

---

their outcome, for the Epigonoi took Thebes and razed its walls to the ground. Nor was there a 'necessary condition' governing the city's capture or salvation, though it is significant that the fall of Thebes coincided with the death, at long last, of the seer Teiresias, who had himself embodied the city's fortunes for several generations.

From deeds of heroic adventure Alkmaion now reverted to matters concerning his family. His domestic situation mirrors that of Orestes, for at the prompting of the Delphic oracle he punished his mother's perfidy by murdering her. Horrific though this act was, it did not infringe the honour of the gods, and so did not (unlike the transgressions of, say, Tantalos or Aktaion) draw down automatic divine chastisement. What it did, again as in the case of Orestes, was to conjure up the presence of the Erinyes, those nauseating but socially indispensable avengers of the shedding of kin blood. The madness which they sent caused Alkmaion to wander from place to place; in Greek myths restless movement is often, as in the case of the maiden-turned-cow Io, a metaphor for psychological distress.

The only way of alleviating this condition was for Alkmaion to find a host who would give him shelter and perform the necessary rite of purification. However, the situation was complicated by the fact that, on Eriphyle's death, Alkmaion had inherited the necklace and robe of Harmonia. In the

district of Psophis (in northern Arcadia), Alkmaion received purification from Phegeus, whose daughter he then married, giving her the deadly necklace and robe as dowry. Yet when the land became infertile, it became clear that Alkmaion's matricidal pollution had still not been fully removed. So his wanderings continued.

A second and more potent purifier now took him in, namely the river-god Acheloös, whose perpetually flowing waters could wash away the deepest stain. Once again Alkmaion married his purifier's daughter. Unfortunately she too wanted the necklace and robe – which were still with the wife whom Alkmaion had left in Psophis. When Alkmaion deceitfully obtained the fatal heirlooms, he was killed by Phegeus' sons, in revenge for the insult to their sister. The modest edifice which was said to be the tomb of Alkmaion was still pointed out to visitors to Psophis in Pausanias' day, in the second century AD.

The cycle of killing had still not run its course. Vengeance murders continued, as the children of Alkmaion's second family destroyed the first. Only one location could offer an end, and a new beginning: Delphi, where Apollo, god of purification and of new beginnings, had his oracular seat. The sons of Alkmaion's second marriage dedicated to Apollo the death-bringing necklace and robe, at last neutralizing the objects' malign power by removing them altogether from human circulation.

Strong Bonds:
Love Between Spouses

Protesilaos, the first Greek to disembark at Troy, was also the first to die, leaving his young bride a widow. Here he is shown armed and ready for the fight, with his ship behind him. Thessalian coin, early 5th century BC.

One of the most powerful agencies of disruption is, paradoxically, the very strength of ties which link family members. It is Orestes' devotion to his father's memory which turns him into a matricide; Deianeira brings about the death of her husband Herakles only because she wishes to rekindle the love between them. In other myths too there are representations of bonds which unite. Since, as we have stressed, Greek myths are thought experiments which sometimes test values 'to destruction', it will be no surprise that these uniting bonds are typically subjected to the ultimate trial: that of death.

Tales of marriage and death: Protesilaos and Laodamia

At once poignant and tragic, the story of Protesilaos and Laodamia is a self-contained vignette illustrating the strength of conjugal passion. Protesilaos ('First of the People') was the first of the Greeks to leap ashore at Troy, in defiance of an oracle predicting that whichever warrior took that bold step would die in the act. Sure enough, he was cut down, by Hektor himself according to one version. What intensified the pathos was that at home he had left behind his bride Laodamia, whom he had only just married. Her longing for the union which would never now be fulfilled expressed itself in an unusual depth of grief: she made an image of Protesilaos, with which she lay to console herself.

This story pattern partially overlaps with that of Pygmalion (who, as Ovid memorably recounted, made a statue of a lovely woman which then came miraculously, and durably, to life), since Hermes, god of mediations, brought Protesilaos back from Hades, for a short interlude. Yet Laodamia's solace was all too brief; when Hermes returned Protesilaos to the Underworld, Laodamia committed suicide, so that, in death at least, the pair could be reunited.

Admetos and Alkestis

No less moving, but laced with bitterness and cynicism, is another tale about a marriage, located in Thessaly. Admetos, ruler of Pherai, was married to Alkestis, a daughter of Pelias (king of neighbouring Iolkos). Admetos' early career was glorious: he participated in the Argonautic expedition and the Kalydonian Boar Hunt, those twin tests of heroic

The painter of this south Italian vase (c. 340 BC) has encapsulated the crisis in the household of Admetos and Alkestis. Having nobly consented to die in place of her husband, Alkestis bids farewell to her young children. Admetos holds his head in grief.

170

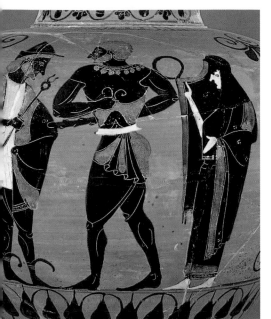

Fortunately, this is one myth which works its way towards a benign resolution. It does so through a notion which pervades the whole Admetos/Alkestis story: that of reciprocity. In the course of his Labours, Herakles received hospitality at the house of Admetos. Herakles characteristically took full advantage of what was on offer, in ignorance of Admetos' state of deep mourning for Alkestis. When Herakles by chance found out the true situation, he wrestled with Thanatos ('Death' – a demonic figure who was a kind of proxy for Hades) and restored Alkestis to life. In this particular thought experiment, the marriage bond, though tested, was not destroyed.

Orpheus and Eurydice

In terms of their influence on subsequent cultural tradition, the tales of Protesilaos and Laodamia, and of Admetos and Alkestis, are far outstripped by the myth of Orpheus and Eurydice, which, especially in music and opera, has resonated in hundreds of later artistic re-workings – in marked

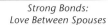

(Left) When a vase-painter has not inscribed names to identify the figures, we are often reduced to educated guesswork. Here, it is likely that what we see is Herakles bringing Alkestis back from the Underworld, accompanied by Hermes (left), the god who takes charge of 'transitions' of many kinds. Attic vase, c. 540 BC.

(Below) One of countless post-classical illustrations of the Orpheus and Eurydice theme. This is a painted panel (c. 1480–90) by the Florentine artist Jacopo del Sellaio. The Centaur pulling Eurydice's hair is evidently a denizen of the Underworld.

prowess; and his capacity for fair dealing was reflected in the fact that Apollo himself was sent to work for him as a herdsman, when the god was once obliged to fulfil a year's penance in the service of a mortal. A divinity did not forget a favour, and, in return for having been well treated, Apollo enhanced the fertility of Admetos' flocks and helped him to win Alkestis as bride.

However – this is an insistent theme in Greek mythology – human good fortune is inherently fragile; otherwise, humans would be like gods. So it happened that at his wedding Admetos forgot to sacrifice to Artemis. Fortunately Artemis' brother Apollo was able to advise Admetos on how to placate her (for she had angrily caused the marriage chamber to abound with snakes). Nor did Apollo's gratitude stop at that: he outwitted the Fates by getting them drunk, and induced them to let Admetos prolong his allotted life-span – provided he could find someone to die in his stead.

This is where the tale, notably as presented in Euripides' *Alkestis*, assumes a grimmer tone. No one would agree to give up his or her own life for Admetos, not even his nearest and dearest, such as his aged parents; life is sweet (compared to the alternative) and the desire to cling to that sweetness is a powerful disincentive to altruism. Only Alkestis was willing to make the supreme sacrifice, an offer which Admetos accepted. Because versions of the story seem to differ over whether or not Admetos had a choice about accepting the Fates' boon, there is a comparable variability about how to evaluate his moral conduct in letting his wife die for him. At all events, Admetos realized the extent of his loss when his wife was no longer at his side.

contrast to its Greek origins, where (unlike the ampler Roman evidence) we have a rather modest corpus of material. At one level the myth concerns the great love between husband and wife, under the pressure generated by the wife's death. But its ramifications extend well beyond that, to embrace maenadic and 'Orphic' rituals, as well as the opposition between wildness and what the Greeks called *mousike* (both 'music' and 'culture'), and that between same- and other-oriented sexuality.

Different stories were told of Orpheus' genealogy. His mother was one of the Muses, his father either Apollo or Oiagros, from Thrace, a region which, as we have mentioned, Greeks from further south tended to characterize as wild and uncivilized. Implicit in Orpheus' ancestry, then, is the double association with sweet harmony and with something potentially more savage. These are the

Between the figures of Hermes (left) and Orpheus (right), Eurydice makes her way towards the world of the living. This marble relief (1st century AD) is one of a number of copies of a classical Greek original.

(Right) Orpheus' death at the hands of Thracian maenads. The lyre, raised by Orpheus in self-defence, offers little protection against these determined women. Attic vase, c. 470 BC.

poles between which the hero's life oscillates.

When Orpheus' wife died of a snakebite, he took a step which only the greatest heroes could contemplate: to try to reverse the inevitable process of mortality by bringing his wife back to the world of the living. His approach was the opposite of that used by Herakles; instead of brute force, he employed singing and lyre-playing, talents in which he outshone all mortals. He could move the very rocks and trees (another mythical musician, Amphion, charmed the stones into place in the walls of Thebes; p. 131). Orpheus proposed to enchant an even stonier audience: Hades and Persephone, the rulers of the Underworld. Our sketchy Greek sources leave some doubt as to what took place, but it seems that Orpheus partially succeeded in his persuasion: Eurydice was released from death, but only on condition that Orpheus did not look back as she followed him up to the light. However, in myth such prohibitions are made to be broken. Being human, Orpheus looked back, and Eurydice receded into the darkness.

Orpheus after Eurydice: Orpheus' later career manifests the wildness, but also, eventually, the sweetness, which we saw to be latent in his genealogy. After the loss of Eurydice, remarriage was ruled out by Orpheus' excess of grief. Instead, the musician roamed the Thracian countryside lamenting his loss, until he was torn limb from limb by a group of maenads. One of the reasons mentioned in

our sources for this savage act repeats a standard theme: Orpheus had offended Dionysos, and so was punished by the god's worshippers. But another alleged reason illustrates, by implication, how Orpheus had turned diametrically away from his previous attachment to marriage: the maenads, it was said, took their revenge on him because he had rejected the love of females altogether, in favour of that of his own sex.

Either way, Orpheus' music could not be stilled by death. His head floated down the Thracian river Hebros and into the sea; the current bore it southwards, past several islands, until it came ashore, singing still, on the island of Lesbos. One of the myth's many functions is thus to provide an aetiological explanation for the exalted poetic reputation of Lesbos, the home of many renowned poets from the 'legendary' (Arion) to the 'historical' (Sappho and Alkaios). And not only did Orpheus' voice live on through the songs of others: it seems that his head was believed to have formed the focus of an oracle, which could be consulted in a shrine at Antissa, on Lesbos. While it may have been Orpheus' uxoriousness which led him to make his heroic foray into the Underworld, what lent him his post-mortem influence was his connection with the world of the sacred, a world which his uncanny musical talent allowed him to penetrate.

(Left) A consultation of the 'oracle' of Orpheus' head, allegedly preserved in a sanctuary on Lesbos. Much about this scene remains uncertain, such as the purpose of the objects held by the bearded man. Attic water-jar, c. 440–430 BC.

173

Same-Sex Eroticism

Relationships between men in ancient Greece

Orpheus was said to have incurred women's wrath by rejecting them in favour of love for other males. Was it the case, then, that one cause of mythological family-disruption was the promotion of homosexual over heterosexual tendencies, with the consequent loosening of the marriage bond? The answer is emphatically: no. This needs some explanation, and that will lead us into the area of Greek social history.

As scholars have increasingly come to recognize, the ancient Greek world did not know of the modern, 'life-style' category-distinction between homosexuality and heterosexuality, according to which those terms are used to designate contrasting psychological or behavioural profiles. Rather, same-sex physical intimacy – which most certainly did occur in ancient Greek life – was mainly viewed in relation to a number of other parameters, especially the perceived 'activeness' or 'passiveness' of the partners, and their age and status. As in every field of ancient life, so too in regard to sexuality, it is overwhelmingly evidence about *male* behaviour and attitudes about which we are best informed; and here we can identify a marked and historically durable pattern. According to this pattern, an adolescent male would typically be courted by an older man: the adolescent was conventionally seen in the role of the passive 'beloved', the older man in the role of the actively desiring 'lover'.

Such relationships did not in themselves earn social disapproval, but they were liable to be stigmatized if the behaviour of either partner threatened the 'ideal' pattern – if, for instance, the adolescent was seen to be willingly submitting to the older man's sexual advances, or if the relationship was prolonged to a stage where the younger partner had himself reached adulthood. If these dangers were avoided, however, the honour of both partners could remain unscathed. Moreover – an absolutely crucial point – it was assumed that each partner was expected also to take a full part in relationships with women: that is, there was no perceived incompatibility between, on the one hand, participation in the older/younger same-sex liaisons, and, on the other hand, marriage.

The evidence for the older/younger, active/passive model derives from several parts of the Greek world. We know most about the situation at Athens

in the Classical period, though Crete and the Peloponnese also provide valuable material. One Cretan custom – whereby youths were 'abducted' by older males, with whom they spent two months hunting together before returning to the 'civilized' world of the city – has given rise to an intriguing explanation for this whole pattern of same-sex intimacy: the pattern would, so this explanation goes, reflect an earlier initiation rite through which older males inducted younger ones into the community's norms. There are problems with this explanation, not least the fact that, in its Athenian form, the pattern did not cater for the induction of an entire age-cohort, but rather depended on affective bonds between individual pairs. Nevertheless, the possible viability of the initiation explanation serves as a reminder of the divide between modern experiences of sexuality and those in Greek antiquity.

Same-sex relationships in myth

These observations about social history should help us to read the evidence of mythology with greater insight. In particular, we can now appreciate why so many of mythology's male–male bondings involve the paradigmatic adolescent/adult age-gap. Laios, while a guest of Pelops, fell in love with his host's son Chrysippos, and abducted him; Apollodoros calls the young man a *pais*, which we may here translate as 'adolescent' – Laios was teaching Chrysippos how to drive a chariot at the time. (The word 'pederasty' is descended from *pais* and *erastes*, 'lover'.) Then there was Herakles' passion for his doomed young squire Hylas, whom the poet Theokritos describes as a 'delightful *pais*' whose hair hung down in curls – far younger and tenderer than the man's man Herakles; indeed when Hylas drowned, tugged into a pool by a love-struck nymph, his errand had been that of fetching water, which eloquently symbolized his role as the girlish, 'passive' partner in his relationship with Herakles.

(Above) The age difference between the partners in this affair – man and boy – is typical of same-sex relationships between men in ancient Greece. Attic cup, c. 480 BC.

(Below) Herakles' sexual appetite embraced young men as well as women. One of his male lovers was Iolaos, seen here at the hero's side in his combat with the Nemean lion. Attic vase, c. 520 BC.

The 'abduction' of Ganymede by Zeus. Zeus, at his least authoritarian, carries a walking stick instead of his usual sceptre. Ganymede holds a cockerel, doubtless a lover's gift. Terracotta from Olympia (c. 470 BC).

Another of Herakles' young male beloveds (Plutarch says there were too many to count) was his Theban protégé Iolaos, cast by numerous myth-tellers as Herakles' helper in his Labours. In Thebes their relationship was enshrined in cult, for in the context of the elite Theban military force known as the Sacred Band – formed in the 4th century BC, and comprising 150 pairs of male lovers – it was at Iolaos' tomb that the lovers swore oaths of loyalty.

Finally we should mention Crete, especially in view of the historical association between the island and same-sex 'abduction' rites. Both King Minos and his brother Rhadamanthus were said by myth-tellers to have succumbed to desire for young adolescent males. In a little-known variant, Minos was even said to have been in love with Theseus; the story did not gain wide currency, but, since this alleged encounter came at a time when Theseus was still unmarried, whereas Minos already had a grown son, we are reminded once more of the fundamental age-and-status differential on which Greek assumptions about 'pederasty' rest.

Same-sex relationships with gods

When one of the participants in a same-sex liaison is a god, the age aspect of the differential between the partners needs rephrasing slightly: for exactly how old is a god? But we have many instances of liaisons involving a divinity and a mortal where there is an obvious difference in 'seniority', as well as in activeness/passivity. Poseidon's desire-driven abduction of Pelops is likened by the poet Pindar to Zeus' abduction of Ganymede, the prototype for relations between the older male and his adolescent beloved. The Megarian poet Theognis (6th century BC) traced what he described as the pleasure of *paidophilia* to Zeus' original abduction of Ganymede to be his nectar-pourer on Mount Olympos.

Now pouring wine is not the same as drawing water (which is what Hylas did), that is, it does not implicitly liken Ganymede to a woman; but it does imply a stark contrast in status between the young, standing attendant and the more senior, reclining drinkers whose pleasure he is serving. Ganymede's status as the 'model' of the beloved boy is graphically expressed in Theokritos' twelfth *Idyll*, which evokes a ritual kissing-contest involving male adolescents in the city of Megara: the poet imagines the contest's fortunate judge as praying to Ganymede that his adjudication be sound.

The god to whom myth-tellers ascribed most same-sex liaisons was Apollo. Once more, these relationships involve a gulf not only in seniority, but also in activeness/passivity. Typical, and most often retold, is the love between Apollo and the handsome youth Hyakinthos (see p. 101), which ended when a discus thrown by the god hit the boy on the head and killed him. Yet this was not the end of the story. First, Hyakinthos' existence was said to have been prolonged in perpetuity when his blood generated a lovely flower. Then, his memory was preserved in cult, above all at the place of his alleged burial at Amyklai (near Sparta), where he was honoured alongside Apollo. Finally, there was even a suggestion (expressed in a cult-song) that Apollo brought Hyakinthos back to life. Some modern scholars have interpreted this evidence as implying belief in a 'rebirth' of the young man, just as most initiation ceremonies involve both the 'death' of one form of existence and the 'birth' of another.

Pairs of 'equal' heroes

Same-sex erotic relationships between those who are equals in age or status do not figure with any degree of prominence in our mythological sources. What of the bonds between such heroes as Achilles and Patroklos, or Theseus and Peirithoös? It is true that some myth-tellers (although not Homer) did interpret the Achilles/Patroklos friendship in homoerotic terms, though significantly there was disagreement about which of the two was the older – as if, in order to make the bond correspond to the assumed behaviour pattern, there just had to be an age difference. In general, the evidence of mythology strongly corroborates that of social history, by emphasizing the ubiquity of the 'older man/ adolescent youth' pattern.

Conclusion

Much of this chapter has been concerned with transgression and disruption, with pathos and death. Greek myths, we have seen, magnify, exaggerate and sharpen the passions and conflicts of everyday life, making them at once more visible and more consequential. Not every, probably not *any* real-life Greek family experienced the traumas suffered by the members of the House of Pelops or the House of Laios. But these stories were thought experiments, told in order to make sense of the world in which real Greeks lived.

Even heroes can feel pain. Patroklos grimaces in anguish as Achilles tends his wounded arm. Achilles' tender care for his companion is clear, though nothing in this image could be said to mark the relationship as more intimate than friendship. Attic cup, c. 500 BC.

The Significance of Place

This chapter will investigate the topography of Greek mythology: we shall be looking at myths against the background of the landscape – both natural and humanly constructed – within which the narratives unfold.

Much of the distinctiveness of Greek mythology derives from its natural environment: mountains, caves, rivers, springs and sea. This environment differs markedly from those of, for instance, Egypt, Mesopotamia, northern Europe, Japan, or the North American plains, regions which have all been the home of myth-telling peoples for whom, as for the ancient Greeks, the particular configuration of their own landscape has profoundly shaped the kinds of tales which they tell.

Human settlements too may constitute distinctive parts of the world of myth. Our examples will be Crete and Troy, each of which has its own special characteristics as a setting for narrative. As it happens, each has also attracted much interest as a result of spectacular archaeological discoveries, which have raised the complex issue of the relation between the world of myth and the 'real world'.

Finally we shall visit a place which no account of the world of Greek mythology can ignore: the Underworld. From the perspective of the anxieties and hopes of the myth-tellers and their audiences, this is a location no less 'real' than more readily visitable regions such as Athens, Thebes and Argos.

The Ladon, flowing through Arcadia, was described by Pausanias as the finest river in all Greece. According to some myth-tellers, Ladon was the father of Daphne, the nymph pursued by Apollo.

VI   A Landscape of Myths

Mountains

Spaces of the imagination

Greece was, and is, a land of bare rocks and rough pastures, of desultory streams that become torrents with the winter rains, of precipitous ravines and unfathomable caves, of marshes and springs and flowering meadows, of a thousand islands set in an untrustworthy sea. Upon this natural world the Greeks imposed their own structures: sanctuaries, houses, farmsteads, villages, cities. The landscape was a blend of the natural and the cultural.

Greek myth-tellers invoked this landscape as a means of giving shape and meaning to their narratives. Such narratives did not simply *reflect* the perceptions of everyday life: rather, they *adapted* those perceptions by selecting and highlighting certain aspects, in such a way that there developed a relatively consistent symbolism of sacred space – or at least, as relatively consistent as was com-

patible with the Greeks' inexhaustible capacity for invention. Our aim will be to set out some of the features of this symbolic world.

What can be seen nowadays is not necessarily identical with what an ancient observer might have seen. Such factors as alterations in coastlines and in river courses, and modifications in land use, have greatly affected what is 'out there' to be seen (in antiquity, grain-growing was much more prevalent, and olive-growing much less so, than is the case today).

Moreover, what is 'visible' is a matter of cultural perception no less than of optics, and in this respect too major shifts have taken place since antiquity; to exemplify the point, we shall include representations of the Greek landscape which were produced by earlier generations of visitors and viewers, in some cases hundreds of years before the invention of photography. In spite of (or perhaps because of) this variability in perception, reading the Greek myths in the light of topography is an indispensable means of coming to terms with their multiple meanings.

Mountains

In Book 6 of the *Odyssey*, when Athene leaves the company of mortals after visiting the land of the

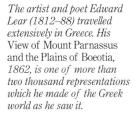

The artist and poet Edward Lear (1812–88) travelled extensively in Greece. His View of Mount Parnassus and the Plains of Boeotia, *1862, is one of more than two thousand representations which he made of the Greek world as he saw it.*

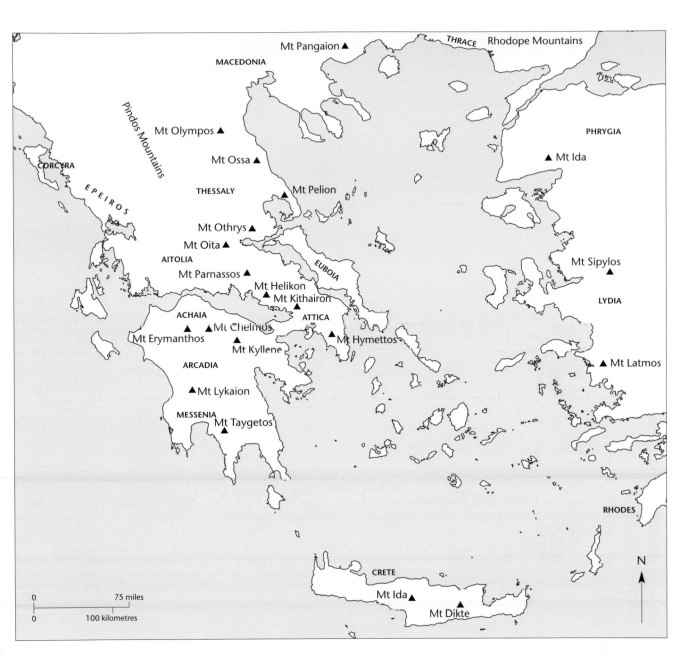

Phaeacians, she returns

to Olympos, where, they say, the abode of the gods
    stands unmoving
for ever, and is not shaken with winds nor
    spattered
with rain, nor does snow pile ever there, but the
    shining bright air
stretches cloudless away, and the white light glances
    upon it.

Though Olympos could be seen from far and wide (from Thessaloniki, on a clear day), the gods' abode was nevertheless felt to be impossibly remote.

No other mountain rivalled the mystique of Olympos, but all mountains had about them something of the sacred, and on any mountain the gods might be active. Hermes was born on Mount Kyllene to the nymph Maia, loved by Zeus. Zeus himself, as a baby, was protected from Kronos' wrath by being sheltered in a Cretan cave, either on Mount Dikte or Mount Ida. The Muses were said to dance and sing with Apollo on Mount Helikon or on Mount Parnassos; Artemis hunted on Mount Taygetos and Mount Erymanthos; Pan was often to be found on the mountains, perpetually in search of a nymph.

Because of this divine presence, a mountain was a place where a mortal might encounter a god or goddess unawares – usually to the mortal's great cost. It was on Kithairon that the hunter

Aktaion made the fatal mistake of disturbing Artemis while she was bathing at a spring; metamorphosed into a stag, he was ripped apart by his own hounds. Less brutally final, but agonizing none the less, was the fate of Teiresias when he saw Athene naked at a spring on Helikon. He retained his life and his physical integrity, in all but one respect: Athene blinded him. A rather different form of encounter with the sacred befell

Pentheus on Kithairon when he finally knew the unrestrained power of Dionysos, as his mother and the other maenads tore him limb from limb; the Messenger in Euripides' *Bacchae* situates the savage dénouement in an appropriately unforgiving spot, the slopes of a rocky, pine-clad gorge, with a torrent surging below.

Sometimes the grim consequences of an encounter with the sacred only revealed themselves

after a certain delay. When Hera, Athene and Aphrodite descended on Mount Ida near Troy, commanding Paris to exercise his judgment, the short-term result was a bribe for the judge in the delectable shape of Helen; only later, when the ashes of Troy lay smouldering, did the true import of the meeting become clear. Paris had not chosen his role as judge; no more did Oedipus choose to be taken to Kithairon as a newborn, and to be

left to die. Paradoxically (the paradox is made explicit in Sophokles' drama *Oedipus Tyrannos*) Kithairon both witnessed Oedipus' 'rebirth', and also sealed his fate: when the hero had been rejected by his real mother and father, his 'foster mother', Kithairon, preserved him for the most hideous of all futures.

The mountains of Greek myth are, then, places where wildness tends to manifest itself as an uncanny and dangerous quality. But there are exceptions, cases where the sacred appears in a more benign light. One example is provided by myths about Mount Pelion in Thessaly, where young heroes were educated under the benevolent eye of the Centaur Cheiron. Mountain wildness here stands for a pre-civilized, transitional state, necessary for the proper development of the future warrior. Achilles and Jason were just two of the many heroes who served their apprenticeship on the wooded slopes of Pelion.

At the end of a hero's life, too, a mountain might occasionally stage a scene of calm solemnity rather than the vengeful rancour associated with the deaths of Aktaion and Pentheus. Such was the role of Mount Oita, the location for the last act in Herakles' earthly drama. On the mountain peak, laid upon his funeral pyre, Herakles made the transition from the world of mortality to that of his new home, on Mount Olympos.

(Above) Mount Pelion in Magnesia (a district of Thessaly) is one of the most beautiful of all Greek mountains: in part wild, in part benign and gentle. It was here that the Centaur Cheiron was said to dwell; he, too, combined the wildness of animal nature with the kindliness of a wise teacher.

(Left) For his Helicon *or* Minerva's Visit to the Muses, *the Flemish painter Joos de Momper (1564–1634/35) drew on a passage from Ovid's* Metamorphoses, *in which the poet described a visit by the goddess to the Muses' home. She had just learnt of a marvellous happening – the creation of a new spring, at the spot where the ground had been struck by the hoof of the winged horse Pegasos.*

Caves

Though less visually dominating than mountains, caves are an equally pervasive feature of the geology of Greece; they also played a significant part in ancient Greek religion. They were a favourite site for the worship of the Nymphs, two of the best known examples being the cave at Vari on Mount Hymettos in Attica, and the Korykian cave

at Delphi on Mount Parnassos. The goatish god Pan was also closely linked with caves, above all after his cult had been imported into Attica during the 5th century BC (he was believed to have helped the Athenians at the battle of Marathon in 490). Although many of Pan's caves were in the country-side, not all were: when the Athenians instituted his cult in a cave on the northern slope of the Acropolis, they were incorporating into the city a small portion of rural wildness. There is a clear symbolic coherence in the constellation of ideas which brought together a god from what was perceived to be 'pre-civilized', primitive Arcadia, with a part of the landscape, the cave, which was itself felt to belong Before. By an analogous symbolism, the 'Holy Ones' (i.e. the Furies) were worshipped at

Nymphs

Nymphs are a class of female divinities with several characteristics in common. They are often closely identified with a particular locality, a fact exemplified by the numerous coins on which nymphs embody the city in question. Nymphs usually have a strong connection with the landscape, for example with mountains, trees, springs, rivers or the sea. Sometimes the generic names given to them make this explicit, as with *neïades/naïades* (nymphs of flowing water, spring nymphs, i.e. 'naiads'), or *druades* (tree nymphs, i.e. 'dryads'), or *orestiades/oreïades* (mountain nymphs, i.e. 'oreads'), though they may simply be called *numphai*, whence the English word 'nymph'. *Numphe* also means 'girl', 'woman', and particularly 'bride', a meaning which points to a connection with sexuality; as archaeological finds have demonstrated, two groups who made extensive dedications to the Nymphs were girls before marriage, and women after childbirth. Sexuality is certainly an important dimension of the nymphs of mythology, whether it be as the objects of erotic pursuit (by Hermes, Pan, satyrs, etc.), or as themselves the active seekers of union with mortals.

Myth-tellers in the Hellenistic period seem to have been especially fond of narrating tales about nymphs whose pursuit of mortals ended in pathos. One example is the infatuation of a naiad for Herakles' young squire Hylas, who had come to draw water:

…as soon as Hylas leant over to dip the pitcher in the stream and the water gurgled loudly as it swept into the echoing bronze, the nymph placed her left arm on his neck and with her right hand on his elbow she drew him down towards her, desiring to kiss his soft mouth. He fell into the middle of the eddying water.

Another whose erotic involvement with a nymph led to his downfall was the Sicilian herdsman Daphnis. His good looks – he was said to have been Hermes' son – caused a nymph to become infatuated with him;

The nymph Arethousa (see pp. 190–91) was loved by the Peloponnesian river-god Alpheios. When she fled westwards to escape his attentions, she turned into a spring in Syracuse. Her head graces Syracusan coins such as this one.

in a fit of jealousy when he slept with another woman, the nymph blinded him. (The traditions about Daphnis are complex; in one version, the songs he sang to console himself in his rustic isolation led to his becoming the originator of pastoral poetry.)

It was a matter of debate as to how long nymphs lived. The consensus seems to have been that nymphs' lives were very long, but finite. The case of tree nymphs was particularly interesting, and gave rise to the notion of 'hamadryad': *hama* means 'at the same time as', and implies that the nymph's life is co-extensive with that of the tree (*drus* means 'tree'). As the *Homeric Hymn to Aphrodite* puts it: 'They belong neither with mortals nor with immortals. They live for a long time… But when the fate of death is near, first those lovely trees wither where they stand, and the bark shrivels about them and the twigs fall, and the soul of both [i.e. nymph and tree] leaves the light of the sun together.' Not surprisingly, to shorten the life of a nymph by felling her tree was an intolerable sacrilege. In his *Hymn to Demeter*, the Hellenistic poet Kallimachos narrates the tale of wicked Erysichthon, who one day took an axe to a poplar sacred to the goddess. The victim's cries of pain were answered by a furious Demeter: the axeman was afflicted with a terrible hunger, which ended only when he consumed his own body.

Already in Homer's *Iliad*, the marine equivalents of the nymphs of tree and mountain are referred to as Nereids, i.e. the daughters of the sea god Nereus; Achilles' mother Thetis is one of their number. The seeming continuity between these beings and the female demon called the *neraïda* (plural *neraïdes*) of modern Greek folklore raises the vexed question of the extent of the 'survival' of ancient Greek religious belief into modern times. The reason why the question is vexed is that it carries with it a weight of ideological implications: to emphasize, or alternatively to deny, such continuity is to make a statement about the 'Hellenicity' of modern Greece, in relation, for instance, to its Ottoman past. As it happens, in the present case it is surely hard to deny *some* element of continuity, since the Nereid/*neraïda* parallels are so close. Already in antiquity we find cases of 'nympholepsy', whereby an individual's

Athens in a cave sanctuary near the hill of the Areopagos; the terrifying physical appearance of these goddesses, and their role in pursuing blood-murderers, lent an obvious logic to their seclusion in a 'wild' part of civic space.

Given that caves were recesses within a goddess – namely Gaia, the Earth – to enter a cave was to make an intimate approach to the sacred. A destination to which one cave gave access was the realm of Hades itself. The traveller Pausanias records that at Tainaron, the promontory at the southernmost tip of the Mani peninsula in the Peloponnese, there was 'a sanctuary which looks like a cave', the spot at which Herakles was said to have brought the monstrous dog Kerberos up from the Underworld.

The representation of caves in mythological

High up on Mount Parnassos, above Delphi, is the Korykian cave. It has a truly impressive central chamber, 50m long by 27m wide (165 by 88 ft), and rising to 12m (40 ft) in height. Like many caves in the Greek world, it was in antiquity sacred to Pan and the Nymphs. 'Of all the caves I have ever set eyes on,' wrote the ancient traveller Pausanias, 'this one seemed to me the one most worth seeing.'

consciousness was believed to have been taken over by the nymphs, reducing him to a state of trance-like devotion: there is inscriptional evidence (end of the 5th century BC), from the cave of Vari in Attica, for the devotion of one such 'nympholept', a man named Archedamos. From the Byzantine period through to the present day, the notion of possession by female demons has persisted as an explanation for otherwise inexplicably strange mental or physical behaviour. In the context of the fundamental God/Devil duality in Christian belief, the *neraïdes* of modern folklore have been regarded as being on the side of the Devil – destructive and malevolent powers who seduce the unwary by adopting alluring female form. That kind of moral polarization is foreign to ancient Greek belief, which lacked the concept of a Devil. The ancient Greek nymphs might, of course, be dangerous, but they could also be beneficent. They had a particular role in nurturing and educating heroes, and even gods, in the skills needed for an effective rural existence. Among their pupils were Dionysos, Apollo, and Apollo's son, the herdsman-hero Aristaios; among the useful skills which these pupils learned from the nymphs were divination, bee-keeping, and how to make cheese.

narratives picks up and develops some of these aspects of worship. Caves are places of habitation, but also wild – shelters, for those who need them, in the world which lies outside constructed human settlements. Like mountains (where, after all, many caves are situated), caves are associated in myth with a time Before. The birth and early nurture of several of the gods took place in caves. Baby Zeus was cared for in a cave, though there was doubt about which one: not surprisingly, several localities vied for the honour, for example in Crete and Arcadia. The infant Dionysos too was looked after in a cave: an iconographically famous moment depicted Hermes handing the newborn over to the nymphs to look after. A remarkable example of the way in which myth could be incorporated into

The survival of any sort of painting from ancient Greece is very unusual, so the discovery in 1934 of four painted wooden tablets was an exceptional event. Found in a cave at Pitsa near Sikyon (northern Peloponnese), the tablets indicate that the cave was sacred to the Nymphs. On the tablet illustrated here, a group of figures is preparing to sacrifice a sheep. The inscription records the names of two women (presumably those making the offering) together with the words: 'dedicated to the Nymphs'.

political ceremony is the fact that this scene was one of the numerous episodes recreated in the extravagant and colossal procession-with-tableaux of Ptolemy II Philadelphos (308–246 BC) in Alexandria. In the words of Athenaios (active AD 200), the writer who records the event:

It would not be right to omit the four-wheeled cart, 33 feet long and 21 feet wide, drawn by 500 men; upon it there was a deep cavern richly overshadowed with ivy and yew. From this, along the whole route, there flew out pigeons, ring-doves and turtle-doves, their feet fastened with ribbons so that the spectators could easily catch hold of them. From the cave also there bubbled up two fountains, one of milk and the other of wine. And all the nymphs standing around him [sc. the baby Dionysos] had golden crowns, while Hermes had a golden staff, and rich garments.

The tableau celebrates one of the earliest episodes in the career of Dionysos, future conqueror of 'The East'. Alexander the Great had seen himself as a new Dionysos; Ptolemy II, inheritor of part of Alexander's legacy, was placing himself in the same tradition, by lavishly displaying the events surrounding Dionysos, including his rearing in the Cave of the Nymphs.

Caves in Homer

Already in the Homeric *Odyssey* we find a range of images of what a cave might be like. Kalypso's cavern, where Odysseus is detained, seems at first sight a paradise: it lies in a grove, with nesting birds, and flowers, and four symmetrically flowing fountains. But the artificial formality of the scene mirrors what has now become the stiltedness of Odysseus' relationship with Kalypso. Another Odyssean cave, that of the Cyclops Polyphemos, again gives an initial impression of being orderly and even idyllic, with lambs and kids neatly divided into pens according to age, and milk and cheese in profusion. But the cave's savage owner belies his dwelling, as he spatters the floor with the brains of his guests, before devouring the remains. Here it is not the sacredness of caves which is in evidence, but their wildness. Only with his return to Ithaca

does Odysseus find himself in a landscape which is neither threatening nor outlandish. The act which convinces the hero that he is finally home is his recognition of the Cave of the Nymphs on Ithaca:

At the head of the harbour, there is an olive tree with spreading
leaves, and nearby is a cave that is shadowy, and pleasant,
and sacred to the nymphs who are called the naiads.
There are mixing bowls and two-handled jars inside it,
made of stone, and there the bees deposit their honey.
And therein also there are looms that are made of stone, very long, where
the nymphs weave their sea-purple webs, a wonder to look on;
and there is water for ever flowing. It has two entrances,
one of them facing the North Wind, where mortals can enter,
but the one toward the South Wind has more divinity. No men
enter by that way: it is the way of the immortals.

(Right) The so-called Cave of the Nymphs on Ithaca, where Odysseus reputedly hid the gifts which his Phaeacian hosts had bestowed upon him. Light falls into the cave from an opening in the roof.

(Below) Caves could be thought of as places of wildness and strangeness. All kinds of threat might lurk there. On this cup Herakles (unusually, beardless) is pulling a fearsome monster from its den in a cave. Attic cup, c. 500 BC.

This Homeric passage was to have considerable resonance in later antiquity. The philosopher of religion Porphyry (3rd century AD) read it in Neoplatonic terms as an allegory about the passage of souls in and out of the cosmos, which, being a place both 'shadowy' and 'pleasant', was symbolized by the Cave of the Nymphs. Porphyry's approach illustrates the apparently limitless capacity of Greek mythology to inspire its hearers, readers and viewers to reinterpret. As for the geographical reality of the cave on Ithaca, there has been a suggested identification with a site in Polis Bay, where excavations have uncovered a large number of bronze tripods dedicated in the 9th/8th centuries BC, as well as later offerings and, from the Hellenistic period, inscriptions mentioning the nymphs and Odysseus. This cave had quite clearly acquired renown already in antiquity, thanks to Homer's narrative.

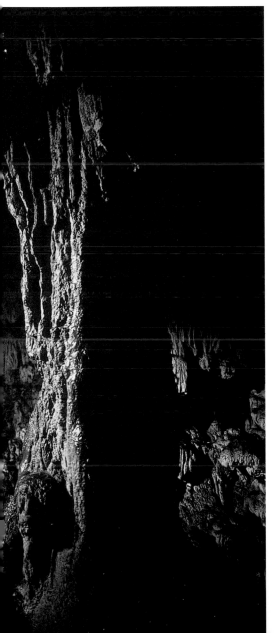

Philoktetes; Minos

The various but partly overlapping connotations of caves which we have noticed so far – primitive savagery, means of access to the sacred, protective seclusion – recur throughout Greek mythology. When Philoktetes, abandoned by his fellow Greek warriors on the way to Troy (see p. 135), dwelt in a cave during his years of painful isolation on the island of Lemnos, he was reduced to a condition hardly better than that of an animal. Other cave-dwellers were not just uncivilized, but ferocious: Zeus' terrifying adversary Typhoeus had a cave for his lair, as did the Nemean lion, victim of one of Herakles' Labours.

The idea that a cave provided a place of privileged access to the sacred is implicit in a story told about Minos, mythical ruler of Crete, who used to go to a cave to converse with his father Zeus, at nine-year intervals (see p. 199).

Selene; Kreousa

As for the characteristic that caves could offer protective seclusion, this often figures in an erotic context. The isolation which caves offered made them ideally suited to secret liaisons. When Selene, goddess of the moon, descended to love the handsome mortal Endymion, their lovemaking took place in a cave near Miletos (in Asia Minor). When Apollo had intercourse with the Athenian princess Kreousa – an event whose near-tragic consequences are explored by Euripides in his play *Ion* – the god chose a cave in which to conceal his deed.

A cave has been Philoktetes' home since the Greeks abandoned him on Lemnos. In this scene (south Italian vase, early 4th century BC) he sits clutching his magic bow in his left hand, while preparations are being made for his removal from the island. Above right is Odysseus, perhaps in conversation with 'Lemnos' (a personification of the island). To the left are Athene and either Neoptolemos or Diomedes, both of whom were said to have been involved in the scheme to take Philoktetes to Troy.

Rivers and Springs

In thirsty Greece, fresh water was at a premium. As well as being self-evidently a requirement for day-to-day existence, it was also needed for numerous religious ceremonies, including purification, sacrifice, weddings and funerary ritual. So for habitations and sanctuaries alike, the proximity of a spring or river was indispensable. Yet neither the landscape nor the climate was particularly generous. There are some sizeable rivers in Thessaly, Macedonia and Thrace, and the Acheloös pours abundantly southwards from its source high in the Pindos range; but elsewhere, and especially in Attica, the Peloponnese and the Aegean islands, rivers can shrink to a miserly trickle, or disappear altogether, in the summer heat.

For the Greeks, rivers and springs were divinities. Rivers, almost without exception imagined as male, supplied seminal energy: even if their waters receded for part of the year, their flow always renewed itself. The creative and nurturing powers of springs, on the other hand, were usually felt to be female, being virtually indistinguishable from the nymphs who embodied their refreshing allure.

The greatest of the rivers of Greece was Acheloös. One of the 3000 children of Okeanos and Tethys, he was himself prolific, siring numerous nymphs/springs, such as Kastalia at Delphi and Dirke at Thebes, as well as the Sirens. His sexual vigour was often represented through the image of a man-headed bull, although this was only one of the shapes which he could adopt. In the famous wrestling match which he fought (unsuccessfully) with Herakles when both were suitors for the hand of Deianeira (see p. 122), he appeared 'now as a bull in manifest form, now as a darting, coiled serpent, now with the trunk of a man and the forehead of an ox, while from his shaggy beard the streams of fountain-water flowed out.'

Genealogy is one of the ways in which myths express meaning. Again and again genealogies convey the cardinal importance of rivers and springs for the flourishing of communities. In the district of Argos the river Inachos, another of Okeanos' sons, is the progenitor of the local culture-hero Phoroneus. But Inachos is a feeble stream, dry except after rains. Why should this be so, if he is divine? The answer can only lie in the superior power of another god. Once upon a time, Inachos

(Right) This head of Acheloös (south Italian terracotta, early 4th century BC) shows a common way of representing the features of the river-god: with bull's horns, but with a man's face and beard.

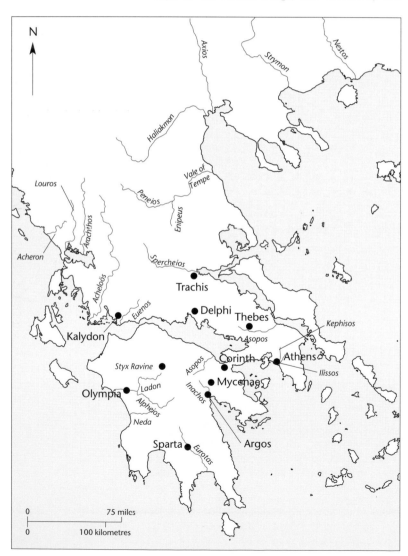

N

75 miles

100 kilometres

The river Peneios in Thessaly was, according to one tradition, the father of Daphne, Apollo's reluctant lover. For part of its length the river flows through the Vale of Tempe, whose beauty was often extolled by post-classical writers and artists.

had been one of the judges who favoured Hera in her contest with Poseidon for possession of the territory of Argos; when the decision went against him, Poseidon reacted angrily by making Inachos' waters disappear.

According to a common mythical pattern, the daughter of a river would be united with a god and would then give birth to a hero, who would in turn be the ancestor of one or another of Greece's future communities. An example is Asopos (several rivers had this name, for example one in Boiotia and one near Sikyon, to the west of Corinth); among his many daughters were the nymphs Corcyra (mod. Kerkira/Corfu) and Salamis, both loved by

Poseidon, and Aigina, loved by Zeus. Unfortunately, the victims of such liaisons were as likely to experience distress as contentment. Inachos' daughter Io, the maiden transformed into a cow, suffered grievously as a result of her liaison with Zeus (see p. 98), though she did eventually resume her human shape, and great heroes – Danaos, Perseus and Herakles – would figure amongst her descendants.

Daphne

No such compensation mitigated the sufferings of the nymph Daphne. According to different myth-tellers, she was the offspring either of the

Sir William Gell's visits to Greece in 1804 and 1806 inspired him to publish several illustrated works on the Greek world. The Valley of Tempe, *1805, is one of his most atmospheric watercolours.*

Arcadian river Ladon, or the Thessalian river Peneios. Either way, her parentage was handsome: Pausanias called the Ladon the loveliest river in Greece, while the Peneios glides between Mounts Ossa and Olympos through the verdant and shady Vale of Tempe, the subject of countless poetical and artistic evocations. In the Peloponnesian version of Daphne's story, she behaved like a mortal equivalent of Artemis, hunting in the wilds with her female companions. When a young man called Leukippos ('White Horse'), son of Oinomaos the king of Elis, fell in love with her, the only way he could get near her was by passing himself off as a girl. For a while the ruse worked, but when Apollo too lusted after Daphne, the god instilled into the nymph and her companions a desire to strip and to plunge into the river Ladon. Leukippos' deception was exposed, and the offended maidens stabbed him to death.

The Ladon–Daphne–Leukippos story would enjoy little resonance in the post-classical mythological tradition. The version of Daphne's fate which caught on was, as in so many cases, the one which had been filtered through the inexhaustibly fertile literary imagination of the Roman poet Ovid. Tailor-made for Ovid's central theme of metamorphosis was a story which made Daphne the daughter of the river Peneios. She rejected Apollo's sexual advances, prayed to her father, and was changed into a laurel, a tree which would thereafter be sacred to Apollo.

Alpheios

No less suited to Ovid's theme, but transmitted (with many variants) in Greek sources too, is the story of another river-god and another nymph. Alpheios, the principal river of the Peloponnese, rises in Arcadia and flows west into the southern

(Left) Daphne's escape from Apollo's amorous pursuit through her transformation into laurel is here represented by the 15th-century Florentine painter Antonio del Pollaiuolo. The change in Daphne's form can hardly be described as understated, yet it all takes place in a 'familiar' context: the landscape resembles that of the valley of the Arno near Florence. Apollo is dressed as a young Renaissance nobleman.

Ionian Sea. Continue almost due west, and the next landfall is Syracuse in Sicily. This fact of geography is developed in the tale of Alpheios' longing for the nymph Arethousa, who used to swim in his waters. She rejected him and fled, but he pursued her, even across the sea. She became the spring which bore her name, rising in the tiny islet of Ortygia at Syracuse, where Alpheios' waters for ever after mingled with hers. The geographer Strabo (1st century BC/1st century AD) ridiculed the idea of a subterranean westward passage by Alpheios – after all, he sensibly observed, the river does not disappear underground, but flows into the sea in full view. Strabo's opinion, it must be stressed, does not prove that the Greeks 'did not believe in their myths'; it just exemplifies one possible view which could be expressed towards the myths' veracity. Scepticism was no less, but certainly no more 'authentic' a reaction than was pious acceptance.

(Right) The marble Apollo and Daphne (1622–25) by Gian Lorenzo Bernini brilliantly captures the protagonists' astonishment. Myth-tellers have often used the tale of Apollo and Daphne to illustrate the opposition between chastity (Daphne's preference) and the pleasures of the flesh (Apollo's aim). For the viewer of Bernini's sculpture it is surely the figures' sensuality which makes the greater impact.

The Sea

In Greek eyes, the fundamental quality of the sea was its ambiguity. The poet Semonides put it like this: 'often the sea stands without a tremor, harmless, a great delight to sailors, in the summer season; but often it raves, tossed about by thundering waves.' (He was making a comparison with a particular kind of woman.) This doubleness of the sea runs throughout our sources.

On the negative side, we can read Plato's *Laws*, a dialogue about what legislation should be introduced in an imaginary colony in Crete. At one point, discussion turns on where the city is to be founded. Should it be close to the sea? But that, observes one

Poseidon ruled the waves with his trident, but he was not the only divinity associated with the sea. On the southern coast of Cyprus, 25 kilometres (15 miles) east of Paphos, is this lovely spot where Aphrodite was said to have been born from the sea-foam.

of the speakers, would have dire consequences, since being near the sea 'fills the land with wholesaling and retailing, breeds shifty and deceitful habits in a man's soul, and makes the citizens distrustful and hostile…'

However, on the other hand, the sea could be represented as a valuable source of livelihood, through fishing and trade. It could even be seen as a symbol of Greekness itself. When Xenophon, Plato's near-contemporary, wrote his account of the astonishing 'March of the Ten Thousand', the most dramatic moment in the whole narrative is when the men of the Greek expeditionary force, having tramped right across Asia Minor, Babylonia and

Armenia, at long last catch sight of the waters of the Black Sea. Their spine-tingling cry, '*Thalassa, thalassa!*' ('The sea! The sea!'), suggests that they have come 'home'.

The sea's ambiguity is explored in mythology. Whereas myths about mountains, caves, rivers and springs involve a seemingly infinite array of divinities, the sea is embodied by a god who, though not the only power active in its waters, is nevertheless comfortably superior to all the rest: Poseidon. His temper is sometimes calm and serene, sometimes furious and uncontrollable.

In Homer's *Odyssey*, Poseidon repeatedly batters Odysseus with ferocious storms; yet he is just as likely to be surrounded by benignly frolicking and acquiescent creatures of the deep. In Moschos' poem about the abduction of Europa by Zeus, Poseidon celebrates his brother's forthcoming nuptials in the midst of a cheerful and musical assembly of sea creatures:

Joyfully from the depths the dolphin gambolled
over the waves. Nereids arose from the sea, and
all advanced in rank mounted on the backs of
sea-beasts. The deep-thundering Earthshaker
[Poseidon] himself made smooth the waves over
the water, and led his brother on his salty way
Around him gathered Tritons, those deep-sounding
musicians of the sea, blowing a bridal song on their
tapering shells.

Several lesser sea-deities, including Glaukos, Nereus, Proteus and Triton, have a shared connection with prophecy; perhaps the implication is that the deep of the sea is parallel to the mysterious profundity of the future. Also powerful at sea (although not thought of as dwellers *in* the sea) were the 'Dioskouroi', i.e. the Dios Kouroi ('Children of Zeus'), namely Kastor and Polydeukes, whom the Romans knew as Castor and Pollux. Their pedigree was classically heroic: as befitted the twin sons of Leda, they counted the Kalydonian Boar Hunt and the voyage of the *Argo* amongst their noble exploits.

But, as with so many heroes, their downfall came about through a family dispute. They were involved in a feud-to-the-death with their cousins Idas and Lynkeus: one version said the Dioskouroi had abducted the two daughters of Leukippos, who were due to be married to Idas and Lynkeus. Thanks to Zeus, however, Kastor and Polydeukes were allowed to be identical after death as they had been before it: each was to spend alternate days on Olympos and in the Underworld. In this unusual posthumous existence they could be called on by mariners in distress; if the mariners' prayer was heard, the twins would ride to the rescue on their trademark white steeds, or in the form of the fiery electrical discharge which can manifest itself around a ship's mast during a storm (St Elmo's fire).

Crete

Androgeos   Glaukos

(Left) Sir Arthur Evans as portrayed by Sir William Richmond (1907). Evans' archaeological work still dominates our view of 'Minoan' Crete. It was he who brought to light the sensational finds from Knossos, revealing a complex civilization of the 2nd millennium BC, predating that of Mycenae.

(Right) This faience figure from the palace at Knossos, usually referred to as 'the snake-goddess', has become an emblem of the 'Minoan' civilization of Crete.

Ever since the excavations by Sir Arthur Evans at Knossos at the beginning of the 20th century, the study of Crete's role in mythology has been dominated by the notion of 'reflections of the Bronze Age'. Bronze Age frescoes of bull-leaping have been interpreted as precursors of the myth of the Minotaur; the intricate remains of the great palace at Knossos have been identified as the source of the myth of the Labyrinth. Such links are implicitly reinforced by the term 'Minoan civilization', which archaeologists habitually, but arbitrarily, apply to Bronze Age Crete. Of course it may be that later Cretan myths about a bull or a labyrinth do indeed preserve, at some level of folk memory, recollections of earlier images or practices. But such a perspective does not begin to exhaust the significance of these

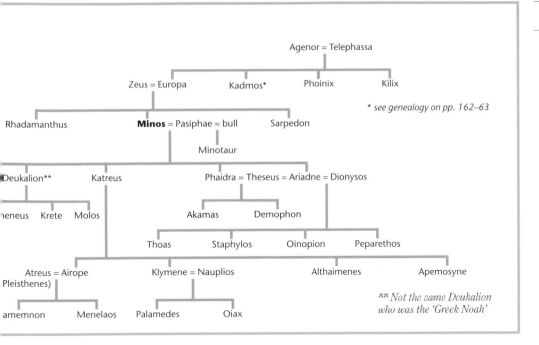

Agenor = Telephassa

Zeus = Europa   Kadmos*   Phoinix   Kilix

* see genealogy on pp. 162–63

Rhadamanthus   **Minos** = Pasiphae = bull   Sarpedon

Minotaur

Deukalion**   Katreus   Phaidra = Theseus = Ariadne = Dionysos

heneus   Krete   Molos   Akamas   Demophon

Thoas   Staphylos   Oinopion   Peparethos

Atreus = Airope (Pleisthenes)   Klymene = Nauplios   Althaimenes   Apemosyne

amemnon   Menelaos   Palamedes   Oiax

** Not the same Deukalion who was the 'Greek Noah'

The Phoenician princess Europa sits on the back of a bull, which is really the metamorphosed Zeus. When she reaches Crete she will give birth to three renowned sons: Minos, Rhadamanthus and Sarpedon. Terracotta, 5th century BC.

stories – just as the meaning of a word is not the same as its etymology. There is much more to be said about myths of Crete than that they contain 'survivals' of what went before.

Within Greek mythology, Crete stands out as an unusual and distinctive place. A good way of appreciating this distinctiveness is to look at Crete's legendary sovereign: Minos. Earlier (see pp. 127–28) we mentioned some episodes in Minos' career which embroiled him with the Athenian hero Theseus; it will now be helpful to set those episodes into context.

King Minos

Minos was the son of Zeus and Europa. In keeping with his illustrious ancestry, he seemed destined to assume sovereignty over Crete from his base at Knossos. However, one day his claim to power was contested; so he prayed to Poseidon to send confirmation of his right to rule, in the form of a bull from the sea, which he would reciprocate by sacrificing. Poseidon sent the bull, but Minos broke his side of the bargain, keeping the special bull and sacrificing an ordinary one instead. Poseidon's reaction was to instill into Minos' wife Pasiphae an unnatural lust for the bull. To fulfil her desire she climbed into an artificial cow prefabricated by Daidalos, Minos' resident technological genius. The two mated, and the strange fruit of their union was the Minotaur: bull-faced, human-bodied and carnivorous. Minos shut it away in another of Daidalos' inventions: the maze known as the Labyrinth.

We have already discussed the story of Theseus' overcoming of the Minotaur, and his escape with Ariadne (see pp. 127–28). Back on Crete, Minos incarcerated Daidalos and his son Ikaros, who escaped (p. 92). Afterwards, according to one tradition, Minos pursued his betrayer Daidalos to Sicily. Daidalos went into hiding, but Minos employed a ruse worthy of the great inventor himself. He had brought with him a pocket labyrinth – that is, a spiral sea-shell: whoever could pass a thread through it would receive a great reward. By attaching the thread to an ant, Daidalos completed the task – so revealing his identity as the only person capable of such ingenuity. But Minos did not manage to punish Daidalos' disloyalty, and died an undignified death, scalded in his bath; some said that Daidalos devised a lethal system of water pipes to do the deed.

Cretan paradoxes

The crucial aspect of Minos' career to stress is *paradox*. As we saw in the episode of Poseidon's bull, one of Minos' principal traits was his tendency to commit transgressions. He was, for example, a serial adulterer: he was even said to have attempted to rape Britomartis, the Cretan equivalent of the goddess Artemis. In revenge, his wife Pasiphae used her powers (she was a daughter of the Sun god Helios) to afflict him with the propensity to ejaculate snakes, scorpions and millipedes. That was the aspect of Minos which led to his description in the *Odyssey* as 'destructive-minded'. But there was another side to him. One source (Hesiod) describes him as 'most kingly of all mortal kings', another (the *Iliad*) as 'Crete's guardian'; he was said to have conversed every nine years with his father Zeus (see p. 199), so that he had the best education of all: education by the sovereign of Olympos. On the basis of

that advice, Minos achieved the reputation of being a supremely wise lawgiver, whose authority did not cease even with his death: Odysseus saw him in the Underworld, 'holding a golden sceptre, issuing judgments to the dead.' Some critics, ancient and modern, have tried to explain the negative spin put onto Minos' achievements as the product of bias by Athenian myth-tellers, against whose ancestors – such as Theseus – Minos was said to have fought; but in fact his Janus-like doubleness is part of a wider picture.

For there is another paradox about Minoan Crete: it is a place both of imprisonment and also of rest-less movement. The Labyrinth is one example of imprisonment; another is the seclusion with which Minos threatened Pasiphae, after her bestial act.

A third example concerns Glaukos, the son of Minos and Pasiphae. While still a child Glaukos fell into a large storage-jar of honey, and drowned. No one could fathom out what had happened to him, so knowledge beyond the ordinary was required. A test set up by Minos to find the best diviner was won by Polyidos ('He who Knows Much'), who then divined the location of the corpse. But Minos wanted his son back alive, so he incar-cerated Polyidos alongside the corpse. When a snake approached the body, Polyidos killed it; but then another snake came along, applied a herb to the dead snake, and brought it back to life; Polyidos repeated this procedure in order to resur-rect Glaukos. True to his tendency to exert control, Minos refused to let Polyidos leave Crete until he had taught Glaukos the skill of divination. Polyidos did so, but then told Glaukos to spit into his mouth – which caused him to forget the seercraft which he had just learned.

The two snakes at the bottom of the image on this Attic cup (c. 470–460 BC), together with the identity of the two human figures – Polyidos and (right) Glaukos – confirm this as a representation of the mysterious events in Glaukos' tomb. By observing how one snake used a magical herb in order to resurrect its companion, Polyidos carries out the same procedure to bring Glaukos back to life.

Minos and the sea

In these episodes Minos' sovereignty expresses itself through the power to restrict and imprison. But there is a different face of Minos' Crete. This is its sea-going aspect, which led Thucydides to say that, 'according to tradition, Minos was the first person to have organized a navy.' (The point has nothing to do with what may or may not have been the actual thalassocratic power of Bronze Age Crete – a topic of major disagreement among archaeologists – rather, the point is about later *perceptions* of what had gone on in 'the time of myth'.) Although it could be argued that sea power is just another aspect of Minos' control, there is a more general point at issue. From Homer onwards, Cretans are repeatedly represented as mobile, travellers, pirates; Crete is a place where people sail from. Typical is a song from Euripides' play *Hippolytos*, in which the perplexed chorus is trying to explain Phaidra's condition (in fact, she is pining away with love for her own step-son). Can it be, the chorus wonders, that bad news has been brought by a ship-borne traveller from Crete – that is, from Phaidra's original home? Crete is the source of many restless things, not least Minos' wife Pasiphae, and their daughters Ariadne and Phaidra herself.

The Crete of mythology illustrates the double-edged quality of power. It is a place of sovereignty, technical prowess and sea-borne domination; but sovereignty can tip over into tyranny (the serial sexual adventures of the 'negative' Minos are typical of the licence which Greek tyrants proverbially allowed themselves), and into the obsessive desire to control; technical prowess is available for ingenious flight, but also for incarceration and bestiality; sea power can take ships to help the Greek cause at Troy – according to the *Iliad*, Crete contributed a large contingent of vessels – or it can facilitate piracy, for which historical Cretans were in fact in later times notorious.

These are some of the paradoxes of power explored in myths about Crete; to that extent, these myths are 'thought experiments'. Perhaps we can go further, and suggest that such stories imply that absolute power must ultimately fail. Minos cannot in the end control Daidalos' technology, or Polyidos' seercraft. When Pasiphae and then Ariadne lust for different aspects of the strange, Minos cannot control them either. In spite of the authority which accrues to him through being Zeus' son, Minos ends his mortal career boiled in a bath.

Crete and the gods

Another aspect of Crete's mythological distinctiveness is its relationship with the gods. The fact that Zeus was said to have been born there did not make Crete unusual: Pausanias observed that 'even a determined person would find it impossible to enumerate all the peoples who maintain that Zeus was born and reared among them.' However, at least according to the Cretans themselves, Crete was a place where *all* the gods originated. According to one writer, 'most of the gods proceeded from Crete to many parts of the inhabited world, conferring benefits upon the races of mankind.' This is a particularly powerful version of the common mythological theme that 'civilization began with us'. More unusual still is another claim made in antiquity, that Crete was where Zeus died. The poet Kallimachos reacted to such an allegation in his

The cave at Psychro, on the slopes of Mount Dikte in Crete, was a place of worship already during the Bronze Age: rich finds of votive offerings have been discovered dating from the 2nd millennium BC into the Archaic period. Whether or not this is the 'Diktaian cave' where Zeus was allegedly born, tradition certainly ascribed many remarkable events to a special cave on the mountain. One tradition located the birth of Zeus here. Another myth related that King Minos used to converse with his father Zeus in the cave, discussing the laws with which Minos governed his kingdom.

Hymn to Zeus, when he ascribed it to the fact that 'Cretans are always liars.' Nevertheless the theme of Zeus' death was taken up by numerous writers afterwards, including gleeful Christian polemicists, who delighted in making fun of pagans who could tell absurd stories about dying gods.

It is not easy to know what to make of the story that Zeus died in Crete. Such an idea was certainly not incompatible with the worship of Zeus, which was a major feature of religion on the island. Some

scholars have seen it as a belief of very restricted circulation, perhaps influenced by the ideas of the Hellenistic author Euhemeros, who wrote a poem alleging that Ouranos, Kronos and Zeus had been mortal kings who were worshipped as divinities by their grateful peoples (see p. 225). Another approach would be to see the story as one more piece of evidence that Crete could be represented as a mysterious and enigmatic place in which religious power flowed in unusual directions.

Troy

Looking at Troy's unique place within the world of Greek mythology can teach us many things, but two above all: the way in which the meanings of myths vary according to the different perspectives of their tellers; and the extraordinary difficulty of any attempt to unravel the opposition between 'real' and 'mythical' space.

Shifting perspectives on the Trojan War

For the Greeks, the Trojan War really happened: it was what we should call a historical event. On the Hellenistic inscription known as the Parian Marble, the Fall of Troy is dated quite precisely to the seventh-last day of the month of Thargelion in the twenty-second year of the reign of King Menestheus of Athens: in modern terms, 5 June 1209 BC. Such confident precision is remarkable, since the inscription dates from 264/3 BC, i.e. almost one thousand years later than the presumed event. Other ancient sources offer a range of different dates, ranging from the late 14th to the late 12th centuries BC.; but what all agree on is the historicity of

the event. Given the plurality of view which characterizes so much of Greek culture, it is no surprise that not all Greeks regarded this historicity in the same light. The 5th century BC historian Thucydides, for example, accepted that the Trojan expedition took place, but queried many logistical aspects of Homer's account; six centuries later Pausanias, in his *Description of Greece*, followed a similarly rationalizing path when he ascribed the fall of Troy – the historicity of which he, too, fully accepted – to a siege engine rather than to a Wooden Horse. The possibility of such rationalizations did nothing to undermine the imaginative power of the story: the conflict between Greeks and Trojans remained the definitive mythical crucible in which to examine the significance of humanity's place in the world.

Like every Greek myth, the tale of Troy was fluid, open to 'negotiation' (as scholars sometimes label the process) according to the interests and attitudes of different myth-tellers. In Homer, for instance, there is no ethnic or cultural opposition between Greeks and Trojans: both sides worship the same gods, and neither side has the monopoly of virtue or vice. By and large the art and literature of the Archaic period follows the Homeric precedent of even-handedness between the Trojans and their Greek foes. It is only in the 5th century BC, especially in Athens, that, in the aftermath of the Persian invasion of Greece, 'Troy' takes on an intensely negative image, and Trojans become the archetypal

The Hellenistic inscription known as the Parian Marble gives a chronological record of what were regarded as important historical events. Amongst the occurrences mentioned are some which we might describe as 'mythical', including the supposed date of the capture of Troy. The Marble survives in two large fragments: one is in the Ashmolean Museum, Oxford; the other is in the museum in Paros.

'barbarians'. A characteristic moment occurs in *Agamemnon*, the first play of Aischylos' *Oresteia* trilogy, when Clytemnestra is trying to persuade her husband Agamemnon, newly returned from the victory at Troy, to walk over a rich purple fabric in order to enact his position of utter triumph. 'What would Priam have done?' Clytemnestra disingenuously enquires. 'He would surely have walked over the fabric,' replies Agamemnon, implicitly confirming the perception of Priam as a typical, luxurious despot.

After the repulse of the Persians in the 480/470s, Greek involvement with the Persian empire continued to dominate the political horizon, until it was overshadowed in the late 5th century BC by the internecine Peloponnesian War, which pitted Athens and Sparta against each other. Throughout this period and beyond it, the Trojan War remained a reference point for political ideology and military action. When, early in the 4th century BC, after Sparta's defeat of Athens, the Spartan king Agesilaos led a Greek expeditionary force against Persia, he explicitly invoked the precedent of the Trojan War by sacrificing at Aulis, as Agamemnon had legendarily done before him. In Athens Troy was 'used' in the same way: when the politician Isokrates (4th century BC) advocated a Greek attack on Persia in order to liberate the Persian-occupied Greek cities of western Asia Minor, he attempted to stoke the fires of patriotism by citing the example of the Greeks' capture of Troy.

But all these 'uses' of Troy pale beside the appropriation of the myth by Alexander the Great. Standing as it did between the 'West' from which Alexander came and the 'East' which he proposed to subjugate, the city of Ilion – reputedly built on the site of ruined Troy – played a key role in Alexander's vision; for he saw himself not, like Agesilaos, as the equivalent of Agamemnon, but as the new Achilles – whose very blood Alexander claimed ran in his own veins, through the ancestral line of his mother Olympias. In theory this might have led Alexander to raze Troy once more; but his vision was more ambitious. Just as his vast military project aimed at uniting West and East in one empire, so his attitude towards Troy embraced the Trojans as well as their erstwhile adversaries. Thus, not content with being Achilles, Alexander also ceremonially appeased the memory of Priam, by sacrificing at the very altar of Zeus on which Priam was said to have been butchered by Achilles' son – and Alexander's alleged ancestor – Neoptolemos.

Real and imaginary Troy

Since Alexander's visit, the fascination exerted by Troy has never been entirely eclipsed, though it has undergone many transformations. In modern times, the focus of that fascination has been the putative physical remains of the city itself. Knowledge of the site's location was lost in the Middle Ages, and it was only in the mid-18th century that the

A photograph taken by Wilhelm Dörpfeld of the excavations of the northeast bastion at the hill of Hisarlik/Troy. The mighty walls leave little room for doubt about the political and military significance of this settlement.

Portrait of Heinrich Schliemann (1877) by Sydney Hodges. Entrepreneur and passionate lover of the Homeric epics, Schliemann made a decisive contribution to our understanding of the Aegean Bronze Age through his excavations, above all at Mycenae and Troy.

matter began to be seriously addressed. But it was not until the 19th century that excavations were undertaken, thanks first to Frank Calvert (1828–1908) and then, above all, to Heinrich Schliemann (1822–90).

Troy and archaeologists

From impoverished beginnings Schliemann had succeeded in amassing a considerable fortune thanks to extraordinary business acumen. He then made a huge investment, of time and energy as well as money, in uncovering Greece's archaeological heritage at Mycenae, Orchomenos, Tiryns and, in culmination, Troy; this labour of love was one which he presented as the fulfilment of a childhood dream.

Schliemann's intuition that the site of Troy was to be found at modern Hisarlik was borne out by his own magnificent finds (in collaboration with the architect Wilhelm Dörpfeld, 1853–1940) of everything from walls and gateways to jewelry and gold. Subsequent archaeological campaigns, led during the 1930s by Carl Blegen (1887–1971) and since 1988 by Manfred Korfmann, have consolidated and expanded the picture. By no means all archaeologists have accepted the inferences which Korfmann wishes to make from his findings; but if he is right, what has emerged, from a combination of archaeological evidence and input from numerous cognate disciplines, notably Hittitology, is that Hisarlik is the site of a city which, in the mid-late 2nd millennium BC, was one of the largest in the entire Near East, with a population of perhaps 5,000–10,000 during the latter part of the 13th century BC.

Not the least astounding piece of evidence which has come to light since Schliemann is that of a treaty (*c*. 1280 BC) between the Hittite king Muwattalli II and Alaksandu of the land of Wilusa (cf. 'Ilion'). It seems perverse to deny the similarity between the names Alaksandu and Alexandros, which was the alternative name borne by Priam's son Paris.

But what can we do with such data from archaeology and Near Eastern studies? What difference can and should they make to our reading of myths of Troy? There can be little doubt that, for most visitors, first-hand acquaintance with the landscape at and near Hisarlik lends immediacy to the Trojan

The discoveries by Heinrich Schliemann and his collaborator Wilhelm Dörpfeld aroused controversy almost as soon as they were announced. For example, the archaeologist Ernst Bötticher alleged that Schliemann and Dörpfeld had not just misinterpreted what they had found, but had actually practised deception. This historic photograph preserves a record of a conference held in 1889 at Hisarlik and attended by all three main players in this academic drama: Schliemann is seated in the centre; Bötticher is second from the left; the dashing figure of Dörpfeld is third from the right.

Aerial view of Hisarlik (above), and excavations in progress (right). The archaeological site is extensive and complex, and continues to provide challenges to the latest generation of archaeologists under Manfred Korfmann from the University of Tübingen, Germany.

story: the massiveness of the walls, the exposed site ('windy' was one of Troy's Homeric epithets), the flatness of the plain (Trojans were famed as tamers of horses), all these can hardly fail to strike a chord of recognition. But what such correspondences should not efface is the fact that, in their ancient narrative contexts, tales of Troy are played out against a *symbolic* landscape which overlies and transmutes whatever topographical and historical 'reality' may or may not have lain behind it.

Troy in the *Iliad*

The prime site for this Troy of the imagination is the *Iliad*, though many other texts and images make their contribution. The principal spatial division in the *Iliad*'s narrative is that between, on one side, the Trojan city, and, on the other side, the Greek encampment beside their beached ships. Within these two polarized areas there are further subdivisions. Inside Troy, two places have special significance. The focus of divine power is the temple of Athene on the city's height; this is the

place where the Trojans express their most ardent prayers for protection, ultimately to no avail. As for the power of humans, this centres on Priam's palace, where he dwells with his extended family:

In it there were fifty rooms of polished stone, built close by each other: there Priam's sons slept beside the wives of their marriage. His daughters' rooms were facing on the opposite side within the courtyard, twelve roofed rooms of polished stone, built close by each other: there Priam's sons-in-law slept beside their honoured wives.

Inside the Greek camp, the single most important location is Achilles' tent, to which he withdraws in anger after the slight by Agamemnon, and to which Priam at last makes his way in order to ransom Hektor's corpse. Also significant is the shore-line. Achilles' marginalization for much of the *Iliad* is expressed by the way in which he repeatedly communes with his mother, the sea nymph Thetis, by the edge of the water. Subsequently, the shore will be where the disgraced Aias, himself marginalized,

(Left) In the third Book of the Iliad Homer describes the scene in which Helen and Priam look down from the vantage-point of the Skaian Gates upon the assembled Greek forces. This lithograph (1907) by Max Slevogt beautifully evokes the contrasting attitudes of those present. On the right is Priam, huddled under his cloak; at the far left, the Elders of Troy chatter busily; in the centre is Helen, glamorous and enigmatic.

(Right) The pitiless brutality of war condensed into one image: as Priam's grandson Astyanax lies stabbed to death on his knees, the blood-stained old king awaits the death-blow to be delivered by Neoptolemos. Attic water-jar c. 480 BC.

The Skaian Gates witness the downfall of even the greatest of the invaders: it is there that Achilles is slain, shot in the heel by the joint agency of Paris and Apollo. But at last the battle shifts from the plain, the walls and the Gates, to the interior of the city itself, as the stratagem of the Horse achieves what brute force could not. Now it is the Greeks who are masters of the walls. In the ultimate gesture of contemptuous power, they extinguish the last fragile hope for the city's future, namely the infant prince Astyanax, child of Hektor and Andromache, either by dashing his little body against an altar or by hurling him from the very ramparts of Troy.

will commit suicide in self-imposed isolation from the rest of the army.

Because Troy's story is about conflict, the points of intersection between Greek and Trojan space are crucial. The prime site of battle is the plain: dusty, blood-spattered, visible alike from the Greek camp and the walls of the city. The best vantage-point is from the top of the city's principal entrance, the mighty Skaian Gates. This is the location for a remarkable episode early in the *Iliad* when the Trojan elders, overlooking the battlefield and chattering among themselves 'like cicadas', notice that Helen too is making her way to the Skaian Gates, where she will converse with Priam as the two of them gaze over the assembled Greek forces. 'No shame that the Trojans and the well-greaved Achaians should suffer agonies for long years over a woman like this,' observe the old men wistfully. 'She is fearfully like the immortal goddesses to look at. But even so, for all her beauty, let her go back in the ships, and not be left here, a curse to us and our children for future time.'

The Underworld

In a vignette from near the beginning of Plato's *Republic* (4th century BC) one of the participants in the dialogue, an old man called Kephalos, describes what he and his elderly friends talk about when they meet. As well as, inevitably, reminiscing about old times, they also ponder what lies ahead:

> when a man begins to realize that he is going to die, there come upon him fear and anxiety about what before did not occur to him. The stories [*muthoi*] that are told of the world of Hades, and of how a man who has done wrong here must be punished there, though he may have ridiculed these stories hitherto, then indeed torment his soul in case there may be some truth in them.

Kephalos' remarks provide yet another example of how Greek myths vary with context. This time the key variable is the age of the person who hears a myth: the same individual may, at one time of life, be scornful of one of the traditional tales, yet at another time be terrified of it. Kephalos also has something to say about the nature of the Afterlife. The idea of punishment after death suggests a tie-in between one's moral conduct while alive and the consequences which will flow from that conduct after death (a theme highly pertinent to the *Republic*, whose argument centres on the nature of justice). But we are still left with a feeling of uncertainty: what exactly will it be like in the Afterlife?

Homer's Underworld

Early in the Greek myth-telling tradition we find one answer to this question. Book 11 of the *Odyssey* narrates the voyage of Odysseus to the Land of the Dead. In order to find this place, he must sail to the edge of the world, beaching his ship on the shore of the Ocean which encircles everything that exists. The spot is dark and gloomy, heavy with fog, and shaded with poplar and willow; two of the rivers of the Underworld, Pyriphlegethon ('Blazing with Fire') and Kokytos ('Lamentation') flow into a third, Acheron (perhaps 'Groaning'). Odysseus sacrifices a ram and a ewe, filling a pit with their blood; the effect is to attract the souls of the dead, who, on drinking the blood, temporarily regain the power to speak to a living person. Through his conversations with the dead, Odysseus learns something about the realm of Hades and his queen Persephone. For all their insubstantiality, the souls of the dead retain the identity and demeanour which they had in life. However, especially for those whose life had been glorious, the contrast with what they now experience is painful indeed.

O shining Odysseus, never try to console me for dying.
I would rather follow the plough as thrall to another man, one with no land allotted to him and not much to live on,
than be a king over all the perished dead.

(Left) The lower course of the river Acheron in northwestern Greece is a secluded and shady backwater, winding its way peacefully to the sea. Further upstream, however, its waters flow through a dramatic gorge. For ancient Greeks, the Acheron was one of the rivers of the Underworld, at once a real river in a real place and a grim feature of the imagined landscape of death.

(Right) The Kokytos, a modest stream flowing into the Acheron, seems to belie its name ('Lamentation'). Yet for ancient Greeks this part of their world had associations with death. The far west was where the Sun set: gloomy and dank.

The words are those of Achilles, obliged by death to leave the spotlight and dwell for ever in the shadows.

Odysseus' account does not offer a clear topography of the Underworld. But his narrative does imply the grouping together of a few notable transgressors, each of whom is suffering exemplary and evidently eternal punishment. Tityos, would-be rapist of the goddess Leto, is having his liver pecked out by two vultures; Tantalos, who was permitted by the gods to share their ambrosia and nectar but who then betrayed that trust, is suffering appropriate torment, as lovely food and drink remain perpetually – 'tantalizingly' – just beyond the reach of his parched lips; Sisyphos, who tried to cheat Death of his due, has endlessly to roll a massive boulder up a hill, only to see it roll down again. The logic of these punishments is fairly evident: it is not just any human crime, but crimes against the honour of the gods, which draw down chastisement upon the perpetrator. But who has assigned these punishments, and by what mechanism? At one point Odysseus mentions that he saw Minos 'seated, holding a golden sceptre and issuing judgments among the dead'. It is not entirely clear whether the former Cretan king is being credited with a special role as judge over all the dead, or whether he is just replicating in the Underworld a role which he played as a sovereign in life, namely that of one who righteously dispenses law to those around him. At all events, Minos is one of the few who seem to retain any significant esteem in the grim Odyssean realm of Hades.

Aristophanes' Underworld

For a riotous contrast to the mist, regret and pain of the Homeric Afterlife we may turn to Aristophanes' sublime farce, the *Frogs* (405 BC). According to the deliciously improbable plot, Dionysos, god of the theatre, travels down to Hades with the aim of bringing back to life one of the previous generation of great tragic poets, whose wise counsel the Athenians sorely need at the present critical juncture of the Peloponnesian War. (The second part of the play will be a contest between the playwrights Aischylos and Euripides for the right to resurrection.)

In the course of Dionysos' hilarious journey we learn something about the geography and resident personnel of this comic version of the Underworld. In order to cross a 'great big bottomless lake' the nervous god has to take a boat trip with Charon, the lugubrious and irascible ferryman of the dead. Having crossed the lake amid the singing, croaking and plopping of the eponymous frogs, and having escaped the clutches of the shape-shifting female monster Empousa, Dionysos bumps into a band of his own Initiates, deceased mortals whose initiation into Dionysiac mystery cults while alive has evidently provided them with a passport to a joyful Afterlife in a flower-strewn area of Hades.

After that, however, Dionysos meets one of the most fearsome of all Hades' denizens: Aiakos, the Infernal Doorkeeper. Though some myth-tellers represented him as a paragon of law and righteousness, the Aiakos who appears in *Frogs* is a kind of pantomime ogre, over-ripe in his language and wildly exaggerated in his sadism:

You loathsome, shameless, audacious creature! You villain, you arch-villain, you utter villain, who drove away our dog Kerberos, that I used to look after – throttled him and took him and dashed off and made a bolt and were gone! But there's no escape for you now –
[*breaking into melodramatic declamation*]
Such is the sable-hearted rock of Styx
and the blood-dripping crag of Acheron
that ward thee, such Kokytos' roaming hounds
and the Echidna hundred-headed, who
will rend apart thine offals, while thy lungs
are gripped by the Tartessian murry-eel,
and while thy bloodied kidneys, guts and all,
the Gorgons out of Teithras tear asunder,
Whom I with swift-foot haste will now go seek.

In the time-honoured tradition of Aristophanic excretory humour, Dionysos reacts to all this bluster by performing an involuntary 'libation'.

Rivers of the Underworld

Antithetical though they are in tone, the Odyssean and Aristophanic visions of the Afterlife encapsulate, if taken together, most of the features which other myth-tellers ascribe to the abode of the dead. Two such features are worth pursuing in more detail: the rivers of the Underworld; and the concept of separate regions set aside for the 'blessed' and for those consigned to post-mortem chastisement.

The two rivers which would become most closely associated with Hades in post-classical tradition were Lethe ('Oblivion') and Styx ('Hatefulness'). Amongst the Greeks themselves, Lethe was seldom

One possible real-world location of the river Styx was in this remote mountain ravine in Arcadia. Wherever it 'really' was, the Styx was eerie and dangerous. Its name in Greek means 'hateful'.

referred to. When myth-tellers did mention it, it was as the river whose water, when imbibed, caused the dead to forget their earlier existence. (This is one more instance of Greek mythology's variability: in the *Odyssey* the dead poignantly *retained* their memories of the world of life.) The Styx, by con-

The shore near Cape Tainaron, the most southerly point of the Peloponnesian mainland. Thanks to its location at what could be seen as one of the 'edges' of the Greek world, this place was appropriately regarded as one access point to the Underworld.

trast, was generally agreed to be one of the central features of Underworld topography. But what, and where, was it? In one of Plato's speculations about existence after death, in his dialogue *Phaedo*, the Styx was a river which flowed into a lake; according to other Greek writers, it was a part of Hades whose source was a stream of icy water plunging 200 metres (650 ft) down a sheer precipice, in the Chelmos range in the depths of northern Arcadia. Pausanias was in no doubt about this stream's eerie power: its water, he reported, brought death to humans and to every other creature. What all were agreed on was that the Styx was especially sacred. When one of the Olympians wished to swear an oath, Iris, messenger of the gods, would fetch a jug of water from the Styx, so that the oath might be solemnized with a libation.

Acheron was another river firmly associated with the Afterlife. According to Euripides, it was across the Acheron that Charon rowed the soul of the dead Alkestis after she had nobly given up her life for her husband (see pp. 170–71). However, like the Styx, the Acheron too has a real-world location to parallel its place in the Underworld. Rising in the Thesprotian mountains of Epeiros in northwest Greece, the river meanders to the sea some way after its confluence with the Kokytos. Why should this modest

(Left) On a low hill not far from the river Acheron is what is believed to be the site of the Nekyomanteion (Oracle of the Dead). Although some have doubted his findings, the Greek archaeologist who excavated the site, Sotirios Dakaris, has persuasively argued that we can identify: (1) a labyrinthine passage through which those who wished to consult the oracle were first led, and (2) an underground chamber into which images could be winched down, creating the impression of ghostly appearances in a kind of 'Underworld'.

river have developed a connection with the realm of Hades? Two reasons suggest themselves. First, the west – the direction of the sunset – was a region which Greek imagination often linked with darkness and foreboding; and Acheron lay, at least from the perspective of many Greeks, in the west. Secondly, the Acheron flowed close to the site of the Nekyomanteion, an oracle where Greeks, in historical times, could go to consult the dead. Some

The body of a young athlete was found with a golden victory-crown still in place on his skull. This unique find, from Hagios Nikolaos in Crete, dates to the 1st century AD. Also in place was a silver coin, on the outside of the dead man's jaw. The coin was payment to Charon, who would ferry the deceased to Hades.

oracular shrines, notably that of Delphi, are situated in remote, mountainous locations; the difficulty of the preliminary journey contributes significantly to the psychological impact of the consultation. The Nekyomanteion poses no such apparent problems of access. But might the preferred mode of approach to this other-worldly sanctuary have been via a river journey along the shaded, winding course of the Acheron?

Charon

Before leaving the topic of rivers, we must revert to the old, cantankerous figure of Charon. Perhaps for the reason mentioned by Kephalos in Plato's *Republic* – that proximity to death concentrates the mind on the possible nature of the Afterlife – vases employed in funerary ceremonies provide us with our fullest evidence for representations of Charon. On several examples of the white-ground vase known as a *lekythos* (an oil-container used to make offerings to the departed) Charon appears in his characteristic role, receiving a soul from Hermes Guider of Souls and preparing to ferry it into the Underworld proper. In literary sources, by contrast, Charon is seldom as prominent as he is in Aristophanes' *Frogs*. But the very nature of his job – that of a menial worker who, for a modest fee (normally the coin known as an 'obol'), ferries every single person who has ever lived, whatever their grandness or humbleness in life – lends itself to exploitation in comic or ironic narratives. The best example is the satirist Lucian (2nd century AD), whose prose dialogues about the foibles of gods and mortals include several portrayals of the Infernal Ferryman who has seen it all before. As Charon wryly observes to Hermes, in the dialogue named after Charon: 'You see what they [mortals] do and how ambitious they are, competing with each other over offices, honours and possessions, all of which

(Left) The bearded ferryman Charon plies his gloomy trade. In front of him is a winged, stick-thin figure known as an eidolon, *an image of the soul of the dead person. Athenian* lekythos, *mid-5th century BC.*

they will be obliged to leave behind them when they come down to us with just one obol.'

It is worth noting that, in some non-Greek and especially post-Greek sources, Charon's remit is far broader. To the Etruscans, who knew him as Charun, he was a fearsome, hammer-wielding death-demon, hook-nosed, bearded, with animal ears and ominous, rectangular teeth. In modern Greek folklore, on the other hand, the figure of Charos (or Charondas, or Haros), although still a personification of death, has come to be situated quite literally on the side of the angels, being regarded either as identical with the Archangel Michael, or as his subordinate. But for all his assimilation into a Christian framework of belief (an assimilation which can be traced back to the Byzantine period), the prospect of encountering Charos is still a terrifying one, since he retains the fateful duty of conveying the soul of the deceased away from life. Here is how a modern Cypriot mother laments her loss:

Cruel Charos, most cruelly you have taken my child,
who was my pride, who was my life.

Places of reward and punishment

Ancient Greek religion was generally oriented towards this world rather than the next. That seems to be the conclusion suggested by the relative lack of emphasis which our surviving texts place upon eschatology (literally, 'the study of last things') – in striking contrast to what we find amongst, for example, ancient Egyptians or medieval Christians or Muslims. Nevertheless in ancient Greece too there were certain contexts, both in mythology and in the practice of cult, where attention was paid towards a posthumous differentiation between, on the one hand, those regarded as specially favoured, and, on the other hand, the wicked. This differentiation was mirrored in representations of the topography of the Afterlife.

According to an idea mentioned sporadically in our mythological sources, a special place was reserved after death for mortals whose lives had been in some way distinguished. This special place was not usually regarded as a sub-division of Hades, but as an alternative to it. An example is the existence which the sea god Proteus predicted for Menelaos:

But for you, Menelaos, o fostered of Zeus, it is not the
    gods' will
that you shall die and go to your end in horse-pasturing
    Argos,
but the immortals will convey you to the Elysian
Field, and the limits of the earth, where fair-haired
    Rhadamanthus
is, and where there is made the easiest life for mortals,
for there is no snow, nor much winter there, nor is
    there ever

At several locations in the Greek world, thin pieces of inscribed gold foil have been found deposited in graves. The inscriptions on them consist of guidance to the dead person about the geography of the Underworld, and about how to behave there in order to achieve a blessed Afterlife. The leaf illustrated below (4th century BC) was discovered at Petelia in the far south of Italy.

rain, but always the stream of the Ocean sends up
   breezes
of the West Wind blowing briskly for the refreshment
   of mortals,
this, because Helen is yours, and you are son-in-law
   therefore to Zeus.

Menelaos is not especially virtuous, just impeccably
well connected, through his marriage to Helen;
indeed some sources affirm that she accompanied
him to Elysion (Latin: 'Elysium'). Occasionally we
hear of other heroes destined to be transported to a
paradisiacal Afterlife: Kadmos, Peleus and Achilles
fall into this category. In their case the destination is
specified as the Isles of the Blessed, an Elysion-
equivalent said to be ruled over by Zeus' father, the
Titan Kronos – still an 'outsider', though this time
imagined as a benign, albeit remote, ruler, rather
than as Zeus' violent adversary. Why, though,
should Kadmos, Peleus and his son Achilles be
singled out for a contented Afterlife (in this variant,
which is recounted by Pindar in his second
Olympian Ode)? As with Menelaos, the answer
relates not to ethical merit but to proximity to the
gods: the Olympians had graced the marriages of
Kadmos and Peleus with their presence, so special
treatment in the Afterlife could be said to be just an
extension of these heroes' already privileged status.

Could ordinary Greeks aspire to a similar translation to paradise? There was no such automatic
assumption, as Kephalos' anxieties in the *Republic*
confirm (see p. 206). Yet one route did offer hope: initiation into one or another of the cults – Dionysiac
or Orphic, for instance, or the Eleusinian Mysteries
– whose beliefs involved a dimension of promised
personal salvation. Archaeological discoveries of
brief texts written on gold leaves, found for
example in southern Italy and Thessaly, have deep-
ened our insight into Afterlife beliefs in an exciting
if enigmatic way (see illustration, left). Such texts
were apparently intended as a combination of mini-
travel-guides for the deceased, and as privileged
passports into the Underworld. One such was found
at Petelia, some 24 kilometres (15 miles), as the crow
flies, to the north of Croton in the toe of Italy. In
Roman times the leaf, encased in a golden container,
was used as an amulet, but the inscription on the
leaf itself has been dated to the 4th century BC. The
text, with its set of instructions to a dead man,
reads as follows:

You will find on the left of the house of Hades a spring,
and standing beside it a white cypress.
To this spring do not even go near.
But you will find another, cold water flowing
from the pool of memory. In front of it are guards.
Tell them: 'I am a child of Earth and starry Heaven;
but I am of heavenly stock. This you yourselves know.
I am parched and perishing with thirst. Give me at once
cold water flowing from the pool of memory.'
And they will themselves give you (water) to drink from
   the sacred spring,
And then you will rule among the other heroes.

The atmosphere evoked by this and similar texts
has been likened to the ancient Egyptian *Book
of the Dead*; one might also find much later
analogies with Mozart's *The Magic Flute*. The
details of what awaits the initiate are not spelled
out, but it will be a future marked not by tantalizing
thirst but by refreshing water, not by oblivion but
by recollection.

Surveying the whole of Greek mythology's
representation of 'paradise', we find a patchy and
inconsistent picture. This is not because Greek
poets/thinkers were incapable of producing a coher-
ent description, but because such a description was
usually called for only if a given context of myth-
telling encouraged a positive, reward-oriented view
of the Afterlife. This is precisely what we find in
some of the dialogues of Plato, where a technical
discussion of moral philosophy is rounded off by a
more speculative account of what prospects the virtuous and the wicked can look forward to after
death. One example is *Phaedo*, the work whose
heartrending conclusion depicts the last moments
in the life of Plato's revered teacher Sokrates, before
his enforced suicide in an Athenian gaol. This is
exactly the kind of context which favours the
setting out of a view in which the virtuous are
promised a just reward after death. Sure enough, the
scenario sketched out by Sokrates as a possibility
('either this or something very like it', is how he puts
it) offers real hope to the righteous, though the
specifics are necessarily hazy:

But those who are deemed to have made outstanding
progress towards living virtuously, these are they who
are released and liberated from imprisonment in these
regions of the earth [the vicinity of the lake of Acheron],
moving upward to their pure dwelling and making their
habitation above ground. And among these, those who
have purified themselves sufficiently through philosophy
live ever afterwards entirely without bodies, and reach
dwellings still more lovely, which are not easy to describe;
nor do we have enough time to do so now.

Representations of the Afterlife which offer the
hope of bliss to the deserving are bound to threaten
bleaker prospects for the unjust. Once more there
are topographical implications. As we saw earlier
in relation to Odysseus' visit to the Underworld in
the *Odyssey*, transgressors are sometimes said to be
punished within Hades itself. But other accounts
talk of a lower, remoter, ghastlier place: Tartaros,
described by Zeus in the *Iliad* as being in 'the
deepest abyss below the earth, where the gates are
iron and the threshold bronze, as far below Hades
as the sky is above the earth.' This too is a place
evoked in Plato's eschatological writings: it is where
the worst transgressors are confined. We have illustrated this chapter with many images of the Greek
landscape, but of Tartaros no image can be offered.
Its nature could be seized only by the imagination,
through antithesis: the opposite of all things light,
airy and optimistic.

A Heritage Constantly Renewed

No aspect of the Greek legacy can rival mythology in the fascination which it has exerted upon successive generations since antiquity. As the 21st century begins, Greek myths still remain influential in many areas of culture, whether it be the re-workings of myths by poets and visual artists, or in the vigorous renewal of the images of gods and heroes in film, on television and in computer games.

In this chapter we shall sample some key moments in the history of Greek mythology's adaptation to new cultural contexts. Beginning with the Romans, we shall follow the retelling and reinterpretation of the stories through the late antique and medieval Christian worlds, and discuss some major artistic and literary representations of Greek myths from the Renaissance to the present day. Since an important part of the story of how Greek myths have been 'received' in the post-classical world relates to diverse interpretations by scholars, these interpretations too will be given due weight in our account.

We turn first to Rome, whose civilization will be incomprehensible to us if we fail to register the imaginative centrality of Greece in general, and Greek mythology in particular, to the Romans' under-standing of themselves and the world.

Artists have imagined the Argo *and its crew in many different ways, according to changing perceptions of heroism and boat construction. This representation, dated to 1484–90, is by the Italian painter Lorenzo Costa.*

VII   Greek Myths after the Greeks

How Rome Re-imagined Greece

early as the 7th century BC. An example is the mixing bowl (c. 650 BC) discovered at Cerveteri, just north of the Tiber. One of the images on the bowl, Odysseus' blinding of the Cyclops, may suggest familiarity not just with the myth, but with the Homeric version of it in the *Odyssey*. An added bonus is the fact that the vase is signed: 'Aristonothos made [this]'; the script is Euboean Greek (Euboeans were prominent in the Archaic colonial expansion, though we cannot tell whether Aristonothos came to Etruria himself, or whether the vase was imported). Such finds stand at the beginning of a rich tradition of mythological narration on objects found in Etruria; sometimes the style

(Above) The image on this vase is virtually an illustration of an episode from Homer's Odyssey: *Odysseus and his men are driving a stake into the eye of Polyphemos. Of all the ancient representations of the blinding, this is arguably the most interesting: the vase is Etruscan, and bears the earliest artistic signature to survive from the Greek world.*

The presence of Greek myths in the Italian peninsula is at least as old as the Archaic period of Greek history. Greek colonial foundations in the south of Italy and in Sicily began already in the 8th century BC, and part of the culture which the city-founders brought with them was story-telling. Further north, in Etruria, archaeologists have unearthed evidence which confirms that Greek myths were known as

(Right) This engraved Etruscan mirror portrays a scene of languid eroticism. The eagle abducting the naked young Ganymede ('Catmite' in Etruscan) is either the symbol of Zeus' power, or Zeus himself in metamorphosed form.

(Far right) The 'Ficoroni Cist' (c. 300 BC) is a superb example of the artistic adaptation of Greek mythology to a Roman context. An engraved copper container designed to hold items of female adornment, it was – as an inscription upon it tells us – made in Rome, as a present from a mother to a daughter. It portrays episodes from the Argonaut myth.

is traditionally Greek, but often a native Etruscan manner is evident, as in the case of the many surviving bronze mirrors decorated with mythical scenes of beauty and eroticism.

All this pales beside the impact of Greek myths at the city of Rome, and in the steadily increasing geographical area which Roman conquests brought within its ambit. Once more our earliest evidence is archaeological: a terracotta representation of Athene and Herakles has been dated to the late 6th century BC. How far such an image would have been felt to be 'extraneous', and how far as Roman – in which case it would be better to speak of 'Minerva' and 'Hercules' – it is impossible to say; this interpretative problem recurs repeatedly in the subsequent history of Rome's encounter with Greek myths. But at least, in time, the evidence relating to the problem becomes more abundant. Indeed the range of contexts within which Greek myths were deployed in Rome soon becomes broader than that evident in Greece itself. Particularly rich are the arts of wall-painting, mosaic flooring, and relief sculptures on sarcophagi, media in which Roman art remade its Greek inheritance and took it in new directions.

(Right) A richly atmospheric wall-painting showing episodes from the myth of Perseus and Andromeda; from the villa at Boscotrecase, near Pompeii.

On a mosaic from the central hall of the Baths of Neptune in Ostia (the port of Rome), Neptune himself is depicted urging on his team of sea-horses. The Baths were dedicated in AD 139.

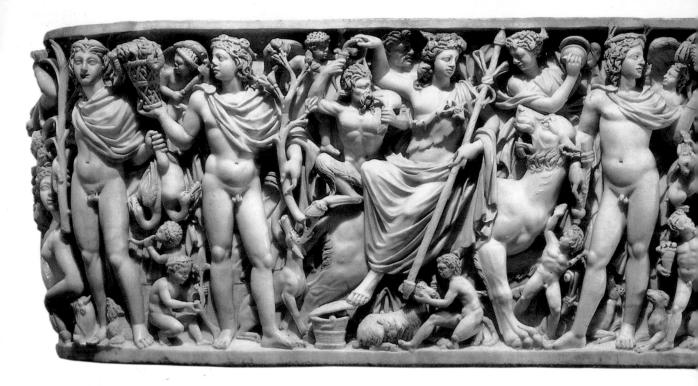

Roman sarcophagi provide us with some of the most intricate and dense groupings of mythological images to survive from antiquity. Here Dionysos/Bacchus is seated on a tiger (centre), flanked by the Seasons, as well as by assorted maenads and satyrs. 3rd century AD.

One aspect of this Roman remaking involves 'equivalences' between Greek and Roman divinities. Such equivalences were made by the Romans from an early date, as a way of establishing connections between their own religion and that of the neighbouring and culturally authoritative Greeks. (There was nothing surprising about this: the Greeks did the same when they equated their own gods to those of the Egyptians: Dionysos to Osiris, Hermes to Thoth, etc.) At a sanctuary of Vulcan in Rome, dating from the second quarter of the 6th century BC, archaeologists have found an Athenian vase depicting Hephaistos; this strongly suggests that the equivalence between these two gods was already being made at that early date. Around four centuries later, the poet Quintus Ennius (239–169 BC) was explicit in his equating of the twelve Greek Olympians with their Roman counterparts.

But some of the equations were more equal than others. Vesta had a far higher profile than her Greek equivalent Hestia, a situation reflected in the centrally important cult of the Vestal Virgins in the Roman Forum. Mars, the father of Rome's founders Romulus and Remus, far exceeded his warlike Greek 'counterpart' Ares in importance, appropriately enough in this Roman community whose ability to sustain its astonishing expansion depended upon the sword. But a plausible case has also been made (by the Dutch scholar H. S. Versnel) for seeing Mars as in some respects analogous not to Ares but to Apollo: for example, both were associated with expiation in the face of disaster, and with a leadership role in colonial expeditions. Mercury, for his part, was associated at Rome with trade and commerce, a trait which sat comfortably enough with the role of his Greek counterpart Hermes as a linker of opposites, but which nevertheless represented a new, Roman emphasis.

At the forefront of Roman attempts to acknowledge correspondences between their own religio-mythic traditions and those of the Greeks, and also

'Equivalences' Between Greek and Roman Divinities

Greek	Roman
Aphrodite	Venus
Apollo	Apollo
Ares	Mars
Artemis	Diana
Athene	Minerva
Demeter	Ceres
Dionysos	Bacchus
Eos	Aurora
Eros	Cupid (Lat. Cupido)
Hades	Pluto
Hephaistos	Vulcan (Lat. Volcanus)
Hera	Juno
Hermes	Mercury (Lat. Mercurius)
Hestia	Vesta
Kronos	Saturn (Lat. Saturnus)
Persephone	Proserpina
Poseidon	Neptune (Lat. Neptunus)
Zeus	Jupiter (Lat. Juppiter)

to stake a claim to their own, distinctively Roman imaginative territory, were the poets. We shall look at four such writers: two composed under the Republic, two under the early Empire.

Poets: Plautus

The comic dramatist Plautus (Titus Maccius Plautus, active 200 BC) was a masterly expositor of farcical situations which turn on the escapades of

(Below) Roman statue of Mars (2nd/3rd century AD). Mars is much more than the 'equivalent' of the Greek Ares. Here the god appears as a Roman general in full armour.

(Right) This 3rd-century AD bronze statuette depicts Mercury in characteristically winged hat and footwear. He has been described as a god of 'circulation' – circulation of goods (as the patron of shopkeepers and businessmen) and of people (as mediator between humans and gods, and between the dead and the living).

eager young freeborn men and their streetwise and rascally slaves, all operating under the presiding star of Fortune. Although most of his plots are drawn from what may very roughly be described as contemporary life, one, *Amphitryo*, takes its plot from mythology. The play depicts the convoluted and hilarious misunderstandings which ensue when Jupiter (Zeus) disguises himself as Amphitryon in order to bed Amphitryon's honourable wife Alcmena (Alkmene). The deceptions are redoubled when Jupiter's henchman Mercury turns himself into a lookalike of Amphitryon's servant. Despite the play's location in the Greek city of Thebes, Plautus' appropriation of the myth is completely convincing, and the retelling ends up by being every bit as much Roman as Greek – a note struck right at the outset when Mercury grabs the audience's attention with an opening gambit more appropriate to Mercury than to Hermes:

> If you want me to prosper your affairs and bring you profit in the buying and selling of goods and in every enterprise…you'll keep quiet while this play is on, and be fair and honest judges of it.

Catullus

Plautus wrote for the public stage. A century and a half later another great artist placed an equally idiosyncratic stamp upon the legacy of Greek myth, but he did so in a style whose scope was intimate and private. Catullus (Gaius Valerius Catullus, *c.* 84–*c.* 54 BC) was a Veronese who, like so many aspiring 'provincial' writers, was drawn to Rome. As a poet whose central theme was erotic passion, he often used myths as a way of giving resonance to his explorations of feeling. Poem 64 gives a flavour of one way in which he transmuted the Greek heritage. An elaborate composition of over 400 hexameters, the work takes as its ostensible focus the narration of the wedding of Peleus and Thetis, that ideal moment when the Olympians forsook their homes to celebrate the union of a mortal with a divinity, gracing the occasion with their presence, and their presents. At the centre of the poem, however, is the evocation of quite a different myth, embroidered upon the coverlet of the newly married couple: the abandonment of Ariadne by Theseus on the island of Naxos.

> There, staring out from Dia's [Naxos'] surf-resounding
>   shore
> And watching Theseus sailing off with his fast fleet,
> Is Ariadne, nursing at heart unmastered passions,
> Nor can she yet believe she sees what she is seeing,
> That very moment woken from deceiving sleep
> To find her poor self left behind on lonely sand.

By juxtaposing the two myths Catullus is able to explore the opposition between faith and faithlessness, and the contrast between a once-heroic age when gods walked the earth, and the grim and unjust here-and-now – themes which also dominate the poet's fiercely intense shorter works, where one of his preoccupations is an unfulfilled longing for stability and permanence in his personal relationships.

When Catullus adapted erotic myths which had previously been told by Greeks, he did so with such conviction as to render those myths totally his own. In breathing new fire and urgency into the tradition of Hellenistic Greek love poetry, he made a statement which was as much about lifestyle and politics as it was about literature: it amounted to a rejection of the world of good-old Roman, public, politico-military virtue.

Virgil

In the work of Virgil (Publius Vergilius Maro, 70–19 BC), the relationship between mythology and

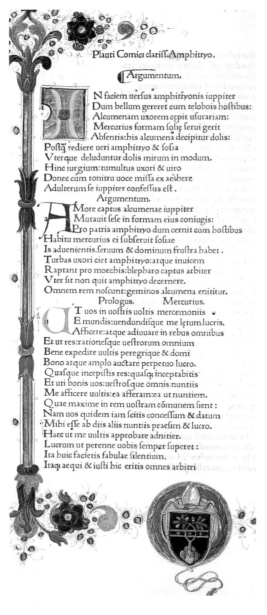

A 15th-century manuscript showing the beginning of Plautus' comedy Amphitryo. *The manuscript was bought in Rome in 1481 by John Shirwood, Bishop of Durham. The coat of arms at the foot of the page may belong to the Italian bishop who originally commissioned the manuscript.*

political context becomes even more important, and much more complex. Virgil lived through the brutal civil strife of the dying Republic, and became closely associated with the new regime of Augustus, whose autocratic rule aspired to put an end to internecine bloodshed. Each of Virgil's three great literary productions needs to be seen against the background of this revolutionary epoch.

Virgil's collection of ten *Eclogues* constitutes a decisive renewal of the pastoral genre, whose previous great exponent had been the Hellenistic Greek poet Theokritos. The *Eclogues'* idyllic landscape, enlivened by the reflective songs of herdsmen, must be seen in a political context: the prevailing mood contrasts sharply with the bloody turmoil of contemporary Rome. Of particular mythological interest is *Eclogue* 5, which includes a lament for the legendary Sicilian shepherd Daphnis (see p. 184). Another notable feature of the *Eclogues*, extremely significant in the light of the future development of pastoral literature and art, is the detail, found in some of the poems, that the location is imagined to be Arcadia. This innovation results from the coalescing of a number of traditions: Arcadia was associated with a primitive and isolated way of life

(though Virgil softens its rough edges); it was frequented by Pan and Hermes, deities whose links to herding and fertility suited them to a pastoral environment; furthermore its people, according to legend, had played a positive role in Rome's own past (see p. 223, on Virgil's *Aeneid*). The invention of a pastoral 'Arcadia' is a clear example of creative myth-telling, and indeed myth-*making*: in later European tradition, this idyllic picture of the world of ancient Greece would come to exercise a powerful hold on the imagination.

In his second major work, the four books known as *Georgics*, Virgil describes and praises the toil of the peasant who cultivates the land; such labour is another kind of bulwark against the lacerations of civil war. After the poem has moved from agriculture to the cultivation of trees, to stock-raising, to beekeeping, in Book 4 Virgil finally relates two intertwined myths. The mythical farmer Aristaios (Latin: 'Aristaeus') unwittingly causes the death of Orpheus' wife Eurydice; as a result, Aristaios is punished when his bees die from disease. On learning the cause of the disease (having forced Proteus, all-knowledgeable sea god, to reveal what he knows), Aristaios performs a

In Thomas Cole's Dream of Arcadia, 1838, *tiny human figures, and the constructions which they have built, are dwarfed by a landscape both serene and grand. Cole was born in England but emigrated to America; his vision expresses an idyllic harmony between humanity and the natural world.*

221

The illuminated manuscript known as the Vergilius Romanus *(end of 5th century* AD*) includes, as an illustration of Virgil's* Georgics, *this image of rustic music-making against a background dotted with animals and plants.*

sacrifice of oxen, from whose bodies bees are miraculously generated.

Enfolded within this myth is another: that of Orpheus' loss of Eurydice; his lonely, inconsolable grief; and his eventual, gruesome death, ripped apart by maenads. Virgil's intricate poetical construction sets one hero (Aristaios), who listens to the gods and is rewarded, beside another (Orpheus), whose story illustrates the inevitable limitations which circumscribe the happiness of even the most

gifted mortal. This is no parasitic, 'secondary' myth, but a bold and novel creation.

The culmination of Virgil's achievement, and one of the twin peaks – along with Ovid's *Metamorphoses* – of Roman myth-telling, is the *Aeneid*, the twelve-book epic which narrates the exploits of the Trojan hero Aeneas (Greek: 'Aineias') from the time of his escape from Troy's destruction to the moment when the Trojans unite with the people of Latium, a union which will form the basis for the subsequent founding of Rome itself. As a poetical composition the work could hardly be more ambitious, since it draws on, rewrites and competes with both the *Iliad* and the *Odyssey*: after Aeneas' Odyssean wanderings come his Iliadic battles.

The *Aeneid* is also a profoundly political poem. Seen against the background of the newly established Augustan regime, the epic makes, by implication, a strongly positive ideological statement, for it celebrates, first the routing of adversaries, and then a new beginning, made possible by the fusing of different ethnic groups, including Greeks (Aeneas meets, and forms an alliance with, a group of Arcadians who have settled at the site of the future Rome).

But, as well as celebrating a victory, the *Aeneid* is also a deeply human poem, which refuses to allow the aspirations of the defeated to be swamped by the onward march of history. Aeneas' love for the Carthaginian queen Dido, an emotion which he decides, under the compulsion of fate, to renounce, retains an imaginative power which, notwithstanding Rome's historical conflict with Carthage, transcends any simple 'Rome good, Carthage bad' polarity. Nor are the native Italian forces who oppose the Trojan intruders consigned to unrelieved condemnation. The act of pitiless fury by which Aeneas slays the local prince Turnus, an act with which the poem abruptly ends, contrasts uneasily with the more restrained conclusion of the *Iliad*, when Achilles and Priam recognize each other's humanity, and Achilles' wrath defers, at least temporarily, to pity.

Ovid

Another Roman poet concedes second place to no one, not even Virgil, in his influence on subsequent European retellings of myth. Ovid (Publius Ovidius Naso, 43 BC–AD 17) incorporates myths into every aspect of his poetical output. His amatory poetry, which explores the experience of love from every conceivable angle, exploits the resources of the web of mythology to multiply the erotic data at his disposal. One of his most innovative works, the *Heroides* ('Heroines'), consists of a series of verse letters allegedly written by female mythological figures to their male lovers/husbands (in some cases there is a pair of letters, one from each partner). Though limited by the fact that they are conceived as being written at a particular moment within the unfolding of the myth – which means that the 'future outcome' cannot be narrated, only ironically hinted at – these imaginary letters nevertheless incorporate a remarkable range of human experience, since their ostensible authors are women as different as Penelope, Dido, Medea and Phaidra (Latin: 'Phaedra').

But even this range is completely overshadowed by the Ovidian mythological masterwork, the *Metamorphoses*. It would seem inconceivable that a fifteen-book epic could be generated from a single mythological motif; yet that was just the kind of challenge which Ovid relished. In the case of *Metamorphoses*, he made the theme of astonishing transformation the linchpin of an exploration of

(Left) Two emblematic scenes from the Fall of Troy decorate the opening of Book 2 of Virgil's Aeneid, *in a late 15th-century Italian manuscript. Above is the Wooden Horse, being wheeled into their city by unsuspecting Trojans. Below is the last departure from Troy of Aeneas, carrying his aged father Anchises on his shoulders.*

(Below) Erysichthon felled a tree sacred to Ceres (the Roman equivalent of Demeter), and was punished with a ravenous and ultimately fatal hunger. The episode was retold by the Roman poet Ovid in his Metamorphoses, *and is here illustrated in a 1570 Parisian edition of Johann Spreng's allegorical commentary on the poem.*

Narcissus in and after Ovid

In the third book of his *Metamorphoses* Ovid tells the tale of handsome young Narcissus (Greek: Narkissos), who fell in love with his own reflection in a forest pool; the nymph Echo, in whom the self-obsessed youth took no interest, pined away to just a voice. Narcissus' futile love reaches its climax when his tears of frustration disturb the clarity of his reflected image:

When he had finished speaking, he returned to gazing distractedly at that same face. His tears disturbed the water, so that the pool rippled, and the image grew dim. He saw it disappearing, and cried aloud: 'Where are you fleeing? Cruel creature, stay, do not desert one who loves you! Let me look upon you, if I cannot touch you. Let me, by looking, feed my ill-starred love.' In his grief, he tore away the upper portion of his tunic, and beat his bared breast with hands as white as marble. His breast flushed rosily where he struck it, just as apples often shine red in part, while part gleams whitely, or as grapes, ripening in variegated clusters, are tinged with purple. When Narcissus saw this reflected in the water – for the pool had returned to its former calm – he could bear it no longer. As golden wax melts with gentle heat, as morning frosts are thawed by the warmth of the sun, so he was worn and wasted away with love, and slowly consumed by its hidden fire. His fair complexion with its rosy flush faded away, gone was his youthful strength, and all the beauties which lately charmed his eyes. Nothing remained of that body which Echo once had loved.

In 1997 the English poet Ted Hughes (1930–98) published a collection of reworkings of Ovid's *Metamorphoses* under the title *Tales from Ovid*. It quickly became a best-seller. Here is Hughes' subtly muscular version of the same Ovidian passage about Narcissus:

Then Narcissus wept into the pool.
His tears shattered the still shrine
And his image blurred.
He cried after it: 'Don't leave me.
If I cannot touch you at least let me see you.
Let me nourish my starving, luckless love –
If only by looking.'
Then he ripped off his shirt,
And beat his bare chest with white fists.
The skin flushed under the blows.
When Narcissus saw this
In the image returned to perfection
Where the pool had calmed –
It was too much for him.
Like wax near the flame,
Or like hoar-frost
Where the first ray of the morning sun
Creeps across it,
He melted – consumed
By his love.
Like Echo's the petal of his beauty
Faded, shrivelled, fell –
He disappeared from his own eyes.
Till nothing remained of the body
That had driven Echo to distraction.

the pathology of love. The myths of transformation, which in their previous Greek retellings had usually been anchored to particular localities, underwent in Ovid a subtle process of universalization, broadening their relevance, and paving the way for Ovid's epic to become a kind of all-embracing mythological handbook for the medieval world. To all intents and purposes, Greek mythology would thereby become *classical* mythology. It is in Roman clothing, and from Roman myth-tellers, that the modern world has inherited its 'Greek' mythology.

Rome's capacity to appropriate and rework the inheritance of the Greeks showed no sign of diminishing under the Empire. The literary successors of Virgil and Ovid continued to exploit the resources of the originally Greek, but now thoroughly Romanized tales. In iconography, too, the imperial successors of Augustus followed his example in adapting the symbolism of Greek myth to the ideological requirements of autocratic rule, as when the brutal emperor Commodus presented himself, in a striking bust dating from about AD 190, as a modern-day Hercules, complete with club and lionskin. But in the midst of such tendencies there developed a new and increasingly powerful movement: Christianity, whose adherents looked at the traditional tales from a fresh and deeply critical standpoint.

Political figures at Rome, as in Greece, liked to present themselves as walking in the footsteps of characters from the mythological past. Lucius Aurelius Commodus (sole emperor AD 180–92) took Herakles as his model, even to the extent of calling himself 'Hercules Romanus'. Like his mythical model, Commodus was prone to extreme violence.

The Impact of Christianity

The marble statue known as the 'Moschophoros' ('Calf-bearer'), c. 575–550 BC, is a genial representation of a man carrying a young animal (top). The same motif is perfectly incorporated into a Christian system of imagery in a sculpture of Christ as the Good Shepherd, 3rd/4th century AD.

Not surprisingly, it was the behaviour of the gods, rather than that of the heroes, which attracted the opprobrium and mockery of Christian apologists. The Christian convert **Clement of Alexandria** (Titus Flavius Clemens, *c.* AD 150– *c.* 211) issued a clarion call in his *Exhortation to the Heathen*, when he ridiculed the absurd and immoral myths of the pagans. Who, he exclaimed, could fail to be shocked by a religion which revered a goddess (Aphrodite) born from a severed penis? Who would not find it contradictory that Zeus was worshipped as 'Baldhead' in Argos but as 'Avenger' in Cyprus?

A century later, the North African Christian writer **Lactantius** (full name probably Lucius Caelius Firmianus Lactantius, *c.* AD 240–320) gave an explanation for some of the pagans' 'irrational' beliefs: namely, that the supposedly divine figures about whom salacious and absurd tales clustered were not gods at all, but merely mortals elevated by poets to divine status: '[Zeus] is said to have carried away Catamitus (i.e. Ganymede) on an eagle. This is poetical elaboration. In fact, he either had him carried off by a legion, which had an eagle for its standard; or else, the ship on which he was placed had an eagle as its tutelary deity, just as it bore the effigy of a bull when he seized Europa and carried her across the sea.'

There were also alternative strategies for explaining away the perceived vagaries of pagan mythology. A generation after Lactantius, the Syracusan Christian convert **Julius Firmicus Maternus** (4th century AD) saw in the divinities of traditional myths nothing but misguided projections of natural phenomena and human passions. The worship of the Sun was an idolatrous deviation from the reverence due to the true Creator; in deifying Zeus the adulterer, Apollo the torturer (of Marsyas), and Ares the mass murderer, pagans were simply deifying their own impious desires.

In deploying such arguments against those whom they castigated as unbelievers, Christian apologists were pouring new wine into old bottles. One ready-made source for them to draw on was the treatise *On the Nature of the Gods* by the orator, politician and writer **Cicero** (Marcus Tullius Cicero, 106–43 BC). Cast in the form of a dialogue between educated Romans of different philosophical persuasions, this work incorporates many arguments for and against this or that view of the gods. Among the opinions advanced are: that the gods of mythology were originally human beings, whom people retrospectively elevated to divinity because of their achievements; and that the gods symbolize cosmic powers, or express moral ideas through the medium of allegory.

Such views have antecedents long before Cicero: indeed, they can be traced back to the very heart of the Greek myth-telling tradition. The notion that the gods were originally deified mortals became associated with the name of **Euhemeros** (see p. 199); in a utopian novel which survives only in fragments, this Hellenistic writer (active *c.* 300 BC) described a voyage to an imaginary island in the Indian Ocean, where, inscribed on a golden column, were set out the exploits of Ouranos, Kronos and Zeus, three deceased mortal kings worshipped by their people on account of their beneficent rule. (It was no coincidence that an early Hellenistic writer should mention such a view, given the prevailing political climate in which several of Alexander's successors received cultic worship from their subjects in return for services rendered.)

As for the view that the gods of mythology should be understood allegorically – that is to say, as standing for cosmic powers or moral qualities – here too it is not hard to find Greek antecedents, for example among the Presocratic and, especially, the **Stoic philosophers**. A succinct account of this approach is provided by scholiasts (ancient commentators) on a passage from Book 20 of the *Iliad*, where the context is a battle in which the gods are ranged on opposite sides. This unseemly divine fight may, the scholiasts note, be interpreted in terms of 'natural and moral' allegory: Poseidon, water, is opposed by Apollo, the heat of the Sun; the virginal Athene, embodiment of prudence, confronts the irrational and adulterous Ares. Other decodings follow: Artemis is the Moon, Hera the Air, Aphrodite lust… This kind of allegorical approach was said to go back at least to the late 6th century BC.

If the anti-mythology arguments of the early Christian apologists had antecedents more than half a millennium earlier, those same arguments also had countless progeny in late antiquity and beyond. But here we meet a paradox. With little or no change, the grounds of the Christians' objections to pagan myths could be, and were, taken as justifying the survival and transmission of those same myths: for if the myths did not 'really' contain shocking or absurd material, what reason could there be for objecting to them? An example of this welcoming attitude is provided by the *Mythologies* of Bishop **Fulgentius** (Fabius Planciades Fulgentius, probably late 5th century AD). Much is uncertain about his biography, but what is not in doubt is the ingenuity with which he used allegorical interpretation, aided and abetted by extraordinary flights of etymological fancy, to render the pagan myths suitable for a Christian audience. Here is his explanation of the meaning of the myth about the nymph Arethousa (Latin: Arethusa), whom the river Alpheios (Latin: Alpheus) pursued across the sea to Syracuse:

Alpheus is in Greek *aletias fos*, that is, 'the light of truth'; while Arethusa is *arete isa*, that is, 'the excellence of equity'. For what can the truth love but equity, or the light, but excellence? And it retains its purity when passing through the sea, because clear truth cannot by any intermingling be polluted by the surrounding saltiness of evil ways.

Given the extraordinarily strong literary and educational authority enjoyed by the works within which Greek – or rather, now, Greco-Roman – mythology was embedded, and given also such interpretative ingenuity as that of Fulgentius, the way was open for the tenacious renewal of the pagan stories in a Christian framework.

The Middle Ages

(Right) Throughout the Middle Ages, Ovid exercised an enormous influence on how the ancient myths were perceived. His poems entitled Heroides *are in the form of letters allegedly sent from mythical women to their lovers. One such is sent by Phaidra to her stepson Hippolytos, whom she is trying to persuade to become her lover. In the scene illustrated (from a manuscript of the* Heroides) *Phaidra hands her letter to the courtly young Hippolytos.*

(Opposite) Taken from a 15th-century manuscript of the History of the Sack of Troy *by Guido de Columnis, this illustration sets the union of Helen and Paris in a very ecclesiastical-looking 'temple of Venus'.*

(Below) In a 14th-century German manuscript, the combat between Hektor and Achilles takes on the complexion of a chivalric duel between knights-in-armour.

Over the next thousand years, allegorical readings would have the cumulative effect of naturalizing Greco-Roman myths within a thoroughly Christianized environment. Thanks to the mental agility

of interpreters, even Ovid, the author so often read in schools, could be seen as a fount of truth and virtue. In the highly influential, 70,000-line poem *Ovide moralisé* (anon., early 14th century), every part of Ovid's *Metamorphoses* was interpreted as Christian edification: thus Phaethon stood for Lucifer, the rebellious angel; Apollo's pursuit of Daphne symbolized the Incarnation, with Daphne representing the Virgin Mary; the quest of Ceres/Demeter for Proserpina/Persephone became the quest of the Church to restore lost souls to the fold.

Euhemerism – the belief that the pagan gods were nothing but deified humans (after Euhemeros, see p. 225) – was another factor which contributed to this process of naturalization. Chronological systems were devised according to which the Christian world-scheme (Creation, Fall of Man, Life of Christ, Last Judgment) was interspersed with the deeds of suitably humanized deities from pagan myth, such as Minerva, the woman who first invented the art of wool-working, and Prometheus, the man who taught his fellows to make fire. Nor was it only divinities who were incorporated into Christian chronology. The deeds of pagan heroes and heroines too became part of one, integrated past: above all, the great deeds at Troy. In the Middle Ages, the Trojan War came to be regarded as a pivotal event in world history, not just because of the mighty 'chivalric' deeds which took place then, but because many families and cities traced their origins back to Trojans who were said to have wandered far and wide after the sack of their city. Franks, Normans, Britons, Venetians, Turks, as well as many European princely families, all claimed to be descendants of the great protagonists of the Trojan War (see p. 228).

Cosmic symbolism was another area where the characteristics attributed to the pagan divinities and hero(in)es constituted not a barrier but a passport to their incorporation into the medieval

sitzen vnd kom zu dem gstat Vnd von dannen einer kleinē schifftige
in die Insulen Citharea ist gebare Ido si paid von den einwanern
vnd andern in grosser ere ist entfangen als die frawe der Insulen
C zu letzt si zunolenden sye gelube den Tempel ist eingangē da
selbst hat si ire opffer der gotin Veneri in vil vnd kostlichen gaben

geraichet C C
Do ein sulichs pa
radi kunt getan
wart die kongin
helena des me
nelai hausfrawe
in ein grossen gesel
schaft vnd vbrau
dende gepar zu dē
tempel sein gan
gen C Paris
nach dem kostlichs
ten gezwet kom
auch darein wā
er het wol gehort
durch die verkū
dūge der lag vor
langst geschehē
die zwelf Castons
vnd Polluas ein
vngelanblichen
schōn graue Do
er die sach do wart

er von stunden der fackel veneris op vnkeusch in dem tēpel Veneris
enzūdet vnd wütet mein angstlichen begir vnd sein kleissiges ge
sichte hat er in die Helena gewendet vnd in sie gelider besūder war in dem
lucher zu besprenget hubschlich hat beschawet C Es hat vmnndt in ir
eins senlichē schemieden glances leuchte frehar welche ein weiss
strich eins snelichē scheines in mittel der schaittel gleich hat getailt
vnd die guldein vädem hie vnd dort gestreut vntter einē gewissen

vor helena

Major figures from ancient mythology were believed in the Middle Ages to be the ancestors of contemporary peoples. Alongside more familiar heroes such as Agamemnon and Paris, this 15th-century woodcut of part of a German 'World Chronicle' depicts 'Turcus' (bottom left) and 'Franco' (bottom right), the founding fathers of the Turkish and Frankish peoples respectively.

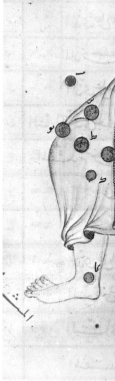

European world-view. Already in antiquity such bodies as Sun and Moon had been regarded as divinities (by Plato, for example), while the constellations were identified with mythical individuals (e.g., Andromeda, Hydra, Perseus) or their attributes (e.g., Lyra, the lyre invented by Hermes/Mercury), which had usually attained permanent transference to the sky through metamorphosis. A further development, from the Hellenistic period onwards, was an emphasis on astrology, that aspect of the study of the heavens which posited complex links between celestial and terrestrial events. In spite of periodic opposition from the Church, such beliefs never

(Right) In a manuscript of the Catalogue of Stars *by the great 10th-century AD Arab astronomer Abd al-Rahman al-Sufi, the 'Medusa' whom Perseus has just decapitated is portrayed – corresponding to Arabic belief – as a male demon.*

228

entirely died out, but they enjoyed a period of exceptional popularity between the 12th and 14th centuries, thanks to newly accessible Greek astronomical/astrological texts which had been preserved by Arab scholars, and which now returned to Europe, in Latin translation, in the wake of the Crusades and via Muslim Spain and Sicily. Such figures as Saturn, Jupiter and Mercury lived on as planetary demons whose physical appearance and dress gave yet one more twist to the enormous adaptability of classical mythology.

(Left and below) A 14th-century manuscript of an astrological treatise depicts two of the planets.
(Left) Saturn changed himself into a stallion in order to deceive his wife Rheia with Philyra. Their offspring was the Centaur Cheiron.
(Below) Mercury at his desk.

From the Renaissance to the 20th Century

The art historian Jean Seznec characterized the Renaissance as 'the reintegration of antique subject matter within the antique form: we can speak of a Renaissance from the day Hercules resumed his athletic breadth of shoulder, his club, and his lion's skin.' The European 'rebirth' of interest in ancient Greece created a context in which this reunited form-and-content of the classical myths came to enjoy a remarkable and long-lasting cultural domination. From Spenser and Shakespeare to Milton and Racine, from Botticelli and Titian to Rubens and Rembrandt, the greatest writers and artists between the 15th and the 17th centuries expressed themselves through a creative engagement with the classical myths (alongside a continuing and constant reference to the tradition of Biblical subjects).

Some Landmarks in the Modern Retelling of Greek Myths

date	author	work
c. 1306–c. 1321	Dante	*The Divine Comedy.* Poem
early 14th cent.	anon.	*Ovide moralisé.* Poem
c. 1486	Botticelli	*Birth of Venus.* Painting
1553–54	Titian	*Venus and Adonis.* Painting
1546–54	Cellini	*Perseus Holding the Head of Medusa.* Bronze sculpture
c. 1567	Pieter Bruegel the Elder	*Landscape with the Fall of Icarus.* Painting
c. 1570–76	Titian	*The Flaying of Marsyas.* Painting
1590	Spenser	*The Faerie Queene.* Poem
1592–93	Shakespeare	*Venus and Adonis.* Poem
c. 1601–14?	El Greco	*Laocoön.* Painting
1607	Monteverdi	*La favola d'Orfeo.* Opera
1609	Bacon	*The Wisdom of the Ancients.* Prose treatise
1622–25	Bernini	*Apollo and Daphne.* Marble sculpture
1635	Rembrandt	*The Rape of Ganymede.* Painting
1636–38	Rubens	*The Banquet of Tereus.* Painting
1742	Boucher	*Diana Leaving the Bath.* Painting
1755	Winckelmann	*Reflections on the Imitation of Greek Works in Painting and Sculpture.* Study in art criticism
1762	Gluck	*Orfeo ed Euridice.* Opera
1788	Schiller	*The Gods of Greece.* Poem
1811	Ingres	*Jupiter and Thetis.* Painting
1818	Keats	*Endymion.* Poem
1820	Shelley	*Prometheus Unbound.* Verse drama
c. 1821–22	Goya	*Saturn Devouring One of His Children.* Painting
1825	K. O. Muller	*Introduction to a Science of Mythology.* Academic study
1856	Kingsley	*The Heroes.* Retelling of classical myths for children
1858	Offenbach	*Orpheus in the Underworld.* Comic opera
1867–75	F. M. Müller	*Chips from a German Workshop.* Academic work on esp. language, religion and mythology
1872	Nietzsche	*The Birth of Tragedy out of the Spirit of Music.* Treatise in which concepts of 'Apolline' and 'Dionysiac' are developed.
1890–1915	Frazer	*The Golden Bough.* Monumental comparative study of ancient and other myths and rituals
1896–97	Waterhouse	*Hylas and the Nymphs.* Painting
1911	Cavafy	*Ithaca.* Poem
1912	Harrison	*Themis: A Study of the Social Origins of Greek Religion.* Academic work
1856–1939	Freud	Psychological study of Oedipus Complex, etc.
1922	Joyce	*Ulysses.* Novel
1927	Stravinsky	*Oedipus Rex.* Opera-oratorio
1934	Cocteau	*La Machine infernale.* Play
1935	Giraudoux	*La Guerre de Troie n'aura pas lieu.* Play
1937	Dalí	*Metamorphosis of Narcissus.* Painting
1938	Kazantzakis	*The Odyssey: A Modern Sequel.* Poem
1943	Sartre	*Les Mouches.* Play
1944	Anouilh	*Antigone.* Play
1963	Dürrenmatt	*Hercules and the Augean Stables.* Comic drama
1963	Columbia (prod.)	*Jason and the Argonauts.* Film
1967	Pasolini	*Edipo re.* Film
1969	De Chirico	*The Remorse of Orestes.* Painting
1977	Cacoyannis	*Iphigenia.* Film
1981	Hall (director)	Production of *Oresteia* at National Theatre, London
1997	Disney (prod.)	*Hercules.* Film
1997	Hughes	*Tales from Ovid.* Version of Ovid's *Metamorphoses*

Needless to say, this engagement with classical antiquity was neither simple nor homogeneous; nor did the 'rebirth' entail a complete break with past attitudes (which is one reason why not all scholars accept the utility of the term 'Renaissance'). One element of continuity was the preoccupation with allegory, though this took on new and extraordinarily diverse forms: Edmund Spenser's exploration of chastity (Diana) and sensuality (Venus) in *The Faerie Queene* (1590) is a world away from Francis Bacon's readings of classical myths in *The Wisdom of the Ancients* (1609); in Bacon's view myths made statements about what we should call science and politics, so that, while Proteus stands for 'the first matter', the tale of Aktaion is a demonstration that those who are close to princes incur great hatred, are liable to be shot at, and therefore 'do lead their lives like stags, fearful and full of suspicion'.

One direction which visual and literary retellings of mythology took in the Renaissance was that of exploring the stories' sensuality. For obvious reasons, myths relating to the goddess Aphrodite/Venus lent themselves particularly to treatment from this perspective. If any single painting has

come to symbolize the Florentine Renaissance it must surely be Botticelli's *Birth of Venus* (c. 1486), yet this was just one of thousands of images of the goddess produced around this time. Of all the myths relating to her, that narrating her liaison with the doomed Adonis offered the greatest scope for pathos. Titian gave a typically rich and intense rendering of the relationship between the two (1553–54), but even this cannot compare with the luxuriant retelling of the myth in Shakespeare's *Venus and Adonis* (1592–93) as when the poet evokes the ardent goddess' attempted persuasion of the reluctant mortal:

'Fondling,' she saith, 'since I have hemmed thee here
Within the circuit of this ivory pale,
I'll be a park and thou shalt be my deer.
Feed where thou wilt, on mountain or in dale;
    Graze on my lips, and if those hills be dry,
    Stray lower, where the pleasant fountains lie.

The dominant cultural authority of classical mythology was not to pass uncontested. In the later 17th century, and more insistently in the first part of the 18th century, that authority became increasingly controversial. When Joseph Addison, writing in *The Spectator* in 1712, referred to contemporary poetic recourse to 'our Jupiters and Junos' as 'downright puerility, and unpardonable in a poet that is past sixteen', he was expressing an unease which many would echo. In pre-revolutionary France, such

unease had a strong moral and political dimension. The royal court was accustomed to witnessing the staging of elaborate musical recreations of classical myths, whose formality found its counterpart in the artificiality of the mythological images painted

In François Boucher's Diana
Leaving the Bath *(1742) the
goddess is depicted as an
improbable huntress, more
like Venus than Diana.
Boucher's calculated eroticism
is plain to see.*

by such artists as François Boucher; this artificiality was conveniently compatible with the objective of offering the viewer explicit sexual titillation, under the cloak of classical mythology's high cachet. Pretentious and precious visions such as

*(Left) Compared with
Botticelli's Venus (pictured
above left), the Venus painted
by Titian offers an altogether
riper and more opulent
spectacle. In* Venus and
Adonis *(1553–54) the
goddess tries to restrain her
mortal lover from going off
to hunt.*

Boucher's attracted the withering criticism of, for example, the Enlightenment philosopher and man of letters Denis Diderot, for whom their remoteness from real-life situations was the antithesis of what artists and writers should, in Diderot's view, be aiming at. It was not the fact of using classical imagery itself to which Diderot objected, but rather the licentious manner in which that imagery was deployed, so as to appeal to the taste of what he regarded as a decadent aristocratic-royalist public.

In France, disillusion with 'mythology as ornament' formed a tiny part of a much wider disenchantment with the existing political system, a disenchantment which led in due course to the 1789 Revolution. Elsewhere, however, attitudes towards classical mythology developed at a different pace and with a different tone. In Germany a decisive moment was the publication in 1755 of a passionate study by J. J. Winckelmann on the subject of Greek painting and sculpture, in the course of which he observed that the only strategy to achieve greatness, or even inimitability, was to imitate the Greeks. Inspired by a similar enthusiasm for Greece, the great German Romantics of the late 18th and early 19th centuries – Goethe, Schiller, Hölderlin, as well as the Austrian composer Franz Schubert in many of his *Lieder* – found in the classical myths – or rather, specifically, in the *Greek* myths – not something dry and stilted, but material brimming with life at its most intense, a life absent

233

*The admission ticket to a
staging of Handel's 'musical
drama' Hercules in 1752,
seven years after the original
performance. The work is
based on Sophokles' tragedy
Women of Trachis.*

Captive Andromache
(c. 1888), by Frederic
Leighton, may be felt by some
to cast a kind of lifeless
rigidity over its subject matter.
But Leighton was greatly
admired in Victorian
England; his elevation to the
peerage was a public sign of
his standing.

from the ignoble present. This attitude was not, it
is worth stressing, shared by contemporary visual
artists in Germany. For them, 'classicism' meant
'following French models' – and that, in the political
atmosphere generated by Franco-Prussian hostility
– was not a viable option. Myths remained socially
powerful.

In England the situation was different again. The
18th century had witnessed significant developments in the transmission of classical myths. One
important medium was opera/oratorio: much of the
output of George Frideric Handel dealt with mythological themes, including his *Admeto, Hercules* and
Semele. Another avenue was translation, notably
Alexander Pope's powerful versions of Homer; but
his elevated and august style had its detractors. In
the early 19th century, the English Romantics dis-
tanced themselves from what William Wordsworth

*A Church of England parson
who became Regius Professor
of Modern History at
Cambridge, Charles Kingsley
is today best known as the
author of* The Heroes; or,
Greek Fairy Tales for My
Children. *The illustration –
Perseus rescuing Andromeda
– is from a 1902 edition of
the work.*

called the 'hackneyed and lifeless use into which
mythology fell towards the end of the seventeenth
century, and which continued throughout the
eighteenth.' Their strategy was not to ignore
mythology, but to breathe new life into it: Keats'
poem *Endymion* and Shelley's verse drama
Prometheus Unbound are two instances among
many. As with the German Romantics, this was not
a return to *classical* myth, but to *Greek* myth. In the
words of Shelley: 'We are all Greeks' – which is to
say, Greeks *not Romans.*

Some of the English Victorians inherited the
Romantics' longing for ancient Greece, but gave it
their own, characteristically ethical spin: Greek
myths – above all, those exemplified in the poetry of
Homer – were a treasure-house of morally improv-
ing examples. This attitude underpins Charles
Kingsley's remark in the preface to his hugely
popular retellings of the Greek myths, *The Heroes*
(1856): '[The Greeks] were but grown-up children,
though they were right noble children too; and it
was with them as it is now at school – the strongest
and the cleverest boy, though he be poor, leads all
the rest.' A similarly moralistic attitude – though,
not surprisingly, without the reference to the British
public school system – can be found in two best-
selling American retellers of the myths, Thomas
Bulfinch and Nathaniel Hawthorne: for these
writers, too, the Greek myths promoted virtuous
conduct (provided that certain morally dubious
tales were left out).

But it would be a mistake to subsume all Victorian perceptions of classical mythology under the
rubric of morally uplifting relevance; the picture
was, as it usually is, more complicated than that.

Scholars have also highlighted a misogynistic Victorian fascination with transgressive mythological figures such as Clytemnestra and the Gorgon Medusa. And – yet another different perspective – in the late Victorian period we find the world of ancient mythology frequently depicted as a place of aesthetic perfection: refined, unattainable, sensuous, but perhaps ultimately frigid.

In Germany, the Romantics' passions fed into an excitingly varied nexus of scholarly activity devoted to the study of classical mythology in particular, and mythology in general. One of the pinnacles of this work is Karl Otfried Müller's *Introduction to a Science of Mythology* (1825). This might sound uncomfortably close to the 'Key to all Mythologies' whose investigation was the life objective of the emotionally shrivelled Mr Casaubon in George Eliot's *Middlemarch*; but Müller's work is in fact lively and open-minded, undogmatically interpreting Greek myths in the light of their religious and historical background.

Less original, but much more influential in his own day, was the work of Friedrich Max Müller (see p. 17), whose study of comparative linguistics led him to interpret Greek myths as misunderstandings of earlier – and, at that earlier stage, intelligible – tales told by the Greeks' Indo-European ancestors, tales whose import concerned elementary cosmic phenomena relating to day, night and the principal celestial bodies (whence the label 'Solar Mythology').

The wildness of Greek myths

It is hard to imagine a greater contrast than that between F. M. Müller, whose funeral was attended by the great and the good from all over the world, and another German scholar/writer who died in the same year (1900), the philosopher Friedrich Nietzsche. Controversial, ultimately mad, and in his own time relatively uninfluential, Nietzsche made one fundamental contribution to the study of Greek mythology: his concepts of the Dionysiac and the Apolline. For Nietzsche, Dionysos and Apollo were not just ancient gods but living aesthetic principles:

Friedrich Nietzsche's concepts of the Dionysiac and the Apolline have proved to be powerful but controversial tools for the understanding of art and culture.

235

*The visionary poet and artist
William Blake painted this
watercolour of Kerberos
(1824–27) as an illustration
for Dante's great poem*
Inferno. *The wildness of the
image contrasts starkly with
some of the more restrained
representations of antiquity
which would become prevalent
in 19th-century England.*

the Dionysiac was the principle of excess, of the
dissolution of boundaries; the Apolline was the
principle of limit, order, clear boundaries. Nietzsche
asserted that it was the coming together of these
principles which led to the genesis of Greek
tragedy, an art-form whose antithesis was the kind
of rationalism associated with the name of
Sokrates. Whatever one makes of this as an 'explanation' of tragedy (or of anything else), it points to a
crucial truth about the ancient Greeks: that they
cannot be understood just as embodiments of
perfection and order, for that is to ignore the uncomfortably disruptive, gruesome and wild aspects of
their culture – aspects which their mythology
repeatedly highlights.

Nietzsche was not the first to notice the wildness
of Greek mythology. The reaction of being scandal-
ized by the stories – a reaction which amounted,
of course, to a backhanded recognition of that
wildness – could count Plato as one of its earliest
representatives, and a similar attitude fuelled many
allegorizing interpretations, up to and including
that of F. M. Müller. What was still rare was a willingness to confront the wildness head-on. Two 19th
century artists who did have the vision to do so
were William Blake and Francisco Goya: each
sensed, as Nietzsche did, the inner violence and
uncanniness which lay at the heart of many Greek
myths. But, like Nietzsche, they were unrepresentative, and to some extent outsiders (even though
Goya did occupy a position at the Spanish court,
his deafness contributed significantly to his sense
of exclusion). Their fresh and radical visions of
ancient myth remained outside the mainstream of
cultural discourse.

Nevertheless, the image of Greece as a place of
graceful perfection was soon to be threatened from
another quarter. In the late 19th and the early 20th

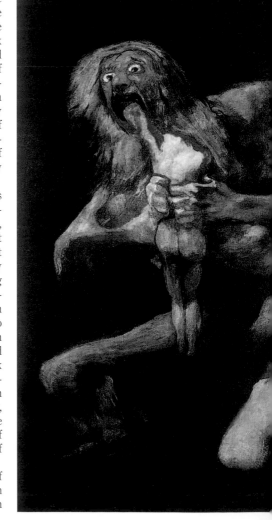

*Hesiod's tale of how Kronos
devoured his children reaches
its ultimate – and hideous –
artistic realization in Goya's
painting* Saturn Devouring
One of His Children
*(c. 1821–22). In antiquity
the figure of Kronos/Saturn
embodied a fundamental
ambiguity: he was capable
of extreme violence, yet he
was also ruler during an
ideal period of the past.
Goya's image leaves no
room for ambiguity: this
god is a terrifying and
nightmarish ogre.*

Jane Harrison's work on Greek religion made important connections between the evidence from classical antiquity and the findings of contemporary students of so-called 'primitive' societies. This portrait of Harrison is by Augustus John.

century, attitudes towards Greek mythology were shaken to their roots as a result of developments in two disciplines: anthropology and psychology. In the view of Jane Ellen Harrison (1850–1928) at Cambridge, and of J. G. Frazer (1854–1941), author of the monumental study *The Golden Bough,* the Greek myths needed to be interpreted in the light of the rituals which underlay them, rituals which, they argued, exemplified patterns found amongst 'primitive' peoples worldwide. Many of these rituals had characteristics to which the Nietzschean term 'Dionysiac' might well be applied. A more or less random selection of the page-headings from Harrison's book *Themis* reads like this: 'Savage Initiations', 'The Thunderstorm and the Bull-Roarer', 'Totemistic Tattoo-marks', 'The Satyrs as Fertility-Daimones'.

Frazer, for his part, focused on what he regarded as a worldwide myth-ritual complex about a king who dies and is reborn, and who thus stands for the annual death and rebirth of vegetation; to these ideas the poet T. S. Eliot, for one, acknowledged his profound debt. The work of Harrison and particularly Frazer received trenchant and often justified criticism at the hands of contemporary and (especially) later scholars, but, by retrieving Greek myths from death-by-decorum, they homed in on what was in general terms, if not in all details, a crucial and neglected aspect of the Greek legacy.

Psychology and politics

If the influence of these British classicists was considerable, it was as nothing compared with the impact of Sigmund Freud (1856–1939). For Freud, myths were significant because they, like dreams, offered access to the unconscious part of the psyche (itself a Greek term denoting 'soul'). Not just that: certain myths, Freud maintained, embodied patterns which were of general import in human psychological development. The myths of Elektra and Narkissos were two such, but the myth to which Freud gave most importance was that of Oedipus. The Oedipus Complex – which was, for Freud, the shibboleth which distinguished the adherents of psychoanalysis from its opponents – encapsulated the developing male child's resentment of the father and attachment towards the mother. Freud's notion of the Oedipus Complex was itself something which developed with time, and his belief in its universality has not been shared by all Freud's adherents, let alone by his critics. Even his reading of what he regarded as the fundamental Oedipal text – Sophokles' *Oedipus Tyrannos* – has been questioned by many classical scholars: one thing from which the Sophoklean Oedipus could not have been suffering when he killed his father Laios was an 'Oedipal' resentment towards *him*, for the

The investigations of Sigmund Freud into the human psyche remain controversial, even generations after his death. But Freud's ideas have exercised a major influence on artists and scholars trying to come to terms with Greek mythology.

Shot on location in Morocco, Pasolini's film version of the Oedipus story created a sequence of brilliant visual images, and reinterpreted the myth in the light of Freud's theories of the human personality.

other myths too were viewed afresh through the Freudian lens; the arresting imagery of the Spanish Surrealist artist Salvador Dalí (1904–89) was avowedly influenced by psychoanalytical theory.

Psychology is one area in which the Greek myths were put to influential use in the 20th century. The myths which raised psychological issues were especially those involving Oedipus and the members of House of Pelops, notably the agonizing moral and familial dilemmas faced by Elektra and Orestes; an example is Jean-Paul Sartre's play *Les Mouches* (1943), in which the eponymous flies are the omnipresent equivalent of the ancient Furies who pursued Agamemnon's children.

Politics too found a mythological voice. Emphasis reverted to the Trojan War, and to the aftermath of the expedition of the Seven against Thebes, when Antigone buried her traitorous brother in defiance of Kreon's edict. Jean Giraudoux's landmark drama of 1935, *La Guerre de Troie n'aura pas lieu* ('The Trojan War will not Take Place'; usually staged in English under the more aggressive title *Tiger at the Gates*), is just one of the many 20th century works which have taken the Greek-Trojan conflict as a vehicle for expressing thoughts and feelings about war. The play dramatizes events immediately preceding the Trojan War; with hindsight, it is hard not to read it prophetically, in relation to the oncoming world conflict. Giraudoux's sophisticated irony cannot mask the play's underlying bleakness: this war is pointless, and yet, for all the efforts of the idealist Hector (who proposes to return Hélène to Ménélas), the war *will* take place. In the end idealism can do nothing against that which is fated, or against such maddeningly human motivations as that of the inveterate war poet who demands a proper subject for his talents. Such a poet is the Trojan Démokos, Giraudoux's own creation (though with a nod towards the Phaeacian bard Demodokos described by Homer in the *Odyssey*). With his dying breath after being struck by Hector, Démokos falsely accuses the Greek Ajax (Aias) of his murder, thus precipitating the war.

Antigone's defiance has proved another rich seam for modern dramatists. One of the most enigmatic versions is Jean Anouilh's *Antigone*, staged in Paris under German occupation in 1944. The play might have been a simple tale of resistance: proud Antigone stands up to the tyrant's decree, and dies for it. But the portrayal of the two principals, Antigone and Créon, will not allow such a simplistic reading. Asked by Créon why it is that she buried her brother, she replies: 'For nobody. For myself.' Créon, for his part, is an unwilling ruler, and admits that what he is doing is absurd; but he is cornered by events. When he finally runs out of arguments to dissuade Antigone from her intransigency, he is obliged to play the role which will lead to Antigone's death and – with the deaths of his son Hémon and his wife Eurydice – the ruin of his own family.

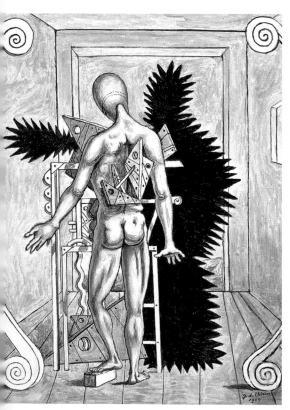

Born in Greece to Italian parents, the artist Giorgio de Chirico drew again and again upon classical themes – though he viewed them through his own extraordinarily distinctive lens. In The Remorse of Orestes (1969), the body of the young man who killed his mother is inseparable from the ominous saw-toothed shadow which is his 'remorse'.

simple reason that at that juncture Oedipus believed that his father was Polybos, king of Corinth. Despite these and similar objections, what is not in doubt is the stimulating and liberating effect which Freudian theory has had on creative artists in various media. In the 20th century attention was focused on the myth of Oedipus more sharply than at any time since antiquity, resulting in such works as Igor Stravinsky's oratorio *Oedipus Rex* (1927) and Jean Cocteau's play *La Machine infernale* (1934), while Pier Paolo Pasolini's film *Edipo re* (1967) approached the myth from an explicitly Freudian perspective. Beyond the myth of Oedipus,

A scene from a 1947 Parisian production of Jean Anouilh's Antigone. *The political and moral confrontation between Antigone and Créon is still of intense contemporary relevance, demonstrating the remarkable durability of the Sophoklean masterpiece which lies behind Anouilh's play.*

These plays by Giraudoux and Anouilh are just two out of a host of politicized reworkings of the myths in 20th century theatre. France has been pre-eminent, though Greece itself, Germany, Britain, the United States and Japan have all made distinctive contributions. The approaches adopted have been astonishingly varied: whereas the Japanese director Suzuki Tadashi set his recreation of Euripides' *Trojan Women* (1974) in the context of (as he depicted it) America's ruthless behaviour towards the defeated Japanese after the Second World War, Andrzej Wajda's *Antigone*, staged in Kraków in 1983, conceived the heroine's defiance of authority in the light of the response of the Polish union Solidarity to state repression. In keeping with the grimness of much post-1914 history, the genre of ancient myth telling which has most influenced modern perceptions has been tragedy.

Tragedy is one way of looking at things; but it is not the only way. In antiquity, as we have seen throughout this book, myths were retold in an astonishing range of tones – including comedy. Successful modern, comic recreations of Greek

Scene from a performance of Suzuki Tadashi's Trojan Women *(1974).*

Jacques-Louis David, Paris and Helen *(1788). The painting presents the loving couple in tender and untroubled mood; their harmony is matched by the lyre which Paris holds.*

mythology are much rarer than one might wish, and certainly rarer than they were in antiquity. The exceptions, therefore, are the more to be savoured. In the mid-19th century the brilliant caricaturist Honoré Daumier produced a series of wickedly amusing deflations of Classicism's cool majesty: in spite of the languid serenity with which Franceschini and David represented Thetis and Helen, it is Daumier's pair of wasp stings which stays in the memory.

Another who ventured to treat antiquity with irreverence was the composer Jacques (born Jacob) Offenbach, whose operetta *Orphée aux enfers* ('Orpheus in the Underworld') was first staged in 1858. The tale of Orpheus and Eurydice had received a series of profoundly moving operatic treatments from, among many others, Claudio Monteverdi (1607) and Christoph Gluck (1762), but Offenbach chose to reinterpret the struggle between music and death as a burlesque comedy

of marital intrigue. Orpheus, a music teacher, is unhappily married to Eurydice, and loves another. Eurydice, meanwhile, is in love with 'Aristaios', who is really Hades/Pluto in disguise. But, when Eurydice is down in the Underworld, Jupiter (disguised as a fly) falls in love with her, and eventually turns her into a happy bacchant. The operetta took Paris by storm, thanks to a damning review by the city's most influential theatre critic, who described it as a desecration of antiquity; thereafter the Parisian public flocked to the box-office, to find out for themselves.

In the 20th century as in the 19th, Greek myth was usually treated as a repository of profound truth rather than humour, but once more there have been exceptions. One of these is *Herkules und der Stall des Augias* ('Hercules and the Augean Stables', 1963) by the Swiss dramatist Friedrich Dürrenmatt. Hercules is no hero: he undertakes his 'labours' in order to satisfy his creditors, who include his

banker Eurystheus, his pawnbroker Epaminondas, his architect Aias and his tailor Leonidas. Hercules' role in Elis (a country whose geography and climate uncannily resemble those of Switzerland) is to rid the place of dung. Taken, with perfect justice, as a satire on the Swiss attachment to cleanliness, the play aroused much opposition from Dürrenmatt's compatriots. 'Aristophanic', in one sense, it certainly is: the omnipresence of ordure is the play's central characteristic. What is missing from this very funny play is Aristophanes' ability to combine filth with sublimity.

Greece since the Renaissance

Our review of modern myth-telling has touched on several countries, but not, so far, on one which for obvious reasons has a very strong claim on our attention. How has the legacy of mythology been 'received' in Greece itself? The most powerful medium for the transmission and re-animation of this legacy has been poetry.

In the context of the protracted and often tormented development of the modern Greek nation state, classical mythology has occupied a variety of positions in cultural and political life, ranging from invisibility to centrality. Wholly marginalized under the Christian Empire of Byzantium, the pagan myths re-emerged as significant points of cultural reference during the 'Cretan Renaissance' of the late 16th and 17th centuries, a period when the island remained under Venetian control until it fell to the Turks in 1669. During this Renaissance, such sophisticated poets as Vitsentzos Kornaros, in his splendid verse romance *Erotókritos*, drew on the ancient stories, almost certainly through the medium of Ovidian retellings. But it was during the independence movement of the 1820s that

the growing sense of national identity was accompanied by a concerted literary strategy of mythological allusion, amongst poets whose own contribution to the cause was to celebrate the struggle for liberation. In this time of bloody heroism, the *Iliad* was a prime point of reference, as in these patriotic lines from the ode 'To Glory' by Andreas Kalvos (1792–1869):

With his immortal measure
divine Homer cheered
the Achaean widows,
and your spirit was kindled
　　by the same melody.

C. P. Cavafy (1863–1933), from Alexandria, also sometimes revisited the *Iliad*, as in his poem 'The Funeral of Sarpedon'. But his most famous journey was back to the *Odyssey*, in 'Ithaca', a meditation on humanity's endless search for experience. A generation later the poet Angelos Sikelianos (1884–1951), from the Ionian island of Lefkas, re-used myths in an intensely lyrical and direct manner. This is how he evokes the momentous transformation of a he-goat into the god Pan:

And then, over the shore's stones and the goats' swelter,
　　dead silence;
and between their horns, as from a tripod, the sun's quick heat
　　shimmered upward.

Then we saw the herd's lord and master, the he-goat,
　　rise alone
and move off, his tread slow and heavy,
　　toward a rock

wedged into the sea to shape a perfect lookout point;
　　there he stopped,
on the very edge where spray dissolves,
　　and leaning motionless,

upper lip pulled back so that his teeth shone,
　　he stood,
huge, erect, smelling the white-crested sea
　　until sunset.

Ithaca

When you set out for Ithaca
ask that your way be long,
full of adventure, full of instruction.
The Laistrygonians and the Cyclops,
angry Poseidon – do not fear them:
such as these you will never find
as long as your thought is lofty, as long as a rare
emotion touch your spirit and your body.
The Laistrygonians and the Cyclops,
angry Poseidon – you will not meet them
unless you carry them in your soul,
unless your soul raise them up before you.

Ask that your way be long.
At many a summer dawn to enter
- with what gratitude, what joy –
ports seen for the first time;
to stop at Phoenician trading centres,
and to buy good merchandise,
mother of pearl and coral, amber and ebony,
and sensuous perfumes of every kind,
sensuous perfumes as lavishly as you can;
to visit many Egyptian cities,
to gather stores of knowledge from the learned.
Have Ithaca always in your mind.
Your arrival there is what you are destined for.
But do not in the least hurry the journey.
Better that it last for years,
so that when you reach the island you are old,
rich with all you have gained on the way,
not expecting Ithaca to give you wealth.
Ithaca gave you the splendid journey.
Without her you would not have set out.
She hasn't anything else to give you.

And if you find her poor, Ithaca has not
　　deceived you.
So wise have you become, of such experience,
that already you will have understood what these
　　Ithacas mean.

C. P. Cavafy

Another writer drawn to the classical heritage was Nikos Kazantzakis (1883–1957), whose many-sidedness and restless passion for voyaging rivalled those of an Odysseus. His most astonishing work is indeed his *Odyssey*, a vast (33,333-line) poetical exploration of the imagined further wanderings of Odysseus after his return to Ithaca. The poem's ambition is as huge as that of its protagonist, who encounters, along the way, characters representing the Buddha, Don Quixote and Christ. On the whole, though, the work has made less impact than some of Kazantzakis' other writings, notably his novel *The Life and Manners of Alexis Zorbás*; the life-affirming eponymous hero ('Zorba the Greek') has become, one might say, a modern myth, being perceived by many outside Greece as an embodiment of what they regard as 'Greekness'.

Alongside the recurrent modern Greek desire to reclaim and renew the ancient mythological legacy is the feeling, strongly felt by some, that that legacy is inadequate, or even to be rejected outright. Much of the poetic output of Yannis Ritsos (1909–90) rests on a dialogue with the ancient legends, predominantly those of the House of Pelops and the Trojan War. But sometimes reality defeats the capacity of an ancient paradigm, even such a powerful one as that of classical mythology, to cope with it. Such was Ritsos' reaction to the tyrannical regime of the Colonels when, in 1968, he wrote a poem called 'Not Even Mythology', from the grim vantage-point of Leros, the island turned into a prison camp for political detainees:

We went inside and again returned to Mythology, searching
for some deeper correlation, some distant general allegory
to soothe the narrowness of the personal void. We found nothing.
The pomegranate seeds and Persephone seemed cheap to us
in view of the night approaching heavily and the total absence.

Ithaca, the longed-for goal of Odysseus' homecoming.

Present and Future

Come Muse migrate from Greece and Ionia,
Cross out please those immensely overpaid accounts,
That matter of Troy and Achilles' wrath, and Aeneas',
    Odysseus' wanderings,

Placard 'Removed' and 'To Let' on the rocks of
    your snowy
Parnassus…
For know a better, fresher, busier sphere, a wide,
    untried domain awaits,
demands you.

These lines, written in 1876 by the American poet Walt Whitman, give trenchant expression to the feeling that 'The Classics' in general, and classical mythology in particular, embody a reactionary and outdated cultural stance; what is needed, on the contrary, is a throwing open of the windows, and a fresh start. There had been countless such attacks on the value of classical learning before Whitman wrote, and there have been countless since; indeed, in the words of Meyer Reinhold, a historian of the role of Classical Studies in the United States: 'The intellectual history of Europe and [the USA] is dotted with assaults against the Classics, and every century and country have had to mount defences against the opponents, who have been indefatigable in marshalling new arguments and attacks against the primacy of the Classics.'

Yet as the 21st century begins, the death of the Classics has not only not occurred, but shows every sign of being postponed indefinitely. Indeed the uses to which classical mythology are being put have expanded dramatically. In Whitman's own New World, university courses in mythology are hugely popular, while creative writers and artists

A Modern Eurydice

In 1984 the Canadian poet and novelist Margaret Atwood took an unblinking look at the tale of Orpheus and Eurydice. In the extract reproduced here, the story's implications for relationships between the sexes leave space for love, but not for romantic idealism.

He is here, come down to look for you.
It is the song that calls you back,
a song of joy and suffering
equally: a promise:
that things will be different up there
than they were last time.

You would rather have gone on feeling nothing,
emptiness and silence; the stagnant peace
of the deepest sea, which is easier
than the noise and flesh of the surface.

You are used to these blanched dim corridors,
you are used to the king
who passes you without speaking.

The other one is different
and you almost remember him.
He says he is singing to you
because he loves you,

not as you are now,
so chilled and minimal: moving and still
both, like a white curtain blowing
in the draft from a half-opened window
beside a chair on which nobody sits.

He wants you to be what he calls real.
He wants you to stop light.
He wants to feel himself thickening
like a treetrunk or a haunch
and see blood on his eyelids
when he closes them, and the sun beating.

This love of his is not something
he can do if you aren't there,
but what you knew suddenly as you left your body
cooling and whitening on the lawn

was that you love him anywhere,
even in this land of no memory,
even in this domain of hunger:
You hold love in your hand, a red seed
you had forgotten you were holding.

He has come almost too far.
He cannot believe without seeing,
and it's dark here.
Go back, you whisper,

but he wants to be fed again
by you. O handful of gauze, little
bandage, handful of cold
air, it is not through him
you will get your freedom.

Although she has no direct classical pedigree, the heroine of the cult television series Xena: Warrior Princess *inhabits a world in which characters (such as Hercules) and locations often echo the ancient myths.*

side' of classical mythology – aspects of the tales not yet told – in order to bring out women's perspectives upon themes hitherto shaped by male myth-tellers; this is just one instance of a 'wide, untried domain' (in Whitman's phrase) waiting to be discovered, within classical mythology itself.

Nor is the enduring attractiveness of the ancient myths restricted to what used to be described as 'high' culture. If film, television and computer software are solid indicators of popular taste, then – to restrict ourselves to English-language productions – the popularity of the films *Jason and the Argonauts* (1963), *Clash of the Titans* (1981), and *Hercules* (1997), and of the TV series *Hercules: The Legendary Journeys* and *Xena: Warrior Princess*, suggest that the decline in the cultural centrality of classical antiquity in most Western countries has far from extinguished the appetite for the ancient stories. Such retellings should not be taken as a sign that the 'true meaning' of the myths has been forgotten or falsified. On the contrary: they are a sign of vigour, and should be welcomed as such. The tradition of Greek mythology will only survive if it never stops adapting to new needs, and, by adapting, continues to stimulate, to unsettle and to inspire.

worldwide continue to draw refreshment from those ancient springs. One example among a hundred possible ones is the *oeuvre* of the Canadian writer Margaret Atwood, who has exploited the 'other

Famous above all for Ray Harryhausen's special effects, the movie Clash of the Titans *(1981) offers a late 20th-century view of the encounter between Perseus and the Gorgon.*

Further Reading

Abbreviations

Bremmer, *Interpretations:* J. N. Bremmer (ed.),
    Interpretations of Greek Mythology
    (2nd edn, London and New York, 1988)
ClAnt   *Classical Antiquity*
CLS   *Comparative Literature Studies*
CPh   *Classical Philology*
CQ   *Classical Quarterly*
EL   *Études de Lettres. Revue de la Faculté des*
          Lettres de l'Université de Lausanne
HSCP *Harvard Studies in Classical Philology*
JHS   *Journal of Hellenic Studies*
MH   *Museum Helveticum*
OCD   S. Hornblower and A. Spawforth (eds),
          Oxford Classical Dictionary, 3rd edn
          (Oxford, 1996)
SMSR *Studi e materiali di storia delle religioni*
SSR   *Studi Storico-Religiosi*
WüJbb *Würzburger Jahrbücher für die*
          Altertumswissenschaft
ZPE   *Zeitschrift für Papyrologie und Epigraphik*

Translations

Most of the original texts relating to Greek
mythology can readily be found in modern
translations into English. Amongst the many
available versions of Homer, the best are still, in
my view, those by Richmond Lattimore: the *Iliad*
is published by the University of Chicago Press
(first publ. 1951), the *Odyssey* by HarperCollins
(first publ. 1965). Other reliable translations are
those of Hesiod's *Theogony* and *Works and Days*
by Martin West (World's Classics: Oxford, 1988),
of Apollonios' *Argonautica* by Richard Hunter
(World's Classics: Oxford, 1993, under the title *Jason
and the Golden Fleece*), and of Apollodoros' *Library*
by Robin Hard (World's Classics: Oxford, 1997).
For the *Homeric Hymns* one may consult the
translation by Michael Crudden (World's Classics:
Oxford, 2001); for Pausanias, the most convenient
version is that by Peter Levi (*Guide to Greece*,
2 vols; revised edn, Penguin: London, 1979). All
the surviving Greek tragedies are available in
sets of translations published by Penguin and
by the University of Chicago Press. Finally,
we should mention the 'Loeb Classical Library'
(Harvard University Press), a comprehensive set
of translations (plus the original text on facing
pages) of all the major, extant writings from
Greco-Roman antiquity. The translations vary
in quality, but the series is an indispensable aid
to study at every level.

Some general and/or especially accessible works in English

Buxton, R., *Imaginary Greece: The Contexts of
   Mythology* (Cambridge, 1994)
Dowden, K., *The Uses of Greek Mythology* (London
   and New York, 1992)
Graf, F., *Greek Mythology: An Introduction*
   (Baltimore and London, 1993; trans. of
   Griechische Mythologie: Eine Einführung,
   Munich and Zurich, 1985)
Kirk, G. S., *The Nature of Greek Myths*
   (Harmondsworth, 1974)

Next, organized by chapter, I list some more
specialized works (though many of them have a
great deal to offer the 'general' reader too). Given the
international character of research into Greek
mythology, it would have been wholly misleading to
restrict this bibliography to writings in English;
works in several other languages therefore figure
prominently.

I Contexts, Sources, Meanings

What is a myth?

Doty, W. G., *Mythography: The Study of Myths and
   Rituals* (Tuscaloosa, Ala., and London, 1986)
Dundes, A. (ed.), *Sacred Narrative: Readings in the
   Theory of Myth* (Berkeley, 1984)
Kirk, G. S., *Myth: Its Meaning and Functions in
   Ancient and Other Cultures* (Cambridge,
   Berkeley and Los Angeles, 1970)
Puhvel, J., *Comparative Mythology* (Baltimore, 1987)
Ruthven, K. K., *Myth* (London, 1976)
Segal, R. A., *Theorizing about Myth* (Amherst,
   Mass., 1999)

Works of reference on Greek mythology

Gantz, T., *Early Greek Myth: A Guide to Literary
   and Artistic Sources* (Baltimore and London,
   1993)
Kakridis, I. Th. (ed.), *Elliniki Muthologia*, 5 vols
   (Athens, 1986–87)
March, J., *Dictionary of Classical Mythology*
   (London, 1998)
Olalla, P., *Muthologikos Atlas tis Elladas* (Athens,
   2001)
Price, S., and Kearns, E. (eds.), *The Oxford
   Dictionary of Classical Myth and Religion*
   (Oxford, forthcoming)

General characteristics of Greek myths

Anderson, G., *Fairytale in the Ancient World*
   (London and New York, 2000)
Brelich, A., ed. P. Xella, *Mitologia, politeismo, magia
   e altri studi di storia delle religioni (1956–1977)*
   (Naples, 2002)
Bremmer, J. N., 'What is a Greek Myth?', in
   Bremmer, *Interpretations*, pp. 1–9
——— , *Greek Religion.* Greece and Rome New
   Surveys in the Classics No. 24, with Addenda
   (Oxford, 1999)
Buxton, R. 'Religion and Myth', in P. Cartledge (ed.),
   Cambridge Illustrated History of Ancient Greece
   (Cambridge, 1998), pp. 320–44
Calame, C., 'Illusions de la mythologie', in Calame,
   *Mythe et histoire dans l'Antiquité grecque: la
   création symbolique d'une colonie* (Lausanne,
   1996), pp. 9–55
Detienne, M., *L'Invention de la mythologie* (Paris, 1981)
Gould, J., 'On Making Sense of Greek Religion', in
   P. E. Easterling and J. V. Muir (eds), *Greek
   Religion and Society* (Cambridge, 1985), pp. 1–33;
   repr. in Gould, *Myth, Ritual, Memory, and
   Exchange: Essays in Greek Literature and
   Culture* (Oxford, 2001), pp. 203–34
Nilsson, M. P., *Cults, Myths, Oracles, and Politics in
   Ancient Greece* (Lund, 1951)
Pembroke, S. G., 'Myth', in M. I. Finley (ed.), *The
   Legacy of Greece: A New Appraisal* (Oxford,
   1981), pp. 301–24
Saïd, S., *Approches de la mythologie grecque* (Paris,
   1993)
Vernant, J.-P., *Myth and Thought among the Greeks*
   (London, 1983; trans. of *Mythe et pensée chez les
   Grecs*, Paris, 1965; 2nd edn, Paris, 1985)
——— , 'Greek Religion', in M. Eliade (ed.), *The
   Encyclopedia of Religion* (New York and London,
   1987), vol. 6, pp. 99–118; French trans., with
   Introduction, appeared as *Mythe et religion en
   Grèce ancienne* (Paris, 1990)
Veyne, P., *Did the Greeks Believe in their Myths?*
   (Chicago and London, 1988; trans. of *Les Grecs
   ont-ils cru à leurs mythes?* Paris, 1983)

On connections with Egypt and/or the Near East

Bernal, M., *Black Athena: The Afroasiatic Roots of
   Classical Civilization*, 2 vols (London, 1987–91)
Burkert, W., 'Oriental and Greek Mythology: The
   Meeting of Parallels', in Bremmer,
   Interpretations, pp. 10–40; repr. in Burkert, *Kleine
   Schriften II* (Göttingen, 2003), pp. 48–72
——— , *The Orientalizing Revolution: Near
   Eastern Influence on Greek Culture in the Early
   Archaic Age* (Cambridge, Mass., and London,
   1992; trans. of *Die orientalisierende Epoche in
   der griechischen Religion und Literatur*,
   Heidelberg, 1984)
Lefkowitz, M. R., and Rogers, G. M. (eds), *Black
   Athena Revisited* (Chapel Hill, N.C., and London,
   1996)
West, M. L., *The East Face of Helicon: West Asiatic
   Elements in Greek Poetry and Myth* (Oxford,
   1997)

On visual representations

Carpenter, T. H., *Art and Myth in Ancient Greece:
   A Handbook* (London, 1991)
Lexicon Iconographicum Mythologiae Classicae
   (*LIMC*) (Zürich and Munich, 1981–99); this
   18-volume encyclopaedia is the indispensable
   starting point for all work in this area
Hampe, R., and Simon, E., *Griechische Sagen in der
   frühen etruskischen Kunst* (Mainz, 1964)
Schefold, K., *Myth and Legend in Early Greek Art*
   (London, 1966; trans. of *Frühgriechische
   Sagenbilder*, Munich, 1964; revised as *Götter-
   und Heldensagen der Griechen in der früh- und
   hocharchaischen Kunst*, Munich, 1993)
——— , *Gods and Heroes in Late Archaic Greek
   Art* (Cambridge, 1992; trans. of *Götter- und
   Heldensagen der Griechen in der spätarchaischen
   Kunst*, Munich, 1978)
——— , *Die Göttersage in der klassischen und
   hellenistischen Kunst* (Munich, 1981)
——— and Jung, F., *Die Sagen von den
   Argonauten, von Theben und Troia in
   der klassischen und hellenistischen Kunst*
   (Munich, 1989)
——— , and Jung, F., *Die Urkönige, Perseus,
   Bellerophon, Herakles und Theseus in der
   klassischen und hellenistischen Kunst*
   (Munich, 1988)
Shapiro, H. A., *Myth into Art: Poet and Painter in
   Classical Greece* (London, 1994)
Woodford, S., *Images of Myths in Classical
   Antiquity* (Cambridge, 2003)

On myth and ritual

Bremmer, J. N., 'Greek Maenadism Reconsidered',
   ZPE 55 (1984), pp. 267–86
——— , 'Scapegoat Rituals in Ancient Greece',

HSCP 87 (1983), pp. 299–320; repr. with Addenda in R. Buxton (ed.), *Oxford Readings in Greek Religion* (Oxford, 2000), pp. 271–93

Burkert, W., *Homo Necans: The Anthropology of Ancient Greek Sacrificial Ritual and Myth* (Berkeley, Los Angeles and London, 1983; trans. of *Homo Necans: Interpretationen altgriechischer Opferriten und Mythen*, Berlin, 1972; rev. edn 1997)

———, *Structure and History in Greek Mythology and Ritual* (Berkeley, Los Angeles and London, 1979)

———, 'Jason, Hypsipyle, and New Fire at Lemnos: A Study in Myth and Ritual', *CQ* NS 20 (1970), pp. 1–16; repr. with Addenda in R. Buxton (ed.), *Oxford Readings in Greek Religion* (Oxford, 2000), pp. 227–49

Buxton, R., 'Wolves and Werewolves in Greek Thought', in Bremmer, *Interpretations*, pp. 60–79

Graf, F., 'The Locrian Maidens', in R. Buxton (ed.), *Oxford Readings in Greek Religion* (Oxford, 2000), pp. 250–70 (trans. and revision of German original, publ. in *SSR* 2.1 (1978), pp. 61-79)

Jameson, M., 'Perseus, the Hero of Mykenai', in R. Hägg and G. C. Nordquist (eds.), *Celebrations of Death and Divinity in the Bronze Age Argolid* (Stockholm, 1990), pp. 213–23

Osborne, R., 'Women and Sacrifice in Classical Greece', *CQ* NS 43 (1993), pp. 392–405; repr. in R. Buxton (ed.), *Oxford Readings in Greek Religion* (Oxford, 2000), pp. 294–313

Segal, R. (ed.), *The Myth and Ritual Theory: An Anthology* (Malden, Mass., and Oxford, 1998)

Versnel, H. S., 'Greek Myth and Ritual: The Case of Kronos', in Bremmer, *Interpretations*, pp. 121–52; revised version in Versnel, *Inconsistencies in Greek and Roman Religion II: Transition and Reversal in Myth and Ritual* (Leiden, 1993), pp. 89–135

On literary sources

Bouvier, D., and Calame, C. (eds.), *Philosophes et historiens anciens face aux mythes*, *EL*, issue 2, 1998

Bowie, A. M., *Aristophanes: Myth, Ritual and Comedy* (Cambridge, 1993)

Brisson, L., *Plato the Myth Maker* (Chicago and London, 1998; trans. of *Platon, les mots et les mythes*, Paris, 1982)

Buffière, F., *Les Mythes d'Homère et la pensée grecque* (Paris, 1956)

Buxton, R., 'Blindness and Limits: Sophokles and the Logic of Myth', *JHS* 100 (1980), pp. 22–37

Calame, C., *Poétique des mythes dans la Grèce antique* (Paris, 2000)

Davies, M., *The Epic Cycle* (Bristol, 1989)

Feeney, D. C., *The Gods in Epic: Poets and Critics of the Classical Tradition* (Oxford, 1991)

Köhnken, A., *Die Funktion des Mythos bei Pindar: Interpretationen zu sechs Pindargedichten* (Berlin, 1971)

Morgan, K. A., *Myth and Philosophy from the Presocratics to Plato* (Cambridge, 2000)

Musti, D., et al., 10-vol. Italian commentary on Pausanias' *Description of Greece* (Milan, 1982–; published in Italian as *Guida della Grecia*)

Richardson, N. J., commentary on *The Homeric Hymn to Demeter* (Oxford, 1974)

Scarpi, P., commentary on Apollodoros' *Library of Mythology* (Milan, 1996; published in Italian as *I miti greci*)

Vernant, J.-P., and Vidal-Naquet, P., *Myth and Tragedy in Ancient Greece* (New York, 1988; trans. of *Mythe et tragédie en Grèce ancienne*, 2 vols, Paris, 1972–86)

West, M. L., commentaries on Hesiod's *Theogony* (Oxford, 1966) and *Works and Days* (Oxford, 1978)

———, *The Hesiodic Catalogue of Women: Its Nature, Structure, and Origins* (Oxford, 1985)

Winnington-Ingram, R. P., *Euripides and Dionysus: An Interpretation of the Bacchae* (Cambridge, 1948; 2nd edn, with introduction by P. E. Easterling, Bristol, 1997)

II Myths of Origin

Bickerman, E. J., 'Origines gentium', *CPh* 47 (1952), pp. 65–81, repr. in Bickerman, *Religions and Politics in the Hellenistic and Roman Periods* (Como, 1985), pp. 399–417

Burkert, W., 'The Logic of Cosmogony', in R. Buxton (ed.), *From Myth to Reason? Studies in the Development of Greek Thought* (Oxford, 1999), pp. 87–106; repr. in Burkert, *Kleine Schriften II* (Göttingen, 2003), pp. 230–47

Calame, C., 'La fondation narrative de Cyrène', in Calame, *Mythe et histoire dans l'Antiquité grecque: la création symbolique d'une colonie* (Lausanne, 1996), pp. 57–162

Caldwell, R., *The Origin of the Gods: A Psychoanalytic Study of Greek Theogonic Myth* (New York and Oxford, 1989)

Dougherty, C., *The Poetics of Colonization: From City to Text in Archaic Greece* (New York and Oxford, 1993)

Edwards, R. B., *Kadmos the Phoenician: A Study in Greek Legends and the Mycenaean Age* (Amsterdam, 1979)

Fontenrose, J., *Python: A Study of Delphic Myth and its Origins* (Berkeley, Los Angeles and London, 1959)

Hall, J. M., *Ethnic Identity in Greek Antiquity* (Cambridge, 1997)

———, *Hellenicity: Between Ethnicity and Culture* (Chicago and London, 2002)

Nilsson, M. P., *The Mycenaean Origin of Greek Mythology* (Berkeley, Los Angeles and London, 1932)

Parker, R., 'Early Orphism', in A. Powell (ed.), *The Greek World* (London and New York, 1995), pp. 483–510

———, 'Myths of Early Athens', in Bremmer, *Interpretations*, pp. 187–214

Prinz, F., *Gründungsmythen und Sagenchronologie* (Munich, 1979)

Renfrew, A. C., *Archaeology and Language: The Puzzle of Indo-European Origins* (London, 1987)

Rudhardt, J., 'Pandora: Hésiode et les femmes', *MH* 43 (1986), pp. 231–46

Séchan, L., *Le Mythe de Prométhée* (Paris, 1951)

Sourvinou-Inwood, C., 'The Hesiodic Myth of the Five Races and the Tolerance of Plurality in Greek Mythology', in O. Palagia (ed.), *Greek Offerings. Essays on Greek Art in Honour of John Boardman* (Oxford, 1997), pp. 1–21

Trumpf, J., 'Stadtgründung und Drachenkampf', *Hermes* 86 (1958), pp. 129–57

Vian, F., *La Guerre des géants: le mythe avant l'époque hellénistique* (Paris, 1952)

———, *Les Origines de Thèbes: Cadmos et les Spartes* (Paris, 1963)

Weiss, P., 'Lebendiger Mythos. Gründerheroen und städtische Gründungstraditionen im griechisch-römischen Osten', *WüJbb* NF 10 (1984), pp. 179–208

West, M. L., *The Orphic Poems* (Oxford, 1983)

Comparisons

Bremmer, J. N., 'Near Eastern and Native Traditions in Apollodorus' Account of the Flood', in F. G. Martínez and G. P. Luttikhuizen (eds), *Interpretations of the Flood* (Leiden, 1998), pp. 39–55

Caduff, G. A., *Antike Sintflutsagen* (Göttingen, 1986)

Cohn, N., *Noah's Flood: The Genesis Story in Western Thought* (New Haven and London, 1996)

Levy, J. E., *In the Beginning: The Navajo Genesis* (Berkeley, Los Angeles and London, 1998)

Luginbühl, M., *Menschenschöpfungsmythen. Ein Vergleich zwischen Griechenland und dem Alten Orient* (Bern, 1992)

III The Olympians: Power, Honour, Sexuality

Arafat, K. W., *Classical Zeus: A Study in Art and Literature* (Oxford, 1990)

Atallah, W., *Adonis dans la littérature et l'art grecs* (Paris, 1966)

Borgeaud, P., *The Cult of Pan in Ancient Greece* (Chicago and London, 1988; trans. of *Recherches sur le dieu Pan*, Geneva, 1979)

Brelich, A., *I Greci e gli dei* (Naples, 1985)

Brisson, L., *Le Mythe de Tirésias: essai d'analyse structurale* (Leiden, 1976)

Burkert, W., *Greek Religion: Archaic and Classical* (Oxford, 1985; trans. of *Griechische Religion der archaischen und klassischen Epoche*, Stuttgart, 1977)

Carpenter, T. H., and Faraone, C. A. (eds), *Masks of Dionysus* (Ithaca, N.Y., and London, 1993)

Clay, J. S., *The Politics of Olympus: Form and Meaning in the Major Homeric Hymns* (Princeton, NJ, 1989)

Delcourt, M., *Héphaistos, ou la légende du magicien* (Paris, 1982)

Detienne, M., *Dionysos Slain* (Baltimore and London, 1979; trans. of *Dionysos mis à mort*, Paris, 1977)

———, *The Gardens of Adonis: Spices in Greek Mythology* (Hassocks, 1977; trans. of *Les Jardins d'Adonis: la mythologie des aromates en Grèce*, Paris, 1972)

——— and Sissa, G., *The Daily Life of the Greek Gods* (Stanford, Calif., 2000; trans. of *La Vie quotidienne des dieux grecs*, Paris, 1989)

Kahn, L., *Hermès passe, ou les ambiguïtés de la communication* (Paris, 1978)

Lloyd, A. B. (ed.), *What is a God? Studies in the Nature of Greek Divinity* (London, 1997)

Neils, J. (ed.), *Worshipping Athena: Panathenaia and Parthenon* (Madison, Wis., 1996)

Piccaluga, G., *Lykaon: un tema mitico* (Rome, 1968)

Sfameni Gasparro, G., *Misteri e culti mistici di Demetra* (Rome, 1986)

Verbruggen, H., *Le Zeus crétois* (Paris, 1981)

Vernant, J.-P., 'Hestia-Hermes: The Religious Expression of Space and Movement in Ancient Greece', in Vernant, *Myth and Thought among* the Greeks (London, 1983; trans. of *Mythe et pensée chez les grecs*, Paris, 1965; 2nd edn, Paris, 1985)

Versnel, H. S., 'Apollo and Mars One Hundred Years after Roscher', in Versnel, *Inconsistencies in Greek and Roman Religion II: Transition and Reversal in Myth and Ritual* (Leiden, 1993), pp. 289–334

IV Heroic Exploits

Brelich, A., 'Theseus e i suoi avversari', *SMSR* 27 (1956), pp. 136–41

———, *Gli eroi greci: un problema storico-religioso* (Rome, 1958)

Bremmer, J. N., 'Heroes, Rituals and the Trojan War', *SSR* 2 (1978), pp. 5–38

———, 'La plasticité du mythe: Méléagre dans la poésie homérique', in C. Calame (ed.), *Métamorphoses du mythe en Grèce antique* (Geneva, 1988), pp. 37–56

Buxton, R., 'The Myth of Talos', in C. Atherton (ed.), *Monsters and Monstrosity in Greek and Roman Culture* (Bari, 2002), pp. 83–112

Calame, C., *Thésée et l'imaginaire athénien: légende et culte en Grèce antique* (Lausanne, 1990)

DuBois, P., *Centaurs and Amazons: Women and the Pre-History of the Great Chain of Being* (Ann Arbor, Mich.,1982)

Ghali-Kahil, L. B., *Les Enlèvements et le retour d'Hélène dans les textes et les documents figurés* (2 vols, Paris, 1955)

Larson, J., *Greek Heroine Cults* (Madison, Wis., 1995)

Lefkowitz, M. R., *Heroines and Hysterics* (London, 1981)

Lyons, D., *Gender and Immortality: Heroines in Ancient Greek Myth and Cult* (Princeton, NJ, 1997)

Malkin, I., *The Returns of Odysseus: Colonization and Ethnicity* (Berkeley and London, 1998)

Mills, S., *Theseus, Tragedy, and the Athenian Empire* (Oxford, 1997)

Reinhardt, K., 'Das Parisurteil', in Reinhardt, *Tradition und Geist. Gesammelte Essays zur Dichtung* (Göttingen, 1960), pp. 16–36

Tyrrell, W. B., *Amazons: A Study in Athenian Mythmaking* (Baltimore and London, 1984)

Ward, A. G., et al., *The Quest for Theseus* (London, 1970)

Metamorphoses

Condos, T., *Star Myths of the Greeks and Romans: A Sourcebook* (Grand Rapids, Mich., 1997)

Forbes Irving, P. M. C., *Metamorphosis in Greek Myths* (Oxford, 1990)

Papathomopoulos, M., commentary on Antoninus Liberalis, *Les Métamorphoses* (Paris, 1968)

V Family Sagas

Bremmer, J. N., 'Oedipus and the Greek Oedipus Complex', in Bremmer, *Interpretations*, pp. 41–59

Clauss, J. J., and Johnston, S. I. (eds), *Medea: Essays on Medea in Myth, Literature, Philosophy, and Art* (Princeton, NJ, 1997)

Delcourt, M., *Oreste et Alcméon: étude sur la projection légendaire du matricide en Grèce* (Paris, 1959)

Gould, J., 'Law, Custom, and Myth: Aspects of the Social Position of Women in Classical Athens',

JHS 100 (1980), pp. 38–59; repr. in Gould, *Myth, Ritual, Memory, and Exchange: Essays in Greek Literature and Culture* (Oxford, 2001), pp. 112–57

Graf, F., 'Orpheus: A Poet among Men', in Bremmer, *Interpretations*, pp. 80–106

Halperin, D. M., 'Homosexuality', in *OCD*, pp. 720–23

Lefkowitz, M. R., *Women in Greek Myth* (London, 1986)

Moreau, A., *Le Mythe de Jason et Médée* (Paris, 1994)

Moret, J.-M., *Oedipe, la Sphinx et les Thébains. Essai de mythologie iconographique* (2 vols, Rome, 1984)

Sergent, B., *Homosexuality in Greek Myth* (London, 1987; trans. of *L'Homosexualité dans la mythologie grecque*, Paris, 1984)

Watson, P. A., *Ancient Stepmothers: Myth, Misogyny and Reality* (Leiden, 1995)

VI A Landscape of Myths

Anderson, M. J., *The Fall of Troy in Early Greek Poetry and Art* (Oxford, 1997)

Angeli Bernardini, P. (ed.), *Presenza e funzione della città di Tebe nella cultura greca* (Pisa, 2000)

Barringer, J. M., *Divine Escorts: Nereids in Archaic and Classical Greek Art* (Ann Arbor, Mich., 1995)

Brewster, H., *The River Gods of Greece: Myths and Mountain Waters in the Hellenic World* (London and New York, 1997)

Connor, W. R., 'Seized by the Nymphs: Nympholepsy and Symbolic Expression in Classical Greece', *ClAnt* 7 (1988), pp. 155–89

Davies, J. K., and Foxhall, L. (eds), *The Trojan War: its Historicity and Context* (Bristol, 1984)

Erskine, A., *Troy between Greece and Rome: Local Tradition and Imperial Power* (Oxford, 2001)

Faure, P., *Fonctions des cavernes crétoises* (Paris, 1964)

Hurst, A., and Schachter, A. (eds), *La Montagne des Muses* (Geneva, 1996)

Larson, J., *Greek Nymphs: Myth, Cult, Lore* (Oxford, 2001)

Malkin, I., *Myth and Territory in the Spartan Mediterranean* (Cambridge, 1994)

Motte, A., *Prairies et jardins de la Grèce antique: de la religion à la philosophie* (Brussels, 1973)

Murr, J., *Die Pflanzenwelt in der griechischen Mythologie* (Innsbruck, 1890)

Muthmann, F., *Mutter und Quelle: Studien zur Quellenverehrung im Altertum und im Mittelalter* (Basel, 1975)

Pollard, J., *Birds in Greek Life and Myth* (London, 1977)

Psilakis, N., *Kritiki Muthologia* (Heraklion, 1996)

Saïd, S., 'Tragic Argos', in A. H. Sommerstein, S. Halliwell, J. Henderson and B. Zimmermann (eds), *Tragedy, Comedy and the Polis* (Bari, 1993), pp. 167–89

Theune-Grosskopf, B., et al. (eds), *Troia: Traum und Wirklichkeit* (Stuttgart, 2001)

Voelke, P., 'Ambivalence, médiation, intégration: à propos de l'espace dans le drame satyrique', *EL* 1992, issue 2, pp. 33–58

Zeitlin, F. I., 'Thebes: Theater of Self and Society in Athenian Drama', in J. J. Winkler and F. I. Zeitlin (eds), *Nothing to do with Dionysos? Athenian*

Drama in its Social Context (Princeton, NJ, 1990), pp. 130–67

Comparisons

Bernbaum, E., *Sacred Mountains of the World* (Berkeley and Los Angeles, 1997)

S. Schama, *Landscape and Memory* (London, 1995)

The Underworld

Ballabriga, A., *Le Soleil et le Tartare: l'image mythique du monde en Grèce archaïque* (Paris, 1986)

Bremmer, J. N., *The Rise and Fall of the Afterlife* (London and New York, 2002)

Burkert, W., 'Elysion', *Glotta* 39 (1960–61), pp. 208–13

Johnston, S. I., *Restless Dead: Encounters between the Living and the Dead in Ancient Greece* (Berkeley, Los Angeles and London, 1999)

Ogden, D., *Greek and Roman Necromancy* (Princeton, NJ, and Oxford, 2001)

Riedweg, C., 'Initiation – Tod – Unterwelt. Beobachtungen zur Kommunikationssituation und narrativen Technik der orphisch-bakchischen Goldblättchen', in F. Graf (ed.), *Aussichten griechischer Rituale* (Stuttgart and Leipzig, 1998), pp. 359–98

Sourvinou-Inwood, C., *'Reading' Greek Death: to the End of the Classical Period* (Oxford, 1995)

Vermeule, E. T., *Aspects of Death in Early Greek Art and Poetry* (Berkeley and London, 1979)

On Charon, see entries under 'Charon I/Charu(n)' in *LIMC* vol. III.

VII Greek Myths after the Greeks

Allen, D. C., *Mysteriously Meant: The Rediscovery of Pagan Symbolism and Allegorical Interpretation in the Renaissance* (Baltimore and London, 1970)

Barkan, L., *The Gods Made Flesh: Metamorphosis and the Pursuit of Paganism* (New Haven, Mass., and London, 1986)

Brumble, H. D., *Classical Myths and Legends in the Middle Ages and Renaissance: A Dictionary of Allegorical Meanings* (London and Chicago, 1998)

Brunel, P., *Le Mythe de la métamorphose* (Paris, 1974)

Brunner, H. (ed.), *Die deutsche Trojaliteratur des Mittelalters und der frühen Neuzeit* (Wiesbaden, 1990)

Burian, P., 'Tragedy Adapted for Stages and Screens: the Renaissance to the Present', in P. E. Easterling (ed.), *The Cambridge Companion to Greek Tragedy* (Cambridge, 1997), pp. 228–83

Chance, J., *Medieval Mythography: from Roman North Africa to the School of Chartres, AD 433–1177* (Gainesville, Fla., 1994)

Edmunds, L., *Oedipus: The Ancient Legend and its Later Analogues* (Baltimore, 1985)

Erzgräber, W. (ed.), *Kontinuität und Transformation der Antike im Mittelalter* (Sigmaringen, 1989)

Feeney, D. C., *Literature and Religion at Rome: Cultures, Contexts, and Beliefs* (Cambridge, 1998)

Feldman, B., and Richardson, R. D., *The Rise of Modern Mythology 1680–1860* (Bloomington, Ind., 1972)

Flashar, H., *Inszenierung der Antike: Das griechische Drama auf der Bühne der Neuzeit 1585–1990* (Munich, 1991)

Galinsky, G. K., *The Herakles Theme: The Adaptations of the Hero in Literature from Homer to the Twentieth Century* (Oxford, 1972)

Gentili, B., and Pretagostini, R. (eds) *Edipo: il teatro greco e la cultura europea* (Rome, 1986)

Graf, F. (ed.), *Mythos in mythenloser Gesellschaft: Das Paradigma Roms* (Stuttgart and Leipzig, 1993)

Impelluso, L., *Eroi e dei dell'antichità* (Milan, 2002)

Jenkyns, R., *The Victorians and Ancient Greece* (Oxford, 1980)

Lamberton, R., *Homer the Theologian: Neoplatonist Allegorical Reading and the Growth of the Epic Tradition* (Berkeley, Los Angeles and London, 1986)

McDonald, M., *Sing Sorrow: Classics, History, and Heroines in Opera* (Westport, Conn., 2001)

Macintosh, F., 'Tragedy in Performance: Nineteenth- and Twentieth-century Productions', in P. E. Easterling (ed.), *The Cambridge Companion to Greek Tragedy* (Cambridge, 1997), pp. 284–323

Mackridge, P., *Ancient Greek Myth in Modern Greek Poetry* (London and Portland, Oreg., 1996)

Manuel, F. E., *The Eighteenth Century Confronts the Gods* (Cambridge, Mass., 1959)

Mayerson, P., *Classical Mythology in Literature, Art, and Music* (New York, 1971)

Miles, G. (ed.), *Classical Mythology in English Literature: A Critical Anthology* (London and New York, 1999)

Morford, M. P. O., and Lenardon, R. J., 'Mythology in Music', in Morford and Lenardon, *Classical Mythology*, 6th edn (New York, 1999), pp. 577–88

Mundy, J., 'Shades of Darkness: Mythology and Surrealism', in D. Ades and F. Bradley (eds), *Salvador Dalí: A Mythology* (London, 1998), pp. 118–42

Reid, J. D., *The Oxford Guide to Classical Mythology in the Arts, 1300–1990s* (2 vols, New York and Oxford, 1993)

Reinhold, M., *Classica Americana: The Greek and Roman Heritage in the United States* (Detroit, Mich., 1984)

Segal, C., *Orpheus: The Myth of the Poet* (Baltimore and London, 1989)

Seznec, J., *The Survival of the Pagan Gods* (Princeton, NJ, 1953; trans. of *La Survivance des dieux antiques,* London, 1940)

Stanford, W. B., *The Ulysses Theme: A Study in the Adaptability of a Traditional Hero* (2nd edn, Oxford, 1963)

Terpening, R. H., *Charon and the Crossing: Ancient, Medieval, and Renaissance Transformations of a Myth* (Lewisburg, Pa., and London, 1985)

Steiner, G., *Antigones* (Oxford, 1984)

Taplin, O., *Greek Fire* (London, 1989)

Tsigakou, F.-M., *The Rediscovery of Greece: Travellers and Painters of the Romantic Era* (New Rochelle, N.Y., 1981)

Vinge, L., *The Narcissus Theme in Western European Literature up to the Early 19th Century* (Lund, 1967)

Warner, M., *No Go the Bogeyman* (London, 1998)
———, *Fantastic Metamorphoses, Other Worlds* (Oxford, 2002)

Winkler, M. M. (ed.), *Classical Myth and Culture in the Cinema* (Oxford, 2001)

Modern academic approaches

Bremmer, J. N. (ed.), *Interpretations of Greek Mythology* (2nd edn, London and New York, 1988)

Edmunds, L. (ed.), *Approaches to Greek Myth* (Baltimore, 1990)

Gordon, R. L. (ed.), *Myth, Religion and Society: Structuralist Essays by M. Detienne, L. Gernet, J.-P. Vernant and P. Vidal-Naquet* (Cambridge, 1981)

On the history of scholarship on Greek mythology

Burkert, W., 'Griechische Mythologie und die Geistesgeschichte der Moderne', in *Les Études classiques aux XIXe et XXe siècles: leur place dans l'histoire des idées* (Fondation Hardt, *Entretiens sur l'antiquité classique* 26) (Geneva, 1980), pp. 159–207

Schlesier, R., *Kulte, Mythen und Gelehrte: Anthropologie der Antike seit 1800* (Frankfurt am Main, 1994)

Vries, J. de, *Forschungsgeschichte der Mythologie* (Freiburg and Munich, 1961)

Sources of Quotations

Almost all the translations from original sources are my own; but there are a few exceptions. For Homer I have cited throughout the versions by Richmond Lattimore (sometimes with adaptations); other exceptions are specified where appropriate. In the case of quotations from ancient texts, virtually all the works from which the quotations are taken may be found in modern translations (see 'Translations' under 'Further Reading'). Quotations are referred to by page number.

19 Pindar, *Pythian* 4, lines 1–8

23 Pausanias, Book 5, ch. 11.9

29–30 Pseudo-Herodotean *Life of Homer*, section 12; available in *Homeric Hymns, Homeric Apocrypha, Lives of Homer*, ed. M. L. West (Cambridge, Mass. and London, 2003)

36 Pindar, *Pythian* 9, lines 1–8

37 Euripides, *Cyclops*, lines 582–7

38 Aristophanes, *Frogs*, lines 200–2

40 'it may well be…' Thucydides, Book 1, ch. 22

'It was, I am inclined…' Thucydides, Book 1, ch. 9

'stealing and committing…' Xenophanes, frag. 166; in *The Presocratic Philosophers*, ed. by G. S. Kirk, J. E. Raven and M. Schofield (2nd edn, Cambridge, 1983)

41 Empedokles, frag. 399, lines 3–4; in *The Presocratic Philosophers*, ed. by G. S. Kirk, J. E. Raven and M. Schofield (2nd edn, Cambridge, 1983)

'Plato attacks traditional mythology': Plato, *Republic*, section 377b–378b

46 'The birth of Aphrodite': Hesiod, *Theogony*, lines 190–206; trans. adapted from M. L. West (World's Classics: Oxford, 1988)

47 Hesiod, *Theogony*, lines 349–54

48 'to be a monument…' Hesiod, *Theogony*, line 500

'the indescribable flame…' Hesiod, *Theogony*, lines 697–99

'Out of his shoulders…' Hesiod, *Theogony*, lines 824–30

50 *Homeric Hymn to Delian Apollo*, lines 117–19

53 Apollodoros, *Library*, Book 3, ch. 4.3

54 Hesiod, *Works and Days*, lines 130–37

59 'round Dodona…' Aristotle, *Meteorologica*, section 352a

'On Zeus' instructions…' Apollodoros, *Library*, Book 1, ch. 7.2

60 Pindar, *Isthmian* 8, line 25

63 Pausanias, Book 8, ch. 1.4

64 Pindar, *Pythian* 1, lines 21–22

68 Homer, *Iliad*, Book 8, lines 19–27

70 'This entire cosmos…' Kleanthes, *Hymn to Zeus*, lines 7–17. The *Hymn* can be found in, for example, the *Penguin Book of Greek Verse* (Harmondsworth, 1971; often reprinted).

'So she spoke…' Homer, *Iliad*, Book 16, lines 458–61

72 'So he spoke…' Homer, *Odyssey*, Book 5, lines 291–96

'it is believed…' scholiast on Lucian, p. 276.7–8 (ed. Rabe)

75 Homer, *Iliad*, Book 1, line 47

76 Homer, *Odyssey*, Book 6, lines 102–4

77 Homer, *Odyssey*, Book 24, lines 1–5

83 Homer, *Iliad*, Book 5, line 890

84 'Jason summons Hekate': Apollonios of Rhodes, *Argonautica*, Book 3, lines 1191–1224; trans. adapted from Richard Hunter (World's Classics: Oxford,

1993). Reprinted by permission of Oxford University Press.

85 Hesiod, *Theogony*, lines 39–43

86 Apollodoros, *Library*, Book 1, ch. 8.2

89 Homer, *Odyssey*, Book 11, lines 587–92

95 'Aphrodite's lament for Adonis': Bion, *Lament for Adonis*, lines 40–66

96 *Homeric Hymn to Aphrodite*, lines 233–38

97 Moschos, *Europa*, lines 95–96

99 'Danae and baby Perseus adrift in a chest': Simonides frag. 543; for what remains of Simonides see *Greek Lyric Poetry*, trans. M. L. West (World's Classics: Oxford, 1994)

111 Apollonios of Rhodes, *Argonautica*, Book 1, lines 1261–62

114 Diodoros of Sicily, *Library*, Book 3, ch. 67.2

129 Euripides, *Suppliant Women*, lines 339–41

136 Homer, *Iliad*, Book 24, lines 507–12

137 Sophokles, *Aias*, line 1365

140 'Strangers…' Homer, *Odyssey*, Book 9, line 252

'Nobody…' Homer, *Odyssey*, Book 9, line 408

144 'The reunion of Odysseus and Penelope': Homer, *Odyssey*, Book 23, lines 205–40

150 Pausanias, Book 5, ch. 13.1

151 Aischylos, *Agamemnon*, lines 1217–22

152 'Athene persuades the Furies': Aischylos, *Eumenides*, lines 870–901

153 'looking like Artemis…' Homer, *Odyssey*, Book 4, line 122

'Into the wine…' Homer, *Odyssey*, Book 4, lines 220–26

165 'Oedipus uncovers the truth': Sophokles, *Oedipus Tyrannos*, lines 1162–96

181 Homer, *Odyssey*, Book 6, lines 42–45

184 'as soon as Hylas…' Apollonios of Rhodes, *Argonautica*, Book 1, lines 1234–39; trans. Richard Hunter (World's Classics: Oxford, 1993)

'They belong neither…' *Homeric Hymn to Aphrodite*, lines 259–72; trans. J. Larson, *Greek Nymphs: Myth, Cult, Lore* (Oxford University Press, 2001), pp. 32–3, after H. G. Evelyn-White, Loeb edn. Used by permission of Oxford University Press, Inc.

185 Pausanias, Book 3, ch. 25.4

186 'It would not be right…' Athenaios, *Deipnosophistae*, section 200b–c

'At the head…' Homer, *Odyssey*, Book 13, lines 102–12

188 Sophokles, *Women of Trachis*, lines 11–14

192 Semonides, poem 7, lines 37–40; the whole poem is available in *Greek Lyric Poetry*, trans. M. L. West (World's Classics: Oxford, 1994)

193 'fills the land…' Plato, *Laws*, section 705a

'Thalassa…' Xenophon, *Anabasis*, Book 4, ch. 7.24

'Joyfully from the depths…' Moschos, *Europa*, lines 117–24

196 'destructive-minded' Homer, *Odyssey*, Book 11, line 322

'most kingly…' Plato, *Minos*, section 320d = Hesiod frag. 144 Merkelbach-West

'Crete's guardian' Homer, *Iliad*, Book 13, line 450

197 Homer, *Odyssey*, Book 11, line 569

198 'according to tradition…' Thucydides, Book 1, ch. 4

'even a determined…' Pausanias, Book 4, ch. 33.1

'most of the gods…' Diodoros of Sicily, *Library*, Book 5, ch. 77.3–5

199 Kallimachos, *Hymn to Zeus*, line 8

201 Aischylos, *Agamemnon*, lines 935–36

204 Homer, *Iliad*, Book 6, lines 243–50

205 Homer, *Iliad*, Book 3, lines 146–60

206 'when a man…' Plato, *Republic*, section 330d–e

'O shining Odysseus…' Homer, *Odyssey*, Book 11, lines 487–91

208 Aristophanes, *Frogs*, lines 465–78; trans. Alan Sommerstein (Warminster, 1996)

211 Lucian, *Charon*, section 20

212 'Cruel Charos…' Cypriot lament cited from M. Alexiou, *The Ritual Lament in Greek Tradition* (Cambridge, 1974), p. 124

'But for you…' Homer, *Odyssey*, Book 4, lines 561–69

213 'You will find…' from R. Parker, 'Early Orphism', in A. Powell (ed.), *The Greek World* (London and New York, 1995), p. 497

'But those who are deemed…' Plato, *Phaedo*, section 114

'the deepest abyss…' Homer, *Iliad*, Book 8, lines 13–16

220 'If you want me…' Plautus, *Amphitryo*, lines 1–16

'There, staring out…' Catullus, poem 64, lines 52–57, trans. Guy Lee (World's Classics: Oxford, 1990)

224 Ovid, *Metamorphoses*, Book 3, lines 474–93; trans. Mary M. Innes (Penguin Classics: Harmondsworth, 1955). Copyright © Mary Innes 1955. Reproduced by permission of Penguin Books Ltd.

Ted Hughes, *Tales from Ovid* (Faber and Faber: London, 1997). Reproduced by permission of Faber and Faber.

225 '[Zeus] is said to have…' Lactantius, *Divinae institutiones*, Book 1, ch. 11.19

'Alpheus…' Fulgentius, *Mythologiae*, Book 3, ch. 12

230 J. Seznec, *The Survival of the Pagan Gods* (Princeton, N.J., 1953), p. 211

231 Bacon, *De sapientia veterum*, section 10 (trans. by Sir Arthur Gorges, London, 1619)

232 ' "Fondling," she saith…' Shakespeare, *Venus and Adonis*, stanza 39

'our Jupiters…' Addison, *The Spectator*, no. 523, 30 October 1712; I owe this reference to G. Miles, *Classical Mythology in English Literature* (London and New York, 1999), p. 13

234 'hackneyed and lifeless…' Wordsworth's note on his 'Ode to Lycoris' of 1817. I owe this reference to Oliver Taplin's *Greek Fire* (London, 1989), p. 94

'We are all Greeks', Shelley, preface to his verse drama *Hellas*, 1822

'[The Greeks] were but…' Kingsley, *The Heroes* (Cambridge, 1856), preface

238 J. Anouilh, *Nouvelles pièces noires* (Les Éditions de la Table Ronde, Paris, 1958), p. 174

242 'With his immortal measure…' Andreas Kalvos, 'To Glory'; there is a modern Greek edition of Kalvos' poetry, by F. M. Pontani (Athens, 1970)

'And then, over the shore's…' *Angelos Sikelianos: Selected Poems*, trans. and with an introduction by E. Keeley and P. Sherrard (2nd edn, Limni, Greece, 1996). Reproduced with permission.

C. P. Cavafy, *Selected Poems*, © 1992 E. Keeley and P. Sherrard. Reprinted by permission of Princeton University Press.

243 Y. Ritsos, *Repetitions, Testimonies, Parentheses*, © 1991 Princeton University Press. Reprinted by permission of Princeton University Press.

244 'Come Muse…' W. Whitman, 'Song of the Exposition', 1876, in Whitman, *Leaves of Grass and Other Writings*, ed. M. Moon (New York, 1965; repr. 2002), p. 165

'The intellectual history…' M. Reinhold, *Classica Americana* (Detroit, 1984), p. 118

Margaret Atwood, 'Eurydice', from Atwood, *Eating Fire: Selected Poems 1965–1995* (Virago: London, 1998), pp. 278–80. Reprinted by permission of Time-Warner Books UK. I owe this ref. to G. Miles, *Classical Mythology in English Literature* (London and New York, 1999), p. 183.

Illustration Credits

Abbreviations:
l = left, r = right, a = above, b = below, c = centre
Measurements are given in centimetres (inches in brackets), height before width before depth.

Ace Stock 51 a, 62–63, 183, 189, 210
Acropolis Museum, Athens: 225a
Photo akg-images, London: Pergamon Museum, Berlin 4–5, 21, 92 a (Villa Albani, Rome), 102–3 (Mykonos Museum), 138 (Bibliothèque Nationale, Paris), 171 b (Museum of Western and Eastern Art, Kiev)
Photo akg-images London/Andrea Baguzzi, 132 br (Museo Archeologico Potenza, Italy)
Photo akg-images, London/Cameraphoto 132 br (138 x 264; 54 ⅜ x 103 ⅞)
Photo akg-images, London/Erich Lessing: 1 (half title; Greek glyptic, Dionysos and Psyches, Hellenistic, 4th century BC/1st century AD; Museum of Archaeology, Naples); 3 (title page); 14–15 (Attic red-figure *skyphos*, Brygos painter, 25 (9 ⅞), Kunsthistorisches Museum, Vienna), 30 b (Archaeological Museum, Eleusis); 42–43, 46 (Museo Nazionale Romano delle Terme, Rome); 48 (Musei Capitolini, Rome); 55 b (Kunsthistorisches Museum, Vienna); 61 (Musée du Louvre, Paris); 85 (Kunsthistorisches Museum, Vienna); 87 a (Relief from a sarcophagus built into the east façade of the Villa Borghese, Musée du Louvre, Paris); 115 b (National Museum of Archaeology, Naples); 117 b (Kunsthistorisches Museum, Vienna); 123 (Kunsthistorisches Museum, Vienna); 142 a (Bibliothèque Nationale, Paris); 143 b (Musée du Louvre, Paris); 146–47 (Olympia Museum); 186–87, 126–27 (Attic red-figure bowl by Elpinikos Painter. Staatliche Antikensammlung und Glyptothek, Munich), 192 (Staatliche Antikensammlung und Glyptothek, Munich), 192–93, 199, 242–43
Photo akg-images London/Pirozzi: 157 (Museo Nazionale Romano delle Terme, Rome)
Antikenmuseum Basel und Sammlung Ludwig, Basel: 122, 137 br, 170 b, 173 (Photo Claire Niggli)
Antikensammlung, Staatliche Museen, Kassel: 153 b (photo Gabriele Böbert)
Archaeological Museum, Agrigento, Italy 143a
Archaeological Museum of Ayios Nikolaos, Crete: 211r
Archaeological Museum, Ferrara, Italy: 101 a (detail of red-figure bowl by the Marlay painter); 73 (Peleus painter, vase painting on black ground from Spina, Valle Trebba, tomb 617)
Archaeological Museum, Florence: 25 a (black-figure volute *krater* by the potter Ergotimos and the painter Kleitias), 83 b, 106–7, 128 (Dokimasia Painter), 160, 168 a (photo Scala)
Archaeological Museum, Ioannina: 100 r
Archaeological Museum, Thessaloniki: 83 a
Archbishop's Palace, Kromeriz, Czech Republic: 90 (oil on canvas, 212 x 207; 83 ½ x 81 ½)
The Art Archive/Dagli Orti: 66–67 (Archaeological Museum Salonica), 104 r (Archaeological Museum Delphi), 109 a (Museo di Villa Giulia Rome), 111 (Archaeological Museum Florence), 214–15 (Museo Civico Padua)
Ashmolean Museum, Oxford: 84, 194 l (oil on canvas, 124 x 90; 48 ⅞ x 35 ⅜), 200, 211 l (Tymbos Painter, *c.* 475–450 BC. The Bridgeman Art Library, London)
Benaki Museum, Athens: 190 (Watercolour, 18.5 x 26.5; 7 ¼ x 10 ⅜)
Bern Historisches Museum: 76
Biblioteca Nazionale di San Marco, Venice: 27 b
Bibliothèque Nationale, Paris: 197, 223 b, 226 a, 228–29 (MS Arab. 5036, fol. 68r)
Bibliothèque Nationale, Paris, Cabinet des Médailles: 38 a (Brygos Painter), 115 a (Stieglitz Painter), 121 a (Inscriptions Painter), 164 a (Achilles painter)
Bodleian Library, Oxford: 27 a
The Bridgeman Art Library, London: 235
British Library, London: King's MS 24, 244 fols., f.73b 223 a
British Museum, London: 31 a, 32 b (Archelaos of Priene), 33 l, 36 b, 45 a, 47 a, 49 r (Didrachm from Epeiros, photo Peter Clayton), 56 a, 56–57 a, 70 a, 80 r, 81 l, 82 a, 87 b, 88, 95 l, 95 r (relief from Camiros), 104–5, 113 a, 114, 119 136 a (Berlin painter, Caere), 137 a, 139 ar, 142 b (Siren painter), 148, 161, 170 a, 188 r, 198, 212, 229 a (MS Add. 23770, fol. 29 v), 229 b (MS Add. 23770, fol. 36r), 234 a
Richard Buxton, 22–23, 23, 39 a, 80 l, 152 (Ioannina Museum), 206
Canellopoulos Museum, Athens: 195
Capitoline Museum, Rome: 224
Peter Clayton 26 br, 58, 71 a, 79 a, 79 b, 93, 141 r (Delphi Museum), 196, 217 b, 219 l, 219 r
Cleveland Museum of Art, Cleveland, Ohio: 99 (oil on canvas 163.5 x 228.5; 64 ⅜ x 90)
Conservatori, Rome: 216 a
Corpus Christi College, Oxford: 220 (Titus Maccius Plautus, *Comoediae*, ed. Georgius Merula, Venice)
Marion Cox: 118 b
Photo DAI, Athens: 201, 202 b
Denver Art Museum: 221 (Oil on canvas, 99.7 x 160.2; 39 ¼ x 63 ¹⁄₁₆ Gift of Mrs Katherine H. Gentry)
© Disney Enterprises, Inc.: 6 b
Photo Michael Duigan: 75
Eleusis Museum, Attica, Greece. 141 l
© Agence Bernand: 239 a (Elisabeth Hardy, Paul Mathos, Marcel Peres and Lucien Barjon. Théâtre de l'Atelier, Paris, 10 October 1947)
Photo © Fáilte Ireland: 18 l (Oliver Sheppard, *Death of Cuchulain*, 1911–12. Bronze sculpture in the General Post Office, Dublin)
Faringdon Collection Trust, Buscot Park, Oxfordshire/The Bridgeman Art Library, London: 57 b (Chalk study)
Photo Alison Frantz: 37 a
Galleria Borghese, Rome: 191 r (242.9; 95 ⅝ photo Scala)
Galleria Nazionale d'Arte Moderna, Rome: 238 b (oil on canvas, 90 x 70; 35 ⅝ x 27 ½. © DACS 2004)
Gemäldegalerie Alte Meister, Staatliche Kunstsammlungen Dresden: 230 a (Oil on canvas, 177 x 129; 69 ⅝ x 50 ¾)
J. Paul Getty Museum, Los Angeles: 38 b (detail of vase showing Aristophanes' *Birds*, *c.* 415–400 BC), 117 a
Photo Heidi Grassley, © Thames & Hudson Ltd, London: 9, 10–11, 17, 35, 39 b, 70 b, 162–63
Photo © Sonia Halliday: 2 (opposite title page), 34–35, 74–75
Robert Harding Picture Library: 7 (Tony Gervis), 50–51 (Adina Tovy), 130 (Robert Frerck/Odyssey/Chicago)
Heraklion Museum, Crete: 194 r
Hermitage Museum, St Petersburg: 120 a (Attic black-figure cup by Psiax)
Photo Hirmer: 16 (grave circle 'A' within the walls of the citadel at Mycenae), 30–31, 36 a, 72, 118 a (Paestum Museum, Italy), 184
Holkham Hall, Norfolk, UK: 40 bc (antique copy of Silanion's original, *c.* 370 BC)
Indiana University Art Museum, Bloomington: 26 a
© Robbie Jack/Corbis: 168 b
Kimbell Art Museum, Fort Worth, Texas: 113 b
Koninklijk Museum voor Schone Kunsten, Antwerp: 182–83
Kunsthistorisches Museum, Vienna: 40 b, 137 bl (Attic red-figure cup, signed Douris, 490 BC)
Le Charivari, Paris, 1841–42: 241 b
Lonely Planet Images: 47 b (Jon Davison), 65 (Bethune Carmichael)
Museum Schloss Fasanerie, Eichenzell, Germany: 60 r
Museo Nazionale, Ferrara, Italy: 29
Musée Baron Gérard: 110 (Oil on canvas)
Museo Provinciale, Lecce, Italy: 166–67
National Archaeological Museum, Athens: 26 b, 50 b, 72–73, 98, 167 b, 185 b
Manchester City Art Galleries: 234–35 (Oil on canvas, 197 x 406.5; 77 ½ x 160)
The Metropolitan Museum of Art, New York: 218–19 (Rogers Fund, 1920, 20.192.16), 217 a (Purchase, Joseph Pulitzer Bequest, 1955, 55.11.5)
MGM/The Kobal Collection: 245
Photo © University of Mississippi: 24
Maps by ML Design, © Thames & Hudson Ltd, London: 12–13, 109 b, 116, 126, 134, 181, 188 l
© MO/Corbis KIPA: 244–45
Museo Archeologico, Palermo: 71 b (photo Scala)
Museum of Fine Arts, Boston: 34 a, 101 b (Attic red-figure cup, Douris Painter, 490–485 BC), 120 b, 151
Musée du Louvre, Paris: 6 a (black figure *hydria* from Caere, Painter of the Caeretan Hydriae), 22, 49 l (photo © RMN – Hervé Lewandowski), 51 b, 55 a (photo © RMN – Gérard Blot), 68 (photo André Held); 86, 94 (photo Peter Clayton); 96 (red-figure *krater* by the Peleus painter. Photo © RMN – Hervé Lewandowski); 121 b (Andokides Painter. Photo © RMN – Chuzeville), 132 a (photo © RMN – Chuzeville), 135 (red figure *skyphos* attributed to Makron. Photo © RMN – H. Lewandowski); 153 a (attributed to Eumenides Painter. Photo © RMN – Hervé Lewandowski); 156–57, 171 a (Swing Painter. Musée du Louvre, Paris. Photo © RMN – Hervé Lewandowski), 172 (photo Michael Duigan), 172–73 (Hermonas. Photo © RMN – Hervé Lewandowski), 174–75 (Briseis painter. Photo © RMN – Hervé Lewandowski), 175 (Amasis Painter. Photo © RMN – Ch. Larrieu), 233 (photo © RMN – R. G. Ojeda)
Musée du Luxembourg, Luxemburg: 240 (Oil on canvas, 146 x 181; 57 ½ x 71 ¼)
Musei Capitolini, Rome: 32 a
Museo del Prado, Madrid: 38 b (oil on panel, 195 x 267; 76 ¾ x 105 ⅛. The Bridgeman Art Library, London), 232–33 (oil on canvas, 136 x 220; 53 ½ x 86 ⅝), 236 b (oil on canvas, 146 x 83; 57 ½ x 32 ⅝). Photo Scala)
Museo Jatta, Ruvo, Italy: 112–13 (Talos Painter)
Museo Nazionale, Rome: 112
Museo Nazionale, Taranto: 53 a
Museo Nazionale di Villa Giulia, Rome: 216–17, 216 b (photo DAI, Athens)
Museo Nazionale Archeologico, Syracuse, Sicily: 187
National Archaeological Museum, Naples: 40 a, 40 ac (photo Scala), 52, 60 l, 105, 133, 149, 205 (Kleophrades Painter)
National Gallery, London: 191 l (Oil on wood, 29.5 x 20; 11 ⅝ x 7 ⅞; Wynn Ellis Bequest, 1876)
National Gallery, Washington, Patrons' Permanent Fund 1990.1.1/The Bridgeman Art Library, London: 230 b (oil on canvas, 98.4 x 131.2; 36 ¾ x 51 ⅝)
The National Museum of Denmark, Copenhagen: 136 b (photo Kit Weiss), 186 (Dept. of Near Eastern and

Classical Antiquities)
National Museum, Palermo: 77 l
Nationalmuseum, Stockholm: 125 r (Sabouroff Painter, from Sicily)
Nemrud Dagh, Turkey: 20 (stone relief from the monumental tomb)
The Principal and Fellows of Newnham College, Cambridge. Photo James Austin: 237 a
Norbert Schimmel Collection, New York: 77 r
Photo © Hakan Oge: 203 a
Oberösterreichisches Landesbibliothek Linz, Austria: 226 b (Cod. 472, fol. 237v.)
Photo Pedro Olalla, *Mythological Atlas of Greece*, Road Editions, Athens 2001: 58–59, 106–7 b, 118–19, 150, 164 b, 178–79, 185 a, 207, 208–9
Olympia Museum: 176
Österreichisches Nationalbibliothek, Vienna: 227 (Cod. 2773, 63r.)
Photo © Fatih Ozenbas: 203 b
Palazzo Durazzo Pallavicini, Bologna: 241 ar
Photo Andreas Pohlmann: 239 b (Tada Keiko as a Trojan woman and Kimura Yasushi as a warrior)
Private collections: 159 (oil on canvas, 154.3 x 111.1; 60 ¾ x 43 ¾), 180 (oil on panel, 24.5 x 38.5; 9 ⅝ x 15 ⅛)
Photo © RMN – Hervé Lewandowski: 31 b (white-ground *lekythos*), 154–55
Photo Scala: 28
Soprintendenza per I Beni Culturali e Ambientali Gabinetto di Numismatica, Syracuse, Sicily: 64 l, 64 r (Tetradrachma from Camarina)
Staatliche Antikensammlungen und Glyptothek, Munich: 81 r (Makron), 82–83, 107
Staatliche Museen, Berlin: 33 r (Douris painter), 89,

100 l, 144, 145 a, 145 b, 177
Staatliche Museen zu Berlin Preussischer Kulturbesitz, Antikensammlung. Photo © bpk, Berlin/Ingrid Geske-Heiden: 56–57 b
Staatliche Museen zu Berlin Preussischer Kulturbesitz, Antikensammlung. Photo © bpk, Berlin/Johannes Laurentius: 63, 156, 162, 167 a
Tate Gallery, London: 236 a (Pencil, pen and watercolour, 372 x 528; 146 ½ x 207 ⅝)
Toledo Museum of Art: 104 l (Attic red-figure *lekythos* by the Providence Painter), 19 (terracotta *hydria*)
Uffizi Gallery, Florence: 232 (tempera on canvas 172.5 x 278.5; 67 ⅞ x 109 ⅝)
Van Buuren Collection, Brussels: 92 b (Oil on panel, 63 x 90; 24 ¾ x 35 ⅜)
Vatican Library: 222 (cod. Lat. 3867, Fol. 44v.)
Vatican Museums: 53 b, 139 al (the Laoköon group. Roman copy, perhaps after Agesander, Athenodoros and Polydoros of Rhodes. Present state, former restorations removed. Museo Pio Clementino), 225 b
Photo John Vickers: 37 b (*Oedipus Rex* directed by Michel St Denis at the New Theatre, Old Vic Company, London)
Virginia Museum, Richmond, Virginia: 125 l (Nikias Painter)
Jean Vinchon, Paris: 25 bl
Photo Giulio Veggi/Archivio White Star: 90–91
Winterthur Museum, 364, 160–61 (Manchester Painter, *c.* 330 BC)
From Mary Wollstonecraft Shelley, *Frankenstein or The Modern Prometheus*, 1934 edition: 18 r
From Konrad von Würzburg, *Trojanerkrieg*, 15th century: 132 bl

Acknowledgments

For advice and assistance on various specific points I would like to express my warm thanks to six friends and colleagues: Mercedes Aguirre, Sir John Boardman, Ed Lilley, Pantelis Michelakis, Eleni Papazoglou and Paul Taylor. I owe an even greater debt to Jan Bremmer and Pat Easterling, who took time from their own work to read through and comment on the whole typescript in draft. At Thames & Hudson, Colin Ridler has been an exemplary mentor, knowing exactly when to encourage and when to cajole; I have also received expert assistance from several others at Thames & Hudson, especially Philip Watson, Geoff Penna and Jenny Drane. Lastly and most importantly, I thank my son George – particularly for his help with the maps – and my wife Tiziana, without whose constant support the writing of this book would have been impossible.

Index